Love, Friendship, and the Self

Love, Friendship, and the Self

Intimacy, Identification, and the Social Nature of Persons

Bennett W. Helm

OXFORD
UNIVERSITY PRESS

OXFORD

UNIVERSITY PRESS

Great Clarendon Street, Oxford, OX2 6DP,
United Kingdom

Oxford University Press is a department of the University of Oxford.
It furthers the University's objective of excellence in research, scholarship,
and education by publishing worldwide. Oxford is a registered trade mark of
Oxford University Press in the UK and in certain other countries

First Edition published in 2010

Published in the United States of America by Oxford University Press
198 Madison Avenue, New York, NY 10016, United States of America

British Library Cataloguing in Publication Data
Data available

Library of Congress Cataloging in Publication Data
Data available

ISBN 978–0–19–956789–8

To Jaime, Jonathan, and Elizabeth, with love

Acknowledgments

Conversations with many people over the course of the last eight years helped me formulate and sharpen the central ideas of this book. Some of my central ideas on love and friendship were initially developed in an APA presentation in 2001, "Friends Are Other Selves," on which Lori Gruen provided helpful commentary. That same year I presented "Love and Friendship" to the Franklin & Marshall College Workshop on Moral Psychology, which provided the opportunity for lengthy discussions with Talbot Brewer, Justin D'Arms, and Daniel Jacobson, all of whom returned the following year to discuss "Values: Loving Oneself." Their joint proddings were enormously helpful to me in helping shape this project at its early stages. (Thanks also to Franklin & Marshall College for making these workshops possible.) A distant successor of this paper, "Self-Love and the Structure of Values," was presented at the Workshop on Ethics, Emotions, and Authenticity at the University of Munich in 2007; I wish to thank in particular Monika Betzler, Peter Goldie, Verena Mayer, and Mikko Salmela for stimulating discussion there. Many of the ideas presented in these papers eventually coalesced into Chapter 4. And over the summer of 2004 I wrote two articles for the *Stanford Encyclopedia of Philosophy* (ed. Edward N. Zalta), which were published in 2005: "Love" (http://plato.stanford.edu/entries/love/) and "Friendship" (http://plato.stanford.edu/entries/friendship/); much of this background work frames my presentation and criticism of alternative accounts of love and friendship primarily in Chapter 1.

In 2002, I presented "Love, Friendship, and the Emotions" at Oberlin College, and I wish to thank the audience for their questions and Todd Ganson for the invitation. Thanks also go to Maria Merritt for her comments on my "Person-Focused Emotions," at an APA presentation in 2003 and to both Maria and Neera Kapur Badhwar for an extended discussion afterwards. In 2006 I presented a related paper, "Affective Intentionality: Holistic and Multiply Layered," at the workshop on Affective Intentionality and the Moral Brain, in Bonn, Germany; my thanks go to Sabine Döring, Peter Goldie, Matthew Ratcliffe—and, especially, Jan Slaby for bringing all of us together for what has proved to be many fruitful discussions. In 2007, I presented "Love and Intimacy: Rethinking Personal Love" at a conference on Love at Franklin & Marshall College, for which I thank Michael Murray and Glenn Ross both for the invitation and for organizing such a stimulating conference. And in 2008, I presented "Personal Love and Intimacy" at the Conference on Love and Hate at Philadelphia University in Jordan, for which I thank the participants, especially Towfic Shomar, for their probing questions. Together, all these papers ultimately became "Love, Identification, and the Emotions," *American Philosophical Quarterly* 46, no. 1 (2009): 39–59, which forms the basis of Chapters 4–5 as well as parts of Chapter 2.

Simultaneously, and partly as a result of an off-hand comment from Tal Brewer in 2001, I was thinking about friendship and, in particular, the way shared activity is a central part of friendship. This generated worries about whether individualistic conceptions of persons (and of shared intention) are adequate to a robust account of friendship, leading to the presentation of "Plural Agents: The Sociality of Emotions and the Rationality of Joint Action" at the Toronto Workshop on Emotions and Rationality in 2003; thanks are owed especially to Richard Boyd, Margaret Gilbert, Karen Jones, and Ronald de Sousa for helpful discussion and, especially, to Jennifer Whiting for organizing and inviting me to the workshop. A substantially revised version of this paper was presented at a third Franklin & Marshall Workshop in Moral Psychology in 2004 and to more lengthy conversations with, this time, Justin D'Arms, Pamela Hieronymi, Daniel Jacobson, David Merli, and Michael Thompson. A still revised version was presented at the Cycle de Conférences at the University of Geneva in 2006 and profited from discussions there with especially Julien Deonna, Kevin Mulligan, Wlodek Rabinowicz, and Fabrice Teroni. I am also grateful to Angelica Krebs, with whom I had a lengthy discussion of the issues raised by this paper in 2006. This paper eventually became "Plural Agents," *Noûs* 42, no. 1 (2008): 17–49 and forms the backbone of Chapter 8.

The final piece of the puzzle began to fall in place in 2006 with a fourth Franklin & Marshall Workshop on Moral Psychology, at which Talbot Brewer, Ruth Chang, David Merli, and Sergio Tenenbaum discussed my "Paternalistic Love and the Development of the Self," which was later presented at the Workshop on the Emotions at the University of Geneva.

My thanks again to participants at both these forums for their healthy skepticism and probing questions.

Finally, I would like to acknowledge support from Franklin & Marshall College and from an National Endowment for the Humanities Fellowship that allowed me to spend academic year 2005–6 working on this book. Above all, my gratitude is owed to Karen, Jaime, Jonathan, and Elizabeth for their love, support, understanding, and tolerance. I just hope that in my attempts to lay out an explicit account, I haven't distorted—either theoretically or practically—the phenomena themselves.

Contents

List of Figures

1

Introduction

Love and friendship are undoubtedly centrally important in our lives. We devote ourselves to our friends and beloveds, investing much time, money, and energy—emotional and otherwise—in them. Yet these common observations can lead us to ask: why should love and friendship have this sort of central importance in our lives? One common answer is that we do this because love and friendship make our lives much better and richer, and because being a lover, beloved,[1] and a friend can help us become better persons insofar as we thereby strive to be better because of that love and friendship. However, understanding this answer more fully and being able to evaluate it requires understanding what exactly love and friendship are, how our lives as persons are different because of them, and whether this difference is somehow central to our being persons at all or whether it is an optional good, like icing on a cake.

My central contention in this book is that our being capable of love and friendship is part of what makes us be persons, and their importance in defining personhood forces us to reject some pervasive assumptions about ourselves and so to rethink what we persons essentially are.

1.1 Preliminary Distinctions

First, however, it will be useful to delineate more clearly what is meant by 'love' and 'friendship,' for the common usage of these terms varies considerably. Love is generally understood to be an *evaluative attitude*: in loving someone or something, we regard it as good or worthy in some

---

[1] Throughout, I shall use the terms 'lover' and 'beloved' to denote the subject and object of our loves. In using these terms, I do not mean to suggest romantic love in particular; indeed, as will become clear shortly, romantic love will hardly be a focus of my discussion at all.

way. Often, we use 'love' simply to emphasize that we like something very much: "I love chocolate (or running)." In other cases, 'love' is used to denote something "deeper": in saying that I love philosophy or being a father, I mean to say that engaging in the activity of doing philosophy or being a certain kind of person is a part of what makes my life worth living; I might just as well say that I *value* these.[2] By contrast, the sort of love at issue in the love of a spouse or child or friend is what we might call *personal love*: a distinctive mode of concern for another person, a concern we have for *his* sake and not for ulterior motives. Of course, in valuing philosophy, I do so not because it brings me great fame and fortune; rather, I do so for its own sake. However, what is different in the case of personal love is that our beloveds themselves can play a role in delineating their own "sakes" and so in defining themselves as the persons they are; that is, they can exercise a capacity for autonomy that is part of what makes them be persons in the first place. Consequently, in personal love we must have a concern for others *as persons* and so not only be attuned to their interests but also respect their capacity for autonomy. In part for this reason, most philosophical accounts of love, including the one presented here, have focused on personal love as a distinctive form of love.[3]

The philosophical tradition from the ancient Greeks on has distinguished three notions that fall under the general concept of love: *agape*, *eros*, and *philia*. *Agape* has come, primarily through the Christian tradition, to mean the sort of love God has for us persons, as well as our love for God and, by extension, our love for each other—a kind of brotherly love. In the paradigm case of God's love for us, *agape* is "spontaneous and unmotivated," revealing nothing about the merits of the beloved but rather something about the lover.[4] Thus the evaluative attitude of love in this case is supposed to *create* value in its object and therefore, on some readings, to initiate our fellowship with God.[5] Consequently, *agape* cannot be justified by an appeal to the beloved or her properties.

---

[2] Indeed, this will be roughly the understanding of valuing that I offer in Ch. 4, understanding valuing as a part of self-love.

[3] One exception is Harry Frankfurt, who treats the love of persons and love of projects, ideals, or causes as essentially the same. See Harry Frankfurt, *The Reasons of Love* (Princeton, NJ: Princeton University Press, 2004).

[4] Anders Nygren, "*Agape* and *Eros*," in *Eros, Agape, and Philia: Readings in the Philosophy of Love*, ed. Alan Soble (New York, NY: Paragon House, 1989), 85.

[5] Ibid., 87–8.

By contrast, *eros* and *philia* are generally understood to be evaluative attitudes not in the sense that they create value, as with *agape*, but rather in the sense that they are responsive to features of the beloved that merit their implicit evaluation. In the case of *eros*, with its connotations of sexual attraction, the evaluation is typically of the beloved's physical beauty, though Socrates (in Plato's *Symposium*) thinks that this narrow responsiveness to physical beauty in particular is a deficient form of *eros* that ought to be developed first into a response to the beauty of the person's soul and, ultimately, into a response to the form, Beauty itself. Perhaps encouraged by this, Alan Soble tries to shift our understanding of *eros* away from the sexual: to love something in the "erosic" sense (to use the term Soble coins) is to love it in a way that, by being responsive to its merits, is dependent on reasons.[6] In so doing, he aims to articulate a sharp contrast between *eros* and *agape*.[7]

Finally, *philia* originally meant a kind of affectionate regard or friendly feeling toward not just one's friends but also possibly toward family members, business partners, and one's country at large;[8] like *eros*, *philia* is generally (but not universally) understood to be responsive to (good) qualities in your beloved. Given this, it begins to look as though the distinction between *eros* and *philia* is to be made simply in terms of the element of sexuality involved in *eros* and absent in *philia*, a way of making the distinction that Laurence Thomas rightly questions: can this adequately account for the real differences we experience between our romantic relationships and our relationships with friends?[9] The distinction between *philia* and *eros* becomes even harder to draw given Socrates' attempt, echoed in Soble, to diminish or eliminate the importance of the sexual in *eros*; indeed, one might rightly ask whether the distinction is one we ought to maintain.

---

[6] Alan Soble, *The Structure of Love* (New Haven, CT: Yale University Press, 1990).

[7] This way of making the distinction between *eros* and *agape* seems to originate in John Brentlinger, "The Nature of Love," in Soble, *Eros, Agape, and Philia*, 136–48. There, Brentlinger poses the *Euthyphro*-like question, "Do we love someone because she is valuable, or is she valuable because we love her?"; *eros*, of course, is the former style of love, and *agape* is the latter. Nonetheless, this distinction is not accepted by everyone: Irving Singer seems to reject it in trying to offer an account of love that combines both *eros* and *agape*, a combination that the *Euthyphro*-like distinction would rule out (Irving Singer, *The Pursuit of Love* (Baltimore, MD: Johns Hopkins University Press, 1994)).

[8] Henry George Liddell et al., *A Greek-English Lexicon*, 9th edn. (Oxford: Clarendon Press, 1940); John M. Cooper, "Aristotle on the Forms of Friendship," *Review of Metaphysics* 30 (1977): 619–48.

[9] Laurence Thomas, "Friendship," *Synthese* 72 (1987): 217–36.

My own sense, which will be defended implicitly in the account of love and friendship to follow, is that although there are undeniable differences between romantic relationships and relationships of friendship (not to mention parent–child relationships, filial relationships, and so on), we ought not trace these differences to a distinction in kind between the evaluative attitudes grounding each. In other words, there is a single more basic kind of personal love underlying each; the differences between these various kinds of relationships can, I believe, be understood in terms of the particular way the parties involved conceive of and negotiate the details of the relationships that emerge from reciprocated personal love. Consequently, we should not try too hard to distinguish *philia* from *eros* in providing an account of personal love.

Moreover, as will become clear shortly (in §1.4), I think the distinction typically made between, on the one hand, *agape* as creating value in the beloved and, on the other hand, *eros* and *philia* as responding to already existing value is misplaced. For this distinction is the result of a more general distinction generally made between cognition and conation in terms of a notion of direction of fit, a distinction that I shall reject as having any application to the evaluative attitudes in general, or to love in particular.

I shall therefore largely ignore the place of sexual attraction in personal love as well as anything distinctively romantic about loving relationships. My paradigms of personal love will be the love we have for our friends and children, and so the target of my analysis might be thought to be something closer to *philia* than *eros*. Yet, as I just indicated, this would be a mistake: the evaluative attitude I am calling 'personal love' is intended to be more basic, a part of the common core that is shared by the attitudes we have toward our friends and those we have toward our romantic partners. Whether this approach ultimately proves fruitful is something that can only be evaluated once the entire theory is on the table.

As I have been describing it, personal love (or henceforth just 'love') is an evaluative attitude, and as such it makes sense to talk about the possibility of unrequited love. Indeed, it is intelligible that we can love others we have never met at all and hence do not have any relationship with, though this will surely be a deficient form of love. Nonetheless, as an attitude toward other persons, love can form the basis of distinctive kinds of relationships between persons. Friendship is one such relationship—a particularly important one in our lives. Although I shall focus my attention on friendship in particular, I intend the resulting account to generalize to other relationships grounded in love, and I will have something to say about how this works in Chapter 8.

Of course, friendship is not just any old relationship based on reciprocated love, even together with mutual acknowledgment of this love. For example, parent–child relationships often involve reciprocated and mutually acknowledged love, but they are generally not considered to be friendships: friendship, it is generally thought, presupposes a kind of equality.[10] Yet even this is not enough: adult siblings may have a relationship involving reciprocated love and equality without their relationship being one of friendship. In part what is needed is to understand friendship as a relationship that involves some form of significant interaction between the friends, interactions that stem from their love and that foster a distinctive kind of intimacy between the friends. Part of the aim of an account of friendship, therefore, is to understand more clearly what sorts of interaction and intimacy are required.

In philosophical discussions of friendship, it is common to follow Aristotle (from Book VIII of the *Nicomachean Ethics*) in distinguishing three kinds of friendship: friendships of pleasure, of utility, and of virtue. Although it is a matter of some dispute precisely how to understand these distinctions, the basic idea seems to be that pleasure, utility, and virtue are the reasons we have for loving our friends in these various kinds of relationships. That is, I may love my friend because of the pleasure I get out of her, or because of the ways in which she is useful to me, or because I find her to have a virtuous character. These grounds for love, it can be expected, shape the kinds of interaction and intimacy that are characteristic of each kind of friendship.

There is an apparent tension here between the idea that friendship essentially involves being concerned for your friend for his sake and the

---

[10] Not everyone agrees, however. Among those who, perhaps through the influence of the historical notion of *philia*, explicitly intend their accounts of friendship to include parent–child relationships, are Amélie O. Rorty, "The Historicity of Psychological Attitudes: Love is Not Love Which Alters Not When It Alteration Finds," in *Friendship: A Philosophical Reader*, ed. Neera Kapur Badhwar (Ithaca, NY: Cornell University Press, 1993), 73–88; Neera Kapur Badhwar, "Friends as Ends in Themselves," *Philosophy and Phenomenological Research* 48 (1987): 1–23; Marilyn A. Friedman, "Friendship and Moral Growth," *Journal of Value Inquiry* 23 (1989): 3–13. To a large extent, this seems to be a merely verbal dispute: although there are certainly important similarities between friendships and parent–child relationships (such as their grounding in personal love), there are also important differences (such as whether the relationship is among equals). Whether we call both kinds of relationships "friendships" is a choice about how to use the term. I shall, however, side with common opinion, understanding friendship to exclude parent–child relationships.

idea of pleasure and utility friendships: how can you be concerned for him for his sake (a part of the love that grounds any friendship) if you do that only because of the pleasure or utility you get out of it? If you benefit your friend only because of the benefits you receive, it would seem that you do not properly love your friend for his sake, and so your relationship is not fully one of friendship after all. So it looks like pleasure and utility friendships are at best deficient modes of friendship; by contrast, virtue friendships, because they are motivated by the excellences of your friend's character, are genuine, non-deficient friendships. For this reason, most contemporary accounts, by focusing their attention on the non-deficient forms of friendship, ignore pleasure and utility friendships.

John Cooper tries to resolve this apparent tension in Aristotle. We should not, he thinks, interpret the sense in which we wish our friends well *because* they are useful to us as providing a justification; the "because" here rather signals a causal connection between our friends' usefulness and our wishing them well:

Understanding the 'because' in this causal way makes it at least as much retrospective as prospective; the well-wishing and well-doing are responses to what the person is and has done rather than merely the expression of a hope as to what he will be and may do in the future.[11]

Consequently, he claims, even pleasure and utility friends are wished well for their sakes rather than for our own. However, Cooper seems to ignore the way in which friendships can change and develop over time in ways that change the social nature of the relationship: what starts out as a pleasure friendship may well develop into something deeper, even though little in what your friend all by himself is and has done has changed. Rather, what changes in this transformation, we might think, is the character of the intimacy and commitment each friend has to the other; these aspects of friendship, I shall argue, are distinctively social in a way that cannot be captured simply by appealing to "what the person is and has done."

Nonetheless, I intend to sidestep this controversy for reasons similar to those which led me to set aside the distinction between *philia* and *eros*. The differences among these various types of friendship, I shall argue, lie in the friends' (possibly implicit) conception of their relationship: of its nature and extent. Although my paradigm of friendship will be something closer to a

---

[11] Cooper, "Aristotle on the Forms of Friendship," 633.

friendship of virtue, that is because my aim is in part to understand how close and intimate personal relationships can get. Friendships of pleasure and utility, however, need not be construed as *deficient* modes of such close friendships: although the friends in the former relationships are not as close as they are in the latter, there need be nothing defective about the former relationships that the parties involved ought to strive to overcome.

1.2 Ordinary Conceptions of Persons

Given this preliminary understanding of what I intend in discussing love and friendship, it is now time to say something about why this discussion is important. Of course, understanding love and friendship is important in its own right because of their centrality in our lives. However, I shall argue, the importance of a philosophical account of love and friendship goes much deeper: to our very understanding of what it is to be a person. One of my central claims will be that two common tendencies in recent philosophical thought about persons prevent us from properly understanding love, friendship, and their importance for the self, so that arriving at an adequate account of love and friendship requires substantial revision to the kind of understanding of persons that is now dominant.

The first of these tendencies is to conceive of our intentional mental states as being divided into two mutually exclusive and exhaustive categories of cognition and conation. The basic idea is often expressed in terms of a notion of direction of fit.[12] Thus, our *cognitions*, which are mental states like belief or judgment, have *mind-to-world direction of fit* in that when there is a discrepancy between what we cognize to be the case and how the world is, it is our minds—our cognition—that ought to change so as to conform to the world in order for our cognition to be successful. By contrast, our *conations*, which are mental states like desire, have *world-to-mind direction of fit* in that when there is a discrepancy between our conations and the world, it is the world that ought to be changed to conform to our minds in order for our conation to be successful—to be satisfied.

---

[12] For a clear and influential account of the notion of direction of fit, see, for example, John R. Searle, *Intentionality: An Essay in the Philosophy of Mind* (Cambridge: Cambridge University Press, 1983).

Underlying this distinction between cognitions and conations is a related distinction between theoretical and practical reason. Reason in general is conceived as a matter of figuring out how to achieve the requisite correspondence between mind and world, given the appropriate direction of fit. Consequently, *theoretical reason* is understood to be a capacity we exercise in figuring out how things are by articulating and applying the norms of epistemic rationality so as to get our thoughts to correspond to the world with the sort of direction of fit characteristic of cognition. Similarly, *practical reason* is understood to be a capacity we exercise in figuring out how to satisfy our conations by articulating and applying the norms of instrumental rationality; by acting in the ways prescribed by practical reason, we thereby aim to impose on the world the sort of world-to-mind direction of fit characteristic of conation.

These related distinctions—between cognition and conation on the one hand and between theoretical and practical reason (or epistemic and instrumental rationality) on the other—are supposed to be mutually exclusive. For in the case of cognition, if the world is to be the source of the relevant standards for assessing the fitness of the connection between mind and world, then the world must have a kind of rational priority over our cognitions. Conversely, our conations must have a kind of rational priority over the world if they are to be the source of the relevant standards for assessing the fitness of the connection between world and mind. It is the direction of rational priority here that makes cognition and conation be mutually exclusive, for no mental state, apparently, could have both kinds of priority; epistemic and instrumental rationality, then, are the kinds of rationality at issue with one or the other direction of priority. Moreover, these distinctions are supposed to be exhaustive. For directions of fit provide normative standards, and there seems to be no alternative source of such standards than either the mind or the world. Consequently, any intentional mental state must be either a cognition or a conation but not both.

The result of this understanding of our intentional mental states is that cognition comes to be seen as intrinsically more rational than conation in two ways. First, only our cognitions are fully rational in that they are always subject to correction by the norms of epistemic rationality given the mind-to-world direction of fit they display. Conations, with their world-to-mind direction of fit, lack a source outside of themselves in terms of which they can be corrected, and so they are intrinsically less rational than cognition. Of course, we can "correct" our conations by subjecting them to norms of consistency and coherence, especially in light of instrumental rationality, but there is nothing outside of conation itself to which they must be answerable, on pain of giving up the world-to-mind direction of fit that makes them be conations rather than cognitions. Second, reasoning itself is understood to be a cognitive ability. For the outcome of a process of reasoning, whether theoretical or practical, will be a judgment containing our best understanding of how things are or of what to do: an understanding that can be explicitly confronted with the world through the application of epistemic or instrumental rationality. The result is that in our understanding of persons it is our cognitive faculties that are emphasized, and it is by exercising these cognitive faculties that we ought to try as best we can to control our conative states of, especially, desire and emotion: to suppress them entirely or at least mitigate their effects on the rest of our thoughts and actions. In this way, our rational nature is sometimes conceived as antithetical to our emotions.

In previous work, I have called this understanding of cognition and conation in terms of the notion of direction of fit, together with the correlative account of epistemic and instrumental rationality, the *cognitive–conative divide*.[13] My claim, to be motivated in §1.4 and argued more fully later, especially in Chapters 2 and 6, is that at least when it comes to the evaluative attitudes including love, the cognitive–conative divide cannot be sustained.

The second tendency in recent philosophical thought about persons that I think we must reject is a tendency toward individualism. This individualism takes two forms, namely an egocentric conception of intimate concerns and an individualist conception of autonomy; I shall consider these in turn.

The egocentric conception of intimate concerns arises when we try to cash out intuitions about what makes an intimate concern be distinctively intimate. The sense of 'intimacy' at issue here can best be conveyed by contrasting intimate concerns like love from non-intimate concerns like compassion. Both love and compassion are directed at particular persons and involve a concern for their well-being as such; however, my compassionate concern for a particular homeless man, for example, is

---

[13] Bennett W. Helm, *Emotional Reason: Deliberation, Motivation, and the Nature of Value* (Cambridge: Cambridge University Press, 2001).

lacking in a kind of intimacy that love involves. Such intimacy does not consist simply in the centrality the concern has for my own life—in the fact that my identity is somehow involved in having such concern. For although I may identify with being the type of person who exhibits such compassion, the connection between my identity and the homeless man is too indirect to be of the right sort. What is needed for the sort of intimacy characteristic of love, apparently, is a kind of identification with my beloved *herself*: I must take her identity "to heart." In "taking her identity to heart," I am concerned with her identity in a way that is somehow analogous to my concern for my own identity—or, for that matter, to her concern for her own identity. Thus, the intuition is that this *intimate identification*, as we might call it, is what distinguishes the kind of concern involved in love proper from other, less intimate forms of personal concern such as compassion.

Although I think this notion of "intimate identification" thus vaguely specified is largely correct, it is so far merely a gesture in the direction of what is needed to understand the sort of intimate concern characteristic of love. The *egocentric conception of intimate concerns* is an attempt to articulate this notion in a particular way: an intimate identification on this conception is one in which your concern for the identity of the other is not merely *analogous* to your concern for your own identity; it is a *part* of it. In identifying with your beloved, you make her cares and concerns, her interests and values, become a part of your identity, so that you care about her as a part of caring about yourself and thereby tie your own well-being to hers: when things go well or poorly for your beloved, they thereby go well or poorly for you. Intimacy, therefore, requires incorporating her well-being into your own.

The egocentric conception of intimate concerns, therefore, construes intimate identification in terms of this sort of incorporation of another's identity into one's own. Thus, the *egocentrism* at issue here lies in the way intimate concerns involve this essential connection to the subject's own identity: it is only by virtue of this connection of the object of my concern to my own identity that this concern is intelligible as distinctively intimate.

The second form of individualism, the *individualist conception of autonomy*, claims that autonomy is a capacity that each of us has individually and cannot be delegated or shared. *Autonomy*, as I shall understand it here, is a capacity not only to determine how one shall act but also and more fundamentally to determine who one shall be; in this way by exercising one's autonomy one can exercise control over one's *identity* or sense of the kind of life worth one's living. So the claim is that our autonomy makes us self-determining: within the limits of the power of our wills, it is fundamentally up to each of us to determine who he or she shall be, what to believe and value, and how to act. Given this, the influence of others in shaping our identities ought to be limited to offering reasons or advice, which we can take or not as we choose; any influence others might have on us beyond this, it would seem, undermines our autonomy.

The individualist conception of autonomy itself stems from two further, plausible thoughts about persons. First is the more general thought that mental states and processes essentially belong to individuals; there is no such thing as a group mind or a mental state that literally belongs to more than one person. Consequently, setting aside cases of brainwashing or other undue influence, it is individuals who are responsible for what they think, and it is individuals who can be charged with irrationality or worse when their thoughts go astray. In particular, the sense of what it is worth doing or who it is worth being, as well as any processes of deliberation we might engage in to arrive at these conclusions through the exercise of autonomy, belong essentially to each of us as individuals.

Of course, just as we might delegate responsibility for some of the things we believe (as when I believe scientific theories merely on good authority), so too we might delegate responsibility for determining our own identities. At this point, however, the second thought comes into play: to delegate responsibility for our own identities is, we might say with an air of paradox, to come to have an identity that is not really our own, that is *inauthentic*. In part this thought is influenced by an acceptance of the cognitive–conative divide. For although there is considerable controversy about whether moral values are proper objects of cognition or conation (hence the debate between cognitivists and non-cognitivists in metaethics), it is uncontroversial (at least among proponents of the divide) that the personal values constituting one's identity are proper objects of conation: they are not (at least not exactly) truth evaluable but are rather subjective in the sense of being relative to each individual person. This is not to deny that our personal values might be constrained by, for example, moral values; rather, the point is that within such constraints there is considerable room for individual choice. This suggests that for a personal value to be authentically mine, I must not merely have it but endorse it as the result of an exercise of autonomy that, given the first thought, must be mine alone. Hence, it seems, autonomy cannot be delegated or shared.

Together, the egocentric conception of intimate concerns and the individualist conception of autonomy form what I shall call the *individualist conception of persons*. Once again, my claim is that we must reject this conception of persons in order to make sense of love and friendship.

I have thus far indicated disagreement with two central tendencies in our ordinary conception of persons: the understanding of our intentional mental states in terms of the cognitive–conative divide and the individualist conception of persons. Yet there seem to be sensible and even powerful reasons for going along with these tendencies, reasons to which I have just alluded. Why, then, would I want to reject these tendencies? My claim, to be motivated in §§1.3–1.5 and for which I shall argue more fully later, is that it is only by rejecting the cognitive–conative divide that we can avoid various problems concerning the justification of love and so restore emotions to their proper place in an understanding of persons as *rational animals*, and it is only by rejecting the individualist conception of persons that we can make sense of the kind of intimacy and shared agency that are possible within love and friendship.

In motivating this claim, I shall divide the most prominent accounts of love into three basic types (love as union, as robust concern, and as valuing),[14] showing how each implicitly presupposes the egocentric conception of personal concerns or the cognitive–conative divide. In §1.3, I suggest that it is ultimately these presuppositions that lead the union and robust concern accounts to an unsatisfactory account of the kind of intimacy that love involves. In §1.4, I suggest that accounts of love that accept the cognitive–conative divide, including accounts of love as valuing, force us to choose—unacceptably—between rejecting the idea that love can be justified for better or worse reasons and rejecting the idea that our loves are

[14] Some accounts of love do not fit into this attempt at categorization, including especially accounts that understand love to be an emotion or a complex of emotions; prominent examples of such accounts include Richard Wollheim, *The Thread of Life* (Cambridge, MA: Harvard University Press, 1984); Rorty, "The Historicity of Psychological Attitudes"; D. W. Hamlyn, "The Phenomena of Love and Hate," in Soble, *Eros, Agape, and Philia*, 218–34; Annette C. Baier, "Unsafe Loves," in *The Philosophy of (Erotic) Love*, ed. Robert C. Solomon and Kathleen M. Higgins (Lawrence, KS: Kansas University Press, 1991), 433–50. For the most part, however, these authors do not aim to provide anything like a complete account of love, thus making attempts at categorization hazardous.

central to who we are and so are partly a matter for self-determination.[15] Finally, in §1.5 I turn to examine the nature of friendship and social action, arguing that alternative accounts of friendship are unable to make sense of the distinctively social relationship that it is because they implicitly presuppose the individualistic conception of autonomy, for it is only by giving up on this presupposition that we can make sense of the kind of social shared activity and shared lives that are possible within friendship.

1.3 Intimacy of Love, the Union and Robust-Concern Accounts

The *union account of love* claims that love—especially romantic love—consists in the formation of some significant kind of union, a "we," in which the boundaries between the lovers' identities become blurred or erased, so that "all distinction between my interests and your interests is overcome."[16] In this way, what formerly had been separate identities have now become a shared identity, a " 'fusion' of two souls,"[17] in which the lovers pool not only their well-beings but also their capacity for autonomy as they come to form this "we."[18] Union accounts use this notion of a shared identity to make sense of the distinctively personal or intimate nature of love: the idea is that what makes love intimate is that it affects our very sense of who we are as persons.

Critics of the union account, of whom Alan Soble[19] has been most vocal, have found these claims to be excessive: union theorists, they claim, take too literally the ontological commitments of this notion of a "we." This leads to two lines of criticism. The first is that union accounts do away with individual autonomy. In line with the individualist conception

---

[15] I provide more sustained arguments against the cognitive–conative divide in Helm, *Emotional Reason*; arguments that stem from the impossibility, once we accept this divide, of properly understanding both rational motivation and deliberation about values.

[16] Roger Scruton, *Sexual Desire: A Moral Philosophy of the Erotic* (New York, NY: Free Press, 1986), 230. For similar claims, see Frankfurt, *The Reasons of Love*, 61–2.

[17] Robert C. Solomon, *About Love: Reinventing Romance for Our Times* (New York, NY: Simon & Schuster, 1988), 24.

[18] Robert Nozick, "Love's Bond," in *The Examined Life: Philosophical Meditations* (New York, NY: Simon & Schuster, 1989), 71. See also Mark Fisher, *Personal Love* (London: Duckworth, 1990); Solomon, *About Love*.

[19] See, for example, Alan Soble, "Union, Autonomy, and Concern," in *Love Analyzed*, ed. Roger E. Lamb (Boulder, CO: Westview Press, 1997), 65–92.

of autonomy, these critics understand autonomy as involving a kind of independence on the part of the autonomous agent, such that she is in control over both what she does and who she is, as this is constituted by her interests, values, concerns, and so on. However, the criticism goes, union accounts, by doing away with a clear distinction between your interests and mine, thereby undermine the sort of independence central to autonomy. If autonomy is a part of the individual's good, then, union accounts make love out to be, to this extent, bad; so much the worse for the union view.[20]

Union theorists have responded to this criticism in several ways, each of which concedes the individualist conception of autonomy the critics presuppose. Robert Solomon acknowledges this "tension" between union and autonomy, but describes it as "the paradox of love,"[21] a view Soble rightly derides: merely to call it a paradox, as Solomon does, is not to face up to the problem.[22] Addressing the problem more forthrightly, Robert Nozick seems to think that a loss of autonomy in love is a desirable feature of the sort of union lovers can achieve, although he does not argue for why such a loss would be desirable;[23] and Mark Fisher, somewhat more reluctantly, claims that the loss of autonomy in love is an acceptable consequence of love.[24] However, such responses, without further argument, seem like mere bullet biting. Moreover, and ultimately more important (as I shall suggest in §1.5), such responses, by accepting the individualist conception of autonomy, do away with what I shall argue is one of the central insights of the union view: the way particular personal relationships can significantly enhance our lives, our activity, and our autonomy by dissolving the social barriers that normally separate people from each other. We need to do better.

The second criticism of union accounts involves a substantive, albeit relatively uncontroversial, view of love; indeed, such a view is already a part of the characterization of personal love I offered in §1.1. Part of what it is to love someone, it is assumed, is to have a concern for him *for his sake*. Insofar as such a concern really is for his sake, it requires the possibility of the lover's sacrificing herself for the sake of her beloved, and this requires

---

[20] Singer, *The Pursuit of Love*, 134–43; Soble, "Union, Autonomy, and Concern," especially §III.

[21] Solomon, *About Love*, 64 ff.

[22] Soble's criticism is presented in the context of similar claims by Erich Fromm (Erich Fromm, *The Art of Loving* (New York, NY: Harper Perennial Library, 1974)), but it applies equally well to Solomon. See Soble, "Union, Autonomy, and Concern," 70.

[23] Nozick, "Love's Bond," 74.   [24] Fisher, *Personal Love*, 28.

that we be able to distinguish between the interests of the lover and those of the beloved. Yet the union account makes the blurring of this distinction the centerpiece of its understanding of love, and this amounts to the lover's simply *appropriating* the beloved's interests for her own, rather than caring about them for his sake.

Some advocates of the union account see this so-called criticism as a point in their favor: we need to explain how it is that I can have a concern for people other than myself, and the union view does this by understanding your interests to be a part of my own; how else, we might ask, can we account for *my* caring intimately about others' goods? Moreover, Neil Delaney, responding to an apparent tension between our desire to be loved unselfishly (for fear of otherwise being exploited) and our desire to be loved for reasons (which presumably involve an attractiveness to the lover given the lover's needs and interests and so have a kind of selfish basis), says:

My inclination is both to accept love for properties [which provide us with reasons] and to countenance the implications regarding the selfishness of would-be lovers. Given my view that the romantic ideal is primarily characterized by a desire to achieve a profound consolidation of needs and interests through the formation of a *we*, I do not think a little selfishness of the sort described should pose a worry to either party. After all, isn't it gratifying to feel needed?[25]

This, however, does not resolve the underlying problem. As Delaney's comments make clear, the result is an attempt to explain the lover's concern for her beloved egocentrically by virtue of the required connection between the lover's identity and the beloved; indeed, the egocentrism here is precisely the egocentrism of intimate concern that forms a part of the individualist conception of persons. Yet critics are objecting precisely to the idea that such egocentrism has a place in an account of love.[26] Although I think this way of putting the criticism is valid for the more extreme versions of the union view, it masks the problem that might be raised for Delaney's more moderate view: to construe intimacy in such egocentric

[25] Neil Delaney, "Romantic Love and Loving Commitment: Articulating a Modern Ideal," *American Philosophical Quarterly* 33, no. 4 (1996): 346. Delaney's view is not the sort of simple union account that Nozick, Scruton, and Solomon offer. He rather conceives of the "we" as a kind of federation of two selves, in which each preserves, at least to a large extent, their own identity and autonomy within that federation. Such a view is developed further by Marilyn A. Friedman, "Romantic Love and Personal Autonomy," *Midwest Studies in Philosophy* 22 (1998): 162–81.

[26] See, e.g., Lawrence A. Blum, *Friendship, Altruism, and Morality* (London: Routledge & Kegan Paul, 1980); Lawrence A. Blum, "Friendship as a Moral Phenomenon," in Badhwar, *Friendship: A Philosophical Reader*, 192–210; Soble, "Union, Autonomy, and Concern."

terms is to fail to capture how such intimacy is an intimacy of concern that is for the beloved's sake precisely because it puts the lover's needs and interests at the focus of that concern. Such a concern, therefore, motivates actions in part prudentially rather than, as love sometimes seems to require, merely for the sake of the beloved. Consequently, it seems, the union account's conception does not capture the sense of intimacy that is essential to love: although such intimacy requires a kind of closeness, it must also not undermine or blur the separateness of the two persons.[27]

The intuitions behind these objections to the union view lead many to adopt what I shall call, following Soble, the *robust-concern account*, which takes concern for the other for her sake to be the central and defining feature of love. Robust-concern accounts try to understand the notion of concern for another for her sake largely in terms that apply equally well to non-intimate sorts of concern, such as those grounded in compassion. Thus, Gabriele Taylor provides a rather generic robust-concern account of love as follows:

To summarize: if x loves y then x wants to benefit and be with y etc., and he has these wants (or at least some of them) because he believes y has some determinate characteristics ψ in virtue of which he thinks it worth while to benefit and be with y. He regards satisfaction of these wants as an end and not as a means towards some other end.[28]

Taylor understands the concern for another for her sake in terms of non-instrumental desires to help and be with another, and these desires are caused by an assessment of the beloved's character.[29] One might ask of this generic account what makes the analysis be one of love in particular rather than compassion. It is not clear that Taylor has much to add here, though other variants of this basic account do better. Thus, W. Newton-Smith argues that

---

[27] For a similar conclusion, offered in the context of an account of friendship, see Wollheim, *The Thread of Life*, 276. This criticism is similar to that offered of the "mirror view" of friendship in Dean Cocking and Jeanette Kennett, "Friendship and the Self," *Ethics* 108, no. 3 (1998): 502–27. The *mirror view* is the idea that "friendship is based on self-love; as such our choice of the friend is based on an appreciation of the similarity of the other to oneself" (506). They characterize such a view as "narcissistic," arguing that it "misrepresents the depth and nature of the engagement which friends have with each other and the impact which each has on the other" (509).

[28] Gabriele Taylor, "Love," *Proceedings of the Aristotelian Society* 76 (1976): 157.

[29] For similar accounts, see Soble, *The Structure of Love*; David O. Brink, "Rational Egoism, Self, and Others," in *Identity, Character, and Morality: Essays in Moral Psychology*, ed. Owen Flanagan and Amélie O. Rorty (Cambridge, MA: MIT Press, 1990), 339–78; Hugh LaFollette, *Personal Relationships: Love, Identity, and Morality* (Cambridge, MA: Blackwell Press, 1996).

this concern must give rise to (or itself involve?) feelings of affection for the beloved as well as a commitment to her that, unlike mere liking, potentially conflicts with one's other (possibly moral) commitments.[30] Richard White adds that this concern for your beloved must both affect your emotional state and transform your identity in some way—in more subtle and indirect ways than simply by identifying with your beloved and so appropriating her interests.[31] Laurence Thomas claims instead that such concern must create a "bond of trust" that enables the lovers to share secrets with each other.[32] And Harry Frankfurt claims that the concern you have for your beloved is not grounded in a positive evaluation of her but rather bestows value on her.[33]

It is not clear, however, that any of these variants of the robust-concern view succeeds in making sense of the kind of intimate concern characteristic of love. Recall that understanding distinctively intimate concern seems to require a kind of identification of yourself with the object of that concern so as to be able to distinguish intimate concern from the sort of concern for another involved in, for example, compassion (see §1.2, p. 9–10). Indeed, it is this intuition that leads to the egocentric conception of intimate concerns as this is embraced by union accounts of love: what differentiates my loving concern for another person from merely compassionate, non-loving concern is that in loving him I must identify with him by tying my well-being to his and so making his interests be my interests. The trouble for proponents of the robust-concern view is that, in recoiling from the excesses of union accounts by appealing to a rather generic notion of

[30] W. Newton-Smith, "A Conceptual Investigation of Love," in Soble, *Eros, Agape, and Philia*, 199–217.

[31] Richard J. White, *Love's Philosophy* (Lanham, MD: Rowman & Littlefield, 2001).

[32] Laurence Thomas, "Friends and Lovers," in *Person to Person*, ed. George Graham and Hugh LaFollette (Philadelphia, PA: Temple University Press, 1989), 182–98; Laurence Thomas, "Reasons for Loving," in Solomon and Higgins, *The Philosophy of (Erotic) Love*, 467–76; Laurence Thomas, "Friendship and Other Loves," in Badhwar, *Friendship: A Philosophical Reader*, 48–64.

[33] Frankfurt, *The Reasons of Love*, 38–9. I cited Frankfurt above as a proponent of the union account (see note 16). However, he also seems to share elements of the robust-concern view insofar as he claims that the essence of love is a kind of "disinterested" concern: a concern that "can be satisfied completely and only by the satisfaction of interests that are altogether distinct from and independent of his own" (Harry G. Frankfurt, "Autonomy, Necessity, and Love," in *Necessity, Volition, and Love* (Cambridge: Cambridge University Press, 1999), 134). Yet if my interests and those of my beloved are independent, it is not clear how it can also be true that "the interests of [a person's] beloved are not actually *other* than his [the lover's] at all. They are his interests too" (Frankfurt, *The Reasons of Love*, 61). As is suggested by my diagnosis below, Frankfurt is trying to have his cake and eat it too in both accepting and recoiling from an egocentric conception of intimate concerns.

the concern we might have for another for her sake, they fail to make sense of that concern as distinctly intimate and so as distinct in kind from non-intimate forms of concern for persons.[34]

Indeed, we can now begin to see that both the union and the robust-concern accounts make the same underlying mistake, which prevents them from providing adequate accounts of the intimacy of concern that is central to love. Union accounts, in trying to make sense of something like what I have called "intimate identification," appeal to a conception of intimacy understood in egocentric terms, such that distinctively personal, intimate concerns are ultimately grounded in one's own interests, so that the actions that stem from these concerns are motivated ultimately by prudence. It is this egocentrism that leads union accounts to understand intimate identification in terms of the blurring of the distinction between my interests and my beloved's, so that love ultimately is understood to involve the appropriation of my beloved's interests. Proponents of robust-concern accounts, correctly seeing that love cannot be construed egocentrically in this way, nonetheless retain the egocentric conception of intimacy. This leads them to reject the idea that intimate identification is central to love, and they consequently fail to make sense of the distinction between love and compassionate concern.

The choice between the union and robust-concern accounts, between an understanding of intimate identification as breaking down the boundaries between persons and the rejection of intimate identification as central to love, is a false one, foisted on us by the unnecessary egocentric conception of intimate concern. The solution, I shall argue, is to reject that egocentric conception of intimacy. As suggested above, we should come to understand what is distinctively intimate about love in terms of a distinctive kind of concern for the identity of another as the particular person he is, a concern that is the same in kind as the concern you have for your own identity but without presupposing that you thereby make your beloved's interests and identity a part of your own. The task, of course, is to articulate how this is possible: how can we provide an account of non-egocentrically yet nonetheless genuinely intimate concern for others? This is a task I shall undertake primarily in Part II.

---

[34] This intuitive criticism of the robust-concern account will be cashed out in more detail later, in the introduction to Ch. 5.

This strategy may seem similar to that advocated by Jennifer Whiting in her accounts of friendship and personal identity.[35] According to Whiting, we ought to understand our concern for our future selves as essentially the same in kind as our concern for our present friends. David Brink adopts an egocentric construal of Whiting's account (or, more generally, any Aristotelian account) of concern, arguing that our personal concern for others must be understood in terms of the conceptually prior prudential concern for ourselves;[36] this is, of course, an acceptance of the egocentric conception of intimate concerns. Whiting, however, explicitly rejects this egocentric construal of her view, arguing that we cannot give conceptual priority to either self-concern or other-concern, but must rather understand each of these in terms of the concern for persons (whether myself or someone else) as having a certain sort of character. Such concern or affection, Whiting claims, is therefore impersonal and disinterested; as she says, this "involves rejecting the importance traditionally attached to the distinction between self and other."[37]

Although I sympathize with Whiting's attempt to overcome an excessive emphasis on individualism and so her explicit rejection of what I am here calling the egocentric conception of intimate concerns, she recoils from this egocentrism not merely to an impersonal account of love and friendship but also to an impersonal account of our sense of ourselves as temporally extended agents. As Brink has subsequently argued, such impersonal accounts "assign only *extrinsic* significance to special concern;... by contrast, common sense attaches *intrinsic* significance to special relationships"[38]—including, we might add, our special relationships to ourselves. At issue here is the question of how a concern can be intimate and personal, involving intrinsic significance, without being egocentric. This in turn raises questions about the justification of the concern we have for ourselves or for our beloveds. We do not ordinarily think that such justification is an objective matter, requiring appeal merely to properties that any (suitably trained) observer could recognize apart from their involvement in a particular relationship; this is what I take Brink to mean in saying that

[35] Jennifer E. Whiting, "Friends and Future Selves," *Philosophical Review* 95, no. 4 (1986): 547–80; Jennifer E. Whiting, "Impersonal Friends," *Monist* 74 (1991): 3–29.
[36] Brink, "Rational Egoism, Self, and Others."   [37] Whiting, "Impersonal Friends," 6.
[38] David O. Brink, "Eudaimonism, Love and Friendship, and Political Community," *Social Philosophy and Policy* 16 (1999): 269.

special concern does not merely have extrinsic significance. Rather, the importance of these relationships and of the concern we have for ourselves or our beloveds, is something that can be appreciated and justified only from within that relationship—only intrinsically, personally. Precisely how we are to understand the nature of such justification is a general problem for accounts of love and friendship, which I shall address in §1.4.

1.4 Justification, Fungibility, and Love as Valuing

How is it possible to justify loving someone? This is a question not about whether love generally is a good thing; it is rather about particular loves for particular persons. Nonetheless, there are two conceptually distinct questions that are relevant here:

Discernment of love: What, if anything, justifies my coming to love this particular person rather than someone else given limited time, energy, and other resources?

Constancy of love: What, if anything, justifies my continuing to love this particular person given the changes—both in him and in the overall circumstances—that have occurred since I began loving him?

Most philosophical discussions of the justification of love focus on the question of the discernment of love, which is typically not distinguished from that concerning the constancy of love.[39]

The answers to these justificatory questions depend on how we construe the kind of evaluative attitude that love is. Given the assumption of the cognitive–conative divide, cognitive states are rationally assessed and so justified in terms of the norms of epistemic rationality in which, roughly, we assess their fit with the world, whereas conative states are rationally assessed merely in light of their overall coherence with other conative states (as well as, indirectly, cognitive states) in part in terms of the norms of instrumental

---

[39] Indeed, not every account of love accepts these as distinct questions or even accepts each of these as valid questions. Thus, David Velleman, for example, thinks there is no question of the discernment of love; see J. David Velleman, "Love as a Moral Emotion," *Ethics* 109 (1999): 338–74. (I shall criticize Velleman's account in §1.4.2.) Nonetheless, pretheoretically these distinctions make some sense and it is worth asking particular theories whether it is appropriate to deny these pretheoretic intuitions.

rationality. Accounts of love that understand it primarily as a form of valuing take an explicit position on whether love is cognitive or conative, giving rise to appraisal accounts and bestowal accounts of love, respectively. It is in this context that I shall raise problems concerning the possibility of answering questions of justification in light of the assumption of the cognitive–conative divide. Although I raise these issues in a discussion of accounts of love as valuing, the problems are general, applying equally to any account of love that accepts the cognitive–conative divide. Thus, robust-concern accounts are generally explicit in conceiving of love in cognitive terms; although other accounts of love may not take an explicit stand on this issue, given the pervasiveness of the cognitive–conative divide in philosophical accounts of the mind it is reasonable to assume that they accept this divide unless they explicitly reject it and so that they fall prey to these general problems.

1.4.1 Justification and Bestowal Accounts

Bestowal accounts understand love to be a conative matter, claiming that love is a matter of bestowing or projecting intrinsic value on the beloved.[40] Irving Singer, the most vocal proponent of the bestowal account of love, understands such bestowal to be a kind of attachment and commitment to the beloved in which one comes to treat him as an end in himself and so to respond to his ends, interests, concerns, and so on, as having value for their own sake. This means in part that the bestowal of value reveals itself "by caring about the needs and interests of the beloved, by wishing to benefit or protect her, by delighting in her achievements," and so on.[41] What distinguishes the bestowal account from the robust-concern account is that whereas the robust-concern account understands such caring to be what love consists in, the bestowal account thinks it is merely the *effect* of the bestowal of value that is love: in bestowing value on my beloved, I make him be valuable in such a way that I ought to respond with robust concern.

Given this brief sketch, what can we say about how to respond to the justificatory questions raised above? The bestowal view, it seems, must

---

[40] Examples of bestowal accounts of love include Irving Singer, "From *The Nature of Love*," in Solomon and Higgins, *The Philosophy of (Erotic) Love*, 259–78; Singer, *The Pursuit of Love*; Marilyn A. Friedman, *What Are Friends For? Feminist Perspectives on Personal Relationships and Moral Theory* (Ithaca, NY: Cornell University Press, 1993).
[41] Singer, "From *The Nature of Love*," 270.

simply reject these questions: insofar as the value at issue in love is bestowed by the lover on to the beloved, what room is there to say that this bestowal happens for better or worse reasons? To attempt to supply justificatory (as opposed to explanatory) reasons here would be, it seems, to appeal to something in the beloved that *merits* the value that is bestowed, which would be to construe love as responding to an antecedent value and so as a cognitive matter, thus contradicting the central claim of the bestowal account. Thus, Singer explicitly claims that love cannot be justified. Marilyn Friedman goes even further in arguing:

> To the extent to which our commitment to someone is contingent upon our high regard for her, then to *that* extent our commitment to that person is subordinate to our commitment to the relevant moral standards and is not intrinsically a commitment to that person.[42]

Friedman's point is that to base our loves on positive appraisals of our beloved's excellences is to undermine the kind of commitment we have to them as particular persons, a commitment that is essential to loving them.[43] Love, therefore, is not the sort of attitude that could be justified.

Friedman's argument is too quick. For to appeal to an appraisal of the good qualities of your beloved's character in order to justify your love is not on its own to subordinate your love to that appraisal. Rather, we might think, in loving someone you must be open to the possibility of changing your evaluative outlook because of that love; when this happens, we might say, you have in effect subordinated your commitment to certain values to your commitment to your beloved. Indeed, that your beloved can have this kind of effect on you is, we might think, central to the intimacy of love—to the way in which you take your beloved's identity to heart in loving him.

More generally, although we have some intuitions pulling us toward bestowal accounts of love and their stand on its justification ("Love is blind"), we also have strong intuitions concerning the discernment of love that pull us in the opposite direction. Given the manifest importance love

---

[42] Friedman, "Friendship and Moral Growth," 6.

[43] Of course, we might think, our loves might be justified by appeal to properties other than excellences in our beloved's character traits. In particular, we ordinarily think that certain familial relationships justify or even demand love: in spite of her many character flaws and few redeeming traits, I ought to love her because she's my sister (or daughter or mother). However, I shall set such cases aside for the moment.

and loving relationships have in our lives, it would be appalling if love were not a discerning attitude, if we could not have better or worse justifying reasons for loving one person rather than another. Could it be, for example, mere historical accident that I love my wife rather than someone else or no one at all? Moreover, if love does involve a commitment to your beloved, why *should* that commitment be sustained? Why shouldn't I dump my wife when she develops Alzheimer's and so becomes an inconvenient burden on me? Conversely, am I required to stand by my wife come what may, including her transformation into a serial killer or some other kind of inhuman monster? The questions concerning the discernment and constancy of love are too central to our understanding and experience of love to be dismissed because of a theoretical commitment to bestowal.

Singer does think there must be a place within love for an appraisal of your beloved's qualities. Bestowing value on someone requires having a clear sense of her well-being and what impacts that well-being positively or negatively, and this in turn requires knowing her strengths and deficiencies, which is a matter of appraising her in various ways. Bestowal thus presupposes a kind of appraisal as a way of "really seeing" the beloved and attending to her. Nonetheless, such appraisal is only required so that the commitment to one's beloved and her value as thus bestowed has practical import and is not "a blind submission to some unknown being."[44] Thus, Singer tries to avoid the conclusion that love is blind by appealing to the role of appraisal: it is only because we appraise another as having certain virtues and vices that we come to bestow value on him. However, the "because" here, since it cannot justify the evaluation (on pain of giving up the bestowal account of love), is at best a kind of contingent causal explanation.[45] In this respect, Singer's account of the selectivity of love makes unintelligible the way in which our loves can be undertaken for better or worse reasons—can be more or less discerning. This is a systematic problem for any bestowal view.

---

[44] Singer, "From *The Nature of Love*," 272; see also Singer, *The Pursuit of Love*, 139 ff. and Irving Singer, *Philosophy of Love: A Partial Summing-up* (Cambridge, MA: MIT Press, 2009), 51–3.

[45] Singer seems to deny this, saying, "Appraisal contributes to love directly, and not merely as a causal factor" (Singer, *The Pursuit of Love*, 141). However, in articulating what he means by "contributing to love directly," Singer seems to say only that in order to bestow value and so come to value the beloved's "desires and ideals" for their own sake, we must first know what these desires and ideals are; this is the point of appraisal. Such an epistemic contribution may not be merely a causal factor, but it does not help us understand the discernment or constancy of love.

In spite of this criticism, there is a kernel of truth in the bestowal view: there is surely something right about the idea that love in a sense creates value and is not merely a response to antecedent value. As I shall argue in §1.4.2, accounts that understand the kind of evaluative attitude that love is in cognitive terms, as a matter of mere discovery, thereby create their own insoluble problems concerning the justification of love. The solution will be to reject the cognitive–conative divide.

1.4.2 Justification and Appraisal Accounts

Whereas bestowal accounts of love understand love in conative terms, a matter of projecting value on to your beloved, *appraisal accounts* of love understand it in cognitive terms: to love someone is to appraise him as having certain valuable properties, such that this appraisal can be held to standards of truth.[46] As with bestowal accounts, appraisal accounts understand love primarily in terms of this valuing; although other accounts of love (including many robust-concern accounts) may involve elements of appraisal, they do not understand such appraisal to be what love consists in. This means that in principle the justification of love on an appraisal account is straightforward: if love is an appraisal, then its justification must be a matter of whether the beloved actually has (or intelligibly seems to have) the valuable properties relevant to the lover's appraisal. In practice, however, it is not so simple.

The difficulty for appraisal accounts arises when we consider what kind of valuable properties are at issue in the appraisal. First, it is clear that these properties must be independent of the lover's attitude of love. This is precisely the difference between the appraisal account of love, which understands love as a cognitive attitude, and the bestowal account of love, which understands it as a conative attitude. Indeed, it is precisely the lack of independence of these valuable properties from the attitude of love that, on the bestowal account, seems to undercut any possibility of justifying love. However, if these valuable properties are independent of the attitude of love, then we run into problems of fungibility.

To be *fungible* is to be replaceable by another relevantly similar object without any loss of value. Thus, money is fungible: if I give you two $5

---

[46] Examples of appraisal accounts of love include: Velleman, "Love as a Moral Emotion"; Niko Kolodny, "Love as Valuing a Relationship," *Philosophical Review* 112 (2003): 135–89.

bills in exchange for a $10 bill, neither of us has lost anything. Is the object of love fungible? That is, can I simply switch from loving one person to loving another relevantly similar person without any loss? The *fungibility problem*, as I shall call it, is commonly put this way: if we accept that love is to be justified by appealing to properties of the beloved, then it may seem that in loving someone for certain reasons, I love him not simply for the individual he is, but because he instantiates those properties. And this may imply that any other person instantiating those same properties would do just as well: my beloved would be fungible. Indeed, there may be another person who exhibits the properties that ground my love to a greater degree than my current beloved does, and so it may seem that in such a case I have reason to "trade up"—to switch my love to the new, better person. However, it seems clear that the objects of our loves are not fungible: love seems to involve a deeply personal commitment to a particular person, a commitment that is antithetical to the idea that our beloveds are fungible or to the idea that we ought to be willing to trade up when possible.

This fungibility problem is distinct from a superficially similar worry raised by Gregory Vlastos in a discussion of Plato's and Aristotle's accounts of love.[47] Vlastos notes that these accounts focus on the *properties* of our beloveds: we are to love people, they say, only insofar as they instantiate the excellences. In so doing, he argues, they fail to distinguish "*disinterested affection for the person* we love" from the "*appreciation of the excellences instantiated by that person*."[48] That is, Vlastos thinks that Plato and Aristotle provide an account of love that is really a love of properties rather than a love of persons, thereby losing what is distinctive about love as an essentially *personal* attitude. As Delaney points out, the solution to Vlastos's problem is relatively easy: we need to distinguish between the object of our love (the person) and its grounds (the properties);[49] in a similar vein, Brink distinguishes between the objects of our loves and the manner in which we love them, which may involve "priz[ing] and promot[ing] their virtue."[50]

The fungibility problem, however, is not that the object of love is a set of properties rather than a person; it is rather that the properties that seem to justify and sustain our loves seem to be repeatable properties, potentially

[47] Gregory Vlastos, "The Individual as Object of Love in Plato," in *Platonic Studies*, 2nd edn. (Princeton, NJ: Princeton University Press, 1981), 3–42.

[48] Ibid., 33, emphasis in the original.   [49] Delaney, "Romantic Love," 343.

[50] Brink, "Eudaimonism, Love and Friendship, and Political Community," 272.

giving us equal if not greater reason to love others than our current beloveds and so seeming to imply that the objects of our loves can simply be replaced with relevantly similar objects without loss. Thus, the fungibility problem is a worry about how we can make sense of the discernment and constancy of love without thereby undermining the idea that love is a response to a particular person rather than a type of person. Any account of love that, like appraisal accounts, accepts a cognitive account of such justification thereby understands justification to proceed by appealing to repeatable, objective properties that others might share, and this seems to imply that nothing of value is lost (or, indeed, that something of value might be gained) by switching our allegiances to another person instantiating these same properties to an equal or greater degree. How, then, can we make sense of discernment without falling into the trap of fungibility?

One tack, taken by David Velleman,[51] is to deny that the fungibility problem is a problem at all: there are no interesting questions to be asked about what justifies my loving this person rather than someone else, and so there is no justificatory worry about whether I should be willing to "trade up"; rather, all people are equally worthy of my love. Understanding this requires understanding the sort of appraisal that love is, distinguishing that appraisal from other positive appraisals of persons, such as respect or admiration, and explaining why we love only some people and not others.

According to Velleman, love is like respect in that it is an appraisal of its object as having dignity—as being a person. What is distinctive of the appraisal that is love, Velleman says, is that whereas respect arrests our tendencies toward self-interest, love arrests

our tendencies toward emotional self-protection from another person, tendencies to draw ourselves in and close ourselves off from being affected by him. Love disarms our emotional defenses; it makes us vulnerable to the other.[52]

This means that the concern, attraction, sympathy, and so on that we normally associate with love are not constituents of love but are rather its normal effects, and love can remain without them.[53] This account therefore

---

[51] Velleman, "Love as a Moral Emotion."   [52] Ibid., 361.

[53] Indeed, Velleman takes this to be a primary selling point of his account: we can, he says, love a meddlesome relative even when we cannot stand being around her and have no interest in promoting her well-being. Such an example, he claims, is not one that robust-concern accounts can make intelligible insofar as they make love consist, perhaps among other things, in the interest to be with and benefit another. However, this conclusion seems too hasty: surely the case of the meddlesome relative

provides a straightforward answer to the question of what makes someone a worthy object of love: that he is a person and so has the sort of dignity as an end in itself that all persons possess. This means that the fungibility problem is a non-starter: things with dignity as the kind of value they possess differ from things with prices insofar as the former are not fungible, whereas the latter are.

This understanding of the justification of love, however, naturally leads us to ask why we love only some people and not others if all are equally worthy of my love. The answer, Velleman claims, lies in the contingent fit between the way some people behaviorally express their dignity as persons and the way I happen to respond to those expressions by becoming emotionally vulnerable to them. The right sort of fit makes someone "lovable" by me, and my responding with love in these cases is a matter of my "really seeing" this person in a way that I fail to do with others who do not fit with me in this way.[54] By 'lovable,' Velleman must mean *able* to be loved, not *worthy* of being loved (given his understanding of love as an appraisal merely of someone as having dignity), and so what he offers is merely an *explanation* rather than a justification of the selectivity of love and so of why my response to another is a matter of love rather than merely respect.

This explanation of the selectivity of love in terms of the "fit" between your expressions of your personhood and my sensitivities to them fails. For the relevant sensitivities on my part are emotional sensitivities: it is the lowering of my emotional defenses that makes me become emotionally vulnerable to you. Thus, I become vulnerable to the harms (or goods) that befall you and so sympathetically feel your pain (or joy). Such emotions themselves are assessable for warrant, and now we can ask why my disappointment that you lost the race is warranted but my being disappointed that a mere stranger lost would not be warranted. The intuitive answer is that I love you but not him. However, this answer is unavailable to Velleman, because he thinks that what makes my response to your dignity be that of love rather than respect is precisely that I feel such emotions, and to appeal to my love in explaining the warrant of these emotions therefore would be viciously circular.

is an example of a deficient sort of love and ought therefore be understood as parasitic on the standard cases. Readily to accommodate such deficient cases of love into a philosophical analysis as being on a par with paradigm cases, and to do so without some special justification, is dubious.

[54] Ibid., 372.

Moreover, even if Velleman's account succeeded at explaining the selectivity of love, it would fail to address the question concerning the discernment of love raised above (p. 20). For the question of discernment is an explicitly justificatory question (what justifies my coming to love you rather than someone else?) that expresses the intuition, deeply embedded in our first- and second-person experience, that love is not merely selective, a matter of picking one person rather than another, but is rather a matter of choosing for better or worse reasons. The same goes for the question concerning the constancy of love, which again is a justificatory question expressing deeply felt intuitions about our experience of love.[55] It might seem that Velleman has already succeeded in rejecting these questions in the course of rejecting the fungibility of persons by understanding persons to have dignity and not price; this, it might seem, is to reject the fungibility problem itself. However, the fungibility problem presupposes that the questions of the discernment and constancy of love are legitimate, and it is in part a problem concerning how those questions are to be answered. To deny that persons are fungible on the grounds that they have dignity rather than price is not so much to reject the problem as to affirm one of the intuitions that makes it a problem in the first place: how can we understand love to be discerning or involve constancy given that persons have dignity and so are not fungible? Indeed, this is a problem for any account of justification that appeals to non-relational properties to understand why love is discerning.

Another proponent of the appraisal account is Niko Kolodny, who takes an approach to the fungibility problem that is fundamentally different from Velleman's by appealing specifically to relational properties. Kolodny claims that to love another person is to believe that you are in a particular relationship with her that is an instance of a finally valuable type of relationship that thereby not only justifies your emotional vulnerability to your beloved and to the relationship itself but also justifies actions on behalf of your beloved and the relationship. So to love someone is to appraise not your beloved directly but rather your relationship with her.[56] The relationships at issue in love, Kolodny claims, are ongoing, depend on a

---

[55] As Delaney notes concerning our second-person experience of constancy, "while you seem to want it to be true that, were you to become a schmuck, your lover would continue to love you, . . . you also want it to be the case that your lover would never love a schmuck" (Delaney, "Romantic Love," 347).

[56] Kolodny, "Love as Valuing a Relationship," 150–1.

historical pattern of concern between two particular people, and give rise to shared activities motivated by that concern. Because it is such relationships that justify our loves, Kolodny claims to have straightforward answers to the questions concerning the discernment and constancy of love and therefore to the fungibility problem. Thus, first, Kolodny argues that we can explain the constancy of love insofar as these relationships can continue when our beloveds themselves change, and even change dramatically. The question of constancy is really a question of whether we can sustain our relationship (or, perhaps, even come to have a relationship of a different, though nonetheless still finally valuable, type) in spite of these changes. Second, concerning the discernment of love, Kolodny claims that the mere fact that someone has the same intrinsic or non-relational properties as my beloved does not mean that I will or even should have the same relationship with him, and so there is no pressure in such cases to switch my allegiances. So far, therefore, fungibility is not a problem.

Of course, Kolodny argues, just as it is relationship *types* that ultimately justify love, it will be possible to have "a 'relationship *Doppelgänger*': a person who has the same relational features as my beloved"; however, here we have no justificatory worries about the discernment or constancy of love:

If my wife and I decide to have a second child, for instance, then we bring into this world a relationship *Doppelgänger* to our first child. The relationship theory implies that we have just as much reason to love the second child as the first. But this is the right implication. We have reason to love both equally, for each is our child.[57]

In short, the only people we have reason to love are those people with whom we already have an established relationship, and so worries about substituting one for the other as the object of my love or about my "trading up" by ceasing to love one but instead loving the other are misplaced: I already love both.[58]

---

[57] Ibid., 147. Note that on its own this fails to address the worries about replaceability that are at the heart of the fungibility problem: surely no one would seriously suggest that a dead child could be acceptably replaced simply by having another. I shall let this pass, however.

[58] As Kolodny notes, this account of justification might seem to be viciously circular. For the relationship is supposed to justify the emotional vulnerabilities and shared activities that themselves constitute that relationship: how could the relationship therefore justify itself (ibid., 161)? In the face of this question, we might ask further, how can we coherently understand love to be an appraisal of the relationship as being of a finally valuable type that can justify itself? In reply, Kolodny distinguishes between the historical pattern of concern and one's present concern, arguing that it is the historical pattern that can, without circularity, "be a reason for one's present concern, a concern that constitutes the relationship going forward" (ibid., 163).

One implication that Kolodny draws out of this account of justification is that once the relationship is present, one ought to continue it; to stop loving someone is to violate these norms of rationality and so to be subject to rational criticism: in failing to continue your concern, you are failing to do what you have sufficient reason to do. In this respect, Kolodny's account is similar to Robert Nozick's otherwise very different response to the fungibility problem, which appeals to the union account of love he endorses:

> The intention in love is to form a *we* and to identify with it as an extended self, to identify one's fortunes in large part with its fortunes. A willingness to trade up, to destroy the very *we* you largely identify with, would then be a willingness to destroy your self in the form of your own extended self.[59]

Like Kolodny, Nozick claims that it is irrational to break off a love once it is begun. Nonetheless, there is an important difference in the kind of irrationality at stake in Kolodny's and Nozick's accounts. For Nozick, the irrationality arises from your undermining your own identity and well-being as the person you are: it is an irrationality that strikes deeply at your sense of yourself. This leads Neera Kapur Badhwar to claim that insofar as Nozick's account implies that you ought not abandon your love no matter who your beloved becomes, what it describes "cannot be understood as love at all, rather than addiction."[60] Badhwar's point is that this account seemingly locks the lover into the love no matter what because the penalty for ceasing to love—self-destruction—is so high. The result is that Nozick's account, by being unable to make sense of the idea that dropping an unwise love may sometimes be the right thing to do, thereby imposes severe limits on our ability to make decisions about how best to live our lives.

For Kolodny, however, the irrationality is minor:

> Whatever kind of criticism the charge of inappropriateness amounts to, it is not blame. It is something like the criticism of the opposite of a phobic response: the absence of fear in the presence of something patently fearsome. What is criticizable is the lack of an emotional response in the context of that which makes it appropriate.[61]

[59] Nozick, "Love's Bond," 78.
[60] Neera Kapur Badhwar, "Love," in *Practical Ethics*, ed. Hugh LaFollette (Oxford: Oxford University Press, 2003), 63.
[61] Kolodny, "Love as Valuing a Relationship," 163–4.

Surely this cannot be right. Once love has flourished and the historical pattern of concern and emotional vulnerability is in place, it may be true that to fail to feel a sympathetic emotion when one's beloved has suffered a disappointment is but a minor lapse for which we can criticize but not blame someone. However, the rationality in light of a broader historical pattern of particular emotional episodes that would continue that pattern and the rationality of the ongoing pattern itself are entirely different. Were someone's interest in Civil War battle re-enactments to begin to occupy his every spare moment to the extent that it obliterates his emotional responsiveness to his children, whom he formerly loved, we certainly would blame him: not, perhaps, for any single emotional lapse, but at least for the overall pattern of failure, which he ought to have recognized and addressed. Moreover, the reason for this blame can be traced to the intuition driving Nozick's response: that love is fundamentally important to us precisely because of the way it touches us so intimately; it is this intuition that Kolodny seems to be denying in providing this account of the justification of love. I shall set this point aside for now but return to it shortly.

Given his understanding of the reasons we have for continuing our loving concern, Kolodny argues that "we can still identify several situations in which those reasons lapse, and failing to have such concern is not inappropriate."[62] Among the more important of these are cases involving the lover's being betrayed or losing respect for the beloved. In the former case, Kolodny claims, the betrayal may result in justified anger or resentment, emotional responses which may "crowd out" or "swamp" your concern for your beloved.[63] In the latter case, insofar as the loss of respect is justified by changes in one's beloved that make her contemptible, for example, such a loss undermines a central background condition of loving relationships: that the participants see each other as equals. Thus, if in coming to feel contempt for your beloved you lose respect for her and so see her as beneath you, you can no longer sustain the sort of relationship that love demands, resulting in the lapsing of the reasons your relationship formerly grounded for continued concern.[64]

---

[62] Ibid., 168.

[63] Ibid., 164. It is not clear, however, how we are to understand these metaphors or how the anger or resentment undermine the reasons we have for continued concern.

[64] Kolodny notes that this is not true of all cases of love: the love between parents and children, for example, does not require this sense of equality. Kolodny thinks that this is what explains why love of a relative is less susceptible to being undermined by loss of respect. (Ibid., 164–5.)

Yet Kolodny here seems to miss an important dimension of the normative constraints on our love. For he seems to assume that resentment and contempt are attitudes that automatically undermine love and the rationality of continuing to love, whereas it may be an important question whether one's love ought instead to undermine the resentment and contempt. Perhaps my love is such that I ought to forgive my beloved for her betrayal or for certain contemptible behavior; indeed, perhaps I ought to help her to see how her behavior is contemptible and so help her become a better person precisely because I love her. The rational connections between resentment and contempt on the one hand and love on the other are bi-directional, and Kolodny's failure to recognize this reveals once again his failure to appreciate the way in which love can be so important to us and to who we are: deciding to initiate and sustain particular loving relationships can be a matter of deciding how best to live my life and so what kind of person I ought to be. Kolodny is surely right that valuing a loving relationship will be a central source of reasons for making such decisions, but the bi-directionality of the rational connections just discussed indicates that these reasons—and the nature of valuing itself—are more complicated than Kolodny acknowledges because they are so vital to our sense of ourselves as persons. The same goes for terminating love and the resulting relationships: it may be that, as I grow and mature as a person, I come to see that my beloved is no longer able to understand my sense of the kind of life worth my living; I decide that he is therefore holding me back and that I should no longer love him—that I should no longer take his identity and his well-being to heart in this characteristically intimate way. Consequently, Kolodny cannot be right in his understanding of the inappropriateness of terminating such valuable relationships.

There are two important points to make about such decisions to sustain or terminate loves. First, they can be made for better or worse reasons of the sort I have just sketched; consequently, our decisions based on these reasons can themselves be wise or foolish, and deliberation about the matter can help us discover the truth here. So far this seems to be in line with a cognitivist conception of love. However, second, making these decisions is a matter of exercising our capacity for autonomy and is in part a matter of self-determination. Insofar as the loves you have contribute to your overall sense of importance and so of the kind of life worth living, they are important in defining your identity as the person you are. This is an additional aspect of the *intimacy* of love that cognitivist accounts of the justification of love miss. For insofar as your identity is at stake in whom you love, and insofar as your identity is something for which you can be responsible through the exercise of your capacity for autonomy, the decision to sustain or terminate a love must be to a significant extent up to you and so must not simply be determined by rational constraints describable from a third-person perspective. Rather, the rationality of such decisions must have its source at least partially within your understanding of who you are to be; thus, to return to Brink's criticism of Whiting raised above (§1.3, p. 19), the justification of these decisions and so of the underlying concern must be consistent with an understanding of such concern as having intrinsic rather than extrinsic significance. This conclusion, central to our understanding of the kind of intimate attitude that love is, is seemingly in line with a conative conception of love.

These two aspects of love—the ideas that love can be justified for better or worse reasons and that love is central to our identities as persons and so is in part a matter for self-determination—therefore seem to be at odds with each other. For if we accept the cognitive–conative divide, it will seem that no single attitude can both be justifiable and so a matter of truth and be up to us and so a matter of self-determination, and we may thus be led to opt for one side or the other, as the bestowal and appraisal accounts of love do. However, I believe, given the centrality of both these aspects to our understanding of love, the right conclusion to draw is rather that we ought to reject the cognitive–conative divide itself and reconceive the kind of evaluative attitude we take love to be. Whether this is a viable strategy or not remains to be seen (and will be the subject of Chapter 2).

Although I have presented my argument here using the bestowal and appraisal accounts of love, the conclusion is important for any account of love. Overcoming the fungibility problem requires making sense of there being reasons to love that not only enable us to answer the questions of the discernment and constancy of love but also are capable of sustaining the kind of intimacy that characterizes love and makes loving relationships central to our identities as persons. The rationality of justification and the intimacy seem to pull us in opposite directions, toward understanding love as a cognitive or as a conative attitude, and this must be reflected in any satisfactory account of love. To reject the well entrenched understanding of our intentional mental states in terms of the cognitive–conative divide as I plan to do will therefore profoundly affect the resulting account of love. In particular, it requires that we reject the standard way of making out the distinction between *agape* as a bestowal account and *eros* and *philia* as appraisal accounts: on my account, love will be none of these as they have been traditionally understood.

1.5 Social Action and Friendship

Thus far my critique of the cognitive–conative divide and the individualist conception of persons has focused on the attitude of love. In part I have argued that love's intimacy requires that we reject the egocentric conception of intimate concerns, which begins to overcome this individualism by requiring that we construe intimacy in a genuinely social way. However, thus far I have had little to say about why we ought to reject the individualist conception of autonomy. My aim in this section is to motivate this rejection by turning from the attitude of love to the relationship of friendship as a paradigm example of a loving relationship.

Insofar as friendship is essentially a loving relationship, we might expect that it essentially involves a richer sort of intimacy than does the attitude of love. After all, friendship does not merely consist in reciprocal love, even reciprocal love among equals: two adult siblings may each love the other and yet fail to be friends. What is intuitively missing from such a case is the kind of dynamic relationship that friendship essentially is: friends must engage each other through their reciprocated love and do so in a way that potentially influences and shapes each other as the person each is. In this way, it is not merely the friends' attitudes to each other that are intimate; the relationship itself becomes intimate. Part of the difficulty in providing an account of friendship is to cash out these intuitions in a convincing way.

My claim will be that friends must in a sense share an evaluative perspective, at least within a certain domain, where this shared evaluative perspective enables each to have the sort of dynamic, rational influence on the other's life that friendship demands. This claim can be motivated, and the implications it has for the individualist conception of autonomy can be made clear, by turning to the idea that friendship essentially involves shared activity. We are often told that friendship involves or requires that the friends engage in shared activity with each other, yet this lip service is almost never supported by an explicit account of what the shared activity characteristic of friendship consists in. Indeed, standard accounts of shared activity or shared intention seem ill-suited to making sense of friendship.

To see this, consider Michael Bratman's account of shared intention and action as a representative theory.[65] Bratman's account is reductive: he understands shared intention in terms of the interconnections among the intentions and beliefs of individual agents.[66] In brief, Bratman understands shared intention as follows:

Shared Intention Thesis (SI thesis): We intend to *J* if and only if

1. a) I intend that we *J* and
    b) you intend that we *J*.
2. I intend that we *J* in accordance with and because of (1)(a), (1)(b), and meshing subplans of (1)(a) and (1)(b); you intend that we *J* in accordance with and because of (1)(a), (1)(b), and meshing subplans of (1)(a) and (1)(b).
3. (1) and (2) are common knowledge between us.[67]

Thus, to use one of Bratman's standard examples, you and I share the intention to plan and host a conference together just in case I intend that we do so and coordinate my planning and activity with you, knowing that you likewise intend that we do so and will coordinate your planning and activity with me. So we will have to decide together what the theme will be, how many speakers to invite, whether to have commentators, and

---

[65] Michael E. Bratman, "I Intend That We *J*," in *Faces of Intention: Selected Essays on Intention and Agency* (Cambridge: Cambridge University Press, 1999), 142–61; Michael Bratman, "Shared Intention," in *Faces of Intention*, 109–29; Michael Bratman, "Shared Intention and Mutual Obligation," in *Faces of Intention*, 130–41; Michael Bratman, "Shared Valuing and Frameworks for Practical Reasoning," in *Reason and Value: Themes from the Moral Philosophy of Joseph Raz* (OXford: Oxford University Press, 2004), 1–27. Other accounts of shared intention include Raimo Tuomela and Kaarlo Miller, "We-Intentions," *Philosophical Studies* 53 (1988): 367–89; Raimo Tuomela, *The Importance of Us: A Philosophical Study of Basic Social Notions* (Stanford, CA: Stanford University Press, 1995); Raimo Tuomela, "We-Intentions Revisited," *Philosophical Studies* 125 (2005): 327–69; Raimo Tuomela, *The Philosophy of Sociality: The Shared Point of View* (Oxford: Oxford University Press, 2007); Margaret Gilbert, *On Social Facts* (Princeton, NJ: Princeton University Press, 1989); Margaret Gilbert, *Living Together: Rationality, Sociality, and Obligation* (Lanham, MD: Rowman & Littlefield, 1996); Margaret Gilbert, *Sociality and Responsibility: New Essays in Plural Subject Theory* (Lanham, MD: Rowman & Littlefield, 2000); Margaret Gilbert, "Shared Values, Social Unity, and Liberty," *Public Affairs Quarterly* 19, no. 1 (2005): 25–49; John R. Searle, "Collective Intentions and Actions," in *Intentions in Communication*, ed. Phillip R. Cohen, Martha E. Pollack, and Jerry L. Morgan (Cambridge, MA: MIT Press, 1990), 401–15; J. David Velleman, "How to Share an Intention," *Philosophy and Phenomenological Research* 57, no. 1 (1997): 29–50.

[66] In this respect, Bratman agrees with Tuomela, "We-Intentions Revisited" and Searle, "Collective Intentions and Actions."

[67] Bratman, "Shared Intention," 131.

so on; as we do this, we will need to divvy up responsibilities, so that I may arrange for catering and you arrange for lodging and transportation. In this way, what we each plan to do in pursuit of our shared goal will appropriately mesh with the other's plans in a way that constrains each of our individual activities in this and other areas of our lives.

Of course, not everything we do in carrying out our shared intention needs to be planned determinately in advance. Bratman allows that precisely what it is that we jointly intend can be to some degree indeterminate, something we work out as the need arises in order to ensure that our subplans continue to mesh appropriately. Consequently, as we begin thinking about whom to invite to our conference, we may realize that we need to define its aim more precisely, a process that may require considerable negotiation, bargaining, and compromise between us in order to sustain our shared intention.

As with other standard accounts of shared intention and action, Bratman intends his account to cover cases in which even complete strangers are able to share intentions and actions. Moreover, Bratman aims to provide an account of shared action even when the parties involved do not share reasons for the intention which they come to share:

Two people may share an intention to organize a conference even if they each have very different reasons for this: perhaps one person's reason is the advancement of scholarship, while the other person's reason has more to do with his professional reputation. Further, even if there were agreement about which reasons are relevant, they may nevertheless disagree about which shared activity would be best. They may arrive at their shared intention by way of bargaining and compromise.[68]

Yet, as I shall now argue, without a significant basis in shared reasons among the participants, the account fails to capture the sort of shared activity characteristic of friendship. The conclusion is not that Bratman is on the wrong track entirely; rather it is that he is trying to reach a different destination, so that he is on a different track from the one that leads to an understanding of the kind of shared activity I shall be concerned with here.

To see this, consider another example. Assume that according to Bratman's SI thesis my friend and I share an intention to spend a day at the beach together: we each intend that we go to the beach together, and we each do so in a way that meshes well with the other's intention because of

---

[68] Bratman, "Shared Valuing," 10.

that intention. Here, it seems, there is a single J, namely going to the beach together, such that we each intend that we J. However, it should be clear that this aim of going to the beach together is to a large extent indeterminate: precisely which beach we shall go to, when and how we shall get there, what we shall do when we get there, and so on all need to be spelled out in order to make the intention determinate. Discrepancies between her and my more determinate conceptions of our shared intention must be resolved as they emerge, even on the fly, via processes of negotiation and bargaining, as we forge a conception of this aim that we each can accept.

Consider, however, precisely how on Bratman's account such negotiation must proceed in cases in which there is no significant basis in shared reasons. Thus, assume that my reason for spending the day at the beach with my friend is that I would find relaxing a day that consists in sunbathing, listening to the sounds of the ocean, reading a good book, and doing all of this together with her. Her reason, however, is that she would find a day at the beach to be a good opportunity to immerse herself in the crowd, walk the boardwalk, and generally allow herself to enjoy the cheesy pleasures of a tourist mecca, all as a kind of experience she shares with me. We must now bargain so as to reach a compromise on how to cash out more determinately our shared intention. Given this lack of shared reasons, reasons which frame what we each see as worthwhile in the shared activity, such bargaining will involve each of us trying to maximize, in some sense, the good to be realized. Even if we each are concerned to act fairly, the negotiations are nonetheless competitive, with each of us trying to secure as many goods as possible while also ensuring that the other does likewise. In this process, our original reasons control what compromises we each are willing to make, such that we would reject attempts at compromise that pull us too far away from our original intentions.

The upshot is that although there is a level of description at which the content of my we-intention is identical with the content of my friend's, we are nonetheless clearly not really "of the same mind" about the matter. With no grounding in shared reasons, we do not really "*share*" an intention in the sense of having "it," a particular intention, in common; rather, we each pursue our individual intentions (which each involve the other person) in a way that involves a commitment to cooperation with the other—to coordinating our subplans—so long as we each are able to secure enough good from the joint activity to make it worth our (individual) whiles.

Bratman's account, therefore, is really an account of what might more accurately be called *"coordinated we-intentions."*

Yet this is not how friends interact when sharing activity. Friends do not normally engage in bargaining and compromise when engaged in a shared activity, negotiating as though their interests are wholly separate and independent, with each concerned ultimately with his own sense of what is worthwhile (a sense that might include a sense of fairness). Rather, friends normally share activity in a richer sense, which we might intuitively capture with the metaphor of being "of the same mind" concerning their shared activities and the point of these activities. My friend's enthusiasm for walking the boardwalk is infectious precisely because she is my friend and because the point of our sharing this activity is in part the very sharing of that activity and the shared pleasures and other experiences it involves.[69] That is, her enthusiasm provides me with a reason, albeit a defeasible reason, to feel likewise, and it ought to be given due weight in my rational responsiveness to what is worthwhile in our going to the beach, potentially sparking in me some anticipation of the cheesy pleasures this would afford us. Conversely, my utter distaste for our making a meal out of the greasy boardwalk fare ought to be a reason for her to be less enthusiastic here: eating such food together on the beach perhaps becomes not so appealing to her. In this way, we mutually "infect" each other, as we grope toward a conception not merely of an end we hope to accomplish together but rather of a shared sense of what is worth doing together.

Such a picture of the shared deliberation among friends is straightforwardly analogous to what goes on within an individual deliberating about what to do. Individuals do not in any literal sense bargain or compromise with themselves. Of course, you might offer yourself a reward as an incentive to finally get yourself to do that unwelcome thing you know you must, or, knowing that you cannot have everything you want given the circumstances, you might decide on a plan that gets you as much as possible of the most important things. However, the character of the incentive structure or the decision making here is quite different from what is faced in normal bargaining or compromise precisely because you have a single, unified point of view: bargaining and compromise presuppose not merely

---

[69] This may sound somewhat like Dean Cocking and Jeanette Kennett's "drawing" account of friendship; see Cocking and Kennett, "Friendship and the Self," 503–6. I shall distance my account from theirs in §8.1.

that there are multiple considerations pulling you in opposite directions but rather that there are multiple points of view on what is worthwhile. In deliberating about what to do from within a single point of view, an individual must balance various competing demands against each other, groping toward a clearer sense of what is worthwhile by trying to achieve something like an equilibrium within her evaluative perspective.

The same is true of friends, or so I shall argue: for my friend and me to be "of the same mind" is for us to aim together at achieving an equilibrium within our shared evaluative perspective. Through this process, each of us seeks to delineate more clearly what is worthwhile *to us* by being rationally responsive to the shared evaluative perspective comprised of the evaluations both she and I (each as one of us) feel emotionally and make in judgment. The resulting shared activity itself takes its character from the sharing of this evaluative perspective as we engage both in that activity and with each other.

This understanding of friends as potentially sharing an evaluative perspective with respect to some shared activity has important implications for our understanding of autonomy. For as I have characterized it, sharing an evaluative perspective requires that the friends must deliberate together to determine what they find worthwhile, so that their sense of what is worth doing in this area of their lives is something they can determine only together. When the shared activity is not merely an amusement, such as going to the beach together, but is more central to their lives, the relevant sense of what is worthwhile will come to include their sense of the kind of persons they should be: their identities. And here we begin to get the sense that close friends—friends who share not merely isolated activities but rather their lives with each other—are people who have come, at least within certain bounds, to share a capacity for autonomy.[70] If this is even possible, then we must reject the individualist conception of autonomy: the rational influence that close friends can have on each other in determining their shared sense of what is important in life need not be a matter either of undue influence undermining their autonomy or of inauthentically delegating responsibility for determining their own identities; rather, it can be central to their exercise of their autonomy in

---

[70] Thus far, this account sounds close to the interpretation Nancy Sherman offers of Aristotle's account of friendship. See Nancy Sherman, "Aristotle on Friendship and the Shared Life," *Philosophy and Phenomenological Research* 47, no. 4 (1987): 589–613.

a way that makes intelligible Aristotle's intriguing yet otherwise puzzling claim that a friend is "another self."

I have not yet offered a clear argument against the individualist conception of autonomy; at best I have suggested that an alternative can help make sense of the kind of shared activity and shared lives that is possible for close friends. There are, nonetheless, important hurdles to be overcome if this alternative is to be viable. In particular, I have come close to suggesting that there can be mental states, namely those constituting the friends' shared evaluative perspective, that belong to the friends together, thereby seeming to reject the plausible claim that mental states belong only to individuals, that group minds are absurd. Nonetheless, as I shall argue in Chapter 8, there is a sense in which we should reject this claim and accept the possibility of something like a group mind, with capacities for believing, desiring, caring, acting, and even exercising autonomy, capacities that they, the friends, exercise only together. Indeed, it is precisely here that we can make sense of one of the central insights of the union view: the way in which, by sharing activity, lives, and autonomy with our close friends we can in a sense dissolve the social barriers that normally separate people from each other and thereby significantly enhance our lives.

1.6 Looking Ahead

Before diving in, it will be useful to provide a brief overview of the structure and content of my account.

I have already indicated that I shall reject the standard account of intentional mental states in terms of the cognitive–conative divide. The motivation for this rejection stems not merely from problems with the justification of love, as I suggested in §1.4, but, as I have argued elsewhere,[71] from problems with the nature and justification of evaluative attitudes more generally, such as caring and valuing as well as loving. As a result, I claim, the assumption of the cognitive–conative divide systematically distorts our understanding of desires, emotions, and the evaluative attitudes. For this reason, I shall begin in Part I with a re-examination of our understanding of the mind quite generally. Ultimately, I shall argue, to have a mind—to

---

[71] Helm, *Emotional Reason*.

be an *agent*—is not merely to be a creature capable of informational states (a bare form of cognition) and goal-directedness (a bare form of conation) but rather to be a subject of cares and concerns and so possessing the sense that things matter—without which the capacity for desire is unintelligible. So how do we make sense of caring or mattering?

The answer, as I shall argue in Chapter 2, must be given at least in part in terms of the emotions given the way emotions involve implicit evaluations: to care about something is roughly to exhibit a certain kind of rationally structured pattern in your emotions and desires that is "focused," as I shall say, on that thing. Yet having the capacity for emotions and desires itself is intelligible only in light of the way the subject's exercise of these capacities gives rise to caring: neither is intelligible apart from the other, and so to make sense of any of them we must go holistic. Consequently, the holism of the mental encompasses not, as is often thought, merely belief and desire in that the capacities for belief and desire each presuppose the other given their mutually dependent functional roles in producing behavior. Rather, the holism of the mental is much broader: the capacities for belief, desire, emotions, and caring together form a single conceptual package, none of which is intelligible apart from the rest. Moreover, the nature of this conceptual package requires that we give up on the cognitive–conative divide.

The account of caring presented in Chapter 2 is rather basic. In particular (given my ultimate concerns with justification) there is so far no room for a distinction between what a creature actually cares about and what it should care about. This is, I believe, appropriate given that the account is intended to apply not only to us persons but to agents more generally, including dogs and cats. Questions of the justification of our evaluative attitudes can arise only for us persons, who are capable of exercising a capacity for autonomy. Consequently, prior to confronting questions of justification head-on in Chapter 6, we need to have a clearer understanding of what it is to be a person. This in turn requires that we extend this basic account of caring considerably, and that is part of my task for Chapters 3–5.

All caring involves a concern for the well-being of something, and yet the notion of something's well-being is intelligible only when we consider that thing under a particular description: as a car rather than as a historical artifact or hunk of steel, for example. Consequently, all caring is caring about something *as* something. This leads to the first extension to the basic account, undertaken in Chapter 3: understanding what it is to care about others as agents in particular. Central to this account is the idea that in caring about someone as an agent, you must care about the things he cares about as a part of caring about him, for the well-being of an agent is constituted in part by his cares. One difficulty here is to make sense of how you can care about what he cares about for *his* sake, without simply taking his cares over as your own (in a way analogous to the union account of love). I present an account of this in terms of my understanding of the focus of the pattern of emotions and desires that constitutes your caring: insofar as you care about this as a part of caring about him, these emotions and desires must be focused on him. And this, I shall argue, requires that you be motivated to *engage* him in activity, in which your emotions and desires are attuned to him and his agency in a way that is very different from when we merely do the same thing side by side.

In Part II, I extend this account of caring into an account of love, starting in Chapter 4 with self-love. The hypothesis, to be confirmed only in Chapter 5's account of loving others, is that love is a concern for someone as a particular person, where the well-being of persons is partly defined not merely by her cares—her sense of what is important—but by her *personal values*: her sense of what contributes to the kind of life worth her living. Analogous to cares, I argue, such personal values (or simply "values," as I shall say) are constituted by rational patterns in one's emotions, in particular emotions like pride and shame, for these are emotions that are focused on *persons* as such and so essentially involve an assessment both of what kind of life is worth one's living and of the extent to which one succeeds in living such a life. Indeed, I argue, particular values can only be understood in terms of the contribution they make to one's overall sense of the kind of life worth living, so that valuing something must be a part of one's overall concern for the particular person one is: a part, that is, of one's love for oneself. In this way, this overall sense of the kind of life worth one's living constitutes one's *identity* as this particular person.

As with the account of caring, this account of love in terms of rational patterns of person-focused emotions is circular, for to love yourself is to have a concern for your well-being as this person, but that well-being itself is determined by your love for yourself. Nonetheless, this circularity is not vicious given its holistic nature, and it is compatible with the thought that in valuing something you can be mistaken—that you can value things that

are not really valuable for you. In part this is because we persons essentially
have a capacity for autonomy, and so the concern we each have for our
own well-being in loving ourselves normally includes being vigilant to
some degree concerning what we value so that we can critically examine
and take some responsibility for these values; this is, I claim, a form of
self-respect that is normally a part of self-love. The critical nature of this
examination and the norms in terms of which it makes sense to say we can
be mistaken about what we value will be discussed in Chapter 6.

In Chapter 5, I examine what it is to love others. My claim (in §1.2)
was that love involves a kind of "intimate identification" in which you
come to have a concern for your beloved's identity that is the same in
kind as your concern for your own. We can understand this, I argue, by
extending Chapter 4's account of self-love as a concern for one's own
identity. What makes this possible is the account of emotions like pride
and shame I offered there, an account that, contrary to the tradition,
understands them not as essentially reflexive, evaluating oneself, but rather
as person-focused: involving a commitment to the worth of their focus as a
particular person. By exhibiting the appropriate pattern of person-focused
emotions focused on someone else, you thereby care about her as the
person she is and, I argue, care about and value the things she cares about
and values as a part of caring about her—for *her* sake. This just is to
share her identity—to identify with her—intimately, given the way it is
analogous to one's concern for one's own identity. In this way, I reject
the egocentric conception of intimate concerns and instead understand
persons in a way that is more social: to be a person is to have the capacity
to love not merely oneself but also others and so intimately to identify
with them.

The argument that this is genuinely an account of love rather than some
other evaluative attitude we might take toward persons is complex and
multifaceted. It partly involves a consideration of the relations between
our attitude of love and feelings of trust and respect toward ourselves or
others, feelings which are often thought to be essential to love. It partly
involves showing how this account fares better than alternative accounts
in making sense of the requisite intimacy of love and so in distinguishing
love from other sorts of evaluative attitudes. And it partly involves the way
this account can make sense of the phenomenology of love and of how to
resolve various puzzle cases that arise concerning love.

One such puzzle case is the fungibility problem, which as I indicated above (§1.4.2) is essentially a problem of justification; I tackle this problem—actually a set of related problems—in Chapter 6. I begin by presenting the outlines of my previous account of the justification of personal values and priorities as in part an exercise of autonomy, thereby going beyond the basic account of caring offered in Chapter 2 and showing how we can distinguish between what one *actually* cares about or values and what one *should* care about or value. (It must be noted that this account is controversial given the way it attempts, through its rejection of the cognitive–conative divide, to find a middle ground between cognitive and non-cognitive accounts. I do not argue for it here but rather summarize the account I offer elsewhere.[72]) I then turn to discuss the implications this has for the discernment and constancy of love, arguing that through the rational interconnections between emotions and judgments, including the way our linguistic concepts both inform and are informed by our emotions, we can make sense of there being reasons not merely for having particular person-focused emotions on the assumption that one already loves someone but rather for coming to love or not or for continuing or ceasing to love someone. Consequently, I argue, to love someone is to find him to have non-fungible import, a finding that I use in presenting an account of the phenomenology of love and loss.

In Part III, I turn from thinking about the evaluative attitude of love to thinking about loving relationships so as to understand more clearly the essentially social nature of persons and the effects that a loving relationship can have on the autonomy of the persons involved. I do this in two ways: first by thinking about paternalistic love in Chapter 7, and then friendship in Chapter 8.

In Chapter 7, I consider how adults, through a loving relationship with a child, can help shape that child's personal values without thereby undermining his autonomy and responsibility for himself. My claim is that in such a relationship, the adult's paternalistic understanding of the child's well-being can provide a kind of scaffold for the child, providing him with access to reasons he could not have on his own, and I try to show how the child and the adult can thereby share responsibility for the child's acquiring or failing to acquire the relevant values; such shared reasons

[72] Helm, *Emotional Reason*, especially Ch. 7.

and shared responsibility, I argue, undermines the individualist conception of autonomy. In the background here is the debate between those, like Bernard Williams, who think that all reasons must be "internal" to our subjective motivational set and those, like John McDowell, who think that some reasons can be "external" in that they are binding on a subject even though the subject does not have access to them. I argue that the reasons adults in loving relationships with children can provide are ones the children, through that relationship, have access to even though they are not within the child's subjective motivational set. In short, the reasons at issue here, because they are essentially interpersonal, do not fit neatly into either category of internal or external reasons. Indeed, this is because that distinction between internal and external reasons itself depends on the individualist conception of autonomy.

In Chapter 8, I further extend this notion of interpersonal reasons and shared responsibility in thinking about loving relationships among equals and about friendships in particular. Fundamental to my account is the notion of a "plural agent": a group of people who do not merely share certain intentions or goals but, more fundamentally, jointly care about certain things. Thus, it is the plural agent itself that is the subject of these cares, which provide the members of the plural agent with genuinely interpersonal reasons for acting, judging, and responding emotionally. Friendships, I argue, emerge when the friends form a plural agent that cares about itself and the relationship they have. This requires that the friends have a joint conception of their relationship as one of friendship, and there are many different types of friendship this can involve, ranging from tennis buddies to romantic relationships. Moreover, by virtue of their joint cares—their joint evaluative perspective—the friends can together deliberate about and justify having or ceasing to have particular cares, including their concern for the friendship itself. Consequently, the continuation or dissolution of a friendship is to be justified only from within the friendship itself.

One particularly important kind of friendship is something like Aristotle's friendship of virtue, in which the friends do not merely hold joint cares but rather hold joint values, grounded in a joint conception of the kind of life worth their living together. In such a case, I argue, the friends form a "plural person" and have a joint evaluative perspective from within which they can deliberate jointly about the personal values that constitute their joint identity as a plural person. In this way, the friends together exercise a single capacity for autonomy in jointly engaging in the pursuit of a certain kind of life, thereby making intelligible their having a joint self (in addition to, and potentially in conflict with, their individual selves). The upshot is that in order to have a proper understanding of intimate social relationships such as these "deep" friendships, we must reject the individualist conception of autonomy and instead understand autonomy to be a capacity we can exercise together with our friends. To be a person, I conclude, is to have the capacity for such friendships and so our rationality and autonomy themselves presuppose our inherent sociality.

It should be clear from the brief overview presented here that my argument in this book does not proceed linearly. As with the account of love, the argument for this account of friendship is complex and multifaceted, depending on its ability to provide insights into a wide range of phenomena. More generally, there is no single argument for why we should reject the cognitive–conative divide, or for why we ought to give up on the individualist conception of persons. Indeed, given my rejection of these philosophical orthodoxies, part of my task in this book is to work the reader into a very different way of looking at a variety of interconnected issues that, taken as a whole, can shed new light on traditional disputes. In doing this, I shall develop some new language to describe familiar phenomena so as to avoid illicitly importing presuppositions antithetical to my basic account. (This explains why I begin in Chapter 2 with a re-examination of the mind generally.) Consequently the account should be evaluated not bit by bit but as a whole: in terms of the extent to which this new outlook succeeds in making better sense than the alternatives of the various and interconnected phenomena of love, friendship, and the nature of persons.

PART I
Caring

2

Agency, Emotions, and the Problem of Import

I indicated in Chapter 1 that there are two tendencies in our ordinary philo-sophical conception of persons that I aim to reject: the understanding of our intentional mental states in terms of the cognitive–conative divide and the individualist conception of persons. In this chapter, I shall begin to address the former. Although the problems I raised for the cognitive–conative divide arise in the case of persons and understanding what it is for us to love, they are more general, arising as well in understanding any evaluative attitude and so, as I shall argue, profoundly affecting our understanding of agency and the mind–body problem quite generally. This needs more explanation.

The mind–body problem arises out of a perceived clash between our scientific conception of nature as mechanistic and our ordinary conception of minds generally. As mechanistic, nature operates according to laws that specify how things will happen or generally tend to happen, and there seems to be no room for normative standards—standards for how things *ought* to happen—to enter into our understanding of the natural world. Minds, on the other hand, are essentially normative, for they essentially can have *intentional* states—states with meaning and representational con-tent—which are unintelligible apart from rational norms. Moreover, minds seem essentially to involve conscious states with a kind of subjectivity that does not neatly fit into our understanding of the natural world as objective; and some minds at least, including those of persons, have the capacity for freedom that again seems not to fit into our understanding of nature as mechanistic. Hence the *mind–body problem* is that of how to reconcile these two seemingly incompatible entities.

In trying to solve the mind–body problem, philosophers of mind have traditionally focused on two main issues central to understanding minds:

intentionality and consciousness. In doing so they have been inadequately sensitive to the ways in which the capacities they analyze get taken up in discussions of moral psychology and the concept of a person. The notion of desire is particularly slippery here, insofar as the concept philosophers of mind have analyzed falls well short of the rich and robust capacity to form genuinely *pro*-attitudes that moral psychology demands. Not recognizing this shortfall, moral psychologists make seemingly innocent presuppositions about the nature of desire, judgment, value, rationality, and the self that cannot be sustained when we try to provide an explicit account of these in terms adequate to solving the mind–body problem. As I shall argue in Parts II–III, one such presupposition is the individualist conception of persons, which ends up preventing us from offering an explicit account, adequate to the mind–body problem, of persons as loving and valuing beings, able to have concerns for others for their sakes and so able to have emotional connections with others that enhance rather than limit our capacities for autonomy and self-determination. Closer to my concerns in this chapter, is the presupposition of the cognitive–conative divide, which is the received dogma in philosophy of mind and yet is one central obstacle to providing a rich account of desire and caring more generally.[1]

In what follows, I shall first, in §2.1, identify more clearly the problems just alluded to for philosophy of mind concerning desire and evaluation, arguing that standard approaches, grounded in the cognitive–conative divide, must fail. I then turn in §2.2 to present an alternative account of the mind and agency that provides emotions with a central place in our understanding of evaluation and motivation quite generally. Finally, in §2.3, I examine the relationship between these emotional or, more broadly, "felt" evaluations and evaluative judgment in defining the agent's evaluative perspective.

2.1 The Problem of Import

Given my background concern with reconciling philosophy of mind and moral psychology, it will be important to lay out without much defense

---

[1] I have argued for this latter claim previously in Helm, *Emotional Reason*; to a large extent, this chapter summarizes these earlier results.

the general approach to the mind—body problem that I shall adopt. I take as my starting point the Davidsonian idea that rationality is the constitutive ideal of the mental.[2] The idea is that what it is for something to be an agent, and so what it is for something to have mental states (such as belief and desire) in the first place is for it to be so structured as to exhibit an appropriate sort of pattern of rationality in its behavior.

Part of the point of this claim is to identify a form of explanation that is distinctive of mental phenomena. Thus, Davidson claims, explanation in the physical sciences works by locating physical phenomena within a broader pattern of other physical objects and events related by laws. Likewise explanation of mental phenomena, including intentional action, proceeds by locating these phenomena within a broader pattern of other such phenomena in such a way as to reveal their rationality. So whereas physical explanation reveals the explanandum as to be expected given the antecedent conditions, psychological explanation reveals the explanandum as what rationally ought to happen.[3]

Of course, to say with Davidson that rationality is the *constitutive* ideal of the mental is to make a claim about what mental phenomena *are* and not just how they are to be explained. Nonetheless, the two ideas are related, for the possibility of explanation in terms of rationality is a condition of the intelligibility of the mental as such. Again, this is true of the physical as well: we could not make sense of something as physical unless we were at least prepared to locate it within a broader pattern of lawfulness in terms of which it can be explained. Bizarre apparent phenomena that cannot be fit into the pattern of lawfulness as we now understand it get rejected as not real, as mere misperceptions or even hallucinations, unless we get solid evidence of their repeatability that forces us to revise our understanding of the relevant laws. In this way, the intelligibility of something as physical presupposes that it fits within a pattern of lawfulness, and it is this fact that guides revisions in our understanding of the relevant laws. Hence, lawfulness is the *constitutive ideal* of the physical in that the possibility of explanation in terms of laws is a condition of the intelligibility of the physical as such.

---

[2] Donald Davidson, "Mental Events," in *Essays on Actions and Events* (New York, NY: Clarendon Press, 1980), 207–25.
[3] See William Dray, "The Rationale of Actions," in *Laws and Explanation in History* (London: Oxford University Press, 1957), ch. V.

The same is true of the mental: mental phenomena are intelligible as such only insofar as they can be located within a broader pattern of rationality in terms of which they can be explained. Hence, their being mental phenomena at all requires their having a place in such a pattern. Of course, not every particular mental state must be understood as rational in order to be a mental state. Irrational beliefs, desires, emotions, and so on are all too common. The point is rather that a creature is intelligible as an agent and so as having various mental capacities only if its exercise of these capacities is for the most part rational. This means that it is possible for isolated occurrent mental states or processes to be irrational, so long as they are isolated, mere "noise" in the overall pattern of rationality. For too much irrationality destroys the essential background pattern of rationality that makes agency, as well as these mental capacities and their exercise, possible. Thus, too many false beliefs, too many failures to be responsive to the truth, too many failures to take the necessary means to one's ends, and so on erode the background of rationality against which having the capacities for belief and desire are intelligible. Conversely, to exhibit such a pattern of rationality just is to have the relevant mental capacities. This is what is meant in calling rationality the constitutive ideal of the mental.

So far, this is really just the outline of a theory of the mind, an outline that I believe is largely correct. Fleshing it out will require specifying more precisely the relevant kinds of rationality and so the relevant patterns a creature must display in order to have mental capacities. It is here that my account differs from the alternatives.

The most prominent and well worked-out articulation of this outline can be found in the work of Daniel Dennett, in which Dennett argues that the relevant kinds of rationality at issue are epistemic and instrumental.[4] Thus, he argues, a chess-playing computer, because it displays a projectible pattern of instrumental rationality in the moves it makes, is a genuine agent, having beliefs and desires concerning the chess game that rationally motivate its actions. What motivates Dennett's appeal to epistemic and instrumental rationality as the constitutive ideal of the mental is apparently an acceptance of the cognitive–conative divide. For as I indicated above (§1.2, p. 7), it is

---

[4] Daniel C. Dennett, *The Intentional Stance* (Cambridge, MA: MIT Press, 1987). Dennett, with his flair for memorable slogans, puts the Davidsonian thesis this way: "rationality is the mother of Intention" (Daniel C. Dennett, "Intentional Systems," *Journal of Philosophy* 68 (1971): 103).

epistemic rationality that governs the sort of mind-to-world direction of fit that cognitions have, and it is instrumental rationality that governs the sort of world-to-mind direction of fit that conations have. Insofar as cognition and conation are mutually exclusive and exhaustive types of intentional mental states, it begins to look like epistemic and instrumental rationality are the only kinds of rationality that enter into the constitutive ideal of the mental. This, I shall argue, is a mistake.

The trouble with Dennett's view, as with other accounts of the mind that accept the cognitive–conative divide and so focus on intentionality and consciousness in solving the mind–body problem, is that it is unable to provide an account of desire or other "pro-attitudes" that are rich enough to sustain the conceptual connection, central to moral psychology, between desire and what is good or worth pursuing. For in focusing narrowly on intentionality, philosophers of mind conceive the task of understanding desire as that of understanding what it is for a creature to represent something as a goal and so use this representation, within a broader system of representations (including both cognitions and conations) structured by both epistemic and instrumental rationality, to determine a course of action that will achieve this goal. Thus, the intentionality of desire is understood in terms of two kinds of standards of correctness: directly in terms of instrumental rationality, for it is this that underwrites the appropriateness of action to goal satisfaction, and indirectly in terms of epistemic rationality, inasmuch as false beliefs may cause one's attempts to achieve the goal to fail. Yet this account of desire cannot make sense of the conceptual connection it has with worthiness of pursuit: the sense of "pro" in "pro-attitude" has been omitted.

To see this, consider a chess-playing computer as an example of something that, although it exhibits the sort of goal-directedness just described, nonetheless fails to be a full-blooded agent (contra Dennett). For a computer to play chess, it must have its behavior organized around the goal of winning the game, and its outputs must be intelligible not merely as legal moves, but as moves that make some sense as attempts to achieve this goal. This means that the computer must exhibit a pattern of behavior structured by instrumental rationality: its moves must generally be made in order to accomplish some sub-goal, which is achieved in order, ultimately, to accomplish the final goal of winning. Consequently, we can understand why, in light of this final goal, the computer would make the moves it does, thereby providing at least the beginnings of an account of the computer as having intentional states like beliefs and desires. Indeed, some philosophers of mind, including Dennett, think that a chess-playing computer really is a full-blooded agent, having beliefs and desires in pretty much the same sense that we do.

Does the chess-playing computer really *desire* to win? Although we might concede that such a computer has the *end* or *goal* of winning the game in virtue of the way this goal structures the computer's behavior via patterns of instrumental rationality, this falls short of an account of desire as a pro-attitude, in which the agent implicitly evaluates the end as being *worth* pursuing—as having *import* of a certain sort. Unlike a dog, which *cares* about going on a walk, and unlike a person who cares about winning a chess game, the computer as described so far[5] cannot care about anything and so, it seems, cannot find anything worthwhile. Thus we ought carefully to distinguish the kind of rationally mediated goal-directedness exhibited by the computer from the sort of action, motivated by the evaluation of the worth of some end implicit in desire, characteristic of genuine agents. Likewise, we ought to distinguish the kind of quasi-agency characteristic of things like chess-playing computers from genuine agency: chess-playing computers are *mere intentional systems*[6] insofar as they exhibit goal-directed behavior mediated by instrumental and (minimal) epistemic rationality. By contrast, to be an *agent* just is to be a subject of import, a subject that can care about things, to whom things can "matter." Understanding agency therefore requires understanding what it is to be a subject of import.

The point here is not merely that certain philosophical accounts of mind, like Dennett's, are mistaken because they imply that chess-playing computers are genuine agents with beliefs and desires. Rather, it is that philosophers of mind, insofar as they are focused narrowly on problems of intentionality and consciousness, ignore the distinction between desire and goal-directedness at their peril. However, given this distinction we need to ask about the place import, as a kind of worth, has in the natural world, for

[5] I do not intend to rely here on the intuition that no computer could care about anything simply by being a computer. Indeed, I believe that it is possible for computers to care, provided that they meet suitable conditions of the sort I lay out in §2.2. My claim here rests on an understanding of mere goal-directedness and the structure of instrumental and epistemic rationality.

[6] The term, 'intentional system,' is Dennett's; see Dennett, *The Intentional Stance*, 15, 28–33.

the natural world, at least as science conceives of it, seems to have no place at all for worth. This is the *problem of import,* and it is a problem that has simply been ignored by philosophers of mind. The result is the mismatch, alluded to above (p. 50), between the accounts of goal-directedness offered within philosophy of mind as a solution to the mind–body problem and the accounts of genuine desire presupposed by moral psychologists.

How, then, can we solve this problem of import? One way of thinking about the problem of import, encouraged by the cognitive–conative divide, is as a kind of Euthyphro question: do we desire things and so find them worthwhile because they antecedently have import, or do things have import because we desire them? To accept the cognitive–conative divide is to find these the only possibilities: to adopt the first option is to conceive of desire as having mind-to-world direction of fit and so as being a cognitive state, whereas to adopt the second is to conceive of desire as having world-to-mind direction of fit and so as being a conative state. Yet neither of these are viable options that fully make sense of the conceptual connection between import and desire.

There are two central problems with understanding desire as a cognitive state. First, such an understanding is counter-intuitive and seems to undermine the idea that desire can motivate us to act so as to satisfy it. For if we accept the cognitive–conative divide, we understand intentional mental states as motivating in light of their intentional content as having mind-to-world or world-to-mind direction of fit. Thus, it is the perceived lack of fit between the content of my mental state and how the world is that motivates me either to change my mind (in the case of mind-to-world direction of fit) or to change the world (in the case of world-to-mind direction of fit). To conceive of desire as a cognitive state is to make mysterious how desires can motivate us to change the world.[7] Second, such an understanding of desire does nothing to solve the problem of import. Indeed, given that import is in the first instance relative to the subject, it is not clear what could solve it. The most plausible solution would seem to be the way the object having import contributes to the subject's biological fitness, so that food, for example, can have import to me because (crudely) it is necessary for my survival. However, such an appeal to biological fitness

---

[7] Of course, we could understand desires to be dispositional states that cause certain sorts of goal-directed behaviors. That, however, would make mysterious how being worthy of pursuit could serve as a reason for such behavior.

presupposes rather than explains import: food is necessary for my survival only instrumentally, and food can therefore be understood as having import to me only insofar as my survival has import to me. But what could explain this import? Again, a cognitive account of desire seems to have nothing to say here.

A conative account of desire, on the other hand, seems to offer a straightforward account of import and its relativity to the subject: something has import to me only if I desire it. The difficulty for such a conative account of desire lies in the apparent objectivity of import: not just any desire succeeds in constituting its object as having import, for we can desire things that do not matter to us, that we do not care about. So it must be only certain desires or other conative states that can somehow automatically constitute their objects as having import. Yet what states would these be? The obvious candidates are pleasure and pain. This would require, however, that we understand pleasure and pain not as pure states of "qualia" but rather as intentional states, evaluating their objects in such a way as to constitute them as good or bad. However, accounts of pleasure and pain that understand them to be intentional in this way do so by understanding them to involve or be constituted by desire,[8] a move that in this context would be viciously circular.

This is not, of course, a knock-down argument that we cannot solve the problem of import if we accept the cognitive–conative divide.[9] Nonetheless, it does motivate seeking out an alternative. The proper solution to the problem of import, as I shall argue in §2.2, is to go holistic: evaluative states like desire and, crucially, the emotions are to be assessed for warrant depending on whether they are proper responses to what has import to us, and yet what it is for something to have import is intelligible only in light of these same evaluative states. In this way, desires and emotions seem to have both mind-to-world and world-to-mind direction of fit, which is impossible if we accept the cognitive–conative divide. Hence we should reject that divide.

---

[8] See, for example, George Pitcher, "Pain Perception," *Philosophical Review* 79 (1970): 368–93; G. Lynn Stephens and George Graham, "Minding Your P's and Q's: Pain and Sensible Qualities," *Noûs* 21 (1987): 395–405; Richard J. Hall, "Are Pains Necessarily Unpleasant?" *Philosophy and Phenomenological Research* 49, no. 4 (1989): 643–59; Natika Newton, "On Viewing Pain as a Secondary Quality," *Noûs* 23 (1989): 569–98; Michael Tye, "A Representational Theory of Pains and Their Phenomenal Character," *Philosophical Perspectives: AI, Connectionism, and Philosophical Psychology* 9 (1995): 223–39.

[9] I have provided stronger arguments against this divide in Helm, *Emotional Reason*.

2.2 Felt Evaluations and the Constitution of Import

What is it for something to have import to a subject? Intuitively, at least part of the answer is that it must be worthy of the subject's attention and action. That something is worthy of attention means not merely that it is permissible or a good thing to pay attention to it; rather, it means that paying attention to it is, by and large, required on pain of giving up or at least undermining the idea that it really has import to one. After all, it is hard (though, perhaps, not impossible) to credit someone with caring about, say, having a clean house even though he never or rarely notices when it gets dirty. This is not to deny that someone who genuinely cares may in some cases be distracted by other things that are more important and so not occasionally notice that it is getting dirty. What is required, however, is a consistent pattern of attending to the relevant object: in short, a kind of *vigilance* for what happens or might well happen to it. Similarly, that something is worthy of action means that acting on its behalf is, other things being equal, required if its continued import is to be intelligible: to care about a clean house requires not only vigilance for cleanliness but also a *preparedness* to act so as to maintain it.

The relevant modes of vigilance and preparedness necessary for understanding import are primarily emotional, desiderative, and judgmental, and I shall argue that we can understand the sense in which objects of import are *worthy* of attention and action in terms of the rational interconnections among these modes. In this section I shall focus on emotions and desires, arguing that these should be understood as species of "felt evaluations"—evaluations that are simultaneously responsive to and constitutive of import. To understand this more fully it is necessary first to establish some vocabulary.

The *formal object* of an emotion is the kind of import that defines that emotion as the kind of emotion it is. Thus, fear of something is to be distinguished from anger at the same thing insofar as in fear you feel it to be dangerous, whereas in anger you feel it to be offensive; these implicit evaluations of something as dangerous or offensive are what make fear be fear and anger be anger and so are their respective formal objects. The *target* of an emotion is intuitively that at which the emotion is directed; more formally, it is that which gets presented in the emotion as having the evaluative property defined by the formal object. In this way, emotions involve implicit evaluations of their targets as having a kind of import. A commonly overlooked object of emotions is their *focus*: the background object having import to which the target is related in such a way as to make intelligible the target's having the property defined by the formal object. For example, I might feel fear as the neighbor kid throws a ball that comes perilously close to smashing a vase. Here the target of my fear is the ball, which the emotion presents as having the formal object—as being dangerous; the focus of my fear is the vase, for it is in virtue of both the import the vase has for me and the relation the ball has to it (as potentially smashing it) that the ball is intelligible as a danger. (Indeed, if it were just an ordinary vase rather than, say, a family heirloom, my fear in this case would be hard to make intelligible.)

In light of this, emotions are intelligible as *warranted* or not in terms of the implicit evaluation of its target, where such warrant has two conditions. First, the focus must really have import to the subject: my fear would be unwarranted if the vase were not something I care about. Second, the target must be, or intelligibly seem to be, appropriately related to the focus so as to have the kind of import defined by the formal object: my fear would be unwarranted if the ball had no real potential to damage the vase (because, say, it is made of light-weight Styrofoam). Given these conditions of warrant, we can understand emotions to be a kind of sensitivity or responsiveness to the import of one's situation: emotions are essentially *intentional feelings of import*.

Part of the point of describing emotions as feelings is to highlight their passivity in contrast to the more active evaluations we make in judgment: the capacity for emotion is a kind of receptivity to evaluative content, and the particular emotions are passive exercises of that receptivity. Conversely, we might say, the import of the situation—of the ball given the danger it presents to the vase and the import of the vase—"impresses" itself on us in our feeling a particular emotion, in something like the way colors impress themselves on us in perception. This means that import must have a kind of objectivity relative to our emotions as that which our emotions apprehend (or misapprehend) and so as that in terms of which particular emotions are to be evaluated for warrant.

Nonetheless, the way we passively apprehend import in feeling cannot be exactly the same as that of ordinary perception, nor can import have the kind of objectivity that secondary qualities have, given the role the emotions play in constituting import and so given the relativity of import to the individual, at least in the first instance.[10] Emotions are often treated as if they were isolated states of feeling, but it is important not to overlook the complex rational connections they have to other mental states. In part, these connections are among the emotions themselves: to experience one emotion is in effect to *commit* oneself to feeling other emotions with the same focus in the relevant actual and counterfactual situations because of the import of that focus. Thus, if you are hopeful that some end can be achieved, then you normally ought also to be afraid when its accomplishment is threatened, relieved when the threat does not materialize, angry at those who intentionally obstruct progress toward it, and satisfied when you finally achieve it (or disappointed when you fail); moreover it would be inconsistent with these emotions to be afraid of achieving the goal, grateful toward those who sabotage it, and so on. In this way, emotions normally come in broader patterns of emotions sharing a common focus.

In general, which situations are "relevant" to these emotional commitments to the import of the focus—'focal commitments,' as we might call them—will be situations in which that focus has been affected favorably or adversely. Thus, we might distinguish *positive emotions*, such as satisfaction and joy, which involve the sense that something good has happened to their focus, from *negative emotions*, like frustration and disappointment, which involve the sense that something bad has happened to their focus. Given this, we can see that a part of the focal commitment one has in feeling a certain positive emotion is a commitment to feel the corresponding negative emotions in situations, both actual and counterfactual, in which something bad happens to its focus, and vice versa; call this subclass of focal commitments 'tonal commitments.' Another part of such focal commitments is revealed when we distinguish, following Robert Gordon, factive from epistemic emotions.[11] *Factive emotions*, like relief and anger, are responses

---

[10] I am qualifying this claim concerning the relativity of import in part to acknowledge that some kinds of import can be interpersonal; indeed, such interpersonal kinds of import will be central to the account I offer of friendship in Part III. However, making sense of import as relative to groups rather than individuals, let alone as being universal (as is the case, I believe, for moral value), will require a much more complex account that builds on the basic account I present here.

[11] Robert M. Gordon, *The Structure of Emotions: Investigations in Cognitive Philosophy* (Cambridge: Cambridge University Press, 1987), 25–7.

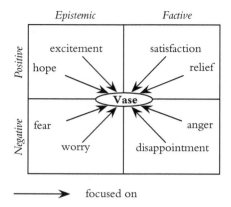

Figure 2.1. Pattern of emotions with a common focus.

to what we know has already happened or, in some cases, will happen, whereas *epistemic emotions*, like hope and fear, are responses to outcomes about which we are uncertain. Part of the focal commitments that particular emotions involve will be to experience transitions from epistemic to factive emotions, depending on whether or not the impact on the well-being of the focus of the epistemic emotion comes to pass: fear ought to become sadness or relief depending on whether the danger materializes or not, for example. (See Figure 2.1.) Call this subclass of focal commitments *'transitional commitments.'*

This talk of emotional commitments needs further explanation in terms of the kinds of patterns they normally involve, patterns that I shall now argue are both rational and projectible. Such a pattern is *rational* in that belonging to it is partly constitutive of the warrant of particular emotions. Thus, other things being equal, my feeling of fear focused on the vase as the baseball hurls toward it would be unwarranted unless I would also feel relief if the vase were to emerge unscathed, disappointment, sadness, or grief if it were destroyed, anger at the neighbor kid for his casual disregard of it, and so on. (Precisely why this is so will be discussed shortly.)

In saying that the patterns are rational, I am not claiming that emotions belonging to the pattern are merely permitted by the import of their common focus. Rather, other things being equal, the failure to experience emotions that fit into the pattern when otherwise appropriate is a rational failure. Consequently, being such as to have these emotions in the relevant actual and counterfactual situations is rationally required, and the resulting pattern of emotions ought therefore to be *projectible*. This does not mean that one must feel emotions every time they are warranted in order for the relevant pattern to be in place; isolated failures to feel particular emotions, though rationally inappropriate, do not undermine the rational coherence of the broader pattern so long as these failures remain isolated. Nonetheless, particular emotions are *beholden* to the broader patterns of which they are a part in the sense that, by virtue of the projectibility and rationality of these patterns, there is a rational requirement to feel these emotions in the relevant circumstances and not otherwise.

At this point we can see that there is a two-way conceptual connection between something's having import and its being the focus of such a projectible, rational pattern of emotions. First, these patterns of emotions depend on import. As claimed above (p. 58), it is a necessary condition of the warrant of particular emotions, as intentional feelings of import, that their focus have import. This means in part that the commitment implicit in these emotions is intelligible as rational only in terms of that import: by feeling the focus to have import, I am in essence feeling it to be worthy of attention and so as calling for other emotions in the relevant actual and counterfactual situations. Particular emotions, therefore, presuppose import as their proper object.

It may now seem that import is conceptually prior to the projectible, rational patterns of emotions, but that would be to ignore the second conceptual connection between them. Insofar as something is the focus of such a pattern of emotions, the projectibility of that pattern ensures that one will typically respond with the relevant emotions whenever that focus is affected favorably or adversely. In effect, the projectibility of the pattern of emotions is an attunement of one's sensibilities to that focus, and this just is the sort of vigilance normally required for import. Yet these patterns of emotions make intelligible not only that one has a disposition to respond to the focus of the pattern. Inasmuch as the pattern itself is rational, one ought to have these subsequent emotions, and so one ought to pay attention to the focus of the pattern, precisely because the past pattern of one's emotions rationally commits one to feel these subsequent emotions when otherwise warranted. Consequently, the rationality of the pattern makes intelligible the idea that the focus of that pattern is worthy of attention. In this way, such a pattern of emotions is presupposed by import, at least insofar as to have import is to be *worthy* of attention: it is hard to make sense of someone as caring about something if he does not respond emotionally no matter what when it is affected favorably or adversely.

Of course, to have import is to be worthy of action as well and, not coincidentally, to feel an emotion is not merely to attend to one's circumstances in a certain way: emotions also move us, in many cases to intentional action.[12] Thus, fear might lead us to escape the danger, and anger or jealousy to seek revenge. In such cases, the emotion explains the action by motivating it in such a way as to make it intelligible within a broader context of rationality: the evaluation implicit in the emotion's formal object justifies the action by revealing it (other things being equal) to have a point, to be worthwhile in the present circumstances.[13] Such a point can be an end to be achieved, as in the examples just provided, but it need not be. Jumping for joy and crying out of sadness each have a point, but that point is not an end these activities seek to achieve but is rather celebration or mourning, and the jumping or crying just is that celebration or mourning, an activity made intelligible by the specific kind of import to which joy and sadness are properly responsive. In this way, such non-goal-directed intentional action can properly be understood to be a *rational expression* of the emotion and so to one's commitment to the import of its focus.

To say that emotions motivate action in this way is not to say that we inevitably act accordingly. For our emotions may be but one of many sources of motivation, and in particular cases these other sources may whether rationally or irrationally, override the dictates of our emotions by, for example, overcoming our fear or stifling our joy. Nonetheless, that the kind of commitment to import emotions involve has some influence on our motivation is a condition of the intelligibility of having the capacity for emotions at all: to feel sad in a particular case without any impulse

---

[12] Emotions can move us to mere non-intentional behavior as well, as when we tremble from fear; such non-intentional behaviors are *arational expressions* of the emotions, and I shall set them aside here.

[13] In saying this, I am rejecting the distinction commonly made between justifying reasons and motivating reasons, the latter of which are supposed to explain action causally. (For more on this distinction, see Michael Smith, *The Moral Problem* (Oxford: Oxford University Press, 1994), especially chs. 4–5.) For detailed arguments for why I reject this distinction and so adopt a form of motivational internalism, see Helm, *Emotional Reason*; Bennett W. Helm, "Emotions and Practical Reason: Rethinking Evaluation and Motivation," *Noûs* 35, no. 2 (2001): 190–213.

to mourn is to have a defective commitment to the import of both the focus and the target, and never to have the impulse to mourn when otherwise appropriate is to fail to have the capacity for sadness in the first place.

That emotions are one of many possible sources of motivation requires that they be rationally interconnected with other such sources so as to make intelligible what we do as normally the rationally appropriate thing to do, all things considered. Indeed, this rational interconnection is precisely what we find between emotions and desires. On the one hand, if something is the focus of a projectible, rational pattern of emotions, it rationally ought to be a focus of desire as well, both as something one is motivated to pursue or maintain and as the source of instrumental reasons for one's pursuit of means to such an end. This is because to display a projectible, rational pattern of emotions focused on a vase, for example, is to be committed to the import of that vase. Insofar as to have import is to be worthy of action, such a commitment must therefore be to have the relevant desires (such as the desire for a display case to protect it from dust and errant baseballs) and so act on its behalf. Consequently, a failure to have the relevant desires focused on the vase and so to be motivated by these desires when otherwise warranted would be a rational failure. Conversely, a consistent failure to have these desires would mean that one is not prepared to act on its behalf, thereby undermining its import and so the rationality of the pattern of emotions. On the other hand, desire also involves a commitment to feel the relevant emotions. For to desire something is not merely to be disposed to pursue it as an end; it rather involves the sense that this end is *worthy* of pursuit. Consequently, if one did not in general feel fear when a desired end is threatened, relief when the threat does not pan out, and so on, it would be hard to make sense of that end as having import and so as being an appropriate object of desire.

The upshot of these interconnections between desires and emotions is that the projectible, rational pattern in one's emotions must include one's desires as well. The projectibility of this pattern, therefore, makes possible not only one's vigilance for import but also one's preparedness to act on its behalf, and the rationality of this pattern makes intelligible its focus not only as worthy of attention but also as worthy of action. This means that to have *import* just is to be the focus of such a projectible, rational pattern of emotions and desires.[14] Indeed, insofar as import is in this way constituted by such patterns of emotions and desires, we can properly understand something's having import to a subject to be a matter of her having a certain evaluative attitude toward it—of her *caring* about it.

It may seem, therefore, that import is simply projected on to the world by our attitudes, so that these attitudes are properly intelligible as conative. That would be a mistake, however. For if these attitudes were conative, they must be conceptually prior to import, but to accept that would be to ignore the first conceptual connection I articulated between something's having import and the relevant projectible, rational pattern of emotions and desires. For our emotions and desires individually are to be assessed for warrant in light of whether their focuses really have the import these states ascribe to them. Moreover, to have the requisite pattern of emotions and desires is to be disposed to respond to situations of a certain kind, where we cannot specify that kind of situation except in terms of the import of the focus of that pattern. Hence, the pattern of emotions is in effect an *attunement*, a habituation of one's sensibilities, to that import. Indeed, we can put this point the other way around by saying that in situations of this kind, the import *impresses* itself on us by not only grabbing and holding our attention but also priming us to act (cf. the intuition expressed above, p. 58). In these respects, import may seem like an object of cognitive attitudes, yet, as I already indicated, that too would be a mistake, implying (contrary to the second conceptual connection articulated above) that import is conceptually prior to these attitudes.

Making sense of the relationship between our emotions and desires on the one hand and import on the other therefore requires that we reject the cognitive–conative divide as applying here and so reconceive the kind of intentional mental states that emotions and desires are. Thus, emotions and desires are commitments to the import of their focuses, commitments which, when they are non-defective, define and institute

---

[14] Actually, things are considerably more complicated than I have indicated here. In particular, evaluative judgment has a place in the broader pattern of evaluations that are simultaneously co-constitutive of and responsive to import, and it is important in a full account to articulate the rational *inter*connections among evaluative judgments, emotions, and desires; I shall sketch this account in §2.3. Indeed, I have argued, these rational interconnections are a central part of what makes intelligible both how motivation can properly be understood as internal to our practical judgments and how deliberation about value is possible. For details on both these points, see Helm, *Emotional Reason*; nonetheless, I shall ignore them here.

a broader projectible, rational pattern that both constitutes that import and makes possible its impressing itself on us, grabbing our attention and motivating us to act. Emotions are, therefore, *felt evaluations* in that they are commitments of this kind: commitments that both are passive responses to attend to and be motivated by import and are simultaneously constitutive of that import by virtue of the broader rational patterns of which they are a part and which they serve to define.

My claim, therefore, is that import and our caring emerge simultaneously in the projectible, rational patterns in our responsiveness to the world. In talking about import as a kind of object to which our emotions and desires must be attuned as a condition of their warrant, we emphasize the first conceptual connection, whereas in talking about our caring as an evaluative attitude constitutive of the import things have, we emphasize the second. These are, nonetheless, two ways of describing the same phenomenon.

In light of this account of emotions as felt evaluations we can understand their *phenomenology*: the sense in which they are pleasures and pains. Emotions are pleasant or painful, they feel good or bad, precisely because, as felt evaluations, they are feelings of positive or negative import, where such feelings are modes of caring about something as a proper focus of one's concern. Thus, to feel fear is to be pained by danger, this distinctive kind of import the target has given its relation to the focus, in the sense that the danger to the focus impresses itself on you, grabbing your attention and motivating you to act; the emotional response, the feeling of this danger, just is the pain. Likewise, to feel joy is to be pleased by some good in the sense that the good to the focus impresses itself on you in feeling.[15]

It should be clear that the feeling of pleasure or pain here involves an awareness not merely of the target having the formal object (i.e., of the lion as dangerous or of the success of my fund-raising efforts as good) but also of the import of the focus (i.e., my life or the opera house). Indeed, the target can have the evaluative property specified in the formal object only because of its bearing on the import of the focus—only because the import of the focus impresses itself on one through its relation to the target. Thus, the pleasure of my joy at my fund-raising success would be a very different pleasure, a very different feeling, if my aim is not

---

[15] For further arguments for this conception of the phenomenology of emotions as pleasant or painful, see Bennett W. Helm, "Felt Evaluations: A Theory of Pleasure and Pain," *American Philosophical Quarterly* 39, no. 1 (2002): 13–30.

to support the opera house but rather to "one-up" a rival by raising more money than he. Likewise, the painfulness of my fear of the lion is phenomenologically very different when the lion poses a danger to my life than when the lion threatens to destroy the only copy of my book manuscript that someone has maliciously tossed into its cage. In each case, the pleasantness or painfulness of the emotion consists not simply in a feeling of the dangerousness of the lion or the goodness of my raising funds but rather a feeling of the dangerousness *to my life* (or the good *for the opera house*) for which, as I feel them, things are going badly (or well): in short, a feeling of the way in these circumstances the import of the focus impresses itself on me.

I have claimed, following Davidson and Dennett, that to be an agent is to exhibit a pattern of rationality in your behavior. I have now understood the relevant kinds of rationality at issue in genuine agency to include not only epistemic and instrumental rationality, but also the sort of rationality characteristic of these patterns of emotions and desires: a *rationality of import*. Consequently, to be an *agent* is to have and exercise the capacities not only to believe and desire but also to have emotions and so to be a subject of import.

2.3 Evaluative Judgment and Single Evaluative Perspective

The account of import provided in §2.2 is intended to apply not merely to people but also to animal agents like dogs and cats, thereby distinguishing them as genuine agents from chess-playing computers.[16] In the case of people, however, things are more complicated insofar as we are capable of evaluative judgment: in our case *felt* evaluations are not alone in constituting import, for deliberation and judgment must also be central. Thus, for example, we can deliberate about what constitutes such vaguely specified ends as a good vacation or a good life, and arrive at judgments that shape the imports things have for us. To decide that you care about something is to confer on its object the status of having import, which

---

[16] For more details on this, see Bennett W. Helm, "The Significance of Emotions," *American Philosophical Quarterly* 31, no. 4 (1994): 319–31.

means that it ought also to be the focus of a projectible, rational pattern of felt evaluations. The failure to exhibit at least large parts of these patterns of felt evaluations therefore undermines the idea that the object really has import, thereby undermining your judgment of its worth. Consequently, deliberation succeeds only if it is able to bring your felt evaluations along with it, and so your felt evaluations, your emotions and desires, impose a kind of constraint on correct deliberation.

This is much too quick, of course. If our felt evaluations are to impose constraints on *correct* deliberation, these constraints must be imposed rationally and not arbitrarily. At this point one might object that evaluative judgments are the primary way in which we make evaluations, for it is by making judgments that we articulate evaluations and so make them explicit to ourselves in a way that allows us to think self-consciously about their justification. So, the objection concludes, the evaluations made explicit in judgment are intrinsically more rational or more fundamental than those implicit in emotion and desire, and the considerations I have just offered are simply irrelevant to understanding how we can deliberate about import.

In reply, I certainly do not want to deny deliberative judgments a central role in constituting import. Indeed, a deliberate, self-conscious endorsement in judgment seems fundamental to our being able to exercise our autonomy over and so take responsibility for what we care about. Nonetheless, I think the objection overstates the role of judgment by assuming that evaluative judgments are always rationally prior to emotions insofar as in any case of conflict between them it is the emotion that ought to be brought into line. As I have argued elsewhere, this is false.[17] Emotions and evaluative judgments are rationally interconnected insofar as each is a commitment to something's having import that simultaneously both is rationally assessable in light of whether that thing really has that import and is partially constitutive of that import. Judgment and emotion are not two separate faculties of evaluation that merely happen to converge on a single object; rather, our judgments and felt evaluations normally provide us with a single, unified perspective on the world, and each therefore can rationally constrain the other inasmuch as norms of consistency apply to this perspective.

[17] Bennett W. Helm, "Integration and Fragmentation of the Self," *Southern Journal of Philosophy* 34, no. 1 (1996): 43–63; Helm, *Emotional Reason*.

In normal cases, these rational connections are obvious. I am angry because, as I believe, John has stolen my car. When I discover that my car has been in my garage the whole time, my belief and my anger simultaneously disappear.[18] We might spell out the rational connections this way: given the evidence, I conclude that he did not steal my car and so did not wrong or offend me, and this leads me to conclude that I have no grounds for anger, where it is this conclusion itself that results in my ceasing to be angry. This observation is supported by the way in which we can rationally assess both the judgment (as right or wrong) and the emotion (as warranted or not) in terms of whether the perspective they afford reveals the world as it is. To draw the inference in judgment and so to achieve the clarity of perspective that inference makes possible is normally to rule out alternative inconsistent perspectives, such as that provided in this case by my anger. Hence, to make the inference in this case just *is* for me to change my emotion as well as my belief.[19]

Of course, emotions and judgments can come apart and so present one with inconsistent perspectives on the world: in spite of my judgment, I may remain angry at John. In such cases, we ordinarily think of the emotion as being at fault. After all, my judgment seems to have a kind of rational priority in part because of its stability and coherence with other things I believe, a coherence that enables me to perceive the situation differently in light of new evidence. However, not all cases of rational conflict between emotion and judgment need to be like this. When walking late at night down a deserted street in an unfamiliar part of town, you may tell yourself that everything is fine, that there is nothing to be worried about, but you may continue to feel afraid nonetheless. In such a case, we might conclude that the persistence of the emotion reveals that one's judgment, rationally isolated as it is from other judgments, is more akin to wishful thinking than your considered view on your circumstances. In such a case, it seems plausible that the best way to resolve the conflict is to give up, at least by withholding, on the belief. Here, we might think, the emotion is revealed to be more rationally appropriate and so

---

[18] Robert C. Solomon, *The Passions* (New York, NY: Anchor Press, 1976), 185.

[19] Indeed, considerations like these even lead Robert Solomon to conclude that emotions just are judgments, in spite of the obvious difficulties that arise concerning the possibility of rational conflict between emotions and judgments. See ibid.; for criticism, see Patricia S. Greenspan, *Emotions and Reasons: An Inquiry into Emotional Justification* (Boston, MA: Routledge & Kegan Paul, 1988), especially Ch. 2.

corrects the judgment in the minimal sense that it provides a reason to reconsider.

The examples thus far have been of conflicts over the targets of the emotions. More interesting examples of rational conflict between felt evaluation and judgment concern cases in which the import of the focus is in question, for examining such cases will clarify the rational interconnections among felt evaluations and evaluative judgments and the role these play in constituting import. The conclusion again will be the same: emotions and judgments are each rationally responsive to the same thing, and each can correct the other in cases of rational conflict. This understanding of emotion and judgment is possible only because import has a kind of limited objectivity as a standard in terms of which we can assess evaluative judgments and felt evaluations for correctness or warrant. I already argued this in §2.2 in the case of felt evaluations. The same is true of evaluative judgments: merely to judge, even sincerely, that something is important does not make it so. In such cases, evaluative judgment may *misrepresent* the import things have.

Consider the following example.[20] Cassie pays much attention to her personal appearance. Thus, she keeps up with the latest trends, eagerly buying current fashions and scorning those who are out of style, and she is fastidious about the condition of her clothes, often getting upset when the dry cleaner does not clean or press them just so. In short, she invests considerable time and emotional energy in her appearance, resulting in a pattern of emotions and desires that constitute the import it has for her. Eventually, however, Cassie begins to think and read systematically about ethics, becomes a confirmed utilitarian, and is articulate about the reasons why. Moreover, she realizes that the money, time, and energy she has been spending on fashion is excessive and ought to be used instead to promote worthy causes, such as helping the needy. She therefore resolves to eliminate or at least to reduce these excesses by, for example, buying new clothes only when the old ones are genuinely worn out: fashion and appearance, she judges, are not very important in the larger scheme of things. In spite of this resolve, however, Cassie continues to feel emotions consistent with her earlier pattern of concern, and becomes increasingly dissatisfied with her appearance and even annoyed at her newfound principles, even as she intellectually rejects these emotions as groundless.

---

[20] Helm, *Emotional Reason*, §5.3.2.

Here Cassie faces a conflict between her emotions (and the coherent, projectible pattern they form) and her judgments (and the pattern of inferences she has come to endorse). In this case it seems that in spite of the narrow coherence of the pattern of emotions that otherwise would constitute her caring about her appearance, her judgments and the patterns of inference they license have a kind of rational priority: her *considered* view is that fashion should not matter to her, that it does not have import to her. Insofar as this is her considered view, it seems that her judgments have corrected her emotions, which now ought to fall in line; their failure to do so merely exhibits the irrationality of these emotions.

Part of what makes these judgments intelligible as articulating her considered view is her ability to justify them in light of a broader evaluative framework. Equally important, however, is the way in which this evaluative framework as a whole generally resonates with her emotions. It provides her with an evaluative perspective on the world that both is consistent with, and in terms of which she can make sense of, those emotions, although perhaps with the exception of a few isolated domains such as fashion. To see this, assume the opposite: that Cassie's intellectual assent to utilitarianism does not generally resonate with her emotions, as when she is forced to make choices between loyalty and devotion to her loved ones and helping others selflessly. For her assent to utilitarianism to represent her considered judgment, the perspective it provides must be able in general to rule out alternative, inconsistent evaluative perspectives and so make the best sense of her overall sensitivity to import. Yet the conflict with her emotions, given their consistency and breadth, is precisely a conflict with an inconsistent evaluative perspective, thus bringing into question the idea that her judgments represent her considered view and so the idea that there is a clear fact of the matter about what she really cares about. In such a case, judgment does not rationally trump emotion and, we might say, Cassie's emotions have corrected her judgment in the minimal sense that, so long as the alternative evaluative perspective they provide persists, she has reason to reconsider.

This example of emotions in this sense correcting judgments is not isolated. Our evaluative judgments can be distorted by peer or other societal pressures, as was the case for Huck Finn judging that he ought to turn Jim in. In such cases one is blind in judgment to the imports one's felt evaluations both constitute and reveal. Moreover, the conflicts between felt evaluations and judgments can occur not merely over whether something has import or not but also over how to balance one's various cares against each other in particular cases. In short, judgments (whether evaluative or not) and felt evaluations are tightly interconnected insofar as they are located within, and assessable in terms of, the same rational framework such that each can correct the other. This means that, when things go right, it is not that two separate faculties of judgment and felt evaluation merely happen to converge on a single object; rather, judgments and felt evaluations provide us with a single, unified perspective on the world. Because of these rational interconnections, changes in one's perspective as the result of changes in either one's felt evaluations or judgments ought to bring the other along with it; if this does not happen, the idea that one's perspective really has changed is undermined, and one's perspective may be fragmented as a result.

This means that evaluative judgments and felt evaluations that share a common focus are a part of the same projectible, rational pattern that simultaneously both is defined by their mutual commitment to the import of their common focus and constitutes that import. The projectibility of this pattern, as defined by these mutual commitments, means that evaluative judgments and felt evaluations must normally be rationally responsive to each other on pain of undermining the coherence of the pattern, thereby fragmenting one's evaluative perspective. By undermining this pattern, such fragmentation therefore undermines the idea that there is a clear fact of the matter about what has import to one. Consequently, as we have just seen, deliberation and judgment on their own do not guarantee success in achieving a new clarity of evaluative perspective and so changing that import. One's felt evaluations may be resistant to new evaluative perspectives one may try to achieve through deliberation, and such resistance, so long as it is systematic and provides one with an inconsistent evaluative perspective, provides one with reason to reconsider.

2.4 Conclusion

In this chapter, I have sketched a basic account of what it is for something to have import to an agent—of what it is for an agent to care about something—in terms of which I distinguished mere goal-directedness from genuine desire, and hence mere intentional systems from genuine agents. The resulting account rejects the cognitive–conative divide: emotions, desires, and evaluative judgments are not cognitions insofar as they serve to constitute their objects as having import, and yet they are not conations insofar as they are rationally evaluable in terms of that import. Rather, as I have argued thus far, import and the rational patterns of felt evaluations and evaluative judgments emerge simultaneously, each presupposing the other in a way that is unintelligible were we to accept the cognitive–conative divide. This account paves the way for an account of love that understands love like caring to be neither simply an appraisal nor simply a bestowal of value; instead, I shall argue, love is simultaneously both.

It should be clear, however, that the account as it was cashed out in §2.2 is intended to apply not just to people but also to some animals, including dogs and cats: they exhibit rationally structured patterns of felt evaluations constituting things as having import to them. Of course, the discussion of the rational interconnections between felt evaluations and evaluative judgments in §2.3 begins to extend this basic account beyond what is possible for animals, which lack a capacity for explicit deliberation and evaluative judgment. Nonetheless, the account of import as its stands is still very incomplete in at least two ways.

First, not all import, not all forms of caring, are the same. Rather trivially, we can care about some things more than others, where this difference is simply a matter of degree.[21] More important is that some forms of caring can be "deeper": richer, more rewarding, more central to our sense of who we are as persons. Thus, although I care about having a comfortable chair to sit in, I care more deeply about my wife and children, where the difference here is qualitative rather than merely in degree. Making sense of this "deeper" sort of caring, including not just loving others but also valuing ends, projects, and so on, will be my aim in Part II.

Second, the account of the objectivity of import and so of the justification of our felt evaluations and evaluative judgments has thus far been quite limited. For thus far import has been understood to be relative to an agent's overall evaluative perspective, such that we can criticize someone for evaluative responses to that which does not in fact have import to her

---

[21] For details on how to understand degrees of import, see Helm, *Emotional Reason*, Ch. 4, some of which can be found in §4.3, below.

or for failing to have an evaluative response to that which does. This is, I believe, appropriate as an account of the kind of import that is possible for animals, but it is clearly inadequate for us persons, for there is no room in the account as it stands to ask whether something *ought* to have import to an agent—whether she ought to care about it. Indeed, it is precisely such questions that are at issue in the justification of love and friendship, and so the account of caring will need to be extended considerably to make sense of these justificatory questions. I shall address these issues at various points throughout Parts II–III.

Before I am in a position to tackle these issues concerning the depth and justification of import, however, I need to address a few other issues. Thus, it is often said that to love someone is to care about him for his sake; what precisely does this mean, and how are we to understand it in the context of the account of caring I have given so far? Providing a preliminary account of caring for another for his sake will be my task in Chapter 3.

3

Caring about Others

Thus far I have provided an account of caring in general: to care about something is for it to be the focus of a projectible, rational pattern of felt evaluations and evaluative judgments, such that one is motivated not only to feel and judge, but also to act accordingly. It might seem, therefore, that the application of this account of caring to others, including other persons and other agents more generally, would be straightforward: to care about someone is for him to be the focus of such a pattern. Thus, you ought to feel joy when things are going well for him, fear when he is threatened, relief when he emerges unscathed, and so on; consequently, you ought to be prepared to act on his behalf when this is called for by the circumstances—by, for example, pushing him out of the way of an oncoming train.

However, this is surely inadequate as an account of caring about others insofar as what is at issue here is not simply the physical or psychological well-being of the one you care about, as if all you care about is his meeting a certain minimum standard of physical and psychological health. Rather, insofar as it is an agent that you care about, at issue is his well-being as such: as being a subject of import to whom things can matter. The well-being of an agent as such therefore depends on how the things he cares about fare; this is something like the notion of "happiness" as traditional utilitarians have used the term. Thus, if someone you care about cares about raising prize-winning pumpkins, he fares in part as his pumpkins fare, and so in caring about him you ought to attend to and act on behalf of his successes and failures in this aspect of his life. In particular, you ought to feel joyful when he (and his pumpkins) win a prize at the state fair, sad or disappointed[1] when he loses, frustrated with and angry at the

---

[1] This is disappointment in that failure, which should not be confused with disappointment in the person who fails. (I shall discuss such disappointment in a person in Part II in the context of my account of person-focused emotions.)

judge who rates his pumpkins much lower than they deserve because of internal politics of the International Vegetable Growers Association, and so on. In this way, his frustrations, joys, fears, hopes, desires, and so on are in an important sense yours as well, for you care about his raising prize-winning pumpkins as a part of caring about him. Caring about other agents, therefore, requires sharing their cares.

Of course, it is possible to care about agents without sharing their cares. Thus, someone might care about his dogs simply as showpieces, as items to be groomed (and, potentially, to be rented out for stud services) and so merely care for their physical well-being and appearance. Such caring, however, is focused on what is only incidentally an agent, and is not the kind of caring I have in mind here. It is also possible to care that something be an agent, to care about its status as an agent, in a way that is not focused only incidentally on its agency. Thus, a psychologist might care that in performing brain surgery on rats she does not damage or destroy their status as agents and so make them useless to her experiments. However, this kind of caring about an agent is still too distant, too "impersonal" (to stretch the use of that term), for my purposes here. For the kind of caring at issue here involves a concern for the well-being of the agent *for its own sake*, and not merely for the sake of something else, such as a psychology experiment or stud fees. My vague talk of "sharing another's cares" is intended to point to this distinctive kind of caring about agents.

So far this is rather metaphorical and intuitive, and the account needs to be spelled out in much greater detail; that is my aim in this chapter. In line with my earlier account of caring generally, providing this account will require articulating the precise rational interconnections of the patterns of felt evaluations and evaluative judgments constitutive of such caring. In particular, how is it that I can share the cares of an agent about which I care—cares which I am rationally committed to sharing by virtue of my caring about the agent—without simply taking them over for my own? And how does this amount to caring about the agent for *his* sake rather than for my own sake?

One further caveat before I begin: my concern here will be with caring about other *agents* generally, not caring about persons as such. For, as I shall argue in Part II, the way we care about persons as such is much "deeper" not merely in its intensity, a mere matter of degree, but in kind. This is because persons and their well-being are distinct in kind from mere agents and their well-being. This distinction between agents and persons, which I shall spell out in detail in Chapter 4, roughly follows Charles Taylor's critique of utilitarianism.[2] For if merely caring about someone involves a concern for her happiness (as a utilitarian would construe it), then such caring is focused merely on what Taylor calls her "weak evaluations" and so ignores the "strong evaluations" constitutive of her identity as this person; by contrast, I shall argue, love involves "sharing," in a certain sense, another's strong evaluations. For this reason, I shall distinguish between caring about agents and loving persons, and it is only the former that is in view in this chapter.

3.1 Caring For the Sake of . . .

The account of caring presented in Chapter 2 is intended to be an account of what it is to care about something for its own sake. In general, talk about that for the sake of which you do something is about your motives or reasons for doing that. In particular, to care about something for its own sake is to care about it in recognition of the import it has and apart from any consideration for other things the import of which might motivate or provide a reason for caring about this. This is exactly the account I have given. Thus, I have said, emphasizing the objectivity of import, to care about something is to have your sensibilities attuned to the import it has, such that this import can impress itself on you in particular circumstances. Consequently, my concern for it is not motivated by an independent concern for anything else, which is to say that I care about it for its own sake.

Of course, we must be mindful that the kind of objectivity import has (at least as explicated thus far) is quite limited, for import is also constituted by the very felt evaluations and evaluative judgments that constitute one's attunement to it. Thus, emphasizing the subjectivity of import, we can say that these evaluations each are a kind of commitment to having other evaluations with the same focus when otherwise appropriate. Yet here too we find that one's caring is not motivated by any independent concern

---

[2] Charles Taylor, "What Is Human Agency?", in *Human Agency and Language: Philosophical Papers 1* (Cambridge: Cambridge University Press, 1985), 15–44.

insofar as the commitment one undertakes to import as a part of one's evaluative perspective is not contingent on other such commitments.

This conclusion can be clarified and further supported by considering what it is to care about something for the sake of something else—that is, by considering the ways in which other things can provide motives or reasons for your caring about this. One way to care about something for the sake of something else is instrumentally, as when I care about making oboe reeds for the sake of playing the oboe. In the remainder of this section, I shall discuss the nature of such instrumental reasons for caring and how they are connected to and partially constitutive of caring about something as an end for its own sake. This will lead to a more general discussion of what it is to care about something as something, which will in turn lead, in §§3.2–3.3, to an account of what it is to care about something as an agent, for its own sake.

In the account of caring or import provided thus far, I have largely omitted any discussion of the importance of instrumental rationality in the articulation of the relevant pattern of rationality. This may seem odd, especially given the plausibility of the following *instrumental principle*: if an end has import to you—if you care about it—then, other things being equal, you ought also to care for the sake of that end about what you believe to be the necessary means to that end. How should we cash out this "for the sake of that end"?

The answer lies in a more careful articulation of the focus of the relevant felt evaluations and evaluative judgments. Given that I believe that making oboe reeds is a necessary means to playing the oboe well, and given that I care about playing the oboe well, I ought to care about making reeds. This does not mean, however, that I ought to have a pattern of felt evaluations focused on making reeds. For to say that this is their focus is, I have claimed, to say that I am committed to the import this has for me for its own sake, in a way that is not contingent on my caring about playing oboe, and this is false: making oboe reeds is tedious, frustrating work that I would not care about doing were it not for its instrumental connection to the end of playing oboe. Hence, my caring about making reeds is a part of my caring about playing oboe, and I would not care about making them were I to cease caring about playing oboe. What is needed, therefore, is a way of making sense of this instrumental connection.

As I have argued elsewhere,[3] we can make sense of instrumental rationality by understanding my desire to make a reed, my frustration at splitting the cane while tying it on to the tube, my hope that this reed will enable me to play low notes softly, my disappointment that it does not, and so on all to be focused not on making reeds per se but rather on playing oboe: what commits me, given the demands of instrumental rationality, to having this desire and to feeling these emotions is my commitment to the import of playing oboe well and not my commitment to the import of making reeds as such (for I have no such commitment). Thus, we might say, such emotions and desires are "clustered" around making reeds, but focused on playing oboe: making reeds is in this sense the *subfocus* of these felt evaluations. (See Figure 3.1.) This makes intelligible how I can care about making reeds not for its own sake but rather for the sake of playing oboe: the demands of instrumental rationality make this pattern of emotions and desires subfocused on reeds a part of the larger pattern of emotions focused on playing oboe and constitutive of import. We might describe this structure in the patterns of felt evaluations constituting caring about something for the sake of something else in terms of the subpattern of felt evaluations subfocused on the means being a *layer* in the overall pattern constituting caring about the end. Indeed, given that there can be multiple means for a given end and even further means for attaining these means, the structure of felt evaluations can be *multiply layered*.

This has three important consequences. First, it confirms my claim that for something to be cared about for its own sake just is for it to be the focus of a projectible, rational pattern of felt evaluations and evaluative judgments. Second, it makes intelligible one way to care about something for the sake of something else in terms of the way instrumental rationality structures the pattern of evaluations constitutive of caring about that something else—of its import. Finally, to slightly extend the instrumental principle articulated above (p. 78), caring about the means to some end is partially constitutive of caring about that end: generally to fail to care for the sake of an end about the necessary means to that end is, other things being equal, to erode the relevant rational pattern and so to fail to care about that end. This is because, given the very concept of an end as something to be achieved (by

---

[3] Helm, *Emotional Reason*, especially §4.4.

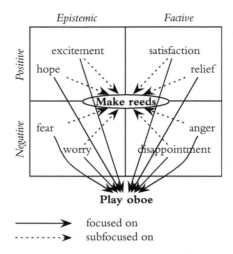

Figure 3.1. Pattern of felt evaluations with focus and subfocus.

taking certain means), instrumental rationality must be a central part of the rational structure of the relevant pattern constitutive of such caring.

Although instrumental rationality figures into the rational pattern of emotions and desires constitutive of caring about anything because of the way in which desire and activity motivated by desire must normally be an element of this rational pattern, it is particularly important in defining the rational structure of felt evaluations and evaluative judgments constitutive of our caring about ends as such. Nonetheless, it should not be assumed that we only care about ends as such. As indicated above, this leads to the question of how an understanding of the kind of thing the focus of your care is can inform your caring about it and so can be central to that caring. For to care about something is to be concerned with its well-being, and yet the idea of something's well-being makes sense only in light of an understanding of the kind of thing it is. This needs further explanation.

Consider, for example, my caring about my favorite water pitcher. On the one hand, I might understand it simply to be a functional item, a tool I care about because it enables me to get the job done particularly well. Thus, it might be just the right size, have a spout that pours well, be well balanced around the handle, and so on, so that I prize it because of its usefulness: I care about it as a tool. In understanding the pitcher in this way, I delimit a conception of its well-being with which I am concerned and to which my felt evaluations ought to be responsive. So, as you carelessly swing the pitcher around I might be afraid that you will bang it on the counter top and damage the spout, for this is central to its functioning as the tool it is and in virtue of which I care about it; however, I may be wholly unconcerned if you scratch the finish, for in understanding it merely as a tool, I do not care about its appearance, so long as this does not affect its integrity as the tool it is.[4] On the other hand, I might in caring about the pitcher understand it to be simply a work of art. Thus, its proportions, its color, the design etched into it, and so on all might make it an item of beauty, and I care about it merely as such. In this case, its appearance is everything. So, whether or not its handle is beginning to loosen, or whether or not it has developed a leak, may be irrelevant to me so long as its appearance is unaffected. Consequently, caring is always caring about something *as* something, though of course a person might care about the same object in multiple ways simultaneously, depending on her understanding of the kind of object it is.

It should not be presupposed that the relevant understanding of the focus of one's care must always be explicitly articulated in judgment (though it may be). Rather, such an understanding may be implicit in the existing rational structure of felt evaluations constitutive of caring about it. Thus, it may be that I come to discover that I care about the water pitcher merely as a tool by virtue of the fact that I find myself unconcerned by its becoming tarnished or scratched or dented. Indeed, such a discovery may even force me to revise my explicit judgments about how I care about it (as I argued in §2.3). Consequently, such an understanding is not one the subject needs to have explicitly articulated, nor need she be able to articulate it clearly when asked. At issue is not a discursive understanding, but a practical one, something like the way in which ordinary people understand what numbers are in being able to make use of arithmetic in their everyday lives: such an understanding is revealed in the way we generally conform our responses in particular circumstances to certain norms of rationality as when, for example, giving correct change or correcting mistakes when

---

[4] This is not to say that I care merely about having a thing—anything—with certain of its properties: that I care merely about having a good pitcher, or that I care about having a good pitcher merely as instrumental to my end of serving drinks. Rather, I might care about this particular thing itself, as would be revealed in the fact that not just any object with these properties will likewise be an object of my concern, given the way in which the pattern of emotions and desires projects into the relevant counterfactual or future cases. (I shall return to the general problem of fungibility in Ch. 6.)

they are called to our attention. Likewise, an implicit understanding of a pitcher as a tool is revealed in the way in which a subject generally conforms his felt evaluations and evaluative judgments to a certain rational pattern constitutive of caring about it as such.

One might object that this is viciously circular, for I have said both that one has an understanding because of the way in which the pattern of one's felt evaluations constitutive of caring about something as something is rationally structured, and that such rationality structures this pattern because one's understanding of something as something informs one's caring about it. Thus, one might ask, which comes first: the rational structure or the understanding? The answer is: neither. The account is circular, but not viciously so, for such circularity is a feature of any holistic account that takes seriously the idea that rationality is the constitutive ideal of the mental.

This understanding of the focus of our cares—and so of the emotions that constitute those cares—as always involving an understanding of the kind of object it is forces a slight change to my earlier account in §2.2 of the phenomenology of these emotions. There, I argued that the pleasantness or painfulness of particular emotions is a matter of my feeling things to go well or poorly for the focus, a feeling of the way the import of the focus impresses itself on me in these circumstances. It should now be clear that the understanding of the kind of object the focus is and so of its well-being that informs the relevant emotions thereby also informs the import of their focus. Consequently, in being afraid that you will damage the spout of my favorite pitcher as you swing it about carelessly, I feel its import *as a tool* impressing itself on me through the danger your carelessness presents to its well-being as such. Such fear would therefore feel subtly different were I to care about the pitcher as a work of art, for although it would still be a feeling of being pained by the danger your carelessness presents to its well-being, its well-being, that import, and so the danger I feel and am pained by will all be different. (This point will become important later.)

3.2 Caring About Agents

This understanding of what it is to care about something for its own sake can now be applied to thinking about what it is to care about another agent for the sake of that agent. Nonetheless, as the discussion of the water pitcher indicates, there can be multiple ways to care about something depending on the agent's understanding of the object of her care. What is at issue here is caring about something as an agent for its own sake, and this needs some clarification.

Compare the owner who cares about his dog simply as a showpiece with the owner who cares about her dog as a "member of the family."[5] In the former case, let us assume, the owner cares about the dog merely as a show dog, as an object of aesthetic appreciation: other things being equal, he is strongly motivated to groom it, admires it when it looks good, gets angry at the kid who gets bubblegum in its hair (and worries whether it will come out), and so on. Here is a pattern of felt evaluations focused on the dog and constituting its import for him. Nonetheless, he does not care at all about its being an agent except insofar as this bears on his concern with its appearance. Thus, although he might hope that this time his dog does not get nervous around the buzz of the hair trimmer and although he might be glad that it readily devours the egg he gives it daily for a shiny coat, his concern with the dog's well-being is limited by this implicit understanding of it as an aesthetic object and does not extend to the dog's "happiness." So, in a sense he cares about the dog for its own sake, albeit merely as an aesthetic object.[6] By contrast, the second owner, who cares about her dog "as a member of the family," has a different set of concerns and so cares about it in a different way that is informed by her implicit understanding of it as an agent. For given this understanding, both her conception of the dog's well-being, of how things fare with it, and so the way in which in caring about her dog she is responsive to what happens to it, will be very different from the conception and caring of the first owner. Of course, the

---

[5] I have used scare quotes here because no one in her right mind would literally treat a dog as a member of the family—as a full-blooded person or as having the potential to be a full-blooded person. As I indicated above (p. 76–7), caring about persons as such is distinct in kind from merely caring about agents as such.

[6] One might be tempted to say that he cares about the dog merely as a part of his caring about appreciating beauty, so that the focus of the pattern of felt evaluations here is not the dog itself but rather beauty or the activity of aesthetic appreciation. Although this may be true in some cases, it need not be true in all. For if the focus were merely beauty or the subject's aesthetic appreciation, then we would expect instances of beauty or objects of that appreciation to be more or less fungible: if another dog were just as beautiful as your own, then you ought to care about it just as much as yours, other things being equal. Yet this need not be the case: the owner might develop a special attachment to his dog and so care about *it* in a way he does not care about other, equally beautiful dogs, even though he cares about his dog merely as an aesthetic object. Here it is clearest to say, as I do in the text, that the owner cares about the dog itself, for its own sake, albeit as an aesthetic object.

first owner will likely also have an understanding of his dog as an agent; after all, he's not blind to its agency. However, his understanding does not inform the way in which he cares about his dog, whereas hers does. What does this mean?

As I argued in §2.1 (p. 54), what it is to be an agent is to have and exercise the capacities not only to believe and desire but also to care about things, and how a particular agent fares depends in large part on how the things it cares about fare. This means that the well-being of an agent as such is determined in large part by that agent through its exercise of the very capacities in virtue of which it is an agent.[7] Because to care about something is to be committed to its import and thereby to its well-being, to have one's caring informed by an understanding of it as an agent is to be committed to its well-being as thus determined and, therefore, to be committed, other things being equal, to caring about what it cares about as a part of caring about it. This does not mean that in caring about my dog, for example, I must normally care about the very things he cares about for *their* sakes, such that I must normally exhibit a pattern of felt evaluations focused on these things. Rather, in caring about them as a *part* of caring about him, I care about them only because I care about him: I care about them for *his* sake. Consequently, the pattern of felt evaluations and evaluative judgments focused on and so constitutive of caring about the agent as such must normally include felt evaluations subfocused on the things that agent cares about. (See Figure 3.2.) To fail in general to exhibit such subpatterns in the overall pattern of felt evaluations focused on an agent—to fail in general to care about what it cares about for the sake of the agent—is to fail to care about the agent as such.

Notice that, in spite of the different ways in which I have described them, there is a close analogy concerning these connections (a) between caring about the agent as such for its sake and caring about the things it cares about as a part of caring about it and (b) between caring about an end and caring about the means for the sake of that end. In the former case, I described the connection in terms of the way in which one's understanding of the object of one's care structures one's commitment to

---

[7] Of course, how an agent fares depends as well on its physical and psychological health, but these in turn depend to a large degree on what it cares about, both because agents normally care about their own health and because being healthy is instrumental to achieving ends they care about.

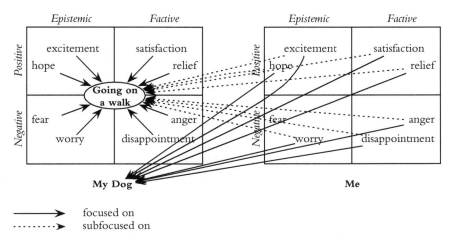

Figure 3.2.   Pattern of felt evaluations focused on another agent.

its well-being and therefore the pattern of felt evaluations constitutive of
one's caring. In the latter case, I described the connection in terms of the
role a certain kind of rationality has in structuring the pattern of one's
felt evaluations constitutive of caring about something. We can now see
that these just are two different ways of describing the same phenomenon.
Thus on the one hand, to have instrumental rationality thus structure
the pattern of one's felt evaluations constitutive of one's caring about
something, just is for one to understand that thing as an end to be achieved.
Likewise, for instrumental rationality to fail to structure this pattern is,
other things being equal, to fail to care about it in a way that is informed
by an understanding of it as an end. On the other hand, to understand
something as an agent, in a way that informs one's caring about it, just
is for the pattern of felt evaluations constitutive of that caring to be
structured by certain norms of rationality in addition to the bare rationality
of import described in Chapter 2. This is because of the way in which
any understanding involves rational commitments to subsequent thoughts,
feelings, and actions; in particular, for an understanding of something to
inform one's caring is for these rational commitments to structure the
pattern of thoughts, feelings, and actions constitutive of one's caring. In
both cases, it is the multiply layered structure of the relevant felt evaluations
that makes intelligible that one cares about the focus as an agent or as
an end.

One might object that my account seems to require that in caring about an agent one cares about everything she cares about blindly and uncritically. Thus, if someone you care about cares about getting her next fix of some illegal drug, then even though you may find this abhorrent, in order to care about her you must care about (her) getting the drug. However, this is not a consequence of my account. The requirement is that in caring about an agent as such you ought normally to care about the things she cares about, other things being equal. Yet this requirement is subsidiary to the overall concern for the well-being of that which you care about: it is only because the well-being of an agent is normally constituted partly by the things she cares about that you ought—normally, other things being equal—to care about what she cares about in caring about her. In this case, however, what she cares about manifestly does not contribute to her well-being, and so other things are not equal, and you ought to instead care that she does not obtain the drug.

Of course in some cases the question of whether what she cares about properly defines her well-being may not be so straightforward, and you and she may disagree about it.[8] And in other cases you may find yourself simply unable to care about something she does, perhaps because what she cares about conflicts with something else you care about so that you cannot consistently care about them both. On their own, such cases need not imply that you give up caring about her, for isolated failures in the overall rational pattern of felt evaluations focused on her, including those subfocused on the things she cares about, need not destroy the pattern constitutive of your caring about her; however, if your failing to care about what she cares about becomes the norm, then that overall pattern may be undermined, and it can be hard to sustain the idea that you genuinely care about her. Nonetheless, it should be clear that this does not mean that in caring that I win a race, I cannot also care, as a part of caring about someone else, that he wins it too. Although it is inconsistent that both he and I win the race, it is not inconsistent for me to care about both, and I may end up both glad that I won and disappointed that he lost—a kind of ambivalence that nonetheless does not involve any rational incoherence because these two emotions have different focuses.

---

[8] In the case of persons, the issue may seem to involve a problematic tension between the intimacy of love and the beloved's autonomy. I address this case in §5.2 as well as, in the case of paternalistic love, in Ch. 7.

3.3 Shared Cares and Engaged Activity

I have argued that caring about an agent as such requires caring about the things he cares about as a part of caring about him, and I have cashed this out in terms of a distinctive rational pattern in one's felt evaluations, a pattern that is informed by an at least implicit understanding of him as an agent; in light of this understanding one ought normally to exhibit subpatterns of felt evaluations subfocused on the things he cares about but focused on him. Thus, if Fred cares about the Pittsburgh Penguins and I care about him, then I ought to exhibit, as a part of a more general pattern of felt evaluations focused on Fred, a subpattern of felt evaluations subfocused on the Penguins. Of course, this subpattern of felt evaluations differs from the normal pattern of felt evaluations constitutive of my caring about the Penguins in that the latter pattern involves felt evaluations focused on the Penguins directly, whereas the former involves felt evaluations subfocused on the Penguins but *focused* on Fred. So, insofar as I lack the former pattern we should not say that I care about the Pittsburgh Penguins for its sake. Nonetheless, because these subpatterns are otherwise identical to the pattern of felt evaluations I have argued would be constitutive of my caring about the Penguins, I nonetheless do care about the team: I get frustrated when they cannot score goals, worried when their star winger goes down, joyful when they pull off a hard won victory, and so on. Given that Fred is the focus of these felt evaluations, we should say in this case that I care about the Penguins for *his* sake.

Sharing another's cares in this way, I have argued, is partly constitutive of caring about him. Nonetheless, it should be clear that such sharing need not extend beyond my caring about him given the way the relevant pattern (and subpatterns) of felt evaluations focused on him is informed by an understanding of him as an agent. Thus, were he to stop caring about something, or were I to stop caring about him, I would (other things being equal) have no reason to continue caring about it.[9] Nonetheless, more needs to be said about exactly what is shared and how. In particular, in

---

[9] This is not to deny that I might through caring about something for the sake of another come to care about it for its own sake. However, this is not rationally required, nor is it to be expected in the kinds of cases I am now considering. (I shall have more to say about a stronger sense in which two people can share cares in my discussion of friendship in Ch. 8.)

sharing the cares of an agent I care about, I ought generally to share his emotions, as when I come to feel the disappointment of a colleague whose paper was just rejected. Such sharing of felt evaluations is, we might say, a kind of sympathy; however, it is a kind of sympathy that needs to be distinguished from other kinds of sympathy.

One kind of sympathy, one way in which we share emotions with others, is something akin to infection. For example, when you walk into a crowd of angry people, you can find yourself being infected by their anger and so coming to be angry yourself, even though you may not know exactly what they are angry at or why.[10] A similar case involves the infectiousness of laughter, as when walking up on a conversation and hearing only the punch line of a joke, you find yourself laughing genuinely along with the others, even though you do not understand what is so funny. As the metaphor of "infection" suggests, these are cases in which our coming to feel what others do is arational, a sort of reflexive response we find ourselves making and which we can prevent only with effort. By contrast, the kind of sharing of felt evaluations at issue in caring about an agent can be evaluated for its rationality, precisely because of the kind of commitment to the import of that agent one undertakes in caring about her. Thus, when the colleague I care about gets a paper rejected, I *ought* to feel her disappointment, other things being equal, and in the absence of compelling excuses I can be criticized for failing to do so. Moreover, unlike the infection cases, I ought to feel her disappointment even when, for whatever reason, she does not, as when she is too busy preparing for class to let the news "sink in."

What makes intelligible this idea that the sharing of emotions as a part of caring about another can be evaluated for its rationality is that, unlike the infection cases, these felt evaluations have determinate focuses. For the

---

[10] One might think that the phenomenon I have just described concerns not emotions but moods: you become infected by the crowd's angry mood. However, moods are not simply objectless emotions, or even emotions that have relatively less determinate targets than emotions; rather, moods persist longer than occurrent emotions (but not as long as the evaluative attitudes, such as caring or loving), and they affect the ways in which we feel emotions and desires in ways that emotions do not. Thus, in being in the sort of sad or depressed mood characteristic of mourning, one's emotions and desires focused on other things are, other things being equal, dampened or suppressed in a way that can explain the phenomenology of things seeming generally "gray." For more on this notion of the dampening of emotions, see Helm, *Emotional Reason*, especially Ch. 4; for more on how this contributes to an understanding of moods, see Bennett W. Helm, Yaroslava Babych, and Aleksandra Markovic, "Moods as a Sense of Priorities" (talk given to MidSouth Philosophy Conference, 1999).

warrant of felt evaluations is intelligible only in terms of the import of their focuses and the connection between these focuses and the targets of the felt evaluations. Of course, the focus of my emotions will be different from the focus of hers: her emotions are focused on her scholarship (or her career, or . . .), whereas mine are focused on her and only subfocused on her scholarship. So we do not share precisely the same felt evaluations, nor, for that matter, do we share precisely the same cares: she cares about her scholarship for its sake, whereas I do so for her sake, and so my disappointment is rationally connected to my caring about her in a way that hers is not. Nonetheless, it seems natural to say that I share her care—and her disappointment—insofar as, given the way my cares and emotions track hers and the non-accidental coincidence of the object of our respective cares, of the kind of emotion expressive of that care in particular cases, and of the target of that emotion.

Indeed, it is the focus of the emotions in these various cases that makes intelligible their phenomenological differences. When I get a paper rejected because of an undeservedly negative referee report, my anger consists in the feeling of the import of my scholarship as such impressing itself on me in the present circumstances in such a way that I am pained by the offense that rejection presents: the rejection feels bad—hurts—in this way precisely because of its bearing on the well-being of my scholarship. Such anger differs from the anger I would feel on behalf of a colleague I care about in similar circumstances: in the latter case, my anger consists in the feeling of the import my colleague has to me as an agent impressing itself on me in the present circumstances, through her concern for her own scholarship, so that I am pained by the offense the rejection presents to her. Thus in being angry on her behalf, the pain I feel consists in part in the feeling not only of the import she (the focus) has to me but also of the import her scholarship (the subfocus) has to her, so that the rejection feels bad because of its bearing on the well-being of both her scholarship and her; in this respect my anger on her behalf differs phenomenologically from my anger at my own paper's rejection. By contrast, when, as a part of a crowd, I come to be infected by their anger without knowing the focus of that anger, the resulting feeling of offense (with or without a determinate target) feels empty or ungrounded precisely insofar as there is no focus the import of which impresses itself on me through the target—through that offense.

Another kind of sympathy to be distinguished from that which is central to caring about an agent as such stems from a distinct kind of caring. Thus, you may care about dogs quite generally, and so care about this particular dog by, for example, sharing its pain or distress and being thus motivated to act on its behalf, or by sharing its joy as you meet and greet each other. This sort of caring, which is directed at particular individuals only inasmuch as they are instances of a certain kind, is focused not on those individuals but rather on the kind. Although such caring about the kind may involve sharing felt evaluations with particular instances of that kind, the motivation for that sharing is very different from the kind of caring about a particular individual with which I am primarily concerned. For, as this identification of the object of caring indicates, the focus of these felt evaluations will be different in the two cases—the kind (dogs in general) in the one case, and the individual (this dog, Max) in the other.

In caring about the kind, therefore, my concern is with the well-being of dogs as such, and so with the physical and psychological capacities and characteristics shared in common among all dogs. Thus, when a dog—any dog—is injured and so has a physical impairment, my caring about dogs generally ought to be expressed, other things being equal, in my sympathetic feelings directed at this dog: I ought to be pained by its injuries as a part of my caring about dogs generally, and so I ought to be motivated to act on its behalf. This will be true whether or not I have encountered this dog before, and so my concern for its well-being is delimited by my understanding of the well-being of dogs quite generally. By contrast, unlike my caring about the kind, in caring about this dog, I do not in any way commit myself to caring about all dogs (let alone all agents). Rather, my caring about this dog gains increased intimacy through my commitment to what it cares about, for in caring about this dog as an agent, my concern for its well-being is delimited largely by the dog itself through the exercise of those very capacities in virtue of which it is an agent. The increased "intimacy" therefore stems not merely from the increased knowledge I must have of this dog in order to respond to circumstances that affect its well-being as thus defined, but, more significantly, from the history of interactions I must have with this dog rather than with dogs generally, in virtue of which I can be said to be truly committed to its import and so truly to care about it. This needs further elaboration.

Thus far I have focused my attention mainly on the way in which caring about an agent as such commits one to having certain *emotions* focused on that agent but subfocused on the things he cares about. It should be clear that this pattern of shared emotions is central to the history of interactions constitutive of such caring. Yet desires are felt evaluations too, and these desires will normally be "shared" as well. Thus, when my dog, whom I care about, cares about a certain end, such as retrieving a bone that was knocked under the couch, I ought, other things being equal, to care about this for his sake, to feel the desire to retrieve it, and so come to be motivated to act accordingly. I therefore share this desire with him in the same sense I share emotions with him, and insofar as such a shared desire leads to our engaging in some activity together, we might say that I "share" this activity with him as well.

Saying that I "share" desires or even activity with the one I care about risks confusion with alternative accounts of shared intention and activity, which are intended to analyze a quite different phenomenon.[11] A problem for any such account is to distinguish cases in which two agents merely happen to be doing the same thing side by side, such as painting a house, from the more interesting cases in which their doing this is not accidental. The standard accounts of shared intention and shared action make this distinction, and so come to understand what it is truly to share intentions or actions in terms of a distinctive kind of coordination among the parties involved: each must intend that they together do what is in some sense the same thing, and they must each coordinate their intentions and actions with the others, in circumstances of common knowledge, so as to satisfy these intentions. However, the kind of "shared" desire and activity I have in mind is quite different.

Insofar as the agent I care about can be a dog or an infant, there is no requirement that the parties involved must know that the other has the intention that we do this together: dogs and infants are not capable of mental states with this sort of sophisticated content about the minds of others. Indeed, on my account, there is no requirement that the one I care about even have a desire that *we* do something together. As in the example

[11] See, for example, Tuomela, "We-Intentions Revisited"; Margaret Gilbert, "Obligation and Joint Commitment," in Gilbert, *Sociality and Responsibility*; Searle, "Collective Intentions and Actions"; Michael Bratman, "Shared Intention," in Bratman, *Faces of Intention*, 109–29; Bratman, "I Intend That We J."

given above, my dog may want to retrieve the bone that is under the couch, and I may come to share this desire—that *he* get the bone—and so fish it out for him. Here it is clearly a stretch to say that the activity is "shared." However, that should not obscure the way in which such action involves him in a non-trivial way: in so acting I am engaged with him precisely because of the way I share his desire because I care about him. My action on his behalf ought, in such a case, to be understood as *engaged action*; this needs further explanation.

In caring about my dog and so coming to share his desires and other felt evaluations as an expression of that caring, I must remain attuned to what he cares about and so to his interests. Consequently, in being motivated to act, it need not be that I simply retrieve the bone for him, thereby taking over the activity from him; other things being equal, this will be appropriate as an expression of my caring about him only when all he cares about is simply that the end state obtain, rather than that it attain through his agency.[12] Alternatively, I might merely offer him encouragement, saying, "That's right; go get it!" as he bats at it with his paw, or I might help him by moving the couch aside, so that his retrieval of the bone is achieved through both our actions. Precisely how it is appropriate for me to act on his behalf will in general depend on his interests and concerns as these have been revealed in the past patterns of his felt evaluations as well as in his present responses, and so in acting I must pay special attention to him and the way my participation in this activity affects his well-being. It is this attunement to him and his agency (including not just his actions and desires but also the underlying cares that motivate them) as a part of my caring about him as an agent that constitutes my engagement with him.

Such engaged action therefore differs from other actions on behalf of an agent that are motivated merely instrumentally. Thus, you might pay me to look after your kid, and I might therefore be motivated instrumentally to retrieve his toy when he drops it. Indeed, in taking care of him, I may have to attend to his desires and emotions in a superficially similar way so I instead help him do it himself when he gets angry at me for taking over

---

[12] I suspect this fine-grained distinction in the content of the desire is not one that intelligibly applies to dogs, except where the dog desires simply to engage in the activity for its own sake, as when it tears up a stick. However, it clearly applies to two-year-old children: as I retrieve the toy my two-year-old daughter has dropped, she may get angry at me, saying, "my do it!"

from him. This does not, however, constitute the sort of attunement I have to my own daughter, whom I care about, in similar circumstances. For in being attuned to her, I ought not merely to come to desire that she do it herself but also come to share her anger at me for undercutting her own agency insofar as I care about her for her sake (and insofar as her anger is warranted). In this way, my action as engaged is essentially embedded within and so motivated by a broader pattern of response constitutive of my caring about her.[13]

In short, in caring about an agent as such, it is this agent, as the focus of one's caring, that motivates one's sympathy and sympathetic, engaged action. Such motivation, moreover, stems from the commitment one has in caring about an agent as such to care about the things he cares about as a part of caring about him.

3.4 Conclusion

In this chapter I have extended my account of caring in general to include a distinctive kind of caring, which I have called caring about an agent as such. This has required first coming to understand what it is to care about something for its own sake in terms of its being the focus of the relevant pattern of felt evaluations and evaluative judgments; caring about one thing for the sake of another I have understood in terms of the one's being the subfocus of a pattern of felt evaluations that is ultimately focused on the other. Second, I have examined what it is to care about something as being of a certain kind in terms of an at least implicit understanding of that kind informing and so structuring the rational pattern of felt evaluations and evaluative judgments constitutive of one's caring. In particular, I have argued that caring about something as an agent requires that the pattern of felt evaluations and evaluative judgments constitutive of one's caring be structured in such a way that one comes to share not only her cares but also thereby her felt evaluations and desires. This means that in caring about an

---

[13] For this reason, not only are cases of engaged action not necessarily shared, but cases of shared action and intention are not necessarily engaged either. For a group of people merely to share a we-intention and coordinate their plans and activities is not yet for any of them to care about the others or to be motivated to act and respond emotionally out of a concern for the others.

agent as such one ought normally to undertake engaged activity with her as an expression of one's caring.

In presenting this account, I have been using dogs as my central example of the focus of one's caring about agents as such so as to make clear that the sort of caring I have been discussing is not intended to apply just to persons, though we certainly can and often do care about persons in this way. Nonetheless, two caveats are in order.

First, in focusing on caring about dogs, I have obscured one important part of the phenomenon of caring about agents as such: reciprocal caring. For, as seems likely, dogs cannot recognize, let alone respond appropriately to, the beliefs, desires, and cares of another (since that would require that they have a deeper understanding of rationality than they seem to have); for that reason, dogs cannot come to care about what you care about as a part of caring about you, and so they cannot care about agents as such. This is not, of course, to deny that dogs can care about other agents, for they surely do in many cases care about their offspring and their owners, just not *as* agents: although my dog has a concern for my well-being, his understanding of my well-being is not informed by an understanding of me as an agent whose well-being is defined in part by my own cares. Nonetheless, reciprocal caring is not only possible but quite common, and it is distinguished by the increased intimacy it brings to the relationship between the two parties. Although I shall not discuss reciprocal caring here, a distinctive kind of reciprocal caring—that characteristic of friendship—will be my focus in Part III.

Second, it should be clear that we persons can care about each other much more deeply than merely as agents. For a person is not merely an agent but a moral agent and as such is subject to the norms of distinctive kinds of practical and theoretical rationality in a way that makes possible distinctive capacities for deliberation, valuing, and self-consciousness. Consequently, caring about persons as such—*loving* them—will require a separate discussion, which is the focus of Part II.

PART II
Loving

4

Values: Loving Oneself

In Part I, I presented an account of caring in general, which culminated in Chapter 3 with an account of caring about another as an agent—that is, of a kind of caring informed by an implicit understanding of the focus of one's caring as an agent. Now in Part II, I turn to provide an account of what it is to care about another not merely as an agent but as a person; I shall argue that this is a distinct kind of caring and is worthy of being called "loving." I shall proceed by first, in this chapter, discussing what it is to love yourself and then, in Chapter 5, discussing what it is to love another person. This account will be central to my discussion in Part III of the nature of friendship.

In order to understand why caring about someone as a person is distinct in kind from caring about someone as an agent, we must first understand how persons differ from mere agents. As I have argued elsewhere, the answer in outline is this:[1] persons are creatures with a capacity to care not merely about things or ends in the world but about themselves and the motives for action that are truly their own. To care about yourself in this way is to put yourself at stake in your engagement with particular things, projects, ends, and so on—things, projects, and so on which thereby become a part of your identity as this particular person. This is, in effect, to define the kind of life it is worth your living. Yet to be a person is not merely to have a capacity to evaluate yourself in this way; it is also to have the capacity to be responsible for these evaluations and so for your identity in virtue of the interconnected capacities to deliberate about what kind of

---

[1] I have deliberately formulated this outline in a way that resonates with the justly influential accounts of Harry Frankfurt and Charles Taylor. (See in particular Harry G. Frankfurt, *The Importance of What We Care About: Philosophical Essays* (Cambridge: Cambridge University Press, 1988); Taylor, *Human Agency and Language*; Charles Taylor, *Sources of the Self: The Making of the Modern Identity* (Cambridge, MA: Harvard University Press, 1992).) I have criticized both Frankfurt and Taylor in the context of offering my own positive account of personhood in Helm, *Emotional Reason*; this positive account will be developed further here.

person you shall be and to exercise a form of control over your cares so as actually to acquire this identity.[2] Of course, we persons need not actually be responsible for ourselves in this way; we need only have the capacity to do so.

Central to this account of personhood is the idea that we persons can have a conception of the kind of life it is worth each of our living, a conception that is implicit in our values. To *value* something, as I shall use the term, is not merely to find it to have worth of some sort, for that is what I have understood by 'caring.' Rather, the kind of worth at issue in valuing is "deeper" inasmuch as it serves to define the kind of life it is worth living and so one's identity as this person; put another way, in valuing something the subject thereby comes to *identify* herself with it. It is their involvement in our identities as persons that makes intelligible the intuitive "depth" of values and so distinguishes them from mere cares. In the paradigm case, therefore, valuing has traditionally been understood to be reflexive, evaluating ultimately oneself and consequently serving to identify oneself with something.[3] Because this notion of valuing is so important to understanding what it is to be a person, I shall henceforth carefully distinguish between valuing and caring as kinds of evaluative attitudes and so between values and cares as kinds of import; 'import' itself will remain a more generic notion.

It should be clear that this notion of valuing is distinctively personal insofar as it is both relative to the individual person and definitive of who she is as a person. Such *personal values*, as we might more properly call them, are distinct from moral or other universal values. In particular, although I might recognize that certain works of art or nature scenes have value, I need not (though I may) personally value these things by finding them somehow to be a part of the kind of life worth living. Moreover, it should be clear that such personal values are a matter of the evaluative attitudes a person in fact has, as distinct from what she should value—from questions of justification. I shall return to these questions of justification in §6.1.

This is, of course, just a brief outline of what it is to be a person. In particular, what it is to value and identify with something is so far only intuitive and stands in need of an explicit account. My claim will be that

[2] For a detailed account of such responsibility for self, see Helm, *Emotional Reason*, especially Part II.
[3] As I shall argue below in Ch. 5, it is a mistake to think that valuing is always reflexive, as many believe.

an account of valuing should be modeled on the account of caring I have already provided: valuing (the evaluative attitude) and values (the relevant kind of import) are constituted by a projectible, rational pattern of felt evaluations and evaluative judgments. The difference between values and cares lies in the distinctive kind of felt evaluations and evaluative judgments at issue in each. In particular, I shall argue, valuing is constituted by a pattern of emotions like pride and shame, for it is these emotions that serve to identify one with their objects, thereby making sense of the intuitive "depth" of values.

Establishing this thesis will require providing an account not merely of pride and shame but also of the more general kind of which these are instances, such that a projectible pattern of felt evaluations of this kind is intelligible as constitutive of values. Thus, in §4.1, I shall critically examine alternative accounts of pride and shame in a way that motivates my positive account, presented initially in §4.2 in terms of the way in which projectible, rational patterns of "person-focused felt evaluations" constitute values. In §4.3 I develop this account further by explicating the connections between a person's values and her identity, thereby coming to understand more fully the intuitive "depth" of values in terms of their place within a broader evaluative attitude I identify as self-love. One of my central claims will be that in order to make sense of this "depth" we must understand values individually as parts of a person's overall identity and as not in general intelligible apart from it. This account of self-love and of the felt evaluations constitutive of it will be further enriched in Chapter 5 by developing a full-blown account of love, including loving other persons.

4.1 Standard Accounts of Pride and Shame

Perhaps the three most influential accounts of pride and shame are those of Arnold Isenberg, Donald Davidson, and Gabriele Taylor.[4] Isenberg defines pride as having three parts: "there is (1) a quality which (2) is approved (or

---

[4] It is no accident that each of these three accounts is inspired by Hume's account of pride in David Hume, *Treatise of Human Nature*, 2nd edn., ed. P. H. Nidditch (Oxford: Oxford University Press, 1978). To avoid controversy in the interpretation of Hume, however, I shall focus merely on these contemporary accounts.

considered desirable) and (3) is judged to belong to oneself."[5] In a similar vein, Davidson's account of pride is this:

the basic structure of pride and its etiology as Hume saw them is clear: the cause consists, first, of a belief concerning oneself, that one has a certain trait, and, second, of an attitude of approbation or esteem for anyone who has the trait. Together these result in self-approval or self-esteem—what is normally called pride.[6]

Likewise, Gabriele Taylor writes:

This completes the analysis of pride the passion: a person who experiences pride believes that she stands in the relation of belonging to some object (person, deed, state) which she thinks desirable in some respect. This is the general description of the explanatory beliefs. It is because (in her view) this relation holds between her and the desirable object that she believes her worth to be increased, in the relevant respect. This belief is constitutive of the feeling of pride [and is the 'identificatory belief']. The gap between the explanatory and identificatory beliefs is bridged by the belief that her connection to the thing in question is itself of value, or is an achievement of hers.[7]

One important difference among these views concerns the "depth" of the evaluation at issue in pride. Isenberg and Davidson understand pride to be grounded in traits that are desirable or praiseworthy; this seems insufficient. After all, many praiseworthy properties are not such that, for most of us, their possession is an occasion for pride, such as the ability to drink soup without excessive slurping: such a property, though praiseworthy, fails to support the kind of "depth" pride intuitively has. What is needed is the idea that the relevant property pertains somehow to my identity as this person, for it is in this way that we can properly distinguish "deep" emotions, such as pride and shame, from their "shallower" counterparts, such as approval and disapproval. In this respect, Taylor's account is better insofar as it involves a notion of identification, and she is generally admirably clear in her account of valuing something and identifying with it. However, Taylor sometimes seems to forget the "depth" of evaluation identification makes possible. Thus, she frequently returns to the example

---

[5] Arnold Isenberg, "Natural Pride and Natural Shame," in *Explaining Emotions*, ed. Amélie O. Rorty (Berkeley, CA: University of California Press, 1980), 357.

[6] Donald Davidson, "Hume's Cognitive Theory of Pride," in Davidson, *Essays on Actions and Events*, 284.

[7] Gabriele Taylor, *Pride, Shame, and Guilt: Emotions of Self-Assessment* (Oxford: Oxford University Press, 1985), 41.

of someone who feels proud of a feast he merely attends and for which
he is in no way responsible; Taylor thinks such pride is "unreasonable
but nevertheless perfectly normal and possibly even common."[8] Yet if
pride does involve evaluations of the sort of depth I have been describing,
such an emotion would be almost unintelligible as pride and would
require a special story explaining away how someone could make such a
mistake.

In spite of this and other differences, these standard views of pride have
three central features in common, features that generally go unquestioned in
their presentation. First, they are *cognitivist* accounts of pride, understanding
it as constituted by antecedently intelligible cognitive states, such as belief
or judgment, and conative states, such as desire or approbation. Second,
they understand the relevant evaluations to be essentially *universal* either by
being evaluations that anyone ought to acknowledge, as with Isenberg's
and Taylor's accounts, or by being such that the subject would also apply
them to anyone similarly situated, as with Davidson's account. Finally, they
are *reflexive*: although pride in part involves a positive evaluation of qualities
or objects in the world, it also and centrally involves a positive evaluation
of oneself.

Standard accounts of shame share these three central features as well.
Thus, Isenberg says: "The analysis of shame runs parallel to the analysis of pride. Shame is the feeling that comes with consciousness of
[one's own] faults, weaknesses, disadvantages—that is, of qualities deemed
undesirable."[9] Likewise, Taylor understands shame to be constituted by a
"self-directed adverse judgement . . .: she feels herself degraded, not the sort
of person she believed, assumed, or hoped she was or anyway should be."[10]
Although both Isenberg and Taylor identify some important differences
between pride and shame, most notably (as Taylor claims) that shame
essentially involves the notion of an audience,[11] the general shape of the
accounts of pride and shame are quite similar. Thus, in each case, shame is
clearly understood to be reflexive, and the accounts given are cognitivist,
and the relevant evaluations are universal in nature.[12]

---

[8] Ibid., 33.   [9] Isenberg, "Natural Pride and Natural Shame," 365.

[10] Taylor, *Pride, Shame, and Guilt*, 64.

[11] I shall criticize this view, which Isenberg explicitly rejects, below (p. 114–15).

[12] Other accounts which understand the evaluation implicit in shame to be essentially universal
include: Stephen Darwall, *Impartial Reason* (Ithaca, NY: Cornell University Press, 1983); Bernard

I shall argue that each of these features must be abandoned in order to provide a proper account of pride, shame, and related emotions.

As I indicated in §2.1, I think we have strong reasons to reject any account of emotions and import that accept the cognitive–conative divide, as these cognitivist accounts of emotions do; instead, I offered my account of emotions as felt evaluations in §2.2. I shall not repeat these arguments here; nonetheless, I shall make two remarks about how these arguments apply to the case of pride and shame. First, it is not hard to imagine counterexamples to the sort of judgmentalism found in these standard accounts, counterexamples like those Patricia Greenspan provides for cognitivist accounts of emotions generally.[13] For example, I may find myself getting swept up in the patriotism following the 2001 attacks on the World Trade Center and Pentagon and so come to be proud of the American response—not merely in the bravery of the rescue personnel but also of the quick rout of Taliban forces in Afghanistan. Nonetheless, I may also simultaneously be a pacifist and so judge the use of military force of any sort to be objectionable. In such a case, there is a rational conflict between my judgment and my pride; however, as Greenspan argues, a cognitivist account misdiagnoses the kind of conflict at issue here. For example, according to Taylor's cognitivist account of pride,[14] my pride in the quick military victory involves a judgment that this victory is desirable; to make this judgment while simultaneously judging that military force of any sort is objectionable is to be rationally incoherent, and this is what on cognitivist accounts explains the rational conflict. However, such incoherence in judgment is in general too strong a diagnosis of that conflict: "we need some special reason . . . for attributing to [such an agent] an unacknowledged judgment in conflict with those he acknowledges."[15] Not only is such a reason not forthcoming in this case, it is not necessary to make sense of such a conflict between an emotion and a judgment. For as I argued about emotions in general (§2.3), making sense of such a conflict requires understanding felt evaluations to be distinct from judgmental

---

Williams, *Shame and Necessity* (Berkeley, CA: University of California Press, 1993); Ilham Dilman, "Shame, Guilt, and Remorse," *Philosophical Investigations* 22, no. 4 (1999): 312–29.

[13] Greenspan, *Emotions and Reasons*, especially Ch. 2, §i.

[14] Isenberg's and Davidson's accounts can make sense of this sort of pride at best only awkwardly: the quality or trait I believe myself to have and that I find praiseworthy must be something like my being a citizen of the country whose military achieved quick victory.

[15] Ibid., 18.

evaluations, and so to be irreducible to independently intelligible cognitive states.

Second, there are related problems with the standard view's approach to the relevant kind of evaluation at issue in pride and shame. If the cognitivist accounts of pride and shame are to be sustained, such an evaluation is to be made intelligible in terms of antecedently intelligible cognitive or conative states, such as judgment or desire. I have already argued that this approach to evaluation will not work in general: we cannot make sense of the evaluations implicit in desires and explicit in evaluative judgments as independent of emotional evaluations, and so neither desires nor evaluative judgments are intelligible as constituents of emotions. The same is true of the evaluations implicit in pride and so of the way in which these evaluations are central to one's identity as this person: we cannot reduce such identification merely to an evaluative judgment, nor even to the richer and more complicated self-conscious endorsement in judgment, arrived at through a process of deliberation, of the desire that something belong to one, as on Taylor's account. For it is possible to identify with certain things while failing to make the relevant evaluative judgments or even while explicitly repudiating in judgment one's identification.

To see this, consider again the example just given of my pride in the quick US military victory. In that example, my pride was the result of my getting swept up in general feelings of patriotism, and it might be thought that, in light of my pacifist judgments, this pride is clearly an irrational aberration and in no way indicative of my sense of my own identity. However, if I were raised a red-blooded American, with patriotic fervor firmly a part of my character, things would not be so clear. For in such a case, I would exhibit a general pattern of feeling pride in American successes and shame at American weaknesses. Moreover, assume that my upbringing instilled these patriotic feelings in me unselfconsciously, without any explicit endorsement or deliberation about whether I ought in this way to put myself at stake in how things fare with America. Now assume, however, that in the fall of 2001, I go off to college and soon fall in with a group of pacifists, finding myself persuaded by the ideals and rhetoric they espouse. At this point, the attack on the World Trade Center and Pentagon occurs, and in spite of my newly formed pacifist views, I find myself subsequently feeling proud of the quick victory in Afghanistan, even while judging that such feelings are inappropriate. In this case, however, it is not clear that my pride is irrational. Rather, in the context of both the pattern of pride and shame felt in response to American successes and weaknesses, and the recent origins of my contrary judgments, we may instead question the sincerity of those judgments precisely because of this conflict. Such a conflict within one's identity is not intelligible on a cognitivist account of pride and shame.[16] Cognitivism about pride and shame must therefore fail, and a richer notion of identification is needed: one which understands the feelings of pride and shame themselves (and not judgmental proxies for these feelings) to have a central role in establishing one's identity.

These brief remarks about the inability of cognitivism to make sense of the sort of evaluations central to our identities point to the second problem with the standard accounts: their unanalyzed assumption that the evaluations at issue in pride and shame are universal. For if pride and shame essentially involve properties that pertain to our identities as persons—if pride and shame essentially involve a sense of my identity as this person being at stake—then we might expect that the evaluations at issue are likewise deeply personal and so not ones that either ought to be acknowledged from within the evaluative perspectives of others, or can be applied generally in assessing the lives of other persons. Indeed, this is precisely what we find: pride and shame differ from feelings of esteem and contempt—feelings that involve evaluations of comparable "depth" by pertaining to their object's[17] identity as this person—insofar as at issue in pride and shame, but not esteem and contempt, is (a) what *I* (and not necessarily others) find to be valuable (b) in *my* life (and not in just anyone's life). Thus, although I do not value having a beautiful face or body in the sense that I find being beautiful to be central to my identity as this person, to the kind of life it is worth my living, I might do so; indeed, other people clearly do value beauty as central to their lives and so are proud or ashamed of their appearance accordingly. Likewise, although I do not value my bladder control, it is not hard to imagine someone who does, perhaps because after a spinal cord injury he finds regaining bladder control to be central to his humanity and so comes to be proud of himself in this respect

---

[16] For similar examples of this sort of conflict, see §2.3 and Helm, "Integration and Fragmentation of the Self."

[17] Note my careful use of 'object' here, which is intended to be neutral with respect to *which* object of these emotions the person is.

(and ashamed—rather than merely embarrassed—of his occasional lapses). Thus, the values central to pride and shame are personal in that they are *mine* and need not be the values of anyone else.

In addition, my valuing or failing to value the beauty of my face or my control over my bladder does not commit me to making positive or negative evaluations with similar "depth" of others who have or fail to have these attributes: even if I hold these values, I need not extend them to others (though I might). By contrast, esteem and contempt involve evaluations that are universal in these ways: to feel esteem or contempt of one person for having certain attributes is to commit oneself not only to feeling esteem or contempt of others having the same attribute; it is also to commit oneself to defending these evaluations in the face of others who disagree with you. Standard accounts of pride and shame, in understanding the values they involve to be essentially universal, either by being shared with others or by demanding similar evaluations of anyone similarly situated, thus blur this distinction and so fail to account for the way in which pride and shame are essentially personal.

In insisting that the values central to pride and shame are personal in these two ways, I am not denying that they can also be held by or applicable to others. In many cases this might be so merely by coincidence. In other cases, there might be sound, perhaps moral, reasons why everyone ought to value certain things. And, most significant for my project here, in still other cases certain values can be shared by members of a group or even can be held jointly by the group itself. I shall return to this issue of shared and joint values, and to understanding its importance in giving an account of friendship, in Part III.

It might be objected that I am here merely stipulating a use of 'pride' and 'shame' and doing so in a way that ignores ordinary usage. Thus, we do often say things like "My young daughter is proud of learning to use the potty, and I'm proud of her for doing so," but this is not, contrary to my assertion above, a case in which she finds her bladder control to be a part of her identity. Hence, the objection concludes, the evaluation implicit in pride need not be "deep" in the way I claim.

In reply, I believe these are cases not of pride per se but the "shallower" emotion of being pleased with something. Thus, my daughter is pleased with herself (or I am pleased with her) for acquiring this ability not because she (or I) values it as part of what makes her life worth living but because she (or I) merely cares about her having this ability. Although in understanding pride as essentially involving such "deep" evaluations I may require a revision of ordinary language, such revision, I shall argue, is necessary in order properly to make sense of the phenomena. In particular, in order to make sense of the distinction between caring and valuing and so in order to understand what it is to be a person and to have an identity as this person, we must distinguish between kinds of emotions in terms of their "depth." So although I may stipulate that 'pride,' 'shame,' and so on are the names for emotions that essentially have this sort of "depth," this does not mean that the resulting dispute between me and proponents of the standard account is merely verbal, for that would be to ignore the larger issues at stake. The appropriateness of this understanding of pride as essentially "deep" in this way, therefore, is something we can assess only in this broader context.

A second objection to my account is that it ignores ordinary usage in a different way. We often say that we are proud or ashamed of other people, but this does not seem to fit the notion of value and identification I have said underlies these emotions. For, it may seem, in being proud of my colleague for receiving a prestigious fellowship, I do not identify with her in the sense that I find her to be a part of what makes my life worth living. Perhaps, then, the evaluations implicit in pride and shame are not personal in the way that I have described.

In reply, I think there is something right about this objection, albeit something which speaks not to the sense in which values are personal but rather to the third feature of standard accounts of pride and shame: their reflexivity.

Standard accounts (including my own previous account[18]) tend simply to assume, without argument beyond the presentation of a few stereotyped examples, that pride and shame involve an implicit evaluation of oneself; in Taylor's case, there seems to be an additional motivation to use reflexivity to make sense of the kind of identification that seems necessary to account for the intuitive "depth" of pride. However, to understand pride and shame as essentially reflexive prohibits our making sense of these cases in which we are proud or ashamed of other people. Thus, in being proud of my colleague, I need not evaluate myself positively, as a reflexive account

[18] Helm, *Emotional Reason*, §4.1.

would require; rather, I may evaluate *her*. Thus, I may not automatically feel better about myself as a part of being proud of her; there need be no positive trait that I have now come to possess because of her; there need be no self-approval or increase in self-esteem; and there need be no self-directed positive judgment. The same can be true of cases in which we feel ashamed of someone else: again, such shame can amount to a kind of evaluation of *him*, not of myself. To deny, therefore, that emotions like pride and shame are essentially reflexive is therefore to reject the idea that the concern involved in pride and shame is essentially derived from the contribution made by the object of that concern to one's own well-being: a kind of egocentrism implicit in standard accounts of pride and shame akin to the egocentric conception of intimate concerns discussed in §1.2 (p. 9).[19]

If pride and shame need not be reflexive, evaluating oneself in terms of the kind of person it is worth one's being, how are we to make sense of the special "depth" of evaluation implicit in pride? If, as I have suggested, we are to make sense of this "depth" in terms of a notion of identification, how can this work? Isn't the notion of non-reflexive identification simply an oxymoron? The answer, which I shall sketch now and argue for in more detail in the remainder of this chapter and in Chapter 5, is this: pride and shame are *person-focused felt evaluations* in the sense that they are always focused on, and so commit one to the import of, a particular person as such. It is this focus on particular persons as such that explains the "depth" of pride and shame. Moreover, to exhibit a projectible, rational pattern of person-focused felt evaluations with a common focus just is to *love* that person (as opposed to merely caring about her as an agent).

Such an account of pride and shame as person-focused can help explain as well the sense in which you identify with particular things, ends, projects, and so on. For in loving yourself, you are concerned with your well-being as this person, as this is defined in part by your values—by that which has import to you as constituents of the kind of life worth your living, as constituents of your identity as this person. What place do such values have in your love for yourself? On the one hand, you cannot love yourself without having certain values, for it is these values that define your identity as this person, as the focus of your love. On the other hand, as I shall

---

[19] Of course, it is possible to feel reflexive pride or shame that target others. I shall say more about the differences between the reflexive and non-reflexive cases and the corresponding notions of identification in §5.1.

argue in §4.3, we can make sense of values as having this kind of "depth" as constituents of your identity only if we understand the commitment to something's import undertaken in valuing something to be a part of a broader commitment to yourself; anything less is to fail to identify with it. This means that you can value something only if you do so as a part of loving yourself. In these ways, values are not independent of your love for yourself, and the upshot is that the felt evaluations that are simultaneously constitutive of both your love for yourself and your values must have yourself, this particular person, as their focus and have the particular things valued as their *subfocus*, much like the desire I have for the means to some end takes that mean as its subfocus, while remaining focused on the end. (See §3.1.) Consequently, your values are constituted by subpatterns within this broader pattern constitutive of your love for yourself and so of your identity as this person.

When the focus of this love is another person, such love explains the sense in which we have a close, personal connection with others in virtue of which our emotions are intelligible as pride or shame, rather than esteem or contempt. For in loving someone and so being both committed to her import as this person and concerned with her well-being as such, my love is informed by an implicit understanding of her as this person—as, that is, a creature capable of having, and deliberating about, a conception of the kind of life it is worth living. That which a person finds central to this kind of life are her values, and these values define her identity and so her well-being as this person. Thus, when the focus of my love is someone else, so that I am thereby concerned with her well-being as this person, her values ought to be central to my feelings of pride and shame focused on her and so to these evaluations of how things fare with her. In effect, as I shall argue in Chapter 5, this means that, other things being equal, I ought to value the things she values as a part of loving her, in much the same way that I ought to desire the means to an end as a part of caring about the end, or that I ought to care about the things an agent cares about as a part of caring about it, other things being equal.

All of this, of course, requires further explication and argument, which will occupy me for the remainder of this chapter and the next. To make the exposition go more easily, I shall for the moment pretend that all person-focused felt evaluations are reflexive—that, as I shall ultimately argue, their focus is always the subject herself. I shall thus in §4.2 provide an alternative account of pride, shame, and the like as felt evaluations constitutive of one's values by virtue of their commitments to the import of that which one values. In §4.3, I shall argue that in order to make sense of the "depth" of one's values as constituents of the kind of life worth one's living, we must understand these felt evaluations to be focused on oneself, implicitly understood as this person, and subfocused on the things valued; such felt evaluations are, therefore, person-focused and so properly constitute not only one's valuing these things but also, and more importantly, one's love for oneself. In Chapter 5, I shall argue that person-focused felt evaluations need not be reflexive and that once we lift this pretense we can provide a proper account of what it is to love others largely in terms of patterns of non-reflexive person-focused felt evaluations.

4.2 Patterns of Person-Focused Felt Evaluations

I argued in Chapter 2 that for something to have import in general is for it to be worthy of attention and action, and that we can make sense of such worthiness in terms of projectible rational patterns of felt evaluations. The same is true of the kind of import I have called "values": for something to have value to one is for it to be the focus of a projectible rational pattern of felt evaluations. Because at stake in one's values are oneself and one's well-being as this person, and so because values involve an implicit understanding of the kind of life it is worth one's living, the felt evaluations constitutive of this pattern and so of these values must evaluate oneself in these terms; these are, of course, emotions like pride and shame, as well as "*second-order desires*": desires to act in a certain way as a part of a concern to live a certain kind of life.[20]

For this account to succeed, two challenges must be met. First, we must be able to understand pride, shame, second-order desires, and so on to have a subfocus[21] and so to involve a commitment to the import of

[20] This way of understanding the notion of a second-order desire and its role in constituting one's values gets around Gilbert Harman's criticisms of Frankfurtian accounts of such desires in Gilbert Harman, "Desired Desires," in *Explaining Value and Other Essays in Moral Philosophy* (Oxford: Oxford University Press, 2000), 117–36. I shall have more to say about this on p. 116.

[21] As I indicated at the end of §4.1, I shall argue in §4.3 that the focus of emotions like pride is a person (currently assumed to be the subject for ease of exposition), and that the particular values pride

that subfocus. (Indeed, the commitment must be distinctive insofar as it involves an implicit understanding of the kind of life worth one's living; I shall return to this in §4.3.) Is this true? Second, the resulting pattern of felt evaluations with a common focus must be sufficiently robust in order to make sense of the idea that this pattern is projectible and rational in a way constitutive of its subfocus as worthy of attention and action and so as having value to one. It might seem, however, that a pattern constituted by merely three kinds of felt evaluations—pride, shame, and second-order desires—is insufficiently robust. What other felt evaluations in addition to these three can be constituents of such a pattern?

To begin, consider an example of pride. Assume that I already value being a good professor and that now, having just been given an honorary chair in recognition of my accomplishments in research and teaching, I feel pride. Precisely what am I proud of? If we stick to ordinary language, there is no single answer, for we often say things like: "I am proud of myself" or "I am proud of receiving the award" or "I am proud of my accomplishments" or "I am proud of being a good professor"; indeed, each of these might accurately describe the same occurrent emotion. How, then, do we map these various "objects" on to an analysis of pride in terms of its target, subfocus, formal object, and so on?

Recall the definitions I provided of the target, (sub)focus, and formal object of felt evaluations in §2.2 (p. 57). The *formal object* of a felt evaluation is its characteristic evaluation, an evaluation made intelligible in virtue of the relation between the felt evaluation's target and (sub)focus. The *target* is that at which the felt evaluation is directed, that which gets felt as having the evaluative property defined by the formal object, in virtue of its connection to the (sub)focus. The *(sub)focus* is the background object having import to the subject whose perceived relation to the target makes warranted (or would make warranted, if the perception were reasonably accurate) the target's being evaluated in this way. How do these apply to the example of pride just given?

In order to make sense of the intuitive "depth" of pride and its inherent connection to a person's identity, I submit, we should understand its formal

---

is responsive to are intelligible as having import only insofar as they are a part of the person's identity. Consequently, to preserve the linguistic convention I shall justify in §4.3, I shall speak here of pride having these values as its subfocus, with the person as its focus proper.

object to be roughly a kind of dignity or nobility.[22] The target of the pride, then, is that which it evaluates as having such dignity or nobility; in this example that object is myself: in feeling this pride, I feel myself to have such dignity, to be positively evaluated in this way. Yet if the formal object of pride is dignity, how does such dignity involve a kind of "depth," lacking from the emotion of being pleased, that involves one's putting oneself at stake in feeling pride? The answer lies in the way in which such dignity bears on one's values: in being proud of myself for receiving the honorary chair, I am putting myself at stake in the value this represents, namely my value of being a good professor. In valuing this, I find this to be a part of the kind of life worth my living, and so in receiving the honorary chair I find myself in circumstances in which success in this aspect of my life is salient. This reveals two things. First, the kind of evaluation central to the formal object of pride is more precisely a kind of dignity arising from one's successfully and notably upholding one's values and so living as one ought, a worthy kind of life. Second, the subfocus of my pride is my being a good professor, for this is the background object having import (indeed, to account for the "depth" of pride, having value) and whose relation to the target—myself—makes warranted the positive evaluation implicit in pride. Receiving the honorary chair, then, is not properly speaking one of the objects of pride, but is rather its cause in that it provides an occasion for pride by making my successes in this aspect of my life salient relative to my other concerns, for it is in circumstances such as these that the import of my success impresses itself on me in feeling pride (see §2.2, p. 64).

As with other emotions, pride is not merely a response to salient circumstances relevant to the import of its subfocus; it is also a commitment to that import and so a commitment to attend to and act on behalf of that subfocus.[23] This means that to feel pride is to be committed to feeling other emotions and desires with the same subfocus, when these are warranted by the circumstances, where such focal commitments include both tonal and transitional commitments (see §2.2, p. 59). In particular, insofar as pride is a factive, positive emotion, evaluating its target positively as a result of

---

[22] In this I am following Charles Taylor; see Taylor, *Human Agency and Language*.

[23] Actually, things are a bit more complicated, as we shall see. If the person is the focus of pride, then it is the import of the person to which you are committed in feeling pride. However, since your identity as this person is constituted by your values, the commitment to your import as this person is thereby a commitment to the import of the things valued.

things that have happened, not things that will or might happen, it involves a tonal commitment to the relevant factive, negative emotions, such as shame. Thus, to be *proud* of myself for being a good professor is to be committed to being ashamed of myself for failures in this aspect of my life, such as the failure to charge with plagiarism the star quarterback out of fear of reprisals by supporters of the athletics department.[24] (*Shame* here, like pride, targets the person, evaluating myself as degraded for notably failing to live as I ought in the aspect of my life specified by the subfocus.) The failure to feel shame in this case, other things being equal, begins to undermine the commitment to import implicit in my pride, and the failure in general to feel other felt evaluations with this subfocus undermines the idea that it really has import to me.

What "other felt evaluations" are these? The focal commitment one undertakes in having a felt evaluation involves not only the sort of tonal commitment just discussed but also transitional commitments: commitments in having an epistemic emotion to having the relevant factive emotions. For example, as I read the star quarterback's paper and find mounting evidence of plagiarism, I may begin to realize the implications and so come to feel uneasy, knowing what I should do, but uncertain as to whether I can muster the courage to do it. This is, we might say, a kind of *anxiety*: a kind of pain in anticipation of a possible failure to uphold one's values (of being a good professor, say), evaluating one's own motives (such as the fear of reprisal) as a threat to these values. Thus understood, anxiety is an epistemic, negative person-focused emotion, and, by committing one to the import of its subfocus, it involves transitional commitments to feeling the relevant factive person-focused emotions, depending on how things unfold. Thus, if I give in to my fear, my anxiety ought to become shame; if, however, I overcome my fear and stand my ground in the face of intense pressure from the athletic department, my anxiety ought to become pride (if my conduct here is laudatory) or, perhaps, a kind of *self-directed relief* (if I merely narrowly avoid acting shamefully). On the other hand, I might not feel anxiety in these circumstances, but a kind of *self-assurance*: a kind of pleasure in anticipation of one's ability to uphold

---

[24] Note how whether or not this is a failure depends on one's understanding of what it is to be a good professor, an understanding that must be at least implicit in the pattern of one's felt evaluations with this common focus. After all, one might think (contrary to what my example presupposes) that being a good professor requires giving special treatment to football stars.

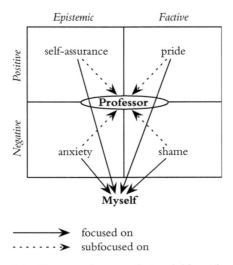

Figure 4.1. Pattern of person-focused felt evaluations.

one's values in the face of such a test. Self-assurance as thus understood is a positive epistemic person-focused emotion, and it involves transitional commitments to feeling typically factive person-focused emotions (such as pride and shame) with the same subfocus. (See Figure 4.1.)

Thus far I have roughly laid out the structure of the various objects of a range of positive and negative, epistemic and factive, person-focused emotions, though I have not had much to say about the way these emotions motivate action. Of course, there are characteristic arational expressions, as when we hold our heads high out of pride or cover our faces out of shame. Such arational expressions, however, do not contribute to an understanding of what it is to have these emotions in general, for we can readily imagine creatures that experience shame—a feeling of degradation at the failure to act in accordance with one's values—even though they do not arationally express it as we do. Insofar as rationality is the constitutive ideal of the mental,[25] what matters in providing an account of a kind of mental state is its rational structure, in particular, in this context, its rational expressions. How, then, should we refine this analysis of these person-focused emotions to include the ways they rationally motivate action?

[25] Davidson, "Mental Events," 223. (See §2.1, above.)

Some person-focused emotions, such as pride, generally do not get rationally expressed in any characteristic way. For example, sometimes we celebrate occasions for pride, and other times we do not, yet neither of these seems either required by or contrary to our feelings of pride (although celebration is certainly made rationally intelligible by pride). On the other hand, we might think that shame essentially involves the motivation to conceal one's failure, so that we should properly understand actions out of this motive to be a rational expression of shame. This could be accommodated within my account by understanding the formal object of shame to be degradation not merely at any failure to act in accordance with one's values but rather at such a failure *worth concealing*. Indeed, in this way we might distinguish shame from an emotion we might call "remorse" or, since remorse tends to involve a negative evaluation not of oneself but of one's actions, "*contrition*": a feeling of pain at a failure to act in accordance with one's values, a failure for which it is worth making amends.[26] After all, contrition would seem to motivate such actions as a public apology, to which shame seems antithetical. Nonetheless, I shall not pursue making such fine-grained distinctions among these person-focused emotions here. For the finer the grain in the distinctions, the more contestable the analysis becomes, and what concerns me here is primarily the overall structure of these emotions and the way they fit into patterns constitutive of value (on which, more presently).

Gabriele Taylor understands shame normally to involve both a reference to an audience and a changed view of the subject in the eyes of that audience to a more degraded position than the subject was in previously. Of course, Taylor claims that this appeal to an audience is only a metaphor that illuminates shame in a distinctive way (distinctive inasmuch as it does not apply to pride, for example). She spells out her "metaphors of an audience and of being seen" as follows:

they reflect the structural features of the agent's becoming aware of the discrepancy between her own assumption about her state or action and a possible detached observer-description of this state or action, and of her further being aware that she ought not be in a position where she could be so seen, where such a description at least appears to fit.[27]

---

[26] In an earlier brief discussion of what I then called "reflexive felt evaluations," I included remorse (Helm, *Emotional Reason*, 103), though I now think that was insensitive to the distinction just made here.

[27] Taylor, *Pride, Shame, and Guilt*, 66.

Consequently, Taylor claims:

a person feeling shame will exercise her capacity for self-awareness, and she will do so dramatically: from being just an actor absorbed in what she is doing she will suddenly become self-aware and self-critical. It is plainly a state of self-consciousness which centrally relies on the concept of another, for the thought of being seen as one might be seen by another is the catalyst for the emotion. The element of drama in the shifting viewpoints and the sudden realization of one's changed position is quite missing in the case of pride.[28]

Although some cases of shame will involve such an element of "drama," it is a mistake to think that all cases of shame do, as is clear when we consider the possibility of transitions from person-focused emotions like anxiety to shame: I can be anxious over whether I will act in accordance with my values and, finding I do not, feel my anxiety turn into shame. Here there is no "drama" of the sort Taylor describes: I am self-conscious the whole time, and there are no "shifting viewpoints" that can be illuminated using the metaphor of an audience. Rather, the relevant point of view from which I evaluate myself remains constant in my commitment to a particular value implicit in both my anxiety and my shame, and shame is no different from pride in this respect. Moreover, the element of "drama" Taylor describes is possible not only for shame but also for pride. Thus, you might engage in a project out of motives you implicitly believed not to be central to your identity, but upon successful completion of the project be startled to find that you feel pride in this accomplishment.

My discussion of the rational expressions of person-focused emotions should not obscure the place of desire in our commitment to the value of a particular subfocus or, therefore, in our motivation to act on its behalf. In many cases, the way we are motivated to act as the result of having a particular person-focused emotion is mediated by desire. Thus, anxious over how I will conduct myself upon discovering the star quarterback has committed plagiarism, I may resolve not to give in to my fear of reprisal and so, by self-consciously attending to the value of being a good professor and the way this impinges on my present circumstances, instill in myself the desire to uphold this value in the face of this contrary motive. (Indeed, such a desire might arise spontaneously either as a direct response to this import

---

[28] Ibid., 67.

impressing itself on me or as the consequence of feelings of self-assurance.) Such a desire is a *second-order desire*: a desire that I be motivated to act in a particular way as a part of my valuing something, as a part, that is, of a commitment to its having a place in the kind of life worth my living. As such, a second-order desire involves a focal commitment to the underlying value and thereby to having the relevant person-focused emotions with that value as their subfocus. Moreover, these other person-focused emotions commit the subject, through their focal commitment to some value, to having not only other person-focused emotions with a common subfocus, but also second-order desires with this subfocus. Second-order desires are, therefore, fully a part of the pattern of person-focused felt evaluations that, I shall argue, is constitutive of value.

This understanding of a second-order desire is much stronger than Harry Frankfurt's understanding of it as merely a desire to desire something else, or even (as with his notion of a second-order volition), a desire to act on some other desire.[29] For as Gilbert Harman argues, many mental states can fit Frankfurt's merely formal definition of a second-order desire (or many of the variants of it in the literature) without having anything to do with its subject's values and so without requiring that we understand that subject to be a person.[30] Rather, as I shall argue in §4.3, second-order desires like the other felt evaluations I have been discussing, are essentially person-focused and so involve a commitment both to the import of yourself as this person and to the value of a subfocus as a part of your identity; consequently, I understand the "depth" of second-order desires to lie not in their form as second-order, but in their content as person-focused.

The upshot is that to experience one of these person-focused felt evaluations is to be committed, other things being equal, to have other person-focused felt evaluations with a common subfocus in the relevant circumstances. To exhibit a projectible, rational pattern of these felt evaluations with a common subfocus is to be disposed to attend to and act on behalf of that subfocus. Moreover, given the rationality of the pattern, a failure to attend to and act in these ways is a rational failure, and so we can understand the subfocus to be worthy of such attention and

---

[29] See, e. g., Frankfurt, *The Importance of What We Care About*; Frankfurt, *Necessity, Volition, and Love*.
[30] Harman, "Desired Desires."

action. In short, to exhibit such a projectible, rational pattern of these felt evaluations is for the common subfocus of that pattern to have import to the subject: person-focused felt evaluations are individually responsive to and jointly constitutive of such import. Because of the way in which these person-focused felt evaluations are "deep," that common subfocus is not merely cared for but valued, thereby putting oneself at stake in how things fare with it.

This last claim needs some justification. I have claimed that what distinguishes values from cares is their "depth," which I have understood in terms of their having import as a part of the kind of life worth one's living. This raises the question of just what it is for a kind of life to be worth living and so of the way in which values are a part of this in such a way that one thereby puts oneself at stake in them. My aim in §4.3 is to explicate this by explicating the sense in which the relevant felt evaluations are focused on persons. I should also acknowledge that the account to be presented here is an account of what a person *in fact* values, rather than of what she *ought* to value—an account of the kind of life she *finds* worth living rather than of what is *really* worth her living. I discuss the justification of values (and priorities) in §6.1.

4.3 Identification: Loving Yourself

Thus far I have proceeded as if it were clear that felt evaluations like pride and shame are person-focused, involving a commitment to the import of their focus—the subject in the reflexive cases now under consideration. Insofar as rational patterns of felt evaluations like pride and shame constitute our values, they must therefore involve a commitment to the import of the things valued as well, but only as their subfocus. Yet why bother understanding the person to be the focus of these felt evaluations at all? Why not instead understand such felt evaluations to be focused on the thing valued and just drop all this messiness of focuses and subfocuses?

The quick, rather unenlightening argument for understanding the felt evaluations constitutive of our values to be focused on persons is this: to value something is to find it to have import as a part of the kind of life it is worth one's living. Consequently, the import a valued thing has presupposes the import of this kind of life: to be committed to the value of something is thereby to be committed as well to the worthiness of a certain kind of life of which it is a part. Insofar as the relevant felt evaluations involve a focal commitment to the value of something, they must therefore also involve a focal commitment to the worthiness of a certain kind of life and so to the import of the person. Consequently, we should understand these felt evaluations to take the person as their focus, and the thing valued as their subfocus. Indeed, this understanding of pride and shame is required by their formal objects: the evaluation implicit in pride or shame of oneself as ennobled or degraded is intelligible only in light of a commitment to one's import as this particular person, as this is defined by one's values. This means that these felt evaluations must involve an implicit understanding of the person as such—of who one is, of one's identity—and of one's well-being as this person, and this must include an implicit understanding of the place their subfocus has within that identity.

This argument, however, is too quick, for it does little to clarify either the precise relationship between one's values and the kind of life worth one's living or the relationship between a commitment to such a life and a commitment to the person as such, and so it does little to clarify what is meant in saying that the relevant felt evaluations are person-focused. Indeed, at this point one might pose what I shall call the *objection from the independence of values*: the account just presented of these felt evaluations as person-focused, even thus vaguely stated, is too strong insofar as it is unable to make sense of the way in which my commitment to one value is independent of my commitment to other values. For one implication of my claim that these felt evaluations essentially involve a focal commitment to the import of the person is that feeling, say, anxiety over my ability to charge the quarterback with plagiarism, in committing me to my import as this person, thereby commits me to responding emotionally in other circumstances in which my well-being as this person is favorably or adversely impacted, whether or not these other circumstances are relevant to my valuing being a good professor. Thus, if I also value being a good husband and father, then my anxiety in the one case commits me to feeling proud of myself for my skillful handling of a potentially explosive family dispute. Yet, one might think, these two values really have nothing to do with each other, so why should we think that my anxiety in the one case, stemming as it does from my valuing being a good professor, commits me also to being responsive to circumstances impacting another, independent value?

A related objection concerns the ontological and conceptual priority of values over the identities they serve to constitute. Thus, we might think, to value something just is to identify with it, where this act or state of identification is what creates or forms our identities. Consequently, our identities as persons are simply the *product* of our valuings, and so are ontologically and conceptually posterior to those valuings. Indeed, this understanding of values and their relation to our identities makes sense of why particular values should be independent of one another, as the first objection supposes.

These assumptions of the priority of our values over our identities and of the independence of one value from another are made tacitly by many accounts, including those of Harry Frankfurt and Christine Korsgaard. The root problem for Frankfurt and Korsgaard is in part to distinguish those actions and motives for actions that are truly your own from those that are in some sense alien forces operating within you. The thought is that what accounts for this distinction just is that by virtue of which you identify yourself with these motives, and so is that which constitutes your identity as this person. Since his landmark "Freedom of the Will and the Concept of a Person,"[31] Frankfurt has understood such identification in terms of "a configuration of the will":[32] we must *care* about things by virtue of having desires for them together with second-order desires that we be moved by these desires.[33] Consequently, Frankfurt says:

It is by these same configurations of the will, moreover, that our individual identities are most fully expressed and defined.[34]

Thus, for Frankfurt it is our antecedently intelligible desires and structure of desires that constitutes our caring and so our identities. As he puts it:

Caring is indispensably foundational as an activity that connects and binds us to ourselves. It is through caring that we provide ourselves with volitional continuity, and in that way constitute and participate in our own agency.[35]

---

[31] Harry G. Frankfurt, "Freedom of the Will and the Concept of a Person," *Journal of Philosophy* 68, no. 1 (1971): 5–20.
[32] See, e.g., Harry G. Frankfurt, "On Love, and Its Reasons," in Frankfurt, *The Reasons of Love*, 42–3. Frankfurt's current understanding of such identification is a development of his early view and is largely consistent with it.
[33] Harry G. Frankfurt, "The Question: 'How Should We Live?'", in Frankfurt, *The Reasons of Love*, 16. It should be clear that Frankfurt's use of the word, "caring," matches my use of "valuing."
[34] Frankfurt, "On Love, and Its Reasons," 50. For a similar account undertaken in the context of an account of pride and shame, see Taylor, *Pride, Shame, and Guilt*, 24 ff.
[35] Frankfurt, "The Question," 17.

In this way, Frankfurt clearly understands our values to be conceptually and ontologically prior to our identities, which are understood as their products. Moreover, it is also clear that Frankfurt views these configurations of the will as wholly independent of each other, so long as the higher-order desires constituting different cares do not conflict with each other.

Korsgaard, like Frankfurt, thinks that understanding what makes certain motives and actions truly your own requires appealing to a kind of identification, although she understands such identification to be not a matter of the structure of your will but rather to be the result of self-conscious deliberation and choice. As rational creatures we demand reasons for our actions, and such a demand "requires that you identify yourself with some law or principle that will govern your choices."[36] Such a principle is a "description under which you value yourself," which Korsgaard calls your *practical identity*.[37] Valuing a particular description of ourselves is something we do piecemeal: the normative standards for correct decisions concerning our practical identities is something she understands in terms of the *form* of a maxim,[38] something we consider in isolation from other possible maxims we might adopt. The result is that "for the average person there will be a jumble of such conceptions" (i.e., of practical identities), which are themselves independent of each other.[39] Consequently, the self-conscious, autonomous adoption of a principle of action is a matter of coming to value oneself in terms of that principle, which in turn is to be understood as a matter of one's identifying oneself with it. Hence for Korsgaard, as for Frankfurt, valuing is conceptually prior to a person's identity.

These two assumptions—of the independence of values and of the priority of values over our identities—are mistaken and present us with a conception of our values and their relation to our identities as persons that is untenable. We get a hint of the trouble when we think about the relative unity of the self, of a person's identity. The qualifier, "relative," is important here. In actual persons, no one's identity is perfectly unified; at best we approximate an ideal of unity (and one might even question how

---

[36] Christine M. Korsgaard, *The Sources of Normativity* (Cambridge: Cambridge University Press, 1996), 103–4.

[37] Ibid., 101.   [38] Ibid., 108.

[39] Ibid., 101. Of course, in calling this a "jumble" of practical identities, Korsgaard does not mean to dismiss the idea that we persons can have a kind of integrity. Thus, she understands integrity to be a matter of "living up to [your] own standards" (393); however, she gives no hint that doing so is to be understood except by considering such standards one by one.

ideal complete unity would be). However, it should be clear that some persons have identities that are so disunited that it seems best to split that identity into two or more distinct identities, each with its own relative unity. Such is the case for persons suffering from Dissociative Identity Disorder (or Multiple Personality Disorder, as it was known formerly). So the question confronting any account of identification is: how can most people have relatively unified identities? What makes it the case that the identity constituted by one value is the same as the identity constituted by another, so that these two different values are each parts of the same overall identity?

It might be thought that we need not look very far for an answer. After all, no one claims that one's identity is constituted by a single value all on its own, and no one thinks that particular values exist in a vacuum. Rather, we might think, the unity of a person's identity is intelligible in light of the interconnections among the various values that make it up. Thus, one's priorities structure one's values more or less clearly, where it is this structure that defines the relative unity of a person's identity.

I agree with all of this. What I think is problematic is that the assumptions of the independence and the priority of values prevents a proper acknowledgment of these facts. For if in valuing something I thereby come to identify myself with it, such valuing, such identification, cannot ignore the potential unity that makes this be *me*. That is, for me to identify myself with something by valuing it, that thing must come to have a place within my identity as this particular person, so that we cannot understand such identification apart from the larger whole of the person's identity that identification presupposes. Consequently, values must always already be embedded within the identity they serve to constitute, so that particular values presuppose the very identity that they jointly compose. If particular values are always already embedded within a person's identity, then we cannot assume that such values are ontologically or conceptually prior to that identity.

One implication of this will be that we cannot understand what it would be for a person to value something wholly apart from the place that value has at least roughly within a system of priorities. Priorities cannot be understood as a kind of ordering of already existing values, slapped on after the fact as an attempt to impose a kind of structure on them. That particular values always already have a place within one's overall identity implies that an at least rough structure of priorities is an essential part of our values and their rational interconnections.[40]

Yet the part–whole relationship between our values and our identities has deeper implications than this. One's identity, I have said, consists in the kind of life worth living for one, and so it presupposes a kind of commitment to living such a life. As much as your values are always already a part of your identity—insofar as in valuing something you find it to have a place within a worthwhile life—the evaluative attitude you have toward things valued must be understood to be a part of a more general evaluative attitude you have toward yourself, where it is this more general attitude that properly speaking constitutes our identities. If this is right, then standard accounts of value, including my own previous account, misplace the relationship between values and the import of the person to himself: the import of the person to himself does *not* derive from the antecedent import of the things valued. Rather, valuing and self-love each presuppose the other, so that although we can continue to say that a person's identity is constituted by his values, these values themselves have the "depth" they do that distinguishes them from mere cares precisely because they are a part of his overall love of himself.[41] I shall argue that this is fundamentally mistaken in a way that obscures the sense in which values are essentially focused on persons as such.

To see this more clearly, consider a case in which these two values motivate contrary actions, as when my daughter breaks her leg and needs to be taken to the hospital just as my class is about to begin. In this case I decide that, although generally speaking teaching classes is fundamental to being a good professor and so to the kind of life worth my living, here and now what matters is my daughter, and so I take her to the hospital. Should I then feel ashamed of or disappointed in myself for failing to uphold my value of being a good professor? Have I therefore failed to live as I ought given the place being a good professor has in defining my identity? Of course not. It is perfectly reasonable to think that such shame would be

---

[40] I have argued for this conclusion in Helm, *Emotional Reason*, §4.3.

[41] My own previous account was, I believe, an improvement on the kind of account Frankfurt and Korsgaard offer insofar as it understands values as essentially structured by an at least rough structure of priorities. Nonetheless, by accepting the priority of values over one's identity, it failed properly to acknowledge the way in which values and self-love are each conceptually dependent on the other, as I shall argue here.

unwarranted: taking care of my daughter in these circumstances just is living as I ought—just is upholding my identity as this person, who has multiple and sometimes conflicting values—and shame or disappointment in myself would be warranted only if I fail to do so.

I claimed above (p. 121) that our values are always already embedded within a person's identity: they must always already have a "place" within that identity. We are now in a position to appreciate more fully what this means. For this example suggests that although taken individually values specify particular ways in which you find life worth living, taken together they must constitute a larger whole: the kind of life it is worth your living overall, a kind of life that is central to your identity as this person. That is, being embedded within an overall identity, within an overall way in which life is worth living, means that the particular felt evaluations that constitute the value in question must be structured in part by that identity and so in a way that is informed by an at least implicit understanding of the particular person you are—of the overall sense of the kind of life worth living that constitutes your identity as this person. In this way, your values, by committing you to the import of something in such a way as to identify yourself with it, thereby presuppose the worthiness to you of a certain kind of life: the import of your identity as this person. Indeed, it is only in this way that we can make sense of the intuitive "depth" of values as involving a kind of identification. (See Figure 4.2.)

In this respect, the relationship between valuing something—caring about it as a part of the kind of life worth living—and caring about your identity as this person (about the overall life worth your living) is analogous to other cases in which we have a multiply layered structure of subfocus and focus in the relevant felt evaluations constituting your caring. In each of these cases, valuing something or caring about it as a means or caring about it for the sake of another is intelligible only in terms of the place it has within a broader instance of caring—about one's identity, about an end, or about another agent—and it is only in terms of the structure of this overall caring that we can make sense of how the individual cases are informed by the relevant concepts—of a person, of an end, or of an agent. Indeed, the point of this account of subfocuses and focuses is to illuminate these relationships and so the overall rational structure among the felt evaluations constituting that caring. So although it does seem odd to say that feeling an emotion subfocused on one thing I value commits me

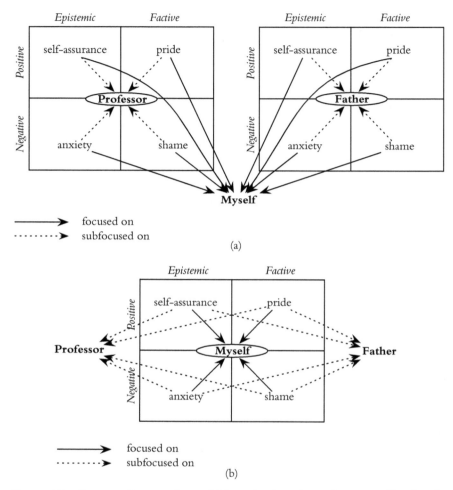

Figure 4.2. Pattern of person-focused felt evaluations focused on oneself and with multiple subfocuses: alternate views.

to feeling in the appropriate circumstances other felt evaluations subfocused on other things I value—just as it seems odd to say that desiring one means to an end commits me to desiring, in other relevant circumstances, other means to that end—this oddness is merely an artifact of our having our attention drawn to the things valued (or to the means) rather than to the broader structure of import that makes intelligible the import the value (or the means) has to me. This is why we must understand the relevant felt evaluations constitutive of our values to be person-focused and so retain the understanding of a person's values as rationally interconnected, thereby rejecting the assumption of the independence of values that motivates the objection from the independence of values. Consequently, in response to that objection, we should ask: why should we think, as the objection supposes, that my two values of being a good professor and being a good father "really have nothing to do with each other"? After all, they are both values of the same person, and part of what they have in common is their constitution of the same identity.

In having felt evaluations such as pride or shame, therefore, I must be responsive not merely narrowly and parochially to the failure to uphold certain values that are these felt evaluations' subfocuses, but more broadly to whether in these circumstances I am living the kind of life worth my living—to, that is, the bearing of these circumstances on the well-being of their focus, the person. The commitment to import I undertake in valuing something, as a commitment to attend to how things fare with it and so to have the relevant felt evaluations, must likewise not be so narrow and parochial: it is a commitment to the import of myself as this person. Consequently, to value something, for it to have import to you as a part of such a life, therefore presupposes having some sense of, and commitment to, how this value is connected within a structure of such priorities to other values—to, that is, one's identity as this person.[42] We must therefore reject the assumption of the priority of values.

It might be suggested that one's priorities are distinct from one's values, and that all my argument has shown is that a person's identity must include not merely a set of values but also a set of priorities. After all, we might think, desires and preferences are independent mental states, and it is always possible to have the same desires but different preferences. The same is true of values and priorities, which I have understood elsewhere to be a kind of preference one values having.[43] Since it is always possible to have the same

---

[42] It is important not to misread my claim here as stronger than it is. I am not saying that a person's priorities must be fully determinate in every case, let alone that her values must be rank-ordered somehow. My claim is only that she must "have some sense" of her priorities, at least as these apply to particular circumstances, such that she has some grounds from which to justify choices among values when they conflict—choices evident not only in her actions but also in her feelings. This is consistent with the incommensurability of the relevant values: with there being no way to specify in general, for any circumstance, which value ought to take priority.

[43] Helm, *Emotional Reason*, especially chs. 4 and 7.

values and different priorities, the objection continues, we must understand
the two to be distinct in such a way that, contrary to the conclusion just
reached above, the commitment to import undertaken in valuing something
really is "narrow and parochial." Consequently, the objection concludes,
my argument has not shown that the felt evaluations constitutive of values
are person-focused after all; indeed, by acknowledging the independence
of values and priorities, we ought to reassert the independence of values
from each other.

This objection, however, fails properly to understand the way in which
our felt evaluations constitutive of import, whether cares or values, essentially belong to a single evaluative perspective. For the singleness of this
evaluative perspective lies not merely in the way in which felt evaluations
and evaluative judgments all with a common (sub)focus are rationally
interconnected; rather, it also lies in the way in which the rational interconnections among felt evaluations and evaluative judgments with different
(sub)focuses make possible a coherent overall responsiveness to import.
Thus, in our overall responsiveness to import, we find that our felt evaluations are responsive in two ways to the degree of import—to how much
import something has to us. First, our desires and emotions ought to be
more or less intense in response to things that have more or less import to
us. Second, particular felt evaluations ought to *dampen* or suppress others
(or be dampened or suppressed by others) as a part of one's response to that
which, in the current circumstances, has the most import: confronted with
a minor annoyance in the context of a great victory, my joy at the victory
ought to diminish the intensity of or even suppress entirely the frustration
I otherwise would feel at the annoyance. Indeed, it is the overall rational
structure of the commitments we implicitly undertake in feeling emotions
or desires of greater or lesser intensity, or in having one felt evaluation
dampen or suppress another, that constitutes both the degree of import and
the relative degree of import things have to us, even while particular felt
evaluations are themselves responsive to that degree of import.[44]

This means that it is false, contrary to the objection just raised, to
think that preferences or priorities are independent of desires or other felt
evaluations: the responsiveness to import one has in caring about or valuing

---

[44] For details on this account of degree and relative degree of import in terms of the intensity of felt
evaluations and the way they dampen and suppress each other, see Helm, *Emotional Reason*, especially
Ch. 4.

something involves a responsiveness not merely narrowly and parochially to what happens to that thing but, more broadly, to import and degree of import quite generally, lest the rational structure constitutive of both one's caring and that import be destroyed. In short, particular felt evaluations, including desires, are intelligible as such only in the context of a single evaluative perspective from which the subject views the world, for they are essentially manifestations of a subject's rational responsiveness to the world as a whole.

It should be clear that this conclusion concerning the singleness of one's evaluative perspective on its own does not imply that the felt evaluations constitutive of values must be person-focused any more than it shows that the felt evaluations constitutive of cares are person-focused (which they are not). The point of this reply is to defuse the attempt to understand values as conceptually independent of each other yet connected by priorities, which themselves are understood as independent of our values. Nonetheless, this does reinforce the central point: although one's values taken individually delineate particular elements of the kind of life worth living, these elements and the particular responses we make to them cannot be rationally isolated from each other but must instead form a rationally structured whole. In the case of values in particular, the part—whole relationship is such that we cannot understand the import of a part, of a particular value, apart from the place it has in partially constituting the import of the whole, of one's identity as this person. Or, to put the same point from the perspective of our valuing things rather than their having value, we cannot make sense of our commitment to the import something has as a value apart from the place this commitment has within a broader rational structure of commitments to the worthiness of one's living a certain kind of life. Consequently, whether or not any particular action (or omission) amounts to notably upholding or trampling on some value, and so whether or not such actions or omissions warrant feelings like pride or shame that evaluate the person as, for example, ennobled or degraded, depends in part on the place that value has within a broader rational structure of values constitutive of one's identity. This part—whole relationship is best illuminated by understanding the felt evaluations constitutive of import, of our valuing, to be focused on oneself as this person and subfocused on the things valued.

This way of putting the point should not mislead us into thinking that all my argument has shown is that a person's identity is constituted not merely by a set of values, but by a set of values together with the priorities that structure them into a relatively unified whole, all of which is consistent with the conceptual priority of your values over your identity. For, as I have argued, we cannot make sense of the essential "depth" of values—that is, of what makes the relevant concern be a matter of valuing something rather than merely caring about it—apart from the place these values have in constituting someone's identity as this person. For in order for a concern to be intelligible as a matter of valuing something, that concern must *presuppose* an identity of which it is a part. That is, we cannot make sense of the commitment to something's import as being a matter of valuing it apart from the place this commitment has within a broader rational structure of commitments to the worthiness of one's living a certain kind of life. Again, this part–whole relationship is best illuminated by understanding the felt evaluations constitutive of import, of our valuing, to be focused on oneself as this person and subfocused on the things valued.

We can now see that Frankfurt's and Korsgaard's conceptions of valuing and identification are too simple. For such accounts understand valuing and identification piecemeal, as if the commitments one undertakes in identifying with one thing are independent of the commitments one undertakes in identifying with something else. As I have argued, if we are to make sense of how these particular identifications add up to a single identity, such that it is intelligibly the same person identifying with all of these things, we must understand the commitment undertaken in identifying with any given thing to be, ultimately, a commitment to its place within this larger whole—one's identity as this person—whose import is thereby presupposed. The assumptions of the independence and priority of values must therefore be rejected.

At this point another objection to my account of values as constituted by person-focused felt evaluations might be posed, an objection concerning what it is to value something *for its own sake*. I have claimed that to exhibit a projectible, rational pattern of felt evaluations with a common focus just is to care about that focus for its sake. In my accounts of caring about something as an end and of caring about another as an agent, I used the notions of a focus and a subfocus to make sense of cases in which I care about one thing (a means or something another agent cares about) for the sake of something else (the end or that other agent). It therefore may seem that in valuing something, insofar as the relevant felt evaluations are focused on oneself as this person and only subfocused on the thing valued, I am understanding such valuing as always being for one's own sake and never for the sake of the thing valued. Yet this seems wrongheaded: typically, it seems, our valuing something is made intelligible by the thing itself. Consequently we often value something not because of the way it contributes to our own identities as persons; rather we find it to contribute to our identities because it is intrinsically valuable. That is, our incorporating something into our sense of the kind of life worth living often, at least, involves our valuing it for its own sake. The objection concludes, therefore, that my account of valuing, insofar as it cannot accommodate such cases, is at best incomplete.

In reply, this objection misses a crucial disanalogy between the cases of valuing and cases of caring about something for the sake of something else. For in cases of the latter sort we have an independent understanding of what the end is for the sake of which we care about this means, or of "who" the agent is for the sake of whom we care about something he cares about. Indeed, it is because this understanding of the end or of the agent is independent of our caring about the means or about what he cares about that we can make sense of the former providing a motive or reason for the latter. However, in the case of valuing something, my caring about my identity as this person is not independent of my valuing the things I do, for my identity is constituted by the rational structure of these values. Consequently, my concern for my own identity cannot itself provide a motive or reason for my valuing some particular thing until I have a determinate conception of my identity as including this thing, but having such a conception just is valuing that thing, and such valuing cannot be a motive or a reason for itself. We cannot therefore understand the structure of valuing as focused on oneself as this person and subfocused on the thing valued in terms of the idea that we value things only for the sake of oneself. Rather, it would be better to say that we value certain things for their own sake as a part of caring about our identities as persons.

I have just argued that individual person-focused felt evaluations as well as the evaluative attitude of valuing are intelligible as such, and as distinct in their "depth" from non-person-focused felt evaluations and from caring, by virtue of their being a part of a more general evaluative attitude focused on the person as such. This more general evaluative attitude, I believe, can properly be understood as love: to *love* yourself just is to find yourself as this particular person to have import for your own sake and so to be committed to your well-being as this is defined by your identity. My claim here is not that loving yourself means finding yourself to have import as *a* person, merely as a being with certain capacities definitive of personhood quite generally, such as the capacity for autonomy. Rather, my claim is that loving yourself means finding yourself to have import as *this* person, as a person with a particular identity as such, for without this it is unclear what could be meant by finding yourself to have import "for your own sake": your "sake," your well-being, is defined by your identity as the person you are. Consequently, loving yourself presupposes that you have a determinate identity as this person.

Why should we think that such an attitude toward oneself amounts to self-love? There is no simple answer to this question, and in the end I shall simply offer the cogency of the account as a whole and the way it is ultimately able to make sense of the phenomena not only of loving oneself but also of loving others and of various loving relationships like friendship. Nonetheless, more needs to be said about the phenomenon of self-love and the way in which it involves attitudes of identification, trust, respect, affection, and so on that have often been used to characterize an attitude of love. That is my task for §4.4.

4.4 Identification, Self-Trust, and Self-Respect

I have claimed that one's identity as this person is fundamentally a matter of the kind of life worth one's living, and that this is determined largely by one's personal values and priorities; after all, we tend to answer questions about who we are by specifying what we stand for, what is fundamentally important in our lives. Thus, when asked who I am, I do not say that I am a 6-foot 4-inch former soccer player who likes chocolate and is susceptible to the gambler's fallacy because although true, these things are not central to who I am, to what I am "about" and for this reason are not particularly informative in response to the question. Rather, I respond by saying that I am a philosophy professor, a father of three, etc., for these are the things important in my life. Nonetheless, this claim can be misleading. For it may sound like a person's identity just is a particular collection of values structured in a particular way by certain priorities, such that any change in your values or priorities amounts to a change in your identity so that you are no longer the same person you were. This would seem to lead to the following objection: thus understood, the commitment undertaken in loving yourself to your well-being as this person is a commitment to maintain your present system of values, no matter how flawed, lest you cease to be this person anymore. Surely this is an unacceptable conclusion: we can be convinced (sometimes rightly so) that our current identities are flawed and stand in need of revision, and we can try to transform our identities accordingly. I agree with all of this, but it is not an objection to my account.

A person, as I have argued elsewhere,[45] is a creature that has the capacity to have a say in defining its own identity as such and so in determining its well-being as the particular person it is; this is our *autonomy*, our capacity for self-determination. Of course, we can be mistaken about what is valuable in our lives and so in what our identities really are. Indeed, the possibility of being mistaken is crucial to our sense that it is not arbitrary what our values shall be. Hence, it is in part a matter for *discovery* what is really valuable in life and so what each of our identities is. This implies that we can make a distinction between a person's understanding of her identity, as this is both implicit and explicit in the present pattern of her evaluations (felt or judged) and what her identity really is. This observation, however, should not lead us to think that a person's identity, and so her well-being as this person, is something determinate in advance. For this would require that we ignore the idea, central to our personhood, that each of us is potentially autonomous and can have a say in defining her identity and so her well-being: what a person's identity is is not independent of her understanding of it.

The conjunction of these two claims—that what a person's identity is is potentially a matter for *discovery* and that we persons can have a say in, and so *invent*, our identities—can seem paradoxical: nothing, it might seem, can simultaneously be both an object of discovery (and so necessarily there in advance) and an object of invention (and so necessarily not there in advance). This is what I have elsewhere called the *apparent paradox of simultaneous autonomous invention and rational discovery*.[46] However, the paradox is only apparent and can be avoided once we give up the

---

[45] Helm, *Emotional Reason*.   [46] Ibid., especially chs. 1 and 7.

cognitive—conative divide: properly understood, the rational constraints that make intelligible the idea that we can discover, through processes of deliberation, what is really valuable in life are internal to the very evaluative perspective we seek autonomously to shape and define in the course of such deliberation. Deliberation about value—about what our identities shall be—is, therefore, neither a cognitive process of pure discovery nor a non-cognitive process of pure invention; it is, rather, a process within which our values, our identities, are *disclosed* as what they are.[47]

The upshot is that a person's identity (and so her well-being) is not a fully determinate, static entity, as the above objection presupposes. In some respects, therefore, a person's identity is like a building that is constantly undergoing remodeling, with parts being demolished, others being added, still others being modified, and all without a fixed, determinate blueprint. Thus, as certain parts begin to take shape, others are seen as inadequate and in need of modification. Consequently, the blueprint, and so the fate of the building itself, is continually evolving and (hopefully) improving, a process from within which it would be artificial to select a moment in time as determinately fixing the "identity" of the building and so as defining its well-being as demanding no further changes. Likewise, no fixed state of a person's evaluative perspective, of values structured by certain priorities, can be understood to define her well-being as demanding no further changes to that perspective: a person's identity may continually evolve in response to new inadequacies that emerge into view as the result of past changes.

Unlike such a continually remodeled building, however, it is the person herself who determines what her identity shall be from within that very identity.[48] The centrality to our personhood of the autonomy that makes this possible means that a person's concern with her identity as this person and so with her well-being as such, a concern that I have claimed constitutes her love for herself, is a concern not simply with achieving the conformity of her actions and attitudes with a predefined conception of the kind of life

---

[47] I present a brief overview of my account of how such deliberation about values is possible in §6.1, though I do not there discuss the relation between such deliberation and our capacity for autonomy in terms of which we can see how a person might try to transform her identity. For details on this, see Helm, *Emotional Reason*, especially chs. 6 and 7.

[48] This clearly involves a kind of circularity, which one might think vicious; I shall articulate and address this worry below, p. 139.

worth her living; it is also a concern with defining her identity and so with exercising her autonomy.

Loving yourself, therefore, normally means being, to some degree, vigilant concerning the content of your identity. Although, as with caring about an agent as such, the understanding you have of your well-being is in part implicit in the patterns of responsiveness you exhibit in your person-focused felt evaluations, the vigilance normally required by loving yourself means that it ought not be entirely implicit. Rather, properly and fully exercising your capacity for autonomy and so taking responsibility for your self means at least sometimes critically examining that which you value explicitly and self-consciously, with an eye to protecting yourself from harm at the very core of your identity as this person. Such self-protection is, in effect, a kind of self-respect. Gabriele Taylor has what might seem a similar understanding of self-respect. As she puts it:

To respect the self, then, is . . . to do that which protects the self from injury or destruction, just as to respect others is not to think well or badly of them, but is at least to abstain from injuring or destroying them, whether physically or morally.[49]

However, the analogy Taylor makes between self-respect and the minimal sort of respect we owe others is flawed: self-respect, at least, involves not merely a negative commitment to abstain from harming yourself, but rather is constituted by a positive commitment to protect your identity as this person by virtue of a commitment to your autonomy. *Self-respect*, in the sense in which I intend it here, is this sort of vigilance concerning the content of your identity and so is a matter of paying due attention to the proper exercise of your autonomy, all as a part of loving yourself.

To say that loving yourself normally involves self-respect is not to say that you cannot love yourself without respecting yourself in this way — without exercising your capacity for autonomy in taking responsibility for who you are; still less is it to say that loving yourself means engaging in constant self-examination and criticism. To love yourself is to exhibit a broad pattern of activity on behalf of, and responsive to, yourself and your identity, and that pattern can be in place overall even if isolated portions of it are absent. Consequently, the Socratic claim that the unexamined life is not worth living is surely too strong: life can be worth living insofar as you

---

[49] Gabriele Taylor, "Shame, Integrity, and Self-Respect," in *Dignity, Character, and Self-Respect*, ed. Robin S. Dillon (Boston, MA: Routledge & Kegan Paul, 1995), 161.

value certain things it is otherwise permissible to value and generally act in accordance with these values even if you fail to exhibit proper self-respect and so fail to be fully autonomous. Nonetheless, a life worth living *ought* to be examined inasmuch as love, this commitment to the import of yourself as this person, involves a rational commitment to self-respect. To fail to exercise autonomy when called for is to fail to respect yourself the way you ought, to fail to exercise due diligence concerning your own well-being, and so to fail fully to live up to the commitment you have to yourself in loving yourself.

The failure to respect yourself in this way results in your simply going along with whatever values you happen to find yourself with, values that might be instilled in you through peer pressure or other external influences. It is a failure, therefore, to take responsibility for your identity, and it results in an identity we might understand to be *inauthentic*.[50] Of course, inauthenticity is a matter of degree, and it is profoundly affected by the relationships we have with other people, especially during our upbringing. I shall return to these connections in Chapter 7.

We are now in a position to understand more clearly the notion of identification at issue in self-love. To *identify* with something is to value it by bringing it into your evaluative perspective as a part of the kind of life worth your living, potentially as the result of the exercise of your autonomy and practical reason. This may sound overly intellectual, as if practical reason were a purely cognitive affair, something we can exercise only self-consciously in judgment. It should be clear, however, that this is not how I conceive of it, for according to my account the capacity for practical reason is exercised in part by having felt evaluations, and deliberation about what to value cannot properly proceed apart from felt evaluations.[51] Consequently, such identification need not (though it may) be deliberate or self-conscious, and it need not (though it may) be something the genesis of which one is responsible for: one may come to identify with certain things as the result of one's upbringing, in the process of coming to be a person in the first place. For something to be brought within your evaluative perspective in this way normally means not merely that it is the subfocus of a pattern of person-focused felt evaluations

---

[50] See, e. g., Taylor, "What Is Human Agency?"; Haji Ishtiyaque and Stefaan E. Cuypers, "Moral Responsibility, Love, and Authenticity," *Journal of Social Philosophy* 36, no. 1 (2005): 106–26.

[51] Helm, *Emotional Reason*, Ch. 7; see also Ch. 7, below.

constitutive of your valuing it, but also that it thereby plays a role in your present (perhaps implicit) understanding of your well-being and in this way helps to delineate who you are as this person. This is what justifies my use of the term, 'identification': to identify with something is for it to play this kind of role in the delineation of your identity as this particular person.

One's *identity* as this particular person, therefore, just is the kind of life worth one's living, as this is defined by one's overall evaluative perspective.[52] Once again, such an evaluative perspective is to be understood not merely as a particular state of one's evaluative system at a particular time (such as, for example, one's current dispositions to make certain evaluations, felt or otherwise), but as a dynamic and evolving system of such states, tied together by the exercise of practical reason that is simultaneously both constitutive of and demanded by the import one has to oneself as this person. To love yourself is to have such an identity, and you cannot have such an identity apart from your love for yourself: the unity of evaluative perspective necessary for this to be a single identity is possible only because the evaluations constitutive of your various values are ultimately focused on yourself as this person in a way that constitutes self-love.

Nonetheless, as Harry Frankfurt has rightly argued, it is a non-trivial question which evaluations are truly your own and so properly belong to your evaluative perspective. He introduces the problem this way:

We think it correct to attribute to a person, in the strict sense, only some of the events in the history of his body. The others—those with respect to which he is passive—have their moving principles outside him, and we do not identify him with these events. Certain events in the history of a person's mind, likewise, have their moving principles outside of him. He is passive with respect to them, and they are likewise not to be attributed to him. A person is no more to be identified with everything that goes on in his mind, in other words, than he is to be identified with everything that goes on in his body.[53]

---

[52] It should be clear than such an understanding of a person's identity is a technical notion that has little directly to do with questions that arise in the literature on diachronic personal identity. For such questions typically concern the locus of personal agency, which is not at all what the notion of a person's identity as defined here is intended to address. Moreover, although for some purposes we might want to include other properties of a person in his "identity," such as his physical attributes and abilities, his past history and accomplishments, and his character traits, I shall construe my technical notion of a person's identity more narrowly than that.

[53] Harry G. Frankfurt, "Identification and Externality," in Frankfurt, *The Importance of What We Care About*, 61.

In particular, it seems, those evaluations that initially appear to constitute your values, your identity, may turn out not to be properly your own at all; consequently, any conflicts between such evaluations and those that do constitute your values will not be internal to your identity. How, though, can we distinguish those cases in which evaluative conflicts are internal to your evaluative perspective from those in which they are not? The answer depends on the overall rational shape of your evaluative perspective, on whether or not a particular conflicting evaluation or even a pattern of such evaluations is intelligible as an isolated failure within that perspective as a whole. For isolated failures—so long as they genuinely are isolated—can be written off as mere mistakes, not properly reflective of your own evaluative perspective or, therefore, of your identity as this person.[54]

For example, someone may be brought up with racist attitudes such that he has ingrained dispositions to feel various negative emotions directed at minorities just because they are minorities. However, he has come to realize what is wrong with these racist attitudes and has made an effort to eliminate them from himself, though with only partial success. Thus, when he encounters a well-dressed black man in the elevator as he leaves his office late at night, he may feel contempt tinged, perhaps, with a bit of fear; these emotions he quickly repudiates, dismayed that after all these years he still finds such racist attitudes within him, and he makes an effort to strike up a pleasant conversation with the man. Moreover, his repudiation here is such that he takes pride in his ability to overcome these racist attitudes, feels dismayed at or ashamed of those few occasions in which he allows these attitudes get the better of him and influence his overt behavior, and so on. It is his reasoned understanding of what is wrong with these racist attitudes, together with his repudiation of his racist feelings and the way in which this repudiation resonates emotionally with him in his feelings of dismay, pride, and so on that isolates these racist attitudes as not properly a part of his evaluative perspective and so not properly a part of his identity as this person: they are, rather, a force external to himself.

Such a structure to his overall evaluative perspective constitutes a kind of *distrust* of the isolated evaluations: a refusal to accept them as a part of his own evaluative perspective and so a refusal to accept the conflicts

---

[54] For a detailed discussion of when such conflicts count as genuinely isolated, see Helm, *Emotional Reason*, Ch. 5, especially §5.3.

such evaluations present with his broader evaluative perspective as internal to himself. This does not imply that such conflicts fail to provide him with any motivation to eliminate the distrusted evaluations, so that these evaluations can be safely ignored; rather, my claim is that by refusing to accept such conflicts as internal to himself, a refusal that normally consists in part in being motivated in this way, he thereby deprives these distrusted evaluations of having any rational weight in his sense of what is valuable in life. In this way, such distrusted evaluations are *external* to his identity: although they are forces to be struggled against, they are nonetheless alien to himself precisely by falling outside his evaluative perspective in this way. Thus understood, distrust is a significant achievement: it is not merely, as Frankfurt claims, a matter of repudiating a particular emotion or desire and so "withdrawing" oneself from it, as if this were simply a decision one can make, a matter of exercising one's capacity for judgment on a particular occasion.[55] Rather, distrust is an attitude reflected in the overall rational structure of one's evaluative perspective, and it is an achievement that requires structuring not merely one's evaluative judgments, but also one's felt evaluations, including especially reflexive person-focused felt evaluations.

Accepting an evaluation (felt or judged) as integral to one's evaluative perspective and so to one's identity is likewise not simply automatic; it rather involves a converse attitude reflected in the overall rational structure of one's evaluative perspective: an attitude of trust. To *trust* an evaluation is to find, by virtue of one's overall evaluative response to it in both felt evaluation and judgment, that it carries some rational weight in the structure of one's identity by virtue of a distinctive pattern within both (a) one's responsiveness to the (sub)focus of that evaluation, a responsiveness to which one is committed by making or feeling the trusted evaluation and that normally constitutes its import to one, and (b) one's responsiveness to conflicts between this evaluation and others. This responsiveness to conflicts in turn involves both (i) a rational structure of dampening relations within one's evaluative perspective (see §4.3, p. 126) such that the import of the (sub)focus of this trusted evaluation comes to have a place in a structure of preferences and priorities, whereby potential conflicts between it and

---

[55] Harry G. Frankfurt, "Freedom of the Will and the Concept of a Person," in Frankfurt, *The Importance of What We Care About*, 11–25. For further discussion and criticism of Frankfurtian notions of identification and withdrawal, see Helm, "Integration and Fragmentation of the Self."

other evaluations can be settled, at least in particular cases; and (ii) being motivated in the face of actual conflicts to second thoughts about one's preferences and priorities or even about the import of the (sub)focuses of the conflicting evaluations and so, potentially, being motivated to exercise one's autonomy so as to re-prioritize that which has import to one or even to cease caring about or valuing one or more of these (sub)focuses.

Such a responsiveness toward your own evaluations is properly understood to be a kind of trust insofar as it is a kind of reliance on the soundness of those evaluations, a reliance in which you put yourself—indeed, your identity as this person—at stake. Moreover, it is not merely a trust in these evaluations themselves; insofar as these evaluations constitute your overall evaluative perspective on the kind of life worth your living and so constitute your identity as this person, it is more fundamentally a kind of trust in yourself: a reliance on your own identity as this person in responding not only to external circumstances but also to your internal situation as you exercise your capacities for practical reason and autonomy.[56] Self-trust therefore requires having a sense of your own integrity as this person, your identity with yourself, where this is a sense which involves a refusal to allow rational conflicts within yourself that could otherwise tear at and destroy your identity as a single person. Thus understood, self-trust is a kind of achievement as providing the kind of unity to one's evaluative perspective necessary to constitute a single identity as this person.[57] Some degree of self-trust, therefore, is essential to loving oneself.

[56] Further reasons for understanding this to be a kind of trust will emerge in my discussion of loving others in Ch. 5. For loving others, as I shall argue, involves both respecting and trusting them in ways analogous to the way in which loving yourself involves self-respect and self-trust.

[57] Given this understanding of self-trust, we can understand Dissociative Identity Disorder (DID) to involve a kind of failure of trust within a single human being. Thus, in cases of DID the evaluations of a given human organism separate themselves into two or more distinct and only partially and coincidentally overlapping evaluative perspectives, each of which is structured by trust within that evaluative perspective but not between them. Of course, more is going on in cases of DID than just this sort of failure of self-trust, such as the structure of the host's and alters' memories and their different physiological responses to the same stimuli; these additional factors are central to arguing that we have in these cases multiple distinct persons within a single human organism. (Indeed, such facts about the structure of the organism's memory can in part support the idea that the distinct evaluative perspectives are only coincidentally overlapping and so really are distinct.) For extended discussions of cases of Dissociative Identity Disorder, see, for example, Nicholas Humphrey and Daniel C. Dennett, "Speaking for Ourselves: An Assessment of Multiple Personality Disorder," *Raritan: A Quarterly Review* 9 (1989): 68–98; Kathleen Wilkes, *Real People: Personal Identity without Thought Experiments* (Oxford: Oxford University Press, 1988).

At this point two objections might be raised: the first concerning what might seem to be vicious circularity in my account, and the second concerning the possibility of self-hate. I shall address these in turn.

The reflexivity of self-love, which includes self-respect and self-trust, gives rise to a kind of circularity in my account, which might seem vicious. Thus, on the one hand, I have argued that to love yourself is to be committed to the import you have to yourself as this person: not merely as *a* person, with capacities for practical reason (such as autonomy) constitutive of persons as such, but also as having this identity as such. Consequently, loving yourself presupposes that you have an identity as this person, for otherwise your love cannot be properly formed because as that to which you are committed in your love is absent. On the other hand, your identity as this person, as I have understood it, is constituted by the evaluative perspective you have on the kind of life it is worth your living; such an evaluative perspective is comprised of the very pattern of reflexive person-focused felt evaluations and evaluative judgments that constitutes your love for yourself. Consequently, we have a rather tight circle: loving yourself presupposes that you have an identity defining your well-being as this person, but having such an identity presupposes that you love yourself. Such a tight circle, the objection insists, is vicious.

Such a circle will be vicious if we understand these presuppositions to involve a kind of priority, whether temporal, ontological, or logical. Should we understand them this way? No: the present circularity is really no different from the circularity inherent in caring about anything, a circularity which gives rise to the dual subjectivity and objectivity of our felt evaluations and of import in virtue of which, I have argued, we should understand import to be disclosed by our attitudes rather than simply being either discovered or invented by them. Thus, I have argued, we can properly describe our felt evaluations as responsive to an object that impresses itself on one in feeling: some import in the world. From this perspective, our felt evaluations are warranted or not insofar as they properly respond to that object, and in this sense they "discover" it. We can also properly describe our felt evaluations as constitutive of that import—not one by one, but by virtue of a broader rational pattern to which one commits oneself in having each felt evaluation that is an element of that pattern. In this sense, then, our felt evaluations "invent" that import. These are two complementary ways of describing the same phenomenon, but it should be clear that neither our felt evaluations nor import is prior to the other, and the inherent circularity is therefore non-vicious. The same is true of the circularity inherent in loving yourself: your identity as this person is the kind of life worth your living, and it is the import of such a life that you commit yourself to in having the felt evaluations constitutive of your self-love. Insofar as such import (and so the kind of life worth your living) is disclosed by your self-love, neither that import (and so your identity as this person) nor your self-love is prior to the other, and the inherent circularity is therefore non-vicious.

This reply is actually a bit too fast, as is signaled by the parenthetical inferences in the last sentence: the relationship between the import you have to yourself and your identity as this person needs to be clarified. Indeed, here an objector might raise anew the worry about vicious circularity, for it might seem that in paradigm cases of caring about something, that which one cares about—the focus of the relevant pattern of felt evaluations—is present in advance of one's caring, and it is only the import such a focus has to one that is disclosed by one's caring; however, in the case of self-love, the trouble is that the focus of the pattern of felt evaluations constitutive of that love, namely the person you are, as having a particular identity as such, is precisely not present in advance insofar as that identity is supposed to be a product of the pattern of felt evaluations constitutive of your self-love. As a *product* of your loving yourself, it might seem, your identity cannot be that to which you are committed in your love.

Nonetheless, the worry is overblown. The determinateness of a creature as this person and the presence in that creature of genuinely reflexive person-focused felt evaluations that form a pattern constitutive of self-love emerge simultaneously as the creature matures. To appropriate a Wittgensteinian metaphor, the light gradually dawns: as an agent's rational responsiveness to the world gradually becomes more complex, these responses gradually become intelligible as the result of its exercise of certain capacities characteristic of persons, in particular of its capacities to have person-focused felt evaluations; however, the kind of complexity of rational responsiveness necessary for the agent to be intelligible as exercising capacities for person-focused felt evaluations is such that its exercise of these capacities must fall into a pattern constitutive simultaneously of the person's love for herself and of her identity as a particular person. This means that for a creature to be intelligible as this person and so as exercising capacities for person-focused felt evaluations, she must already have an identity as this person: without such an identity, the rational pattern that makes the creature's responses intelligible as person-focused felt evaluations would be absent. Consequently, a person's identity as such and her genuinely exercising the capacities characteristic of persons emerge simultaneously, with neither prior to the other.[58]

The second objection concerns the possibility of self-hate. I have argued that to have an identity as this person, indeed to value anything at all, presupposes that you love yourself. At best this sounds odd and contrary to common sense: after all, is it not possible to hate yourself—an evaluative attitude contrary to love—and do so without ambivalence? It might seem that if we accept my account, such an attitude would be impossible, for there would be no "you" to hate absent your love for yourself, which seems ruled out by the lack of ambivalence. How can my account accommodate this intuition?

The answer depends on how precisely we are to understand the notion of self-hate. Thus, on the one hand, we might understand self-hate to be a response to the failure to live the kind of life you find worth living—not merely in some particular respect but rather more or less across the board. Understood this way, self-hate presupposes that you have an at least implicit understanding of the kind of life worth your living, an understanding constituted by your self-love. Such self-hate would then be comprised of widespread feelings of shame, anxiety, disappointment in yourself, and so on: all negative person-focused felt evaluations that are not contrary to self-love but are rather rationally demanded by that self-love. Consequently, on this understanding, self-hate turns out to be, seemingly paradoxically, a particular mode of self-love. Nonetheless, it should be clear that such self-hate is a *deficient* mode of self-love. For what gives rise to the self-hate is at least in part a general failure to be properly motivated to act in accordance with the values constituting one's identity, thereby bringing into question precisely what one's overall evaluative perspective, including one's values and identity, really is.

On the other hand (and somewhat more radically), we might understand self-hate to be the sense that your current values, your current sense of the

---

[58] Of course, there are genuine questions about how it is possible for the light to dawn this way—about how it is possible for a child to come to acquire the capacities for person-focused felt evaluations. This is an issue I address in Ch. 7.

kind of life worth your living, is fundamentally misguided so that, even though you may be living up to these current values, you nonetheless are not living as you ought. In short, understood this way self-hate is the sense that your identity as you now understand it is somehow rotten. On this construal, self-hate is once again the result of a concern for yourself, for your well-being as this person: it is a part of that vigilance concerning the content of your identity that is at the core of self-respect and so is central to self-love. To fail to attend in this way to the content of your identity is to fail to love yourself in the way love ultimately demands. What I have just described involving self-love and self-respect is clearly a positive force, namely a concern for yourself that ought to motivate at least second thoughts concerning the kind of life worth your living and potentially resulting in improvements in your identity. As a negative force, self-hate on this construal would turn out to be a deficient mode of such self-love and self-respect: a matter of simply being "down on yourself" in a way that fails to motivate such positive changes. Understood this way, self-hate is deficient once again in that it fails in this way to motivate action on behalf of yourself.

In normal cases lacking such self-hate, however, we generally have a kind of affection for ourselves, and this discussion of self-hate points the way to understanding such affection. We must not forget that emotions are not merely commitments to import; they are essentially feelings—*evaluative feelings*. Thus, to feel pride is to be pleased by your notably upholding your values, and to feel shame is to be pained by your notably flouting your values. Indeed, I have argued, such pleasure and pain are not mere phenomenal accompaniments of the emotions, but are themselves identical to the kind of commitment to import that emotions are.[59] It is such feelings, both positive and negative, that constitutes your emotional attachment to and identification with yourself: that constitutes your *affection* for yourself.

In short, the overall evaluative attitude toward yourself constituted by reflexive person-focused felt evaluations and evaluative judgments is an attitude of concern for your own well-being as this person, an attitude that essentially involves elements of identification, respect, trust, and affection. All of these are commonly thought to be central to an understanding of

---

[59] See §2.2, p. 65; for more detailed arguments, see Helm, "Felt Evaluations."

what love is, thus in part justifies my understanding of this attitude as self-love.

4.5 Conclusion

I have argued that to love yourself is to exhibit, both in your felt evaluations and evaluative judgments, a pattern of concern for your well-being as this particular person. Central to this account is a certain kind of self-respect and self-trust: loving yourself means in part maintaining, through vigilance and the exercise of autonomy, a single evaluative perspective on the kind of life worth your living—a rationally defined structure of person-focused felt evaluations and evaluative judgments—that constitutes your identity as this particular person. In articulating this account, I have proposed a significantly new understanding of emotions like pride and shame as person-focused, and, consequently, of the nature of identification.

Nonetheless, this argument is incomplete in several ways. First, a central motivation for understanding emotions like pride and shame to be person-focused and so for rejecting standard accounts of these emotions as essentially reflexive, is the idea that pride and shame need not be reflexive in that they essentially evaluate the subject as ennobled or degraded: we can be proud or ashamed of others without these feelings involving our having a changed sense of our own worth as persons. Yet this idea needs to be sharpened and defended by carefully examining a variety of cases in which other persons figure prominently in our feelings of pride and shame. A second and related motivation for this understanding of pride and shame as person-focused is my claim that we ought carefully to distinguish the sense in which we identify with projects, ends, properties, and so on by valuing them from the sense in which we identify with others in loving them. After all, pride and shame when directed at other persons presuppose that the subject has a close personal connection to them, and part of the question is how this close personal connection, intelligible in terms of a kind of identification, is to be understood. My claim, thus far undefended and crucial to defending my account of these emotions as essentially person-focused, is that we can make sense of the ways in which pride and shame can be directed at others only by understanding them to be person-focused and so only by understanding them to be the foundation of the subject's love for these other persons. My aim in Chapter 5 is to explicate and defend these claims.

Finally, it is not entirely clear that the account I have provided here is of something that ought to be called "love"; nor is it clear that the "respect" and "trust" I have argued are elements of such "love" really are respect and trust. To justify my use of this language, I must show how this account of such "self-love," "self-respect," and "self-trust" gibes with an account of loving, respecting, and trusting others, an account that does justice to our everyday conceptions of these notions. Again, this will be part of my aim in Chapter 5.

5

Love as Intimate Identification

In Chapter 4, I presented an account of what I called self-love: to love yourself is to find yourself to have import for your own sake as this person and so to be committed, in large part through your person-focused felt evaluations, to your well-being as this is defined by your identity. But why should we think this is an account of self-*love* at all? An objector might challenge this account as follows. Love, we might think, is a more specific feeling of approval, say, whereas the kind of attitude of "self-love" I have described, is instead largely a matter of having a self-understanding that grounds not only feelings of approval but also feelings of disapproval, such as self-hate; how can such a self-understanding be the attitude of love at all?

Like any evaluative attitude, love is a mode of concern for the well-being of something or someone. Because something's well-being depends on how it is described, I have argued that the evaluative attitudes, including love and self-love, must involve an at least implicit understanding of the kind of thing their focuses are. In the case of self-love, this will include a self-understanding, but it should be clear that such a self-understanding is merely a part, albeit an essential part, of the mode of concern that self-love is. In addition, the evaluative attitudes essentially involve both a vigilance for and preparedness to act on behalf of their focuses as exhibited in the projectible, rational pattern of felt evaluations of the subject. In the case of self-love, such felt evaluations include positive person-focused felt evaluations of a sort we might describe as "feelings of approval," but they are not limited to these. For the kind of concern you have for yourself that is love must also involve an attunement to when things go badly not only in the ways your environment affects you but also within your self, and the resulting negative person-focused felt evaluations will not and should not be simply feelings of approval. Thus, to fail to feel ashamed when you flout your own values, for example, is to fail to have the kind of concern for yourself that self-love essentially is.

Although I began to defend the claim that this really is self-love in §4.4, I acknowledged (p. 130) that the best argument for this account depends in part on the sense it is able to make of love more generally, including in particular love of others. My aim in this chapter is to defend an account of loving others that is roughly parallel to this account of self-love: to love another is to find her to have import for her sake as the person she is and so to be committed, in large part through your person-focused felt evaluations, to her well-being as this person.

A second kind of challenge that might be raised for my account thus far stems not from skepticism concerning whether I have been discussing anything that might properly be called 'love' but rather from skepticism concerning whether anything more needs to be said. I have, after all, presented an account of what it is to care about others in Chapter 3; why not think this just is an account of what it is to love someone? Thus, Irving Singer understands love to be a matter of bestowing value upon another, where this is done

by caring about the needs and interests of the beloved, by wishing to benefit or protect her, by delighting in her achievements, by encouraging her independence while also accepting and sustaining her dependency, by respecting her individuality, by giving her pleasure, by taking pleasures with her, by feeling glad when she is present and sad when she is not.[1]

Similarly, Harry Frankfurt says:

When we love something, however, we go further [than merely finding it to be important to ourselves]. We care about it not merely as a means, but as an end. It is in the nature of loving that we consider its objects to be valuable in themselves and to be important to us for their own sakes.

Love is, most centrally, a *disinterested* concern for the existence of what is loved, and for what is good for it.[2]

More generally, robust concern accounts of love understand love to be at its core a matter of caring about another for her sake.[3] Most of this sounds

---

[1] Singer, "From *The Nature of Love*," 270–1. [2] Frankfurt, "On Love, and Its Reasons," 42.
[3] See, for example, Newton-Smith, "A Conceptual Investigation of Love"; Soble, *The Structure of Love*; Thomas, "Reasons for Loving"; LaFollette, *Personal Relationships*; White, *Love's Philosophy*.

very much like the account of caring about others I have already provided: to care about another is to find him to have import as an agent and so to care about the things he cares about for his sake, to respond emotionally to things that affect his well-being, thereby sharing in his pleasures and pains, and to participate in engaged activity with him. So why not think that my account of what it is to care about another for his sake is sufficient as an account of love or, at least, of the kind of concern for another that is central to love?

The issue here returns us to the dispute raised above (§1.3) between the union and robust-concern accounts concerning the nature of the kind of intimacy that is characteristic of love. For love must be distinguished from other, intuitively less intimate attitudes of caring toward others, such as compassion, and it seems that we must do so at least in part by articulating more clearly the kind of intimacy that is characteristic of love. In doing this, recall, union accounts implicitly appeal to a notion of identification construed as union: your concern for another is intimate just in case it involves your identifying with him by blurring, in your mind at least, any distinction between his interests and your own. However, as I noted above, this appeal to union seems excessive in that (a) it questionably undermines one's autonomy and distinctness from one's beloved and (b) it unsatisfactorily construes intimacy in egocentric terms and thereby fails to make sense of the idea that in love we have a concern for our beloved for *his* sake. Recoiling from these excesses, robust-concern accounts appeal directly to a generic and largely unanalyzed notion of caring about another for his sake, but in so doing they fail, I suggested, to distinguish loving concern from compassionate concern.

Having provided in Chapter 3 an analysis of a rather generic sort of caring about another for her sake, we are now in a better position to see why such an account is inadequate for understanding *personal* love, which is what I aim to elucidate. For understanding the kind of concern we have for our beloveds for their sakes must involve considering the way in which a concern for the well-being of a person as such differs from a concern for the well-being of an agent as such, which in turn requires understanding the difference between the sort of well-being a person has and that of a mere agent.

To be a person is to be a creature not merely with cares but also with values that define one's identity as such; moreover, persons do not merely have values, but they are capable of exercising a capacity for autonomy in deliberating about and so determining which values they shall have and so what their identities shall be. Consider, then, the difference between merely caring about something and valuing it. For example, in caring about playing oboe, I ought to feel a range of non-person-focused felt evaluations in the relevant circumstances: frustration when my reed is not working well, pleasure at my playing something well (or disappointment when I do so poorly), a desire to practice, annoyance or anger at obstacles to my practicing, and so on. In having these felt evaluations, I am in each case responding to the import playing oboe has to me and so the way other things bear on this import. By contrast, in valuing playing oboe I ought, in addition to caring about it, to feel the relevant person-focused felt evaluations when called for by the circumstances: pride at pulling off particularly well an original interpretation of a difficult piece, shame at my failure even to attempt an imaginative interpretation, anxiety or self-assurance before an audition that might launch my musical career, and so on. In having such person-focused felt evaluations, I am responding not merely to the import of playing music (or even *my* playing music); rather, I am responding to the import I have as this particular person, and my having such felt evaluations, therefore, is a commitment to my living a certain kind of life. In particular, to feel shame is to be pained by the way I have let myself down: not merely in the sense that my reed can sometimes let me down, as a failure of competence, but rather in the sense that I have failed to live as I am committed to living, a failure that strikes at my very identity as this person, putting that identity at risk insofar as it is a failure to uphold the rational pattern of felt evaluations constitutive of my identity. My well-being as this person, dependent as it is on my identity as this person, is therefore distinct from the well-being of agents as such.

If the well-being of persons is different in this way from the well-being of mere agents, then the kind of concern we can have for persons must be similarly distinct from that which is possible for mere agents. For if caring about another as an agent centrally involves sharing its cares, then caring about another as this person centrally involves sharing her identity; it is in terms of such sharing of another's identity that we can understand the distinctive intimacy of love. It is because such intimacy is not a part of caring about another as an agent that the appeal to such a generic notion of caring fails to provide an adequate account of love.

To share another's identity just is, we might think, a matter of *identifying* with her. At this point it might be thought, in a way that is analogous to the robust-concern account's attempt to make sense of love in terms of a more generic attitude of caring, that we already have an appropriate notion of identification available to use in making sense of the intimacy of love. For, as I argued in §4.4, we identify with particular things by valuing them and so incorporating them into our own identities. This thought may be what motivates the union account's central claim that to love another is to identify with her in the sense of merging your identity with hers and "pooling" your and her well-beings.[4] Indeed, that this is the right way to understand the motivation behind at least some union accounts seems clear from the way Frankfurt blurs the distinction between valuing something and loving a person. Thus, Frankfurt speaks indiscriminately of our loving other persons, a country, a tradition, or an ideal,[5] and it is in this context that he says:

It is by these nonvoluntary tendencies and responses of our will that love is constituted and that loving moves us. It is by these same configurations of the will, moreover, that our individual identities are most fully expressed and defined.[6]

However, we can now see in a somewhat different way why this attempt to make sense of the intimacy of love in terms of union is misguided. For valuing, as I have understood it thus far, is a mode of self-love in which one understands the thing valued to have a place within the kind of life worth one's living. As such, valuing is an evaluative attitude constituted by person-focused felt evaluations where, as I have understood it thus far, the focus of these felt evaluations is oneself. By blurring the distinction between identifying with something in the sense of incorporating it into your own identity by valuing it and identifying with someone by sharing in her identity, union accounts assimilate loving concern for another to valuing and thereby reveal an underlying egocentrism evident in the Frankfurt quotation above: love of another is ultimately grounded in a

---

[4] Nozick, "Love's Bond," 70; see also Robert Solomon's claim that "intimacy—and love—consist in *shared identity*" (his italics; Robert C. Solomon, *Love: Emotion, Myth, and Metaphor* (New York, NY: Anchor Press, 1981), xxx).

[5] Frankfurt, "On Love, and Its Reasons," 41.

[6] Ibid., 50. A similar problem can be found in Gabriele Taylor's failure to distinguish the sense in which we identify with things valued from the sense in which we identify with other persons; see Taylor, *Pride, Shame, and Guilt*.

concern for oneself. To avoid such an egocentric conception of the sort of intimacy characteristic of love, therefore, we need to make a clear distinction between the sort of concern at issue in love and that which we have for the things we value. As Larry Blum puts essentially the same point in a discussion of friendship:

The sense of identification involved in genuine friendship is not a matter of self-interest at all, and caring for the friend is not simply an extension of caring for oneself. This mistaken conception of friendship trades on an ambiguity within the notion of 'identification,' which can have either an egoistic or a non-egoistic sense.[7]

The trouble, of course, is to provide an explicit account of such a non-egoist (or non-egocentric) notion of identification in ways that make clear just how it is possible to care about your beloved for *her* sake and do so with the distinctive kind of intimacy that is characteristic of love. My central aim in this chapter is to do precisely this, and it is the notion of person-focused felt evaluations that makes this possible.

Before I begin, however, it will be useful to note several things. First, for an account of love to be successful, it must shed some light on some important features of love as well as various problems that have arisen in the philosophical literature. In Chapter 1 I raised two central problems of love: worries about whether the object of love is fungible and about the nature of the justification of love; these two problems will be addressed in Chapter 6. Other issues that ought to be addressed by a satisfactory account include an understanding of the phenomenology of love, including the ways in which love can be not just pleasant but also painful; the relationship between loving someone and the willingness to sacrifice yourself for his sake; and whether love can be voluntary or something for which we can be responsible.

Second, we ought to resist providing an account of love in terms of other attitudes that are themselves left unanalyzed. Far too often accounts of love are presented in a piecemeal and seemingly reductionist fashion, understanding love in terms of largely unanalyzed notions of disinterested concern, or concern for the beloved for his sake, and identification. As I have already pointed out in this chapter, generic accounts of concern fail to capture what is distinctively personal and intimate about love, and

---

[7] Blum, "Friendship as a Moral Phenomenon," 200.

this becomes apparent only when we provide an explicit account of such concern. Yet ultimately the worry is deeper: without an explicit account of such concern we will make presuppositions about it that cannot be sustained upon a closer examination as we try to fit a given understanding of love into a more general picture of the mind and its place in the rest of nature (see p. 50). In particular, there is a significant risk that the sort of intimate identification I have plumped for as central to love will fall into the same trap. Merely to understand this as a kind of identification that both is intimate in being a concern with your beloved's identity that is somehow analogous to your concern for your own identity, and is non-egocentric in that this form of concern is not conceptually posterior to your concern for yourself, is not enough without an explicit, positive account of this kind of identification and how it can be both intimate and non-egocentric.

Third, the apparent reductionism of many accounts of love is also something we ought to resist, even if the account is fleshed out fully. Although it may be true that love involves respecting, trusting, identifying with, being sympathetic to, and caring about another person, for example, and even if we have a general account of what it is to trust, respect, identify with, be sympathetic to, and care about another, the kinds of trust, respect, identification, sympathy, and caring involved to love may seem to differ from ordinary kinds not involved in love precisely because of that involvement. For, it seems, the intuitive "depth" and intimacy of love seems to "infect" these individual aspects of love, so that the trust, respect, identification, and so on involved in my attitude toward my beloved are distinct from those involved in my attitude toward my neighbor whom I do not love because of the intimacy they acquire from being embedded within an overall attitude of love. Part of my aim in this chapter, therefore will be to articulate in the context of a non-reductionist account of love more clearly precisely why this is so.

Finally, as I indicated in Chapter 1, one of my central aims in this book is to argue against the tendencies, all too common in philosophy, to understand our mental states in terms of the cognitive–conative divide and to offer (or presuppose) an individualist conception of persons. Although it will not become clear until I offer my account of the justification of love in Chapter 6, the account of love presented here is neither cognitive nor conative, and it is in part for this reason that I will be able to offer a satisfactory account of justification. Moreover, although I shall focus in this chapter on making clear how the account of intimate identification I offer is non-egocentric, thereby rejecting the egocentric conception of intimacy that is a part of the individualist conception of persons, it will not be until Part III that it will be clear how this understanding of love makes possible a more genuinely social conception of persons.

5.1 Person-Focused Felt Evaluations

In §4.1, I suggested that felt evaluations like pride and shame need not be reflexive, contrary to standard accounts of these emotions: when I am proud of my colleague for receiving a prestigious fellowship, I need not evaluate myself positively but instead evaluate her. Such emotions, therefore, should be understood to be not essentially reflexive but person-focused: committing the subject to the import of their focus as this person. I then claimed that we can understand love generally as an evaluative attitude constituted by rationally structured patterns of person-focused felt evaluations, where the object of love is the common focus of the felt evaluations constituting this pattern. In the case of self-love, the focus of this pattern will be oneself, and I spent the bulk of Chapter 4 fleshing out and arguing for this understanding of self-love. The application of this account to loving others should be obvious, at least in outline: loving another person consists in exhibiting the appropriate rationally structured pattern of person-focused felt evaluations focused on him. Before fleshing this out and identifying some significant differences between self-love and love of others, however, I need to justify more fully this understanding of emotions like pride and shame as person-focused and so not as essentially reflexive. That is my aim in this section.

Consider several examples of pride, starting with clearly reflexive cases. In what we might call *directly reflexive* pride, I am proud of my doing something or for exhibiting certain admirable qualities, especially qualities of character. Thus, if I am proud of my skillful handling of a tricky situation with my teenage daughter, I am in feeling this pride implicitly evaluating myself as living up to my value of being a good father as a part of the kind of life worth my living. In this case, not only is the focus of the pride myself, but the target of the pride is also myself or a property or action of mine.[8] It is only because of such a direct connection between the target of the pride (my action) and its focus (myself), only because this target directly enters into my sense of the kind of life worth my living so that I *identify* with it in this sense, that we can make intelligible the evaluation of the target that is implicit in pride.

By contrast, in what we might call *indirectly reflexive* pride, the evaluation of the target of my pride is intelligible only in light of an indirect or representative relationship between the target and the focus (myself). Thus, I can be proud of my house, or of owning such a fine house, where such pride may be intelligible not because I understand my identity as this person to be wrapped up in the kind of house I own (as would be the case with directly reflexive pride) but rather because my house represents something I do value: my wealth, power, or social status, for example. Of course, for the house to represent *my* wealth in particular, it must be that I have some special connection with the house—by owning it, for example; in other cases, I might be proud of the house because, having built it, it represents my skill as a craftsman.

An important subclass of indirectly reflexive pride involves our being proud of other people, as when I am proud of the members of the US National Soccer Team for putting on such a good showing in the World Cup. How are we to understand this case? In feeling such pride I am affirming the value of a certain kind of life and so coming to feel better about myself, so it is a case of reflexive pride. What explains the connection between the players' doing well and my affirming my own value can only be that I identify with them. Yet the relevant notion of identification at issue here should not be construed in the same way as when I am proud of a particular accomplishment—that is, in terms of my making them directly a part of my identity as this person. After all, I may never have met any of them or seen them play before, so such identification would be too far-fetched. Rather, I identify with them in that I see them as representatives of something else I value: I value being a US citizen and see them as representatives of US citizens generally. Such an explanation presupposes

---

[8] It might be thought that the target in this case is ambiguous: am I proud of my handling of the situation, or am I proud of myself? This is, I believe, a distinction without a difference. For if we were to say that the target is me, so that I am evaluated positively in the feeling of pride, that can only be because my handling of the situation was similarly admirable.

that I at least implicitly understand athleticism or prowess in sports to be features of the US or its citizens generally, features in virtue of which I find my citizenship to be valuable. Consequently, their good showing reflects well on me because they represent a larger group the membership in which I value and so with which I identify in this more direct sense. My pride in them is therefore reflexive—focused on myself—with my citizenship in the US as its subfocus.

My claim is that there is a further kind of pride, which we might call *loving pride*, that is distinct from these reflexive cases of pride. To see this, consider my pride in my wife for winning a bagpipe competition: *must* such a case be construed as either directly or indirectly reflexive pride? Of course we *can* construe it that way. One way to understand this as a case of directly reflexive pride is to appeal to the union account: my wife and I together form a "we" such that there has come to be no distinction between her interests and mine, thereby blurring our identities and our capacities for autonomy. It is this union that explains how her actions become a proper object of my pride. However, I have already argued against the union account as involving an excessive egocentrism and as undermining the autonomy and distinctness of persons. Moreover, in this case such a union is clearly false: I have no interest in playing the bagpipes (heaven forbid!) and yet can still treasure her interest in it as a part of loving the distinct person she is.

We might avoid these excesses of the union account and yet preserve the understanding of my pride as directly reflexive by reinterpreting the target of my pride: what I am proud of is not really her but rather my having fine musicians as friends, as a kind of adornment on my life; or I am proud of myself for my responsibility in making her be such an accomplished piper (as when I am her teacher), and her winning the competition is not the target but rather the occasion calling attention to and warranting this special pleasure in my role in her success. Although these may be proper descriptions of some cases of pride in another person, they are not accurate descriptions of other cases; in particular, such an understanding seems not to apply to the sort of case at issue in healthy, loving relationships, for in such a case my pride really is in my wife, whose import to me explains why on this occasion I evaluate her positively in feeling the pride.

If some cases of "loving pride" are not intelligible as directly reflexive, perhaps they are indirectly reflexive. Thus, I may be proud of my wife in that I find her to be representative of something else that I value. Once again, this is intelligible as a case of pride only if there is some special connection I have with something she represents that explains how her doing well can reflect well on me (so as to preserve the reflexivity). For example, if I am responsible as her teacher for her accomplishments as a piper, I can experience indirectly reflexive pride in her because she represents my skill as a teacher.[9] Or perhaps she and I belong to the same pipe band, membership in which I value, so that I come to identify with her as a representative of this group; her winning the competition therefore reflects well not merely on the band but also on me insofar as I value my membership in the band, and this is what makes intelligible my pride in her. Yet once again these fail to be proper construals of "loving pride," for they are insensitive to the way in which the pride in someone I love is in part an expression of that love—a love which is simply missing from the construal of pride as indirectly reflexive. For as an expression of love it ought to involve a concern for her for her sake and not merely as representing something that I value. This possibility is simply missed by accounts of pride that understand it to be essentially reflexive.

Any account of pride must be able to explain why, in cases in which I am proud of someone else, it is appropriate for *me* to feel this pride in her: what special connection do I have to her that can explain how my emotion is deeply personal in the way characteristic of pride as opposed to esteem? Standard accounts of pride have a ready answer: we should construe such a special connection reflexively, as a matter of identifying with her. Such identification can be understood either directly in terms of my valuing her or finding her directly relevant to something I value, or indirectly in terms of my finding her to represent something I value. Identification, thus understood in terms of something's relation to the subject's own values or identity, is therefore essentially reflexive in this way; indeed, this is precisely the construal of identification we would expect from the egocentric conception of intimate concerns. The trouble with these reflexive accounts of my loving pride in my wife is that they fail to recognize that the value to which I am responding in feeling such

---

[9] Notice how construing the pride in this case to be indirectly reflexive rather than directly reflexive, as in the previous paragraph, does not require that we reinterpret the target of my pride.

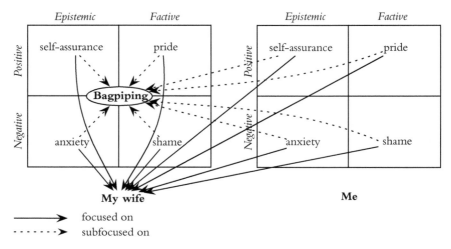

Figure 5.1. Pattern of person-focused felt evaluations focused on another.

pride is the value bagpipes have *to her* and not to me, and what make intelligible why pride is an appropriate emotion to feel here and now are therefore the place this value has in her life and so the way in which the present circumstances reveal in some significant way her success in upholding this value. Consequently my pride in my wife for winning the bagpipe competition cannot be understood as a case of either directly or indirectly reflexive pride. How, then, are we to understand it?

The solution is to understand pride to be a person-focused emotion, committing one to the import of its focus as this person, that need not be reflexive. Thus, in being proud of my wife for winning the bagpipe competition, my pride is focused on her and subfocused on her playing bagpipes. (See Figure 5.1.) To feel this pride is to be committed to the import she has as this person and so to the import bagpipes have as a part of her identity as such. Such commitments are, therefore, to feeling other person-focused felt evaluations with the same focus. Indeed, these will be person-focused felt evaluations I ought to share with her: when she is proud, ashamed, anxious, self-assured, and so on, where these are emotions focused on herself, I ought similarly to feel pride, shame, and so on for her sake.

As was the case with caring about another agent as such (see §3.3), in saying that I must *share* these person-focused felt evaluations with her, I mean not merely that I must have sympathetic echoes of emotions and desires that she antecedently has. Annette Baier is right to say that love

is a *coordination* ... of two (or more) persons' emotions, and it is more than sympathy, more than just the duplication of the emotions of each in a sympathetic echo in the other.[10]

For the commitment I undertake in being proud of my wife to her import as this particular person and so to her values as these define her identity as such, is a commitment to respond in felt evaluation to that which significantly impacts her well-being positively or negatively. This may require that I feel, say, anxious on her behalf, even when she does not yet recognize the impending threat to her identity. In effect, for me to share these person-focused felt evaluations with her is for me to share the rational pattern of such felt evaluations focused on her and subfocused not just on bagpiping but also on the other things she values, insofar as these values constitute her identity and so her well-being.[11] This is for me to *value* what she values not for my sake in that I make this a part of my identity but *for her sake*, as a part of my commitment to the import she has to me.[12] To value something for her sake is for this pattern of felt evaluations to be focused on my wife and subfocused on the thing valued. Consequently, it is only as contributing to her well-being that her piping is valuable to me, so that I share not just her person-focused felt evaluations but also, in this sense, her values and, therefore, her identity as constituted by these values.

To be concerned for another's well-being by virtue of a projectible, rational pattern of person-focused felt evaluations focused on him, a pattern that involves your sharing his person-focused emotions focused on himself

----

[10] Baier, "Unsafe Loves," 442.

[11] Just as for self-love, the commitment I undertake for her sake to her playing bagpipes, because this involves a commitment to her import as this person, essentially involves as well a commitment to the import of other things constituting her identity as such.

[12] I therefore find inadequate Baier's way of cashing out her insight that the sharing of emotions in love is more than just sympathy. Baier does so by appealing to ordinary sympathy plus

appropriate *follow-up* responses to what one knows by sympathy that the other is feeling—mischievous delight at the other's temporary bafflement, a frisson of fear at their feigned aggression, glory in the other's surrender. [Ibid., 443.]

However, she has no clear proposal (beyond presenting a few examples) for what follow-up responses really are at issue in love. By contrast, my understanding of the sharing of emotions involves a distinctive type of (what might be called) sympathy: one grounded in the rational structure of person-focused felt evaluations that, I shall claim, constitutes my love for another.

and so sharing his identity, constitutes his having import to you as this particular person. In such a case, the requisite identification with him—the special connection you have with him—in virtue of which your felt evaluations are intelligible as person-focused with its "depth" of evaluation, is constituted not independent of your feeling pride, shame, and so on for his sake but rather by the overall pattern of felt evaluations constituting his import to you: your pride in him is intelligible as pride rather than esteem, for example, only insofar as that pride is already embedded within a broader pattern of concern constituting your concern for him as this person. Indeed, this sharing of his identity is *intimate identification*: a concern for the identity of another that is same in kind as the kind of concern you have for your own identity (see §1.3, p. 18). I submit that such an intimate concern for the well-being of a particular person as such is love.

5.2 Intimate Identification

As I already noted in §1.3, one important topic on which many accounts of love disagree concerns the place of autonomy and respect in love. Union accounts of love, because they understand the kind of identification involved in love to be a matter of blurring boundaries between the individuals involved, tend to claim that love involves giving up on individual autonomy. By contrast, robust-concern accounts, rejecting the union accounts' understanding of identification, are able to preserve individual autonomy, though, I suggested, at the cost of losing the intimacy of love. My claim is that we do not have to choose between intimacy and autonomy: we can keep both so long as we reject the egocentric conception of intimate concerns that gives rise to this apparent conflict. With the account of love in terms of rational patterns of non-reflexive person-focused emotions just given, we are now in a position to see how this can work.

I claimed that to love someone is to have a concern for his well-being as the particular person he is. Yet by whose standards ought I to assess what affects his well-being positively or negatively? That is, whose conception of his identity ought I to use in responding in these ways: mine or his? And under what circumstances, therefore, ought I to feel the person-focused felt evaluations constitutive of my concern for him? On the one hand, the answer cannot simply be that it is his conception, for I ought not to be proud of him for upholding values I think are generally abhorrent; nor could I more generally share this value with him, even if it is for his sake. For to do so would be for me to be inadequately sensitive to the value these things intelligibly can have (by my lights), and I would thereby fail in my commitment to his well-being. On the other hand, the relevant conception of his identity cannot simply be mine, for then I would be inadequately sensitive to his identity as this person and, in particular, to the place his autonomy ought to have in defining his identity as such. For example, when I value for his sake something he takes to involve excessive hedonism and so am proud of him for being what by his lights is weak willed, he might with justification take my pride to be a patronizing insult rather than an expression of my love for him.

The middle ground between these two extremes, of course, involves respect. Because in being committed to the import he has as this person I am committed to the proper exercise of those very capacities defining his personhood, including his autonomy, I ought in general to defer to his view, at least so long as his view is arrived at in ways that do not subvert the exercise of his autonomy. However, such respect does not require complete deference. In cases in which his view has been distorted by undue external influence such as peer pressure or in which he is not thinking clearly enough properly to exercise his autonomy, as when he is self-deceived or even simply too immature: in such cases, perhaps, I ought to intervene out of my concern for his well-being as this person.[13] Yet even in such cases, my intervention ought to be motivated by my paying due attention to the proper exercise of his autonomy in ways motivated by a concern for the content of his identity; this just is the kind of *respect* I ought to pay those I love. This understanding of respect for others directly parallels the account given in §4.4: love, whether of yourself or others, normally requires respect, and a widespread failure of such respect tends to undermine the rationality of the pattern of person-focused felt evaluations constituting that love.

This understanding of respect implies that loving someone normally requires considerable agreement in what it is impermissible or mandatory

---

[13] I shall discuss paternal love and the role it can have in the formation of a person's identity, in Ch. 7.

to value or do. For if my beloved is about to embark on a course of action I find prohibited not just for myself but for anyone, or if he fails to value something I think he must, then, other things being equal, I ought to object out of a concern for his well-being. For in such a case simply to defer to his view would be, according to me, harmful to his well-being and so contrary to my concern for him; indeed, if he continues in this way, then I ought to be ashamed of him for failing to live as he ought in this respect, regardless of his failure to be ashamed of himself. Here there is a rational conflict between my sense of what is mandatory (or impermissible) and his, which I ought to share for his sake, and such a conflict, like any other rational conflict, demands resolution by, for example, my helping him to see that he ought (or ought not) to value this, or my coming to see that he can permissibly fail to value (or continue to value) this after all. Once again, isolated failures of this sort can be tolerated within the overall rational pattern of person-focused felt evaluations constituting love for another; however, widespread failures about what it is impermissible or mandatory to value will tend to destabilize not only the rationality of that pattern but also, therefore, the love itself—not in the sense that it makes love impossible but rather in that it involves a kind of rational conflict internal to the love that makes continued love difficult and even painful.[14]

Precisely how I ought to proceed to resolve such a conflict depends on my sense of whether there are factors like peer pressure, self-deception, or immaturity that might explain his failure to agree with me and so that rationally motivate a kind of paternalism at least in this case. In the absence of these factors, respect for myself ought, other things being equal, to lead me to question whether I am seeing things correctly here. It might be suggested (although I shall not), that this is a kind of "trust" in my beloved, parallel to the account of self-trust given in §4.4, for I am finding his evaluative perspective to provide me with reasons at least to reconsider my own. However, if it is a kind of "trust," it is one that does not depend on love or the kind of respect I have identified as central to love, for it is a kind of responsiveness that, because it is motivated by self-respect, I might owe

---

[14] I suspect Marilyn Friedman would disagree here, claiming that making your love depend on such an evaluation of your beloved is a matter of subordinating "our commitment to that person . . . to our commitment to the relevant moral standards" (Friedman, "Friendship and Moral Growth," 6). However, it is not clear either that such subordination is a bad thing or even that it is a feature of my account. I shall return to this point in a discussion of unconditional love in §6.2.2.

myself to make to the evaluative perspectives of relative strangers, rather than a kind of response I owe to my beloved. Nonetheless, there is a kind of trust that is characteristic of love and that we owe to our beloveds.

Loving someone, I have claimed, involves valuing what she values for her sake, and I have articulated what it is for me to value something for her sake in terms of the relevant pattern of person-focused felt evaluations being focused on her. It should be clear, however, that although I value these things for her sake, *I* am the one who values them. This means not merely that I am the subject of the relevant feelings of pride, shame, and so on that constitute my valuing these things for her sake, so that I am the one that feels pleasure or pain depending on how she fares. It also means that the relevant pattern of felt evaluations constituting my valuing these things for her sake must normally include desires that motivate me to act on her behalf; such desires include second-order desires insofar as they are a part of my valuing these things, and my actions (or failures so to act) may well provide proper occasions for me to be proud or ashamed of myself, where these are evaluations of myself as ennobled or degraded. Thus, I may be ashamed of my failure to be properly supportive of my beloved out of mere laziness; my shame in this case targets me on the occasion of that failure and is focused on my beloved, subfocused on the thing she values, and sub-subfocused on my supporting her in her endeavors with respect to this value.

In addition to this feeling of shame focused on her and targeting me, I ought as well to feel shame that not only targets myself but also is focused on myself. For we cannot understand my love and the values I share with my beloved to be isolated from the rest of what I care about; rather, my love and shared values must have a place within my overall sense of import as this is structured by my priorities. Hence, to fail to support my beloved out of mere laziness is a failure to uphold my priorities. In part in order to understand the intuitive "depth" priorities have relative to our preferences, I have elsewhere understood priorities as a matter of valuing having certain preferences.[15] Consequently, this failure to uphold my priorities is a failure to which I ought to respond with person-focused emotions that, because these are my priorities that structure my sense of my identity as this person, are focused on myself. This means that what is at stake in my loving her is not simply my responsiveness to the import she has to me and, through this,

---

[15] See Helm, *Emotional Reason*, §4.3.

to the import of the things she values, a responsiveness that is focused on her. For insofar as my love for her is embedded within the kind of life worth my living, love requires as well a responsiveness to my successes or failures to live the kind of life I find worthwhile, a responsiveness that is focused on myself.

The upshot is that loving another is not merely a matter of sharing her values but also exhibiting a rational pattern of self-focused felt evaluations constitutive of valuing the place your love for her, and so the values you share with her for her sake, have within your life. In this way, my sharing in her identity is something that I find to partially constitute my own identity, so that my identity, my sense of the kind of life I ought to live, has become dependent on my responding properly to her values. This means that to love someone is normally to *trust* her to have such an impact on one's own identity; as a part of the rational pattern constitutive of love, such trust is something we owe our beloveds insofar as we love them. This understanding of the kind of trust involved in loving another preserves the parallel to the sort of self-trust discussed in §4.4: it is a matter of finding an evaluation—in this case the valuings of one's beloved—to be internal to the evaluative perspective defining one's own identity, so that one comes to rely on such evaluations in a way that puts one's own identity at stake.

All of this serves to bolster the intimacy of the sort of identification involved in love. For we now have a clear way to cash out the metaphor of "taking someone's identity to heart" that I claimed in §1.2 (p. 10) is central to making sense of the kind of intimate identification essential to love. To value the things your beloved values for her sake, as I argued in §5.1, is to "share her identity" as it is constituted by these values. Yet I have now argued that sharing her identity in this sense also requires that you value the place this has within your overall sense of the kind of life worth your living, thereby making your upholding her values for her sake itself be a part of your identity, so that you thereby make your own identity dependent on her values—on her identity. This just is for you to "take her identity to heart": this just is *intimate identification*.

It should be clear that this account of the kind of intimate identification essential to love requires that the lover has a reasonably accurate understanding of the beloved's identity. For unless you generally understand what someone values and so what his identity consists in, you cannot value what he values for his sake and so cannot take his identity to heart. (Of course, some degree of inaccuracy is possible here without undermining the overall pattern of felt evaluations focused on him and constituting your taking his identity to heart.) This just is a part of having an understanding of his identity inform the way you care about him in the way necessary for love: to love someone is to care about him as this particular person, as this is defined by his identity. As before, this understanding of the beloved, this conception of the object of your concern that informs that concern, need not be something the lover can articulate explicitly in judgment; all that is required is that the lover respond with the appropriate pattern of felt evaluations constituting his valuing the things she values for her sake, so that such an understanding can simply be implicit in those emotional and desiderative responses.

We can now understand more clearly the kind of "special connection" you must have in cases of non-reflexive pride and shame that makes intelligible the intuitive "depth" of these emotions as opposed to emotions like esteem and disapprobation: that special connection just is your taking her identity to heart. This implies that genuinely to feel non-reflexive pride and shame for another is normally possible only when such feelings are embedded within a broader rational pattern of such felt evaluations constituting your love for her, such that your current pride or shame is an expression of that love. For to fail to exhibit that broader pattern of felt evaluations constitutive of love is to fail to identify intimately with another in a way that makes intelligible that what you feel now is genuinely pride or shame rather than some non-person-focused emotion.

By failing to incorporate some such notion of intimate identification, robust-concern accounts fail to distinguish the evaluative attitude of love from "shallower," less intimate evaluative attitudes. Consider, for example, Alan Soble's discussion of the kind of identification at issue in love. According to Soble, we identify with others in one of two ways: either by "imagin[ing] what they are feeling by noticing what *we* would feel" in similar circumstances (which he calls "wearing the other's shoes") or by "imagin[ing] what y would be feeling, not by invoking what x would feel but by invoking y's beliefs and values" ("wearing the other's shoes *and* hat.")[16] Soble claims that only the second sense of identification is involved in loving someone:

X's being able to imagine how y feels requires only that x know y well, not that x psychologically incorporate y's perspective. Hence, x's viewing as bad what is

---

[16] Soble, *The Structure of Love*, 271.

good for *y* in *y*'s sense does not force *x* to have contradictory beliefs, because *x*'s wanting for *y* what is good for *y* in *y*'s sense does not automatically translate into *x*'s believing it is good. ... To assert otherwise would be to claim that *x* could never empathize with *y*, and be concerned for *y*'s well-being, without in part *becoming y*.[17]

Soble is here rejecting the idea that love involves a distinctively intimate form of concern in part motivated, as I suggested in §1.3, by Soble's tacit understanding of such intimacy in egocentric terms. However, this leaves him unable to distinguish the kind of empathy we can have for people we know well but do not love from the sort of empathy involved in our more intimate concern for others. The result is that Soble is unable to distinguish the kind of concern we have for others in loving them from merely caring about them as agents.

Nonetheless, the kind of intimate identification I have just described should not be confused with the sort of identification at issue in union accounts of love. For the point of identification as union is precisely to break down the distinctions among persons so as to come to understand a person's concern for his beloved's well-being egocentrically in terms of his concern for himself. By contrast, I have offered an account of our concern for another's well-being as this person in terms of non-reflexive person-focused felt evaluations; this account is non-egocentric in that your concern for your beloved, though intimate, is not to be explained in terms of your incorporation of his identity into your own. Of course, insofar as loving another normally involves trusting him and so putting your own identity at stake in him, love of another is not fully independent of your concern for yourself. However, this lack of independence from your concern for yourself does not raise any worries about egocentrism; to the contrary, your concern for yourself is relevant to your love for him only because you make your concern for yourself dependent on his values, and not the other way around. Consequently, such a lack of independence does not blur the distinction between his values or identity and yours given the way the focus of the relevant felt evaluations must track either you or him. Thus my account of intimate identification, of taking another's identity to heart, does not merge the identities of lover and beloved as the union account requires.

---

[17] Soble, *The Structure of Love*, 273.

By rejecting the union account's understanding of intimate identification, I am therefore able to preserve the individual autonomy of both the beloved and the lover. The beloved's autonomy is preserved through the central role respect plays in the kind of concern for another's well-being as this person that love is. Although I have indicated that there may be occasions for the lover to intervene and so try to reshape the beloved's evaluative perspective, these will be occasions in which the beloved fails properly to exercise his capacity for autonomy, and such attempts, therefore, normally aim, as a part of the overall concern for his well-being that love is, at getting her to gain or regain its proper exercise.

This implies that it is false to say, as many proponents of the union account do, that when something good or bad befalls my beloved, that same good or bad also necessarily befalls me. Although in sharing the values of my beloved I ought to share in her pleasures and pains, in particular her feelings of pride and shame focused on herself, because my emotional pleasures and pains here are motivated by my love for her and so focused on her, they are responses to what has import to her rather than what has import to me. So the good or bad things that befall her are not good or bad for me, though in loving her I ought to feel them just the same.

Nonetheless, we must not ignore potential threats to the lover's autonomy, especially in accounts of love like mine that involve the lover's own well-being coming to depend in some way on the beloved. If the lover is to retain control over her well-being so as to be ultimately responsible for her identity as this person, love must be to some extent voluntary. This is not to imply that we can come to love or stop loving at will: Robert Solomon's claim that love is chosen, an action that we can undertake voluntarily, is surely too strong.[18] Yet to recoil from this to the opposite extreme and claim that love is essentially involuntary and out of our control is equally misguided.[19] I shall argue in Chapter 6 in discussing the justification of love, that love, like valuing, essentially involves the simultaneous invention and discovery of import in a way that can preserve our common-sense understanding of love as an essentially emotional and so passive response to

[18] Solomon, *Love*, 48. Solomon arrives at this conception of love by understanding love to be an emotion and understanding emotions to be, at root, judgments that we make. For a similar claim in which he identifies voluntariness as an "essential feature" of love, see Solomon, *About Love*, 44.

[19] For claims that the attitude of love is not under our voluntary control, see, e.g., Thomas, "Friendship," 221; Thomas, "Reasons for Loving," 472; and Frankfurt, "Autonomy, Necessity, and Love," 136.

import and yet also as an attitude that is under our indirect control in ways that preserve our autonomy as lovers.

This all suggests that the capacity to have person-focused felt evaluations is a capacity whose emergence in an individual does not come in two stages: first reflexive, giving rise to your love for yourself, and then non-reflexive, giving rise to your love for others. Rather, the capacity to love another and the capacity to love yourself emerge simultaneously with the capacity to have person-focused felt evaluations, whether the focus of these felt evaluations is oneself or someone else. Of course, at this point it is merely suggestive; I shall argue for this more fully in Chapter 7, in which I shall consider how a young child can develop into a full-blown person with an independent identity.

One might object to this account of intimate identification as central to love as follows. I have claimed that to love someone is to take her identity to heart and so share her values for her sake. However, I have claimed that to love someone is to allow her and her values to affect your own well-being. Together, these two claims seem to imply that love ought to be transitive: we each ought to love those whom our beloveds love, for whom they love will affect their well-beings as this person, and love just is a concern for someone's well-being as this person. This in turn seems to imply that to love anyone requires loving if not everyone then at least a wide selection of people many of whom you may not even know. That, the objection concludes, is wildly implausible.

Indeed, this would be wildly implausible; in fact, it seems to be a direct consequence of accounts of love that understand love to involve the breaking down of the distinction between the identities of lover and beloved—accounts such as the union account. However, my account does not imply this result, for the imagined objector arrives at this conclusion by subtly misrepresenting my account of intimate identification. In loving someone, I share her values, her concern for her own identity, though I do so for her sake. If she loves someone else and so shares his values, then she does so for his sake. There is, therefore, no requirement that I similarly share his values and so identify with him, for the values that I share with her, insofar as I do so for her sake, will be values focused on her, not on him, even when she is the one valuing these things for his sake. That is, the values of hers that I normally ought to share in loving her are those of her values that are focused on herself, not on other people. Of course, I have also claimed that in loving him her well-being has become dependent on his values, but this is a limited sort of dependence that falls short of union. For in trusting him and so sharing his values for his sake, she must be motivated to act in support of those values in such a way that her actions and motivations in this regard can be the basis of her feeling pride or shame in herself, thereby evaluating herself in ways that affect her identity as this person in light of her support of his values, all as a part of loving him. In loving her, then, I ought in part to be concerned with whether she is properly supportive of those she loves and so share such pride and shame for her sake. However, such a concern for her for her sake once again clearly falls short of my loving him—of my caring about his identity as the person he is for *his* sake. The regress, therefore, never gets started.[20]

It might seem, however, that there is the potential for a related kind of regress of concern that arises in the case of two people who each love the other. If by loving you my identity has come to depend on my being supportive of you—that is, if by loving you I value my being supportive of you, where such a value is constituted by felt evaluations focused on myself—then you, if you love me, ought to share my value of being supportive of you. Indeed, you ought yourself to value being supportive of my values, including this one, and the infinite regress gets started. However, such a regress is not worrisome, for it is analogous to an innocent regress of motivations. Thus, if I care about doing something, then for instrumental reasons I ought to care about motivating myself to act accordingly, and I ought therefore to care about motivating myself to get motivated to act, and so on. In this case the appearance of an infinite regress is innocent because of the structure of instrumental reasons. If I care about doing something, then being motivated to act accordingly is simply a part of my caring about doing it. To the extent to which it makes sense to say that I care about motivating myself to act or that I care about motivating myself to get motivated—because, say, I get frustrated at my failure to set up incentives to motivate me to act—these "cares" are merely instrumental

---

[20] Of course, this conclusion does not mean that I should be indifferent to the people she loves. Insofar as they have import to her, I ought to have a concern for them, albeit for her sake and not for their own. In particular cases this may require, within the limits imposed by my respect for her, that I be concerned with whether she is loving the right people: whether her loves really do have a positive impact on her well-being.

to my more fundamental care to do it, and as such they have doing it as their focus and getting motivated as their subfocus (or motivating myself to get motivated as their sub-subfocus). So there really is no "regress" of cares or motivations at all. The same goes for the apparent regress of values among two people who love each other: the appearance of a regress is innocent because of the rational structure of love. Thus, your valuing being supportive of my value of being supportive of you just is a part of your loving me, and it involves no distinct value beyond your concern for me and my well-being as this person (including your place in it).

5.3 Love, Sacrifice, and Phenomenology

I have claimed that love is an essentially intimate evaluative attitude, and I have now offered an account of that intimacy in terms of intimate identification: to identify intimately with someone just is to have a concern for him that involves not only valuing what he values for his sake but also respecting and trusting him in such a way as to make your identity come to be dependent on his in the way just outlined; such identification is intimate insofar as the concern for another it involves is the same in kind as your concern for yourself. In order to justify this as an account of love, however, I need to show that this account of intimacy enables us to make sense of a variety of phenomena commonly thought to be a part of love.

Soble, in his criticism of union accounts of love, argues that we must be able to understand the lover and the beloved as distinct persons, for to somehow "fuse" their personhood, as union accounts seem to suggest, is to fail to make sense not only of how they can be autonomous individuals but also of how the lover can be motivated to sacrifice herself for the sake of her beloved.[21] Although my account of love as intimate identification is much closer to the union account's appeal to identification as union than is Soble's robust-concern account, it should be clear that my account avoids this problem with autonomy as well. For insofar as love is a concern for another as this person, where his personhood includes his capacity for autonomy, love essentially involves a concern for his autonomy in a way that demands respect. Intimate identification on my account, then,

---

[21] Soble, "Union, Autonomy, and Concern"; Soble, *The Structure of Love*, §12.4.

preserves the distinction among persons Soble rightly worries about. It is less clear, however, how my account can make sense of the possibility of self-sacrifice.

To sacrifice yourself for someone else is not—at least not necessarily—to behave irrationally, giving up something more important for the sake of something less important, and so to say that love may sometimes demand self-sacrifice is not to say that love sometimes demands that we behave irrationally. Rather, the question of self-sacrifice is a question of whether the reasons for acting in a particular way for someone else's sake can sometimes outweigh the reasons you have for acting in another way for your own sake, including preventing certain harms to yourself that might result from some action. This just is a question of priorities: can your concern for someone else's well-being as that particular person sometimes be more important than your concern for your own well-being as this person? That is, can your love for someone else sometimes be more important than your love for yourself? Were this not possible, Soble argues, we could not make sense of your concern for another to be genuinely for *his* sake rather than for your own: necessarily to subordinate your concern for another to your concern for yourself would be to fail to be concerned for him for his sake.

As I have argued, love, as an evaluative attitude, is a commitment to the import of someone as a particular person. As such a commitment, it must have a place within the subject's overall evaluative perspective, a perspective in which not only do things have varying relative degrees of import but their import also can become relatively more pressing in particular circumstances (see §4.3). Thus, although I may love myself more than I love you,[22] I ought to feel your pain in response to the loss of your child more strongly than I feel my pride in receiving a certificate of appreciation from the soccer team I coach: in these circumstances, your well-being is impacted much more severely than mine is. Consequently, I may forgo attending the awards ceremony—something I would otherwise like to do—in order to be with you in your time of need, and I do this for your sake, out of my love for you. Similarly, you may forgo an opportunity to take an exciting yet minor promotion overseas because doing so would

[22] Of course, there is no compelling psychological reason why this must be so, but I shall set aside cases in which I may love someone more than myself as too controversial to use to make the point.

require that your spouse give up his job and his opportunities for career advancement in order to accompany you; in such a case, you might come to feel, the negative impact on his well-being from such a move outweighs the benefits to your well-being, and so you decline the offer out of love for him, for his sake. In such cases, the commitment to the import of another as a particular person that you undertake in loving rationally requires that in circumstances of the right sort you forgo benefits to yourself or even cause harm to yourself for the sake of your beloved; this just is self-sacrifice. There is, therefore, no reason to think that intimate identification undermines the possibility of self-sacrifice; to the contrary, it may in particular circumstances rationally demand it.

Another aspect of love that must be handled by any account by any satisfactory account is its phenomenology. I shall present a basic account here and return to the issue in §6.3, where I discuss, in the context of the fungibility problem, the phenomenology of mourning—of the feeling of the loss of someone you love.

The phenomenology of love—whether love of yourself or of another—can be understood in large part in terms of the phenomenology of the person-focused felt evaluations that constitute it, a phenomenology that differs from that of non-person-focused felt evaluations. Consider first love of yourself. If I value being a philosopher, my pride in giving a particularly good talk feels good—is pleasant—insofar as the import of my being this particular person impresses itself on me in feeling my circumstances to involve a kind of dignity. This pleasure differs from the pleasure I would feel were I merely to care about this, and it does so in virtue of the person-focused emotion's "depth" of content: what impresses itself on me in feeling is the import of my identity and, in particular, the place doing philosophy has within it, so that my feeling of pride is, we might say, a *feeling of identification*. This feeling of identification is a matter of having the target (the talk I just gave, for example) feel good or bad—be pleasant or painful—in a distinctive way precisely because of the way my value of doing philosophy and, more fundamentally, the import of my identity, impress themselves on me in my awareness of the target, so that my good feelings cannot be understood independently of this import. Consequently, the "depth" of content central to person-focused felt evaluations gives rise to a corresponding "depth" of feeling that is simply absent in the case of non-person-focused felt evaluations. The same is true of love of another:

my pride or shame in another feels the way it does because of the way the import of my beloved's identity as this person—and the relevant value as a part of that identity—impresses itself on me pleasantly or painfully in the current circumstances, where the pleasure or pain I feel cannot be separated from that feeling of import.

Of course, our experience of our beloveds will be more complicated than what I have just indicated given the way our person-focused emotions motivate us, either directly or indirectly through our desires. Recall that import impresses itself on us not simply by grabbing and focusing our attention but also by motivating us to act, where the feeling of import is in part the feeling of our being so moved (see §2.2). In part this means that the phenomenology of love arises from our person-focused felt evaluations quite generally, including not just our person-focused emotions but also our second-order desires. In particular, in the case of self-love, negative person-focused emotions like shame, especially if a response to a habitual failing, will normally motivate us (perhaps ineffectually) to change ourselves as a part of the kind of self-respect that is normally a part of our self-love—of our concern for our well-beings as the persons we are. In the case of love of another, however, our respect for our beloveds requires that, in giving due weight to their autonomy as a part of their well-beings, we do not simply impose, even paternalistically, our conception of their well-beings on them. In some cases this can lead us to feel considerable ambivalence, in both emotion and motivation, as we struggle to balance our respect for our beloveds with our sense that they have a misguided sense of the kind of lives they ought to live. Consequently, the phenomenology of love consists not merely in the phenomenology of individual felt evaluations, but involves a sometimes ambivalent amalgam of them. Indeed, as with self-love, such person-focused felt evaluations for another—such feelings, both positive and negative—constitute your emotional attachment to and identification with your beloved; this just is your *affection* for your beloved.

One might be worried that these experiences of delight or displeasure in our beloveds are simply a matter of our living vicariously through them. The worry would be that as vicarious they are somehow merely sympathetic and so mere substitutes for experiences that could in some sense more truly be called our own; such substitute experiences could hardly be properly central to our lives in the way that emotional expressions of love manifestly are. However, it should be clear that although these shared emotional experiences I have appealed to in my account of love might be called "vicarious" insofar as we experience them as having import for the sake of another person, and so although we might understand such experiences to be in some sense "sympathetic," they are not "vicarious" or "sympathetic" in a sense that ought to give rise to this worry. After all, the cares and values of my beloved that I share are not cares and values that I merely imagine having; nor are they merely sympathetic echoes of emotions she already feels (see p. 157). Rather, they are cares and values that I genuinely have for her sake, even when she does not, and so they have become a stable part of my evaluative perspective. This means that the particular felt evaluations I experience as a part of having these cares or values are rationally required of me in particular circumstances, and they are in this way expressive of my love for her. Merely vicarious or merely sympathetic felt evaluations that are not in this way a part of a broader rational pattern of felt evaluations constitutive of my evaluative attitudes toward something are therefore *deficient* as felt evaluations.

So far this is similar to what I have said in §3.3 about the distinction between "mere" sympathy and the kind of sympathy involved in caring about another as an agent. Yet the shared cares and values involved in loving someone also become a part of the lover's identity as this person through her intimate identification with her beloved. For in loving him, she must normally value the place her love for him and the values she shares with him have in her life. This means that these shared values and the felt evaluations that constitute them are far from being substitute experiences that are not properly her own, and so they are not vicarious in any sense that gives rise to the worry.

5.4 Conclusion

To love someone, I have argued, is to be intimately concerned for his well-being as this particular person. Such intimate concern I have cashed out in terms of intimate identification: having a concern for his identity, understood in terms of the sharing of his cares and values for his sake, that is analogous to, but not identical with, your concern for your own identity.

This account of love, I have claimed, enables us to make sense of the idea that love is essentially for particular persons, the way love essentially involves trust and respect, and the intuitive depth of our feelings of pride, shame, and other person-focused emotions focused on others. Moreover, I have shown how, in light of this account of love, we can make sense of various phenomena of love, including self-sacrifice for the sake of your beloved and the phenomenology of love.

Throughout, I have been concerned to avoid providing an egocentric account of the kind of concern love essentially involves and thereby to avoid the excesses of the robust-concern and union accounts of love. Thus, in contrast to robust-concern accounts, my account embraces the intimacy of love, thereby enabling me to distinguish the kind of concern involved in love from other, less intimate forms of concern for others, such as caring, in ways not possible for robust-concern accounts. Moreover, in rejecting an egocentric account of intimate concerns, my account is able to preserve the idea that the lover and beloved are and remain distinct persons in spite of the love, thereby preserving their autonomy, all in ways not possible for union accounts.

This rejection of the egocentrism that implicitly grounds alternative accounts of love opens the door for a more social conception of persons. Indeed, I have in effect argued that to be a person just is to have the capacity for love. For to be a person at all is to have the capacity to love yourself and so to value particular things in the world in such a way as to constitute your identity as this person. This capacity to love yourself gets cashed out in terms of the capacity to have person-focused felt evaluations, a capacity that can be exercised both reflexively in loving yourself and non-reflexively in loving others. To be a person, therefore, is to have the capacity to love others and so intimately to identify with them. Of course, this is still a relatively weak sense of the sociality of persons, though it gives rise to much stronger forms of sociality through the relationships this understanding of love makes possible, as I shall argue in Part III.

Finally, the account of love I have presented is non-reductive, avoiding the reductionism I claimed at the outset of this chapter we ought to resist (see p. 151). Indeed, as I have now shown, the sort of respect, trust, identification, sympathy, and concern for another person that are central to love must all be distinguished from their counterparts in other cases precisely because they are embedded within love and so take on the kind of intimacy that is characteristic of love. Indeed, it would be improper to think that I have reduced love even to the person-focused emotions, for I have argued that apart from the embedding of these emotions within a broader rational pattern that is constitutive of love, we cannot make sense of them as instances of pride, shame, and so on.

It might be thought that the account of love I have offered is idealized, for I have presented it in terms of a kind of rationally structured pattern of person-focused emotions. This might suggest that on my account, love is a kind of ideal that particular loves must meet in order to count as cases of love, so that to the extent to which they fail they are deficient, not really genuine cases of love at all. However, this would be a mistake. For although the rationality of this pattern is normative, and so presents what might be considered a kind of ideal, and although it may be that someone on an occasion fails to respond to her beloved as she rationally ought and so exhibits a deficiency of response, this does not mean the love itself is deficient. Rather, the love itself will be deficient when there is a systematic pattern to the deficiency of responses it involves. One such case is love that is *improperly paternalistic* in that it involves the lover's failing properly to respect the beloved and so failing to be properly deferential to the beloved's autonomous sense of her own identity as this person.[23] Such a failure in (improperly) paternalistic love is a rational failure, and it is this irrationality that underlies its deficiency; nonetheless, so long as such irrationality does not undermine in general the overall pattern of felt evaluations I have argued constitute love, we can still acknowledge paternalistic love as genuinely a case, albeit a deficient one, of love. Another deficient type of love is love that is *deferential* in that the lover respects and trusts the beloved too much, thereby failing in his concern for her well-being.

---

[23] Note that paternalistic love as I describe it here differs from the kind of proper paternalism one might take toward young children, a paternalism that is rationally motivated by the beloved's immaturity or failure properly to exercise her autonomy. Such proper paternalism is a normal part of the concern for another's well-being as this person that is love and, as I shall argue in Ch. 7, can be important to the development of the beloved into a full-blooded person.

6

Justification and Non-Fungibility of Love

I have presented an account of love as an evaluative attitude toward persons as such, and I have cashed out this attitude in terms of projectible, rational patterns of person-focused felt evaluations. When the focus of this pattern is another person, it constitutes your intimately identifying with her by sharing for her sake the cares and values that constitute her identity as this person. In presenting this account, I have argued against the union and robust-concern accounts of love largely by presenting an alternative that avoids the unnecessary and unsatisfactory egocentrism that is implicit in these accounts. We need not, I have argued, understand intimate concerns in terms of my making my beloved's interests be a part of my own; rather, intimate concern ought to be understood in terms of the way in which my concern for my beloved's identity is analogous to my concern for my own identity, and I have cashed out this account in terms of capacities for person-focused felt evaluations, capacities which can be exercised either reflexively (generating a concern for yourself as this person) or not (generating your love for others).

For this to be a satisfying account of love, however, I need to show how it can provide satisfying solutions to problems concerning the justification of love, including what I have called the fungibility problem.

Why should we think that love is the sort of thing that stands in need of justification? It is important not to misunderstand what is at stake here. Laurence Thomas rejects the idea that love can be justified, claiming that

no matter how wonderful and lovely an individual might be, on any and all accounts, it is simply false that a romantically unencumbered person must love that individual on pain of being irrational. Or, there is no irrationality involved in ceasing to love a person whom one once loved immensely, although the person has not changed.[1]

Thus, Thomas concludes, "there are no rational considerations whereby anyone can lay claim to another's love or insist that an individual's love for another is irrational."[2] Yet these claims seem to be simply false, especially when applied more broadly than Thomas's focus on romantic love. My son does have a claim on my love precisely because he is my son; other things being equal, we would think there is something wrong with me if I did not love him. Similarly, my wife has a claim on my love, and if my love failed to persist with no reason for that failure, we would think there is something wrong with my love, if not with me.

Nonetheless, there does seem to be an element of truth in Thomas's claims here. Love, as I have argued, is deeply personal in a way that strikes at our identities as persons. Consequently, the question of whether to love a particular person is a question that must be decided at least in part by us through the exercise of our capacities for agency, lest we lose an important part of our autonomy as persons. Indeed, this just is the "creative" aspect of love that bestowal accounts of love have focused on and which I provisionally endorsed in §1.4.1. However, that we can have a say in whom we love does not imply that we do so arbitrarily, for no reasons. In general, the reasons we have for coming to love someone do not dictate that we shall love him; they are rather considerations in favor or against doing so.[3] To construe the notion of a reason for love as compelling us to love, as Thomas does, is to misconstrue the place such reasons have within our agency.

Even given this clarification, however, the question of whether love can be justified remains. As I suggested in Chapter 1, the difficulty arises from our being pulled in two seemingly opposed directions concerning the nature of love. For first, insofar as we think that our loves are not simply arbitrary, that it does matter whom we love, we think of love as an attitude that is properly responsive to a kind of worth other people have, and in this sense love *discovers* that worth. Accounts of love that construe it as a matter of appraisal, as in effect a cognitive matter, can make sense of such

---

[1] Thomas, "Reasons for Loving," 471.   [2] Ibid., 474.
[3] On this point, see LaFollette, *Personal Relationships*, 63.

discovery straightforwardly.[4] However, these accounts fail to make sense of the second intuition we have concerning the nature of love: inasmuch as love essentially involves intimate identification, our loves are important in defining our sense of what is important in life and so our sense of our identities as persons. For insofar as we are responsible and can be held accountable for our identities as persons, it seems that our loves, and the decision to sustain or terminate our loves, must be to some degree up to us. That is, the rational constraints there are on our loves must have their source at least partially within each of our understandings of who we are to be, so that loving others is in part a matter of autonomously *inventing* ourselves. Thus, the "creative" aspect of love identified by bestowal accounts is revealed as a part of its *intimacy*. Accounts of love that understand it to be a cognitive matter are unable to make sense of this dependence of the value to which love responds on our loving attitudes themselves—of this aspect of the intimacy of love—and to this extent are inadequate. On the other hand, accounts of love as bestowal,[5] as in effect a conative matter, can make sense of how love creates the values things have to us and so can be something for which we can be held responsible. However, such accounts cannot make sense of the way in which our loves are non-arbitrary and so a matter of discovery. Given this, how can we make sense of love simultaneously as intimate and personal and as potentially non-arbitrary and rational?

The issue here is, of course, the same as that raised above in §4.4: insofar as whom we love affects our identities as persons, and inasmuch as our identities are potentially a matter simultaneously of non-arbitrary discovery and autonomous invention, there must be reasons for love, reasons that, in some sense, we autonomously construct. The apparent paradox involved in the idea of non-arbitrary reasons that we construct, of simultaneous discovery and invention, is a genuine paradox only if we accept that our evaluations, and the reasons to which they respond, must be either cognitions or conations; if instead we reject this cognitive–conative divide, we can reconcile the authority of reasons and the autonomy and intimacy of our loves in a way that Thomas could not envisage. Indeed, the account of love I have offered is one that rejects that divide: the attitude of love

---

[4] Such cognitivist accounts of love include: Whiting, "Impersonal Friends"; Velleman, "Love as a Moral Emotion"; Kolodny, "Love as Valuing a Relationship."

[5] Singer, "From *The Nature of Love*"; Singer, *The Pursuit of Love*; Friedman, *What Are Friends For?*

and the distinctive import of others as persons to which it responds form a conceptual package, neither of which is intelligible as existing apart from the other. On my account, therefore, the two directions to which we are pulled in our understanding of love are not incompatible, at least on the face of it: love is simultaneously an appraisal *and* a bestowal of value.[6]

Nonetheless, much work is needed to articulate how the justification of love is possible. It is one thing to show (as I did in my general account of import in Chapter 2) that particular felt evaluations are to be rationally assessed for warrant depending on whether their focuses have import or not, where that import itself is constituted by rational patterns of felt evaluations with it as their focus; it is quite another to show that this whole pattern can be justified in a way that goes beyond mere internal rational coherence. That is, the question of justification is not merely whether I ought to feel, judge, or act a particular way *given* that something has import to me; it is rather whether I ought to care or value or love the things that I do in the first place.

I have already provided a solution to the general problem of the justification of values elsewhere.[7] Although this solution provides an understanding of how we can justify the worth of a certain *kind* of life, what is at issue

---

[6] This idea that autonomous invention is central to the intimacy of love implies that love is in a way a voluntary matter: it is to some extent up to us whom we love and, indeed, what our reasons for such love are. This is not to say that we can simply choose, by making a judgment, to love someone. Robert Solomon holds such a view (calling it an "essential feature" of love: Solomon, *About Love*, 44), though it seems clearly too extreme, for we may well find ourselves unable to love someone even though we decide to, and we may find ourselves loving someone even though we decide not to. The patterns of felt evaluations that partly constitute our loves are not simply under the control of our judgments in the way Solomon seems to require.

On the other hand, this does not mean that love is entirely non-voluntary, as Harry Frankfurt claims (Frankfurt, "Autonomy, Necessity, and Love," 135–6; see also Thomas, "Reasons for Loving," 472 for similar claims). Given the rational interconnections between our evaluative judgments and felt evaluations, we can through evaluative judgment exercise some control over what we care about, value, and love. For details on how such control and the resulting "freedom of the heart" is possible, see Bennett W. Helm, "Freedom of the Heart," *Pacific Philosophical Quarterly* 77, no. 2 (1996): 71–87 and Helm, *Emotional Reason*, especially Ch. 6.

[7] Ibid., especially Ch. 7. This solution is, of course, controversial, and I can only mention that controversy here. Cognitivist accounts of (moral) value assume that such values are things to be discovered and hence exist independent of our attitudes toward them, so that our evaluative attitudes are cognitive, with mind-to-world direction of fit. Non-cognitive accounts reject this, assuming that (moral) values are things we project on to the world with our attitudes (perhaps attitudes that are suitably adjusted given full information, etc.); such attitudes are therefore conative, with world-to-mind direction of fit. I have already presented some arguments against such accounts in part through my rejection of the cognitive–conative divide as it applies to import: import quite generally, including that of personal values, is an object of neither cognition nor conation; indeed, when it comes to personal values, the apparent paradox of simultaneous autonomous invention and rational discovery (see §4.4)

in the justification of love seems importantly different. For with love, the question concerns not how to justify the import to you of a particular kind of thing but rather how to justify the import to you of a *particular* person, and not merely as an instance of a particular kind. Indeed, this throws us right into the heart of the fungibility problem: if all we can do in justifying love is to justify loving a certain kind of person, then it seems we can always substitute for our current beloved someone else who is relevantly similar without any loss of value: our beloveds would be fungible. Indeed, this fungibility seems to be a fundamental problem for any account of justification: justification, it seems, *must* appeal to properties that can, at least in principle, be multiply instantiated in order for that appeal to be rationally binding on anyone similarly situated.[8] As Niko Kolodny puts the point:

The claim that nonrelational features are reasons for love implies, absurdly, that insofar as one's love for (say) Jane is responsive to reasons, it will accept any relevantly similar person as a replacement.[9]

As I indicated in §1.4.2, it is common to understand the fungibility problem in terms of the possibility of trading up: if love is to be justified by appealing to properties of the beloved, then it seems I have reason to trade up when someone new comes along exhibiting these properties

---

provides an additional reason to reject it. Of course, such arguments on their own are inadequate to resolve the controversy, but I cannot say more here.

[8] This claim seems to run contrary to Robert Nozick's understanding of the reasons we have for romantic love:

Since a romantic mate eventually comes to be loved, not for any general dimensions or 'score' on such dimensions . . . but for his or her own particular and nonduplicable way of embodying such general traits, a person in love could not make any coherent sense of his 'trading up' to *another*. [Nozick, "Love's Bond," 82]

It is not clear, however, what Nozick means in talking of the "particular and nonduplicable way of embodying" a trait. What he seems to mean is not just that my wife has a disposition to kindness, but the particular way in which her disposition to kindness is manifest in her life. Although it may be highly unlikely that such a highly specific trait would be duplicated in another person, especially once we include the many other specific dispositions to desirable traits she has, it is still duplicable in principle and as such does not seem to solve the fungibility problem. Moreover, it is highly questionable whether the reason I love my wife rather than someone else who is, in some sense, equally kind or even kinder comes down to the precise dispositions my wife has to exhibit kindness in particular situations, a disposition that must be specified with such a fineness of grain that it distinguishes her from everyone else. Would the reasons I have to love my wife be in any way changed if her disposition to kindness were to change so as to conform to someone else's? Surely not.

[9] Kolodny, "Love as Valuing a Relationship," 135. Kolodny puts the point here in terms of non-relational features; he goes on to argue that we can justify love in terms of relational properties, acknowledging that even relational properties can be multiply instantiated and so lead to replaceability of our loves, though this is a bullet he is prepared to bite. See above, §1.4.2, pp. 28 ff.

(and so the same justification) to a greater degree, a prospect that seems to undermine the kind of commitment we normally take love to involve. Common solutions, then, involve either biting the bullet,[10] denying that the problem is a problem in practice because it is very unlikely that another would duplicate the relevant properties of your beloved,[11] or construing the kind of commitment love involves in such a way as to lock the lover in to having just one beloved.[12] Each of these solutions involves a misconstrual of the problem.

The point of my calling this the *fungibility* problem is to emphasize that the worry is not simply about whether we can be justified in replacing our beloveds but is rather about whether they are replaceable *without loss*. Of course, there is a sense in which our beloveds can be replaced: they may die or move away, and someone new may come to occupy something like their place of prominence in our hearts. Indeed, even less dramatically we might through a gradual process come to love someone new and have that love gradually become more important to us than, and eventually displace or even replace, one or more of our old loves. None of this implies that we have in any way failed in the kind of commitment we make to someone in loving her or that our coming to love the new person is in some way unjustified. Nonetheless, what does seem to be required is that in loving someone you find her to have a kind of worth such that to lose her is to lose something of value for which we cannot simply be compensated by a new love, even of someone with similar properties. The fungibility problem starts from this observation and raises the question of what justifies our love for another and what might happen if we have the possibility of trading up from our current beloved to someone else whom we would be, in some sense, more justified in loving.

In this chapter, after presenting a brief and necessarily inadequate overview of my account of the justification of values and priorities in §6.1, I shall then take on the fungibility problem directly in §6.2. Given that the issue with fungibility is that of replaceability without loss, when

---

[10] See, for example, Nico Kolodny's discussion of "relationship *Doppelgängers*" in Kolodny, "Love as Valuing a Relationship," 147. See also Badhwar, "Friends as Ends in Themselves"; Badhwar, "Love."

[11] Ibid., 63; Soble, *The Structure of Love*, Ch. 13.

[12] According to Nozick, romantic love involves forming a "we" with them, such that you cannot form a "we" with two others independently and simultaneously. See Nozick, "Love's Bond," 78.

JUSTIFICATION OF VALUES AND PRIORITIES   181

you do not yet love someone, when she does not yet have this distinctive import to you, the issue of loss, of your losing that import, cannot yet arise. Consequently, I shall distinguish the question of the *discernment* of love (what makes someone worthy of your potential love or more worthy of that love than others?) from the question of the *constancy* of love (what justifies your continuing—or ceasing—to love someone?). Worries about fungibility arise, therefore, only in the case of justifying the constancy of love. Finally, I shall turn in §6.3 to examine the kinds of losses to which we are subject in loving someone so as to have a better understanding of what non-fungibility—irreplaceability without loss—comes to in the case of love.

6.1 Justification of Values and Priorities

To love someone is to find him to have import to you as this particular person. In providing an account of import in general and of love in particular, I have focused primarily on felt evaluations: it is projectible patterns of felt evaluations with a common focus that constitute the import of that focus to you. Although I have acknowledged at various points (such as in §2.3) that evaluative judgments have a place in the rational pattern that constitutes import, I have emphasized felt evaluation and, in particular, the emotions largely for rhetorical purposes: in general, I believe, too much emphasis has been placed on the role of judgment and belief and, consequently, too little attention has been paid to emotions and the indispensable role they play in our mental lives, including their role in constituting import. Nonetheless, when it comes to deliberation, the explicit articulation of thoughts made possible by judgment is indispensable.

The indispensability of evaluative judgment in deliberation about value, however, should not be overemphasized. As I already argued in §2.3, we should not conceive of the evaluations we make explicit in judgment as being somehow intrinsically more rational or more fundamental than those implicit in emotion. Rather, felt evaluations and evaluative judgments that share a common focus are a part of the same projectible, rational pattern that constitutes import, such that the failure to have the appropriate felt evaluations consistent with your evaluative judgments is a rational failure that brings into question not only whether that focus really does have import to you but also thereby the truth of those evaluative judgments. Consequently, deliberation succeeds only if it is able to secure, by and large, consistency among our evaluative judgments and felt evaluations, and providing an account of deliberation about import therefore requires uncovering the rational interconnections between emotions and judgments.

In deliberating about import, you must bring to bear both in judgment and felt evaluation certain evaluative concepts that enable you to articulate and endorse the import you find things to have. The content of these concepts is determined in both denotation and inference in part by their expression and use in language as this is determined within a linguistic community, as well as by the way in which these concepts make intelligible broad patterns of emotional responsiveness of members of this community.[13] Nonetheless, when we set aside universal moral values and instead focus on those evaluative concepts relevant to distinctively personal values (that emerge from self-love) and to our loving others, it should be clear that the content of these evaluative concepts is not entirely determined by the broader community in this way. For insofar as the kind of import at issue in our loves (including self-love) serves to define our identities as the persons we each are, it must be to some extent up to each of us not merely what we in fact value in these ways but also, if deliberation is to be possible, what we ought to value in these ways, so that such import is to this extent relative to the individual. In other words, although we can and should all agree that being kind, courageous, and so on are good and that being miserly, self-indulgent, and so on are bad, and although we can and should all agree about certain paradigm examples of these thick evaluative concepts, reasonable people can disagree about whether a particular case should be characterized in terms of courage or miserliness, and so reasonable people can disagree about precisely how these concepts ought to be understood. It is only because we can with good reason arrive at different refinements of particular thick evaluative concepts that we can arrive at different conclusions about what should have import to us.

---

[13] Precisely what such intelligibility consists in is something I shall address shortly.

A central question in deliberation about import, therefore, concerns what reasons you can have for a particular refinement of one of these evaluative concepts, a concept that then gets used to justify the import something has to you. It is in answering this question that we must examine more closely the rational interconnections among evaluative judgments and felt evaluations with a common focus.

Of course, it is not enough merely to articulate and endorse in judgment a refinement to an evaluative concept. Given the way evaluative judgments and felt evaluations together form a single evaluative perspective, any such proposed conceptual refinement ought to inform not merely our judgments and inferences but rather our entire evaluative outlook, including our felt evaluations. Moreover, as I have argued, the failure to exhibit a substantial part of the pattern of felt evaluations and evaluative judgments with a common focus can undermine the rationality of that pattern and thereby bring into question what really has import to one. This is true not merely in cases in which I judge that something has import to me but fail to feel the relevant pattern of felt evaluations; it is also true in more fine-grained cases concerning the precise understanding of the well-being of something I care about, as when the understanding of its well-being that is implicit in my felt evaluations does not correspond with that which I explicitly articulate in judgment. In such a case, I may try to impose my explicit understanding on my felt evaluations by applying rational pressure on them via self-interpretation and by more overtly trying to instill in myself through the exercise of my will the relevant habits of response that constitute this pattern of felt evaluations.[14] Yet in such a case the failure of my felt evaluations to fall in line ought to call into question the correctness of the fine-grained understanding of its well-being I have articulated explicitly in judgment. Insofar as such an understanding is articulated in terms of newly refined evaluative concepts, calling this understanding into question is a matter of calling the refinement of these evaluative concepts into question.

It should be clear that such a refinement is a non-trivial achievement: we cannot simply elucidate evaluative concepts any way we please, for they must remain true to our experience of import in felt evaluation. For

---

[14] Precisely how we can do this is a matter of how "freedom of the heart" is possible; see Helm, "Freedom of the Heart."

to be intelligible as a genuine refinement or improvement in an evaluative concept, a particular elucidation ought to inform your felt evaluations by articulating more clearly their implicit understanding of import and of their focus. Although the result may be that your felt evaluations simply fall in line with your explicit understanding of the relevant evaluative concepts, this need not be the case, as I hinted above. For to revise in judgment your understanding of these concepts is to commit yourself to altering the rational structure of the patterns of your felt evaluations, and yet your felt evaluations may be generally recalcitrant, thereby undermining that commitment. Consequently, it may take considerable and sustained effort to instill in yourself the habits of response that are properly informed by the concept. Indeed, such an effort may require successive refinements in your understanding of the concept before the concept can succeed in making sense of your felt evaluations. In this way, you can come to articulate in terms of the newly refined concept how your former evaluative perspective was confused and so why, in light of that confusion, portions of your experience of import were mistaken. In this way, we can understand that refinement as a genuine improvement, as a *discovery* of the imports things have to us.

Nonetheless, it should also be clear that this refinement is potentially the product of the exercise of the subject's autonomy. For it may require considerable creativity to arrive at a proposed refinement of an evaluative concept, and it may require sustained effort and will power to get this concept to inform your felt evaluations, thereby revealing it to be true of your experience of import. Indeed, as I have argued, the very process of self-interpretation that is central to this effort itself creates indeterminacies in your patterns of felt evaluations, the resolution of which requires making decisions that delineate these patterns in new ways. When an exercise of such rational control over what we care about and value is successful, both in creating a new and improved understanding of the relevant concepts and in exercising control over your evaluative perspective, you have thereby had a say not merely in how it is appropriate to refine your sensitivity to import but also in the import that this sensitivity enables you to discover. This just is a matter of *autonomous invention* that is fully compatible with the discovery of import precisely because, in rejecting the cognitive–conative divide with respect to our evaluative perspectives, import and our responses to import are understood to be conceptually on a par.

What I have just presented is a rather abstract and compressed overview of how deliberation about values is possible. Deliberation about priorities, as I have argued elsewhere, proceeds in essentially the same way: we come to understand certain values as being more important than others, at least in particular situations, in terms of the worthiness of the kind of life informed by such a priority, a life made intelligible as, for example, honorable or self-indulgent. Of course, this abstract overview is far from a complete account. I have provided more complete arguments for it elsewhere,[15] and I shall provide examples of how this abstract account can be applied in the case of the discernment and constancy of love in §6.2.

6.2 Discernment and Constancy of Love

I have argued that love is a matter of intimate identification in which you come to have a concern for the identity of your beloved that is the same in kind as your concern for your own identity. Indeed, this intimacy, which I have cashed out in terms of your sharing your beloved's identity for her sake and valuing the place that shared identity has in your own life, is absolutely central to understanding the relevant evaluative attitude as that of love: absent this sort of intimacy, I have argued, we cannot properly distinguish love from other, less personal attitudes toward others, such as compassion. An account of the justification of love, therefore, must preserve the intimacy by making intelligible why I should not simply admire this person but actually love him and thereby identify with him intimately.

To try to answer this question by appealing to properties of your beloved seems problematic precisely because of the fungibility problem: the properties justifying your loving this person seem equally to justify your loving others who share those same properties. Indeed, this problem is not eliminated when we consider relational properties, since those might well be shared,[16] and it is unclear how historical properties, which would be unique to an individual, could provide any justification for love. So, it

---

[15] Helm, *Emotional Reason*.
[16] This is a problem for Kolodny's understanding of justification, as I noted above (§1.4.2, p. 28).

seems that those like me who want to provide an account of the justification of love must have some bullet biting in store.

The worry here is overblown, however, and we can address worries about fungibility without backtracking from the idea that in justifying love we do so at least in part by appealing to properties that might well be shared by others.

Part of what many responses to the fungibility problem forget is that we do not simply love one person at a time.[17] When you encounter a new person you might come to love, the question is not normally whether you should love this new person *instead* of someone you already love but rather *in addition* to your current beloveds. Of course, coming to love someone new will not leave your current loves unaffected, for the new love will make demands on your time, attention, physical and emotional energies, and so on, all of which, given our limited capacities, will affect the amount of time, energy, and so on that you can devote to other people you love or other things you value. Indeed, in this respect the impact of adding a new love to your life is similar to the impact of adding a new value (or even of changed circumstances involving an existing value), and in each case the question of what justifies adopting a new love or value is similar: it is a question ultimately of priorities and so of the place the new love or value can justifiably have within your overall evaluative perspective. Thus, the prospect of a new job across the country or even just a promotion involving new responsibilities and corresponding commitments may force me to rethink the place of particular loves in my life in much the same way that the possibility of acquiring a new love may do so, as when a divorced parent must weigh her priorities and the place her love of her children has in her life in deciding whether to begin dating to search for a new love.

This means that the considerations that justify initially coming to love your current beloved will normally be different from the considerations that justify now coming to love someone else sharing all relevant properties with her precisely because you already love your current beloved precisely because your background evaluative perspective will be different between these two cases. Consequently, adequately addressing the concern with

---

[17] Contra Nozick, "Love's Bond," 78. Nozick's claim is false even when we constrain ourselves, as he does, to romantic love.

justification at issue in the fungibility problem requires providing an account that does not simply focus on the justification of a particular love in isolation from other loves. Standard presentations of the fungibility problem miss this fundamental point, which implies that we should be careful to distinguish cases in which the concern is with justifying coming to love someone from those in which the concern is with justifying continuing an existing love. I shall treat these separately.

6.2.1 Discernment

Consider first how we can justify coming to love someone. I have argued that love is discerning: a particular person may have certain properties that make him more worthy of love for you than other people are. In part, these properties are intrinsic to that person: his virtues or sense of humor, for example. Yet they can also be relational properties; for example, we might think, the fact that someone is a close relation normally gives us reason to love her. Thus, when your parents adopt a child, it would seem that his being your adopted brother provides you with a reason to love him. In some cases, these properties—especially relational properties—seem to provide the person with a kind of claim to your love. In other cases, the reasons these properties provide can be outweighed by other considerations, leaving room for choice as to whether to love him or not. In these latter cases, the question of how love can be justified clearly involves showing how the reasons provided for love are also consistent with individual choice, so that to be discerning in choosing your loves is in part an exercise of autonomy. After discussing such cases, I will argue that autonomy is properly involved even in the former cases.

The kind of autonomy we have in determining our loves is clearly not absolute. We cannot simply decide to love someone and have that settle the matter; nor is it always possible for us in every case to exercise control over our motivations, emotions, and other evaluative responses to get ourselves to love someone, even after much effort. Nonetheless, this does not imply, as Harry Frankfurt seems sometimes to suggest, that because love is not simply a matter of choice ("love . . . is not under our *direct and immediate* voluntary control"), it is not under voluntary control at all: "the issue is not up to [us] *at all*. . . . In matters like these, we are subject to a necessity that forcefully constrains the will. . . . Loving is circumscribed by a necessity of that kind: what we love and what we fail to love is not up to us.''[18] We can exercise some degree of direct control over our felt evaluations and so over what we care about, value, and love. Clarifying the nature of this control will also reveal how in loving we are responsive to reasons that we, in some sense, simultaneously create for ourselves.[19]

Assume that Arthur has recently met Bill, someone he finds easy to get along with. Initially the attraction he feels for him stems from certain interests and tastes they have in common: they both like similar kinds of music, are both dedicated volunteers for Habitat for Humanity, and both enjoy playing semi-competitive badminton. Consequently he finds his thoughts immediately turning to Bill when he learns of a concert he wants to attend, and he is pleased and excited by Bill's acceptance of an invitation to go together. One day, as summer approaches, Bill tells Arthur that he has just received an award and promotion; "with this," he says as Arthur begins to feel something like pride for Bill welling up in him, "I can pursue in earnest my goal of seeing a baseball game at every major and minor league stadium in North America!" This remark takes Arthur aback: he never knew Bill had such an obsession with baseball. As they talk and it becomes clear that this is no passing fancy but a life-long dream to which he has already devoted considerable time, effort, and money, Arthur begins to question whether he can or ought to forge an intimate connection with someone who is capable of putting so much stock in such a trivial and insignificant pursuit as this: given the centrality of this plan to Bill's identity, sharing his value here conflicts fundamentally with Arthur's sense of what is worthwhile in life.

Thoughts like these lead Arthur to question what sort of relationship he has had with Bill all along. Does he identify with Bill in a way that makes intelligible feelings of pride at Bill's promotion? Or is the pleasure he feels at this news merely joy for Bill's sake, a joy that does not involve the same intimacy of identification? Having now learned about Bill's obsession with baseball, Arthur may reinterpret his past feelings and find that he comes to feel differently about Bill in the future: he's an enjoyable companion and someone Arthur cares about, but not in a way that involves the kind of

---

[18] Frankfurt, "On Love, and Its Reasons," 44–6, my emphasis. Although Frankfurt later says that "it may at times be within our power to control [what we love] indirectly" (49), he provides no clear account of how this is possible, and it seems to be inconsistent with his insistence that our loves are not arbitrary insofar as they are determined by "the contingent necessities of love" (48).

[19] I will not be able to provide a complete account here. For details, see Helm, "Freedom of the Heart," and Helm, *Emotional Reason*, especially ch. 6.

intimate devotion and trust of his values characteristic of love. Thus Bill's properties—including not just his integrity, intelligence, inquisitiveness, and taste but also his obsession—are what Arthur appeals to in coming to decide that, all things considered, he ought not love him, a decision that he can use, through self-interpretation, to shape not just past and future felt evaluations but also, thereby, the entire pattern constituting his caring for him.

Of course, if this appeal to certain of Bill's properties is to be intelligible as an appeal to reasons for love, it must be possible for it to be mistaken. Perhaps Arthur's decision does not succeed in bringing his felt evaluations along with it: although he tries to interpret his feelings of pleasure at Bill's promotion to be a matter of joy, he nonetheless feels there to be more "depth" to it than this, and in spite of his intellectual dismissal of Bill's "obsession," he nonetheless feels motivated to engage Bill in activity in pursuit of this dream. That is, he feels it to be no mere obsession but rather finds that he emotionally trusts Bill's sense of its importance to him. Consequently, he ends up going to some local minor league games with Bill and finds that he comes to share Bill's excitement and enthusiasm for attending (though feels like he would not go on his own). The resulting conflict between his emotional experiences and his judgments leads him to question his intellectual assessment of Bill's valuing attending baseball games as a frivolous obsession, for he finds that he can share the feeling of its worth. As he thinks about it, he comes to realize that this value is not what he formerly thought—a foolish dedication to a boring game in which little happens—but rather a value of the social phenomenon that a baseball game is: seeing a baseball game is not simply a matter of being a passive observer of events that take place elsewhere in the stadium but is instead a matter of being an active participant in certain traditions with others with whom one comes to feel a kind of camaraderie, all of which differs from stadium to stadium. Through his trust in Bill, Arthur has come to appreciate, in a way in which he could not before intellectually recognize, the import this can have for others.

The upshot is that Arthur has come to a new appreciation of Bill: not as a philistine who squanders his time and talents on frivolous pastimes but rather as having more rather than less refined sensibilities that are trustworthy responses to that which can intelligibly have a place within a rich and rewarding life. This in turn makes it possible for him once again to reinterpret his felt evaluations potentially as person-focused, with Bill as their focus and so once again to exhibit the pattern of felt evaluations constitutive of love. It should be clear that Arthur's coming to see this is not simply a matter of his coming to see the import that was there anyway. The issue is not simply a matter of discovering exactly what it is that Bill values; we can assume that he was previously able to articulate this accurately as the result of conversations with Bill. What he was formerly lacking and has now acquired is what I have called an "appreciation" of the import this has to Bill: a full understanding, including an emotional understanding, of its worth to him. This is to a significant extent a matter of his coming to understand Bill himself: such an appreciation involves a sense of the place this has within the overall life Bill leads, a life itself that Arthur can understand to be worthwhile, even if not a life for himself.

This understanding of Bill is not value neutral. For it is to this understanding of Bill and his properties (as having trustworthy and refined sensibilities rather than as being a philistine) that Arthur appeals in justifying his love and so his sharing of Bill's values, including the value of being a spectator at baseball games, albeit for Bill's sake. Moreover, because this understanding successfully informs—and enables Arthur to make sense of—his felt evaluations, both past and future, we can understand it to be an *improvement* on his previous understanding. In this way, Arthur's resolution of the rational conflict between his judgments and felt evaluations is intelligible as a discovery of the relevant properties of Bill justifying that love. Nonetheless, it is also a conclusion Arthur arrives at as the result of the exercise of his autonomy in interpreting and articulating not only his sense of the kind of person Bill is but also his own felt evaluations. When successful (as we have assumed in Arthur's case), such an articulation makes determinate these felt evaluations in ways that shapes their subsequent patterns and constitutes the import of their focus; in this sense, Arthur has simultaneously invented the import Bill has come to have for him.

All of this implies that, in a sense, Frankfurt is right in claiming that reasons for love depend in part on whether we find ourselves capable of loving.[20] Whether the appeal to a particular person's properties succeeds

---

[20] Harry G. Frankfurt, "On Caring," in Frankfurt, *Necessity, Volition, and Love*, 179. Frankfurt's claim is that our being able to love *itself* is a reason for loving, a claim which I find hard to make sense of.

in providing reasons for our loving her depends in part on whether an understanding of the person as having these properties succeeds in informing and so shaping the felt evaluations constitutive of our love. Similarly, we can now see that David Velleman is also partly right in claiming that the way in which love is discerning depends on the contingent fit between the beloved's dignity and the lover's receptivity to it.[21] Of course, for Velleman this contingent fit is intended to explain without justifying why we love one person rather than others, for he claims that what makes someone worthy of love is precisely their humanity, which they share equally with everyone else. By contrast, my claim is that one's emotional receptivity to someone can be part of what justifies his love insofar as it has a place within an overall evaluative perspective that is informed by an understanding of particular evaluative properties of his beloved, an understanding that is elucidated from within through processes of deliberation and reinterpretation. In this way, he can justify his love in part through an emotional responsiveness that makes that love be ineliminably personal inasmuch as it is arrived at only through the exercise of his autonomy. Hence, contra Velleman, the discernment of love is justificatory.

I have claimed that in justifying coming to love someone, we appeal to her properties. Even setting aside worries about fungibility, which I have indicated do not yet apply when we are concerned with coming to love someone inasmuch as the issue of loss is not yet on the table, it may seem that this is an impersonal basis for love, contrary to what I have just claimed. Indeed, Jennifer Whiting argues that in justifying love we must appeal to properties that others might well share, so that the justification you have for loving one person will be the same as the justification you have for loving a relevantly similar person whom you have never met. Although we can explain but not justify why you come to love the one person rather than the other by appeal to "historical and psychological accident," the justification of love itself is in this sense an impersonal affair.[22] This is a mistake, for three reasons.

First, I have argued that love is a matter of caring about someone as the particular person she is, as having a particular identity that is defined by her values. Hence, the properties we appeal to in justifying loving someone are an appropriate basis for that love only if they are more or less central to her

---

[21] Velleman, "Love as a Moral Emotion," 372.   [22] Whiting, "Impersonal Friends," 23.

identity, for otherwise we would not love her for who she is and so would not properly love *her*. However, I have also argued that particular values are not intelligible apart from their place within that identity: to value something just is to find it to be a part of your identity as this person, and I have understood this by understanding the emotions constitutive of your values to be focused on yourself and so constitutive of, ultimately, your love for yourself. This means that what justifies my love for someone cannot be traits taken in isolation of their place in defining her identity overall. Of course, this does not imply that in loving someone I do so for *all* the traits that enter into her identity; I may with good reason wish that she had a different identity in certain respects. Nonetheless, it does imply that we should not conceive, as Whiting apparently does, of these traits as a kind of checklist: to be relevantly similar with respect to those traits that form the basis of my love is for these traits to have as well relevantly similar places within the overall identities of the person in question.[23] Consequently, although what does the justificatory work is not just the traits but the type of role they have in defining a person's identity, it nonetheless seems a bit of a stretch to understand the appeal to these traits in justifying love to be impersonal.

Second, we can strengthen the case against the idea that the justification of coming to love someone is impersonal by recognizing, as I argued above, that what makes certain traits and their place within a person's identity justify my coming to love him is in part the way in which I find myself able, partly through an exercise of autonomy, to respond to him in finding him trustworthy and so in sharing his values for his sake. This means that whether certain traits-within-an-identity succeeds in justifying my love is not something that is determinate in advance of my encountering and responding to the particular person. It is always possible that, in encountering someone who seemed to be relevantly similar to someone else I am justified in coming to love, I find myself unable or unwilling to respond to him as I did to her, and this may lead me to refine my understanding of precisely what traits-within-an-identity were the basis of my coming to love her.

Third (and related), we must not forget the place one's priorities play in the justification of coming to love someone. The willingness to trust

---

[23] Niko Kolodny seems to make this same mistake, though he understands the properties on the basis of which we love others to be relational properties, as is indicated by his talk of "relationship *Doppelgängers*"; see Kolodny, "Love as Valuing a Relationship," 147.

someone and so share his values for his sake itself, and consequently the justification of coming to love him, depends on the fullness of your own life and whether there is room for an additional love, with all its demands on your time, attention, and other resources.[24] Consequently, Whiting is wrong to think that historical and psychological accidents can explain but not justify love: what makes the justification of coming to love someone ineliminably personal is precisely the way in which that justification itself depends on such historical and psychological accidents—without undermining the idea that it is genuinely justification at issue. This means that what justifies a particular love is not just that the beloved is *a* person who has certain traits (as on Whiting's impersonal construal), but rather that the beloved is *this* particular person.

6.2.2 Constancy

So far I have discussed how we can justify coming to love someone; it is now time to consider how we can justify continuing a love—or giving up on it. It is here that worries about fungibility become important; nonetheless, in this section I shall present only a partial solution to the fungibility problem, focusing as I shall on issues of justification. Another important way to address worries about fungibility is to think more clearly about the nature of the sort of loss that is at issue when we lose or give up on a love; I shall do this in §6.3.

Shakespeare begins Sonnet 116 as follows:

> Let me not to the marriage of true minds
> Admit impediments. Love is not love
> Which alters when it alteration finds . . .

Although there seems to be something deeply right about this—genuine love is constant, steadfast—we must not take it too literally: love should not be a rigid straitjacket, locking the lover in no matter who the beloved becomes.[25] Rather, as Amélie Rorty notes, love ought to be "dynamically permeable" insofar as our loves—and we ourselves—are changed in response to changes in our beloveds.[26] Yet why should we think that love

---

[24] Of course, this raises questions of fungibility: perhaps faced with this new person I ought instead to cease loving someone else to make room for him. I shall address such questions in §6.2.2.

[25] See Neera Kapur Badhwar's criticism of Nozick's rigid union account: Badhwar, "Love," 63.

[26] Rorty, "The Historicity of Psychological Attitudes," 77.

demands a kind of constancy? Rorty offers two reasons. First, "we sense ourselves [to be] fragile, vulnerable in the world," so that we treasure those who treasure us and can protect us when things go badly for us.[27] Second, in some cases we find ourselves being defined by our lover's (or hater's) perceptions of us; in such cases

> it is important to us that our enemies and lovers—the objects of psychological attitudes—perceive us aright, sensitive to the changes in us. Because we crystallize around what they focus, it is important that they continue to love or hate us for what we are.[28]

What is striking about both of these answers is that they are concerned fundamentally with what the beloved gains out of being loved with an appropriate constancy. Consequently, Rorty understands the constancy of love to be extrinsically valuable insofar as it is justified by reasons having little to do with the love itself. This is, I believe, a mistake. For the value of the constancy of love ought to be understood in terms that are intrinsic to the love itself: in terms, that is, of the import the beloved has to you as this person. As I have argued, love is essentially a concern for the well-being of someone as the particular person she is; insofar as persons are normally autonomous creatures, such concern for a person's well-being must involve not only a kind of respect for the understanding she has of herself that is a part of her self-love and that defines her identity but also a kind of trust in that identity so that you come to share her values for her sake and value the place your love for her has within your own identity. It is this aspect of love that makes intelligible its constancy: other things being equal, our loves ought to exhibit constancy as a part of the kind of concern for another's well-being as this particular person that love is, a concern that is essentially constituted by rational patterns of felt evaluations that project into the future and counterfactual situations. The constancy of love is intrinsic to love, and its value cannot be separated from the value of love itself.

This does not mean that our loves must be unconditional; indeed, that is the point of the "other things being equal" clause just above. As I indicated in my discussion of respect and trust above (§5.2, p. 159 ff.), there can be

---

[27] Rorty, "The Historicity of Psychological Attitudes," 80. A similar view can be found in John M. Cooper, "Aristotle on Friendship," in *Essays on Aristotle's Ethics*, ed. Amélie O. Rorty (Berkeley, CA: University of California Press, 1980), 301–40.

[28] Rorty, "The Historicity of Psychological Attitudes," 80–1.

considerable tension between your concern for someone's well-being as this person and your respect and trust of his values when, for example, you disagree on what it is permissible or mandatory to value. Such was the case, perhaps, with Zacarias Moussaoui, convicted of involvement in the terrorist attacks of September 11, and his mother, Aïcha el-Wafi. After hearing Moussaoui's rants in court, damning the US and swearing allegiance to Osama bin Laden, she was quoted as saying that he was no longer her son.[29] Without knowing the details of this particular case, it nonetheless seems reasonable to interpret this remark in part to mean that she thereby renounces her love for him and does so because she finds that she can no longer share his values for his sake and so can no longer identify with him: she rejects and, indeed, is scornful of his sense of what is important in life.[30] It is this scorn—not merely for some of Moussaoui's values but for those values that are most fundamental to his identity—that seems to justify her giving up her love.

How exactly would such justification work? We might imagine el-Wafi to deliberate as follows.[31] The mere fact that it is difficult for her to share Moussaoui's values is not on its own a reason to give up loving him. After all, she already has some reason to continue loving him: he is her son. Indeed, this might lead her to think that she ought to love him and so ought to work harder to get herself to identify with him. However, such attempts may fail utterly, and this failure ought to lead her to question the concept of a son that informs her judgment that she ought to love him. Reflecting on the possibility of foster and step sons, she may come to realize that she ought to construe the concept of a son not merely in biological terms, but in more social terms: as a matter of having certain sorts of social roles within the social structure that is a family. After all, mere biological ties cannot on their own make it that he is worthy of her love. Were Moussaoui otherwise a reasonable or even marginal member of the family—a brother to his siblings, a son to his father—it would not seem appropriate to draw the conclusion that he is no longer her son, but he is not: he has completely

---

[29] *Time Magazine*, March 13, 2006.

[30] For some relevant background, see Aïcha El-Wafi, Matthias Favron, and Sophie Quaranta, *Mon Fils Perdu* (Paris: Plon, 2006).

[31] Given my account of justification (§6.1), it is important that she herself do the deliberating and arrive at the conclusion, for such deliberation is in part an exercise of her autonomy. Hence I am here imagining what she might have been thinking and feeling—imaginings that, while based in some historical facts, are certainly fictionalized in other respects.

rejected them all and so, she concludes, is no longer her son. In this context, what formerly justified her sustaining her love for him (his being her son) has proved no longer to be true in the relevant sense, and so her inability, her unwillingness, to identify intimately with him, to trust and respect him, reveals an understanding not only of his identity as unworthy of support but also therefore of him as unworthy of love.

Thus imagined, it should be clear that el-Wafi's unwillingness to identify with Moussaoui is not a mere refusal to do something unpleasant, the result, perhaps, of a whim or even simple exhaustion. It is rather an unwillingness that is rationally required from within certain central parts of her evaluative perspective, and it is precisely this unwillingness that makes possible a new overall understanding of what is important, an understanding that, through its elucidation of relevant evaluative concepts, comes to inform that very unwillingness. It is the mutual reinforcement of this conceptual elucidation and her overall evaluative perspective that makes intelligible both the elucidation and the resulting evaluative perspective as improvements on their predecessors, improvements which in turn supply reasons for the conclusion that Moussaoui is unworthy of her love.

The story need not end here, however. El-Wafi reportedly changed her mind, saying subsequently, "He's my son, and I love him no matter what."[32] Once again we can imagine (with only a partial basis in fact) reasons why this might be so. Throughout her adult life, el-Wafi struggled and sacrificed on behalf of her children; it is reasonable to think, then, that she valued being a mother to her children. Perhaps, then, she felt ashamed: not only of herself for failing, in her rejection of Moussaoui, to be a good mother but also of him for his hurtful outbursts in court. Such shame conflicts with her prior claim that he is no longer her son: to abandon him in this way is to fail to be the kind of mother that she aspires to be, and her continued shame in him reveals a continued identification that belies her claimed rejection of him. Thus, her attempted elucidation of the concept of a son merely in terms of extant social roles is revealed as inadequate because it has failed in this way to inform her felt evaluations. Hence she is led to a new conclusion: we ought not construe the concept of a son in terms of current social relations, for the biological and historical bonds between them cannot be so easily dismissed. To be a genuine son,

---

[32] Interview with Bruce Crumley, *Time Magazine*, April 20, 2006.

one meriting the love of a parent, is not merely to occupy certain social
relations but to be such that you ought to do so; this comes to be true of
someone by virtue of biological relations and a history of social interactions
which together institute demands for a kind of dutiful loyalty that parents
and children have to each other.

Assume that this further elucidation of what it is to be a son (and
a mother) comes to inform and make intelligible her felt evaluations,
including the feelings of shame both of herself and of Moussaoui. Thus
el-Wafi can understand her feeling of shame in response to his courtroom
rants to be focused on him, a part of a larger pattern of person-focused
felt evaluations focused on him and constituting her love for him. This
provides some evidence of the validity of this elucidation of the concept
of a genuine son as meriting love, of Moussaoui as remaining a genuine (if
flawed) son, and so of the validity of the reason it provides for continuing
to love him. Nonetheless, let us assume, this interpretation of her shame
and other felt evaluations focused on him remains in conflict with her
continued unwillingness to share his identity, and so the concept of a
son, thus elucidated, seems to fail to inform the overall pattern of felt
evaluations that would constitute her love for him. Such a conflict may
seem to undercut the validity of this elucidation and so of the reasons it
provides for continued love.[33]

In the face of this conflict, there is at least one way to make sense of
el-Wafi's claim that she loves her son no matter what, one that is consistent
with other details we know about the case. Although she was unwilling to
say that Moussaoui was mentally ill, even for the sake of helping him avoid
the death penalty, she did acknowledge that he was in effect brainwashed
by what was in effect a kind of cult, whose effect on him was seriously to
degrade his capacity for autonomy. This means that she can consistently
love him and so have a concern for his well-being as this person without

---

[33] Notice that the conclusion here is not that these reasons *are* undercut. Whether or not she has
reason all things considered to love him may well depend on factors she has not yet brought into view,
or it may be (as before) that she simply has not yet tried hard enough to get herself to identify with
him and so to remove the conflict. One source of complication that I am here largely ignoring is the
way in which she would respond in felt evaluation to her attempts to exercise control over her felt
evaluations as she, for example, makes an effort to identify with him. Thus, she may feel proud of
herself for making the effort to share his pride, even when this pride is expressive of values she finds
reprehensible; such pride in turn may lead her to question the reprehensibility of that value, which
can itself be an object of deliberation for her. Clearly this is an open-ended process of dialectic, which
cannot be neatly circumscribed in a simple example.

respecting and trusting his sense of his own identity precisely because of that loss of autonomy.[34] In this way, her unwillingness to share his values for his sake would not undercut the validity of her understanding of what it is to be a genuine son or the reasons it provides for continued love.

This conclusion that she ought to continue to love Moussaoui can be understood in one way as a kind of discovery. For el-Wafi has now come to understand more clearly than she did before the relevant concept of a son and how, in virtue of certain biological and historical bonds, it applies to him; this improved understanding therefore enables her to articulate the reasons justifying the constancy of her love. Yet in another sense it amounts to a kind of invention. For it rests on her exercise of her own autonomy in interpreting and shaping the patterns of her felt evaluations, an autonomy that itself rests on other things she cares about and values, cares and values that themselves are shaped through this dialectical process. Consequently, others might well arrive at other conclusions and so come to justify alternative attitudes toward their sons in relevantly similar circumstances. The unconditionality of el-Wafi's love for Moussaoui, therefore, is something she simultaneously both discovers through a process of reasoning and autonomously invents, and it is therefore consistent with the idea that love is also discerning.[35]

A similar example can bring out more clearly the way in which questions of whether to continue to love someone depend on one's sense of priorities. Assume that your lifelong friend is going through a period of clinical depression. Initially you were happy to do what you could for him: talking with him, sitting with him, helping with daily tasks—cooking, cleaning, paying bills—that are too overwhelming for him to face, getting him out and engaged in activities he cares about, and so on. As the months drag on, however, these efforts become increasingly draining and, with his (uncharacteristically) thankless and even hostile response to you, painful. You may therefore find yourself wondering whether it is worth it, whether you shouldn't just abandon your friend and so free up time and energy to pursue other valuable things in life.[36] After all, in some real sense he is no

---

[34] See p. 174, n. 23

[35] As I have noted above (§6.1), such simultaneous invention and discovery is intelligible only if we reject the cognitive–conative divide.

[36] Among these other valuable things might be other loves, a possibility which raises again worries about whether our beloveds are fungible, even if only in particular circumstances.

longer the person you befriended, for in his depression he seems to have lost his sense that anything is valuable anymore and thereby to have lost his identity. Thus, you may think, to continue to love this person as if he were your friend is painful precisely because it is a farce.

Yet in the face of these judgments you may find yourself ashamed of yourself, and you may come to articulate your shame here in terms of a failure of devotion: it is shameful to give up on a beloved just because that love is painful, all the more so when your beloved is going through what must be an extraordinarily difficult period of his life. This may lead you to a clearer understanding of your circumstances: to fail to look out for your friend's well-being as this person is to harm your friend, and to attempt to define away your responsibilities to him through a trick of personal identity is shamefully and selfishly to dishonor your friend.

This deliberative conclusion is essentially about what shall take priority in your life—your friendship or your other values—and so about the kind of person you find worth being as these priorities structure your identity. The conclusion to stand by your friend is justified by an attempt to interpret your own motives. Insofar as that interpretation gains traction by informing and shaping your subsequent felt evaluations it is confirmed as a kind of discovery of the imports and relative imports things have had to you all along, even though it may require considerable effort on your part to instill in yourself felt evaluations that are thus informed.

It should be clear from this discussion that deliberation about whether or not to continue an existing love is not something that depends on the beloved's properties alone—even her relational properties. For the question is not simply whether she merits your love but in addition what place if any that love ought to have within your life as a whole. This further question is to a large extent a question of the priorities that define your identity as the person you are; answering it therefore is to a significant extent a matter of the exercise of your autonomy in determining and so taking responsibility for your own identity. It is by exercising your autonomy in such cases that you can come simultaneously to discover and invent reasons for loving her. Hence Montaigne was in a sense right in saying:

If a man should importune me to give a reason why I loved him, I find it could no otherwise be expressed, than by making answer: because it was he, because it was I.[37]

---

[37] Michel Montaigne, *Essays of Montaigne*, ed. William Carew Hazlitt, trans. Charles Cotton (London: Reeves & Turner, 1603/1877), Ch. XXVII, "Of Friendship".

To claim that this is *all* we can say is overblown insofar as it seems mistakenly to imply that there can be no justification for love. Yet the kernel of truth here lies in the acknowledgment of the way in which these reasons depend essentially on the particular persons involved—especially on the lover's exercise of his autonomy. Indeed, as I shall argue in Chapter 8, once we consider the kind of reciprocity at issue in friendship, which was the sort of loving relationship of which Montaigne was speaking, we will see that the beloved's autonomy is relevant as well.

6.3 Love and Loss

As I indicated above, this understanding of how we can deliberate about both coming to love someone and whether to sustain a love for her does not on its own solve the fungibility problem, which concerns in part the kind of loss that can be felt, and in many cases ought to be felt, in loving someone. Consequently, my aim in this section is to tackle this question of loss directly.

If an object having import to you is such that its being taken away ought to be experienced as a loss regardless of the status of other objects that might have or come to have import to you, then, I shall say, that object has *non-fungible import*. The question, then, is: in what way does love involve finding a particular person to have non-fungible import? There are two issues here: one concerning what it is for our love to be for a particular person and the other concerning what it is for love to involve non-fungible import. I shall consider these in turn.

I have claimed that to love someone is to find him to have import to you as this particular person. This requires that the object of your concern is understood (perhaps implicitly) not only as *a* person but also as having a particular identity, so that you come to share that identity with him. In particular, the person-focused felt evaluations constituting your sharing his identity must project into the future in the right way, tracking his and only his potentially changing cares and values. Indeed, that the pattern of felt evaluations projects in this way is what constitutes your having the implicit understanding of the object of your love as a particular person and so is necessary for your attitude toward him being that of love. Nonetheless, it is clear that other evaluative attitudes, like valuing or caring, can be focused in the same way on a particular, as I already discussed.[38]

The second issue concerning the non–fungibility of our beloveds is a bit trickier and will require a slight detour into a discussion of the proper response to losses of various sorts, including, ultimately, what it is to mourn the loss of a beloved.

To lose something that has import to you is, of course, for something bad to happen, and you ought, therefore, to respond to this in having the appropriate felt evaluations. Thus, if I have grown attached to my car after many years of driving it, I ought to be saddened at the prospect of having to give it up, regardless of the reasons I have for doing so—for example, because it is just too unreliable anymore, because I have just totaled it in an accident, or because, in the midst of a mid-life crisis, I now want a flashy sports car. Thus, I may feel ambivalent not only when I trade it in and drive a new car off the lot (excited by the new car but saddened by not having my old one anymore), but also subsequently when I find myself coming face-to-face with the fact that I am no longer driving my old car, as when out of habit I reach for the light switch in the wrong place on the dashboard. In these ways, then, I *miss* my old car; indeed, insofar as I care about that particular car, such confrontations with the fact that it is gone *ought* to sadden me, other things being equal, for this just is a part of the projectible, rational pattern of felt evaluations constitutive of my caring about that car.

A similar phenomenon occurs when you lose something you value: such a loss rationally demands that you respond in having certain appropriate felt evaluations. Of course, which felt evaluations are appropriate here will differ from the case of losing something you merely care about because in valuing something you come to identify with it: you find it to have a place within the kind of life worth your living. For in such a case, the loss strikes a blow directly to your identity, and it may require that you significantly alter your sense of your own identity. Thus, a student may have his heart set on becoming a philosopher, may value this, and yet come to discover, perhaps through failure to pass his oral exams or to land a job, that this is not to be. In such a case, merely feeling sad is not properly to acknowledge the import that this has to him given the way he identifies

---

[38] See §3.3, p. 90; see also p. 81, n. 4

with it. Rather, in the face of such a loss, we normally feel *heartbroken*, unable for a while, at least, to regain a clear sense of how to prioritize our lives.[39] Indeed, as with the example of missing your car, this feeling of loss can crop up again and again, even many years later, as your circumstances confront you with the fact of the loss, as when the student returns many years later for a college reunion and encounters his old philosophy teachers. The extended recurrence of such feelings of loss might well be called a kind of "mourning" of that loss, though I shall reserve that word to describe the loss of a loved one.

To mourn the loss of a beloved is very different from missing your old car or even from the heartbreak in response to losing something you value, for the pattern of felt evaluations constitutive of loving someone is very different from that constitutive of caring about or even valuing something. In particular, loving someone involves intimately identifying with him, where such intimacy is simply absent in the case of caring about your car or valuing being a philosopher. Nonetheless, to lose a loved one is once again to lose something that has import to you (albeit a special kind of import), a loss that rationally demands that you respond to this in having certain felt evaluations whose appropriateness is in this case shaped by the intimacy of identification with your beloved. In part this intimacy consists in your sharing his identity by valuing the things he values for his sake. When he dies, for example, he may have left certain things he values *unfulfilled*, perhaps by never accomplishing some goal that he has as a part of valuing something or even by no longer being able to engage in certain activities for their own sakes (and not for the sake of some further goal to be accomplished), such as listening to a favorite piece of music. Were he alive, he ought to feel heartbroken at his being unable to fulfill these values. This implies that, insofar as you value this for his sake, you similarly ought to feel heartbroken for his sake, and your heartbreak ought to extend to all of his values left unfulfilled. Once again, this heartbreak ought, other things being equal, to recur in the future as you encounter circumstances confronting you with the fact of his loss, as when years after

---

[39] In this way, one may not only feel the heartbreak in direct response to the loss of something valued, but also be thrown into a mood that dampens other positive felt evaluations. For a sketch of such an account of moods as persistent states in which certain types of felt evaluations are dampened or suppressed, see Helm, Babych, and Markovic, "Moods as a Sense of Priorities." Moreover, if the loss of the thing valued is central enough to our sense of our own identities, such an inability to prioritize our lives may persist, and we may find ourselves in a full-blown identity crisis.

his death you come across an early manuscript of his for a book project he never completed.

Clearly such heartbreak in the face of the death of a loved one can be quite painful, compounded by the simultaneous loss of many values left unfulfilled. Yet in some cases a beloved may not have significant unfulfilled values, having lived a long life and accomplished many of his hopes and dreams (or long since given up on others). Yet this does not mean we do not mourn the loss of such a beloved. Moreover, we can experience the loss of a loved one even when she does not die, as when you move far away or she simply wants nothing further to do with you even though you continue to love her. Such physical or psychological remoteness need not (let us assume) affect her ability to fulfill her values, and yet that you ought in these cases experience her loss indicates that there must be another important source for the sense of loss of a beloved. This source is provided by the other part of intimacy involved in loving someone: your valuing the place your love for her and the values you share with her have within your life.

To love someone, I have argued, is in part to share her values for her sake. Although I value these things for *her* sake (so that the relevant felt evaluations are focused on her), I am nonetheless the one who does the valuing, and this is for *me* to have a concern for its well-being that ought to motivate my taking some responsibility for it through my own agency. The relevant motivations, undertaken for her sake because I share these values with her, are for engaged activity with her (see §3.3, §5.2). Insofar as these values and consequent motivations are mine, they must have a place within my overall evaluative perspective as this is structured by my priorities, and this implies (as I argued in §5.2) that I value being motivated appropriately by these values. Thus, were I to fail to be motivated to act on behalf of my beloved for bad reasons leading to a gross transgression of the place these motives ought to have in my life, I ought to be ashamed of myself. Similarly, were I to manage courageously to get myself to act on this motive in the face of significant pressure not to, thereby upholding my priorities, I ought to be proud of myself. Such pride and shame, because they are part of my sense of my own priorities, take me as their focus.

Given this, were my beloved to die or become physically or psychologically remote, my continued sharing of her values (inasmuch as I continue to love her) requires continued vigilance and engagement. Thus, if she values supporting the local opera company, I ought to continue to attend to its well-being, noticing, for example, when planned "improvements" to downtown would negatively impact it. In such cases, however, engaged activity simply may not be possible, given her death or remoteness, even though it is rationally called for by my love for her. I ought, therefore, feel not merely a kind of sadness or frustration at my inability to do what I am motivated to do, for insofar as I value the place these values and the motive to which they give rise in my life, such an inability will be something I feel as an inability to live as I ought, as striking at my identity, and so I ought to feel it via person-focused emotions focused on myself—as, we might say, a feeling of *desolation*.[40] Moreover, my failure here, and so the warrant of my feeling of desolation, will remain even if (as in a case of psychological remoteness) my beloved is still around and is successful in maintaining the well-being of the opera.

My claim, then, is that the feelings of loss we ought to have at the loss of a loved one include not merely feelings of heartbreak at our beloved's inability to uphold his values and so pursue the kind of life he finds worth living, but also feelings of desolation at our own inability to act in support of our beloved. Taken together, these feelings of loss constitute, in the case of the death of your beloved, your *mourning* that loss, a sense of loss that clearly will last as long as you continue to love him. In cases in which you have lost your beloved not through death but through physical or psychological remoteness, only the latter sense of loss is operative, and we might mark this distinction by saying that you feel *sorrow* at his loss or that you feel a kind of "*yearning*" for him.[41]

It might be thought that this account of mourning and sorrow or yearning does not go far enough. After all, it might seem, our loving relationships with others can be significantly more central to our sense of

---

[40] English does not have a single word that identifies the relevant person-focused emotion here. 'Frustration' or 'sadness' are words I have used to describe the relevant non-person-focused emotions; words like 'anguish' typically are understood as differing from these merely in their intensity and not—at least not necessarily—in their "depth." It is such "depth" as person-focused that I aim to invoke in using 'desolation,' with its connotations of emptiness and abandonment.

[41] As before (n. 40), English does not clearly mark the distinction I aim to convey here. I have said that we feel the loss of things we care about by "missing" them; what is needed here once again is a word that conveys the kind of "depth" in the feeling of loss at issue when we lose someone we love. Both 'sorrow' and 'yearning' are normally distinguished from 'missing' by their intensity rather than their depth, which is not what I hope to convey, yet I cannot find any better word.

who we are than I have acknowledged here, so that the loss of a loved one can be totally debilitating in ways that I have so far failed to acknowledge. I think this is right. For I have so far been discussing love, understood as an evaluative attitude we take toward other persons, rather than particular relationships we might have with others whom we love. Thus, as I shall argue in Chapter 8, friendships are relationships that essentially involve considerably more intimacy than is apparent just by considering the loving attitudes that ground them. The loss of a close friend, including a spouse, will therefore involve further, potentially more debilitating kinds of loss than I have described thus far.

In addition to the dramatic cases of permanent loss (including remoteness) of a beloved that I have described, there are temporary cases, as when your beloved is away on a trip for a significant period. In such cases, you may still have feelings of desolation insofar as you are temporarily unable to engage with her, though the intensity of your desolation will normally be mitigated by the knowledge that her remoteness is only temporary. Thus, as we ordinarily say, you "miss" her.[42] Insofar as these are temporary cases, however, the pain of "missing" your beloved normally ought to give way to pleasure at reunion. Such pleasure is, we might say, a kind of person-focused satisfaction of your second-order desire, implicit in "missing" her, to re-engage with her.

It should now be clear how loving someone involves finding him to have non-fungible import. For given the way we intimately identify with someone in loving him, his loss rationally requires that we respond with mourning or yearning, patterns of painful emotional experiences that can persist over long periods of time. Although we may come to acquire new loves even as we lose old loves, this does not alter the fact of our loss, so that it would be improper to understand this as a genuine replacement. Indeed, this will be true of all cases in which we value particular things: the value I find in being a philosophy professor is not something of which its place in my life can simply be filled by some other value without loss or without it being such that I ought to feel that loss. Thus, although I may be willing to trade in being a professor for being

---

[42] This use of "missing" someone you love should not be confused with the account of missing something you care about I gave above (p. 201). For to "miss" your beloved in this case is to feel person-focused emotions, unlike the non-person-focused emotions at issue in missing something you merely care about (see n. 40).

a stay-at-home parent in certain circumstances, such a willingness does not at all imply that I need not feel the heartbreak at no longer being a professor.[43]

The non-replaceability inherent in non-fungible values or loves does not preclude our being able to make comparisons between one non-fungible value or love and others in particular situations. Indeed, we have to be able to make such comparisons and arrive at reasonable conclusions about which one is more important here and now if we are to be able to function as rational agents. Thus, in some circumstances, it may be that my love of my daughter ought to take priority over my value of being a philosophy professor (as with the earlier example of my daughter's broken leg in §4.3, p. 122), and sometimes it should be the other way around, as when I find that giving a talk at a conference takes priority over my attending my daughter's soccer game. In such a case, certain kinds of ambivalence may well be called for—ambivalence that does not call into question our decision about which ought to take priority here and now. Thus, although I may have done the right thing in going to the conference, it may be that, even so, I ought to feel regret or sadness for missing her soccer game.[44]

6.4 Conclusion

In this chapter, I have briefly sketched a general account of how we can deliberate about what ought to have import to us. One strength of this account is the way in which, through its rejection of the cognitive–conative divide, it makes intelligible how deliberation about values can be simultaneously both a matter of autonomous invention, as we thereby take responsibility for the constitution of our own identities, and a matter of rational discovery, insofar as we can be mistaken or overcome our mistakes so as to achieve an improved conception of what is worthwhile in life.

[43] Of course, as with loves, a newly acquired love or value may mitigate the feeling of loss in this case, but if what I value really is for this particular thing, it ought not suppress that heartbreak entirely.
[44] Nonetheless, not just any kind of ambivalence is appropriate here: I ought not to feel ashamed of myself for missing her game (as I should if I were simply too lazy to attend), for such shame would normally indicate that I have made a mistake in acting as I did, contrary to my assumption that this is the right thing to have done.

In extending this account to the case of justifying both initially coming to love someone and continuing or breaking off that love, I have argued that we can, in effect, have our cake and eat it, too. We need not choose between, on the one hand, bestowal accounts of love, which seek to acknowledge the way in which love is deeply personal by focusing on the historical relations between particular individuals at the expense of an understanding of how love can be justified, and, on the other hand, appraisal accounts of love, which focus on repeatable properties in order to make sense of justification, thereby blinding themselves to the unique and particular and to the creativity of love in terms of which we can understand the essentially personal nature of love. Rather, once we reject the cognitive–conative divide we can see that these two possibilities are not mutually exclusive: we can reconcile the deeply personal, historically grounded, creative nature of love with the idea that we love and continue to love for reasons that justify that love.

Finally, this account of love solves the fungibility problem in several ways. First, by recognizing that the problem is not simply that of justifying replacing a love but doing so without loss, I have separated questions of justifying coming to love someone from those of justifying continuing that love; fungibility is an issue only for the latter given that loss is not an issue for the former. Second, the justification of love is in part a matter of priorities, where it makes a difference what your current loves and values are. Thus, having justified coming to love one person on the basis of certain traits, you may also justify refusing to come to love another person with those same traits on the grounds that you do not have room in your life for an additional love, which would involve undertaking commitments that would compromise your existing loves. This may raise the question of whether you ought in a particular case to trade up: to replace a current love with another person who exhibits to a greater degree the relevant traits justifying your existing love. However, third, to seek too readily to trade up would raise the question whether your attitude toward your current beloved is actually that of love at all, for love is constituted by a projectible pattern of felt evaluations that essentially involves a kind of trust and respect that make intelligible the kind of intimate identification that love is. Moreover, even when your love is not itself in question (as when your love is already well established), seeking to trade up raises the question of the kind of person you would be if you did so; this is a matter of priorities, and there can be perfectly good reasons for resisting the move to trading up.

Nonetheless, the implication so far is that we can sometimes justify replacing one love with another. However, this does not imply that what justifies our loves is only the beloved's being a certain type of person or that our loves are fungible. For, fourth, justifying a love is a matter of the contingent fit between the beloved's identity as the person she is and the lover's willingness, as partly an exercise of his autonomy, to love her, a willingness in a particular case that need not require for consistency a similar willingness to extend that love to other similar cases. Insofar as the justification of love is partly a matter of invention, what gets justified is the love for a particular person. Finally, fifth, to love someone is to find him to have non-fungible import, such that to lose a beloved through death or physical or psychological remoteness rationally requires experiencing that loss in ways that deeply touch your own identity, through mourning or sorrow or yearning. Hence, although we may substitute old loves with new ones, the new ones will not be genuine replacements. Consequently, the account of the justification of both coming to love and continuing to love (or breaking off a love) that I have provided does not imply that our loves are fungible.

As I indicated at the end of Chapter 5, the account that I have provided here in Part II is in terms of an idealized, rational pattern that actual loves only approximate. Isolated failures to have particular emotions and desires that fit into this pattern do not on their own undermine the existence of the overall pattern and so of the love itself, and for this reason the love need not be deficient. My claim in Chapter 5 was that loves are deficient when the failures of response are systematic. However, it should now be clear that this claim needs qualification, for particular loves must be understood to have a place within an overall life, and we can be justified in limiting the scope or extent of one love to make room for other things that make a life worthwhile without that love's being deficient.

Nonetheless, to say that this account of love involves an ideal is not to say that it describes as full and rich a kind of connection between persons as is possible. For I have confined myself to understanding love as an evaluative attitude, setting aside as much as possible the kinds of relationships that might stem from love. Indeed, we might think, love gives us at least instrumental reasons to pursue relationships with our beloveds, insofar as loving someone requires that you have a reasonably accurate conception of her identity as this person, a conception which can be facilitated by some such relationship. Moreover, love motivates us, through our sharing the beloved's values, to engage our beloveds in activity for their sake, a kind of engagement that tends to promote certain kinds of relationships. Pursuing these relationships provides us with more satisfying connections to others than mere love on its own essentially involves. My aim in Part III is to flesh out certain important kinds of such loving relationships, specifically those at issue between parents and children and between friends. Indeed, I shall argue, fleshing this out will reveal something fundamental about the ways in which individual autonomy depends on the relationships we have with others.

Marilyn Friedman offers an account of loving relationships in which she draws what might seem to be a similar conclusion. Thus, she claims, (romantic) love involves a kind of interaction between the lovers that somehow gives rise to their constituting a "federation of selves"—a third entity that does not require the two lovers to blur the boundaries between them and so does not undermine their individual autonomy, as seems to be the case for the union account.[45] To the contrary, she argues, there is in love the potential for the gain of autonomy, inasmuch as being in a loving relationship might enhance autonomy both directly by enabling you better to know yourself, including both your vices and virtues, so as to make better choices about your life and indirectly by promoting the growth of various skills, such as that of critical self-evaluation, that foster autonomy. These are tantalizing claims, yet Friedman has not fully fleshed them out in a way that makes them convincing. In particular, we need a careful account of what sort of "third entity" such a federation is and so precisely how being a member of such a federation can enhance your individual autonomy.

My aim in Part III will be in large part to make some sense of the nature of loving relationships and the connection between being a part of some such relationships and the proper development and exercise of your capacity for autonomy. In particular, I shall argue, friendship is a

---

[45] Friedman, "Romantic Love," 165.

relationship involving a certain kind of reciprocal love in which the friends together form what I shall call a "plural agent": a single subject not only of goal-directed action but also and crucially of import. As members of a plural agent, I shall argue, friends to a certain extent enhance their autonomy by sharing it.

PART III
Friendship and the Self

7

Paternalistic Love and External Reasons

My aim in this book has been not only to provide an account of love and friendship but also to reveal the ways in which such an account is important to an understanding of persons. I argued in §1.2 that our ordinary understanding of persons is individualistic in two respects. First is what I called the "egocentric conception of intimate concerns," according to which we understand such intimacy in terms of the concern for others being incorporated into our concern for ourselves. To a large extent, my aim in Part II has been to argue against this egocentrism by providing a positive account of love and its requisite intimacy that avoids this egocentrism. Thus, I argued, the intimate identification of love is a concern for the beloved's identity for his sake that is analogous to—but not a part of—your concern for your own identity. Indeed, loving others involves an exercise of the very same capacities involved in loving ourselves and thereby constituting our own identities as the persons we each are. Consequently, having the capacity to love others is therefore a necessary part of being a person; we persons are in this sense essentially social.

In Part III, my aim is to argue against the individualist conception of autonomy by examining more closely at least some of the kinds of relationships between persons that love makes possible. As I articulated it, this individualist conception of autonomy is the idea that our autonomy, our capacity to decide not only how to act but also what to value and care about and so what identity to have, is one we each can exercise only individually. For, it is thought, mental states and processes essentially belong to individuals, and it is therefore only through individual endorsement of particular values that we each determine an identity that is genuinely and authentically one's own as the result of the exercise of one's own autonomy. Consequently, any attempt by others to go beyond offering reasons or advice concerning matters of personal values is an attempt to undermine our autonomy in ways that can only harm our well-beings as the persons we each are. As I shall argue, such an individualist conception of autonomy in effect blocks an adequate understanding of the more intimate social relationships we can have with others.

I shall argue this in two stages. First, in this chapter, I shall examine the sort of properly paternalistic loving relationships loving caretakers —parents—ought to have with children. My claim will be that we must at least begin to relax the individualist conception of autonomy if we are to make sense of the ways in which parents can have some control over their children's upbringing by helping to instill particular values in them, without thereby undermining the children's responsibility for who they become. For, I shall argue, parents can provide their children with reasons for caring or valuing in a particular way, reasons that, by having their source in the loving relationship, others are not in a position to provide; as such, these reasons are distinctively interpersonal in a way that calls into question whether we can make sense of the child as exercising his growing capacity for autonomy all on his own, as the individualist conception of autonomy requires.

Paternalistic loving relationships normally involve a kind of inequality between those involved, an inequality that justifies that paternalism. In Chapter 8, I shall turn my attention to loving relationships among equals and to friendship in particular. In this context I shall argue more strongly that making sense of friendship requires postulating cares and even values that belong not simply to the one friend or the other but rather to both jointly. Consequently, the kind of control over and responsibility for these joint cares and values must involve the joint exercise of autonomy. All of this requires that we reject the individualist conception of autonomy, and it leads to a still richer sense in which we persons are essentially social.

7.1 The Problem of Childhood

According to Tamar Schapiro, children rightly have a kind of special status evident in the everyday ways we treat them differently from adults.[1] This

---

[1] Tamar Schapiro, "What Is a Child?" *Ethics* 109, no. 4 (1999): 716–17.

special status consists in their lacking, at least fully, the kind of authority in their consent or dissent, and so in their words and actions, that we adults have, and this explains both why we treat them differently by holding them responsible for their words and deeds in ways that are different from the way we hold ourselves and other adults responsible and why we have certain special, paternalistic obligations toward them. Thus, I may require that my daughter eat her vegetables even when she protests, and I may punish her when she does not, because I view her protestations as not having the relevant kind of authority: I know better than she does what is good for her in this case.

Given this, Schapiro rightly construes the distinction between children and adults to be not merely an empirical, biological issue but rather a normative one: the immaturity of children is not something we can simply articulate in the merely descriptive terms of natural science but rather requires that we bring in moral notions of rights and responsibilities. That is, children's development into adults is a development into what is in some sense a fundamentally different kind of thing than they were before: into full-blooded, moral persons. Such a development, Schapiro claims, true to her Kantian roots, requires that the child come to acquire an authoritative will in virtue of which we can recognize her actions as truly her own rather than the result of alien forces within her,[2] so that we are warranted in bringing the moral concepts of rights and responsibilities to bear in our dealings with her.

This raises the question of how children are able to make this transition: how can a creature that starts off lacking an authoritative will ever come to acquire it? To have what I am calling an 'authoritative will,' Schapiro says, is to be capable of adjudicating potential motivational conflicts and taking sides on the basis of "an established constitution, that is, a principled perspective which would count as the law of her will"—or, as I would put it, on the basis of an evaluative perspective that constitutes her identity as this person.[3] Now Schapiro claims that children are already "reflective": they are capable of recognizing motivational conflicts and so recognizing that they can choose sides in this conflict—and are indeed able to make these choices.[4] What they lack, she claims, is the established constitution

---

[2] See Frankfurt, "Freedom of the Will and the Concept of a Person."   [3] Ibid., 729.

[4] Presumably Schapiro thinks this is a requirement on genuine agency; I disagree. After all, dogs are agents, though they are not reflective in this sense; this indicates, perhaps, that Schapiro has a somewhat different conception of agency than I do, as essentially involving being able to have a kind of (moral?)

in virtue of which such a choice can be made authoritatively, as expressing their own will. Consequently,

for lack of an established constitution . . . the condition of childhood is one in which the agent is not yet in a position to speak in her own voice because there is no voice which counts as hers.[5]

To acquire her own voice and so to have the kind of authoritative will essential to being a person, "the requisite critical perspective must organize the fundamental constituents of the agent's motivational world" and thereby provide her with a '*basic structure*' as a person.[6]

This understanding of children, Schapiro says, raises the following predicament concerning how their development into full persons is possible. On the one hand her acquiring an evaluative perspective constitutive of her identity as this person cannot be something that just happens to her, the result of forces external to her will acting on her, for if the resulting identity is to be authoritatively hers, she must somehow have a say in determining the requisite evaluative perspective and recognizing it as normatively binding on her. Yet on the other hand that acquisition cannot be simply the result of an action or series of actions of hers, for prior to acquiring it she has no basis on which to choose one evaluative perspective, one set of cares and values, rather than another. How, then, are children to become adults? This predicament she calls the "*problem of childhood.*"

Schapiro's solution to this problem is that children come to form an evaluative perspective through play. To *play*, Schapiro says, is to try on a persona (the critical perspective defining a particular person's basic structure—an identity), act from it, and see whether, ultimately, the principles on the basis of which such play-actions are chosen are principles the agent can adopt as his own. Consequently, such play-action and the principles that underwrite it have a merely provisional status insofar as they do not straightforwardly express the agent's own will, and so "it is inappropriate to take play-action seriously in the same way we take action

---

responsibility for what you do. Nonetheless, even construing agency in something more like the way Schapiro does, I cannot understand how it is possible for a creature to have a capacity for reflective choice without also simultaneously having the sort of constitution that could provide the reasons for such a choice.

[5] Schapiro, "What Is a Child?" 729.   [6] Ibid., 730.

proper seriously."[7] As a child play-acts, she gradually comes to be able, at least within certain limited domains, to make her own decisions and choices and so to act non-provisionally. Moreover, because the principles on the basis of which she acts in one domain will normally have implications for how she ought to act in other domains, she will gradually acquire authority over ever increasing domains of life until she becomes a full-blown moral person.[8] Thus, the predicament in which children find themselves is an "obstacle to morality" that they must overcome on their way to becoming mature adults.[9]

Given this conception of the development of children into adults, Schapiro claims that we adults have certain obligations toward children: a negative obligation to refrain from interfering with that development, and a positive obligation to help them overcome this predicament. This latter obligation we can fulfill

by modeling autonomy ourselves, by making sure that the family and wider culture provide children with good models of autonomy to "choose" from, and by helping children to "choose" among such models. Discipline is one way of guiding such "choices," but in using disciplinary force, the idea should always be to act as a surrogate conscience.[10]

Thus, we ought to explain the principles behind our help and discipline so as "to awaken children to a sense of their own freedom and responsibility rather than to remind them of their subjection to an external authority."[11] The idea seems to be that in acting "as a surrogate conscience," we adopt a *two-pronged strategy*: by rewarding and punishing the child, we aim to shape her existing, typically self-interested motives in more appropriate directions, and by providing the explanations and justifications of the relevant background principles we aim to get her to achieve a new understanding and so to acquire new motives for action. These two techniques are intended to reinforce each other: the external sanctions

---

[7] Ibid., 733.   [8] Ibid., 734.

[9] Ibid., 735, 737. This understanding of the condition of childhood as an *obstacle* to morality is at least misleading, for it suggests that it might be possible simply to remove that obstacle for a child so as to allow her to proceed smoothly and directly to adulthood. Rather, we ought to understand the condition of childhood as something more like a stepping stone or a series of stepping stones: a part of the path to adulthood without which that passage would not be possible. I'm not sure whether or not this is a mere quibble.

[10] Ibid., 736. Note how Schapiro uses scare quotes to indicate that these choices initially have the merely provisional status of play.

[11] Ibid., 736.

aim to shape her existing motives to ensure that the understanding of the relevant principles succeeds in informing those motives.

There are two problems with Schapiro's account of childhood and the passage from childhood to adulthood. One concerns how we adults are to distinguish those domains in which a child's activity is merely provisional from those in which it is not, a distinction we must make if we are to know when to hold them fully accountable for their actions and when to be paternalistic and intervene so as to help them make better choices. The answer cannot simply be that the child is responsible when she can articulate reasons for her choices, since these reasons themselves might have merely provisional status as play. Moreover, we want to be able to hold a child responsible even when he is currently unable to formulate reasons, for in some cases he *should* have thought about the matter, at least more fully than he did. Nor can the answer be that the child asserts that this is really his view, that he is acting on his own authority, since it might always be that such an assertion itself has the merely provisional character of play. Indeed, it now begins to look as though whether a child's action or avowed reasons have this status as merely provisional, merely "playful," is not something we can determine independently of a determination of whether to hold her responsible; instead, we might turn this around and say that a child's words or actions are merely provisional to the extent to which she is not to be held fully responsible for them. So it is not clear that Schapiro's distinction between play and action proper in terms of the appeal to having a merely provisional self rather than having an established deliberative perspective can explain the degree to which we ought to take them seriously and so the extent to which we ought to hold the child responsible.

A second problem, one that is more important for present purposes, concerns Schapiro's conception of the way in which we adults are able to intervene paternalistically on a child's behalf, especially when the child is already going off track. For such a child may, if we make the external sanctions strong enough, choose to act as we want her to act, but for the wrong reason: merely because of the sanction and not because of the underlying principle. Moreover, our explanations and justifications of the relevant principles may simply fall upon deaf ears. The result is that the two-pronged strategy Schapiro outlines seems impotent in the hard cases when we most need it to work.

To see this, consider a typical outburst of a seven-year-old child revealing her cares and concerns. Thus, as her twin brother and sister come home from a birthday party with party favors, my daughter may scream, "It's not fair! They have to share some with me!" It may seem that this outburst is indicative not of a concern for fairness but rather for some selfish surrogate, which we might label *shmairness*: the equal distribution of goodies when this benefits me. In the face of this selfish concern, I may adopt the two-pronged strategy. Thus I impose external sanctions on her, rewarding her when she is fair, punishing her when she is not; I explain to her why fairness is good and how it essentially involves being able to see things from others' perspectives and giving their perspectives due weight in making your own choices, and so on. Yet she may simply dismiss these explanations in ways that manifest her underlying selfishness: "I don't care about them," she may say, "I just want what they have." The principles and explanations I provide may fall on deaf ears precisely because, given her current state of selfishness, she may not be in a position to understand the reasons to which I appeal and for this reason may simply reject them as not relevant to her. This implies that the rewards and punishments I impose on her work only through that very selfishness, so that she is motivated to share her toys with her siblings not out of a concern for fairness but rather only because she knows I will take them away from her otherwise, something she does not want to happen for selfish reasons. How, then, can I instill in her a concern for fairness itself? This is the problem of childhood from the parent's perspective, and the two-pronged strategy outlined by Schapiro seems unhelpful in such a case.

Surely we are not as impotent as this may make it seem. What is at stake here is not merely my getting my daughter to develop some established evaluative perspective or other on the basis of which she makes some choice or other and so becomes an adult whom we can hold accountable for her actions proper. Rather, what is at stake is my being able to help her instill in herself an acceptable deliberative perspective, an ability to make good choices, so that when she starts to go off track I can do more than just throw up my hands and write her off as a bad apple. Indeed, here it seems to matter, in ways Schapiro does not acknowledge, what kind of relationship I have with her: parents or other adults in a loving relationship with her can properly have more influence than mere strangers without thereby undermining her autonomy. My words and my actions matter, or at least ought to matter, to her in ways relevant to my helping instill in her particular values because we love each other. Moreover, the way this matters to her might seem to make possible my having a kind of influence on her that is mediated not merely by external sanctions or explanations that she is unable to understand by the very condition I am trying to remedy. Such an influence, I shall argue, is one in which I provide her with reasons that she can find normatively and motivationally binding on her—reasons of fairness, for example—even though she is not in a position to understand what those reasons are. Indeed, she can come to understand such reasons because of her access to them, an access made possible by our loving relationship.

This may sound impossible: how can my daughter choose on the basis of considerations (of fairness, say) that she is not in a position to be able to understand, considerations that are therefore outside her mental grasp? Why not instead understand her as choosing (provisionally, if you like) on the basis of a concern for shmairness, which more accurately reflects the apparent substance of her choice? In the background motivating such a reinterpretation of this case seems to be the individualist conception of autonomy. For if the capacity to deliberate and choose is essentially one we exercise as individuals on the basis of mental states and processes that again belong to us essentially as individuals, then it seems absurd to say that someone could choose on the basis of something she cannot grasp. One way to cash out the resulting conception of practical reasons is in terms of Bernard Williams's notion of an subjective motivational set:[12] my daughter, selfish as she is, is not concerned with fairness and so, from the perspective of the concerns she has and the understanding of what is important that informs these concerns, does not in a sense have any reason to be fair: we could not charge her with a failure of rationality for disregarding considerations of fairness. Such considerations provide what Williams calls 'internal reasons': reasons internal to her subjective motivational set.

Of course, Williams's notion of an subjective motivational set is not simply that of the concerns that the subject actually has right now. It may be that, although a person does not now recognize it, it would be possible for him correctly to deliberate in such a way as to move from the concerns

---

[12] Bernard Williams, "Internal and External Reasons," in *Moral Luck: Philosophical Papers 1973–1980* (Cambridge: Cambridge University Press, 1981), 101–13.

he now has to some further concerns; if so, this would be enough for him to have internal reason to be motivated by these further concerns. In general, Williams characterizes the elements of an agent's subjective motivational set as those motivational elements he has or would arrive at as the result of both correcting any false beliefs and deliberating properly. Moreover, Williams has a very broad, loosely specified conception of what such a sound deliberative route consists in, so as to include not merely instrumental reasoning but also constitutive reasoning (about what a particular end consists in) as well as certain thought moves grounded in imagination.[13]

This broad understanding of an agent's subjective motivational set leaves it unclear as to whether considerations of fairness would count as internal reasons for my daughter. For Williams's specification of what a sound deliberative route is may well be loose enough as to include some rational method, perhaps mediated by my influence on her, whereby she might arrive at a proper appreciation of considerations of fairness. Indeed, this very looseness makes it difficult to assess Williams's account of internal reasons, for it might seem that any proposed counterexample to the account could all too readily be incorporated into it by an extension of what we understand a sound deliberative route to include: can we understand the reasons a child has to acquire a concern for fairness to be intelligible in terms of a deliberative route, especially when that acquisition is mediated by the influence on her of others in loving relationships with her? Perhaps, we might think, the very presence of that sort of influence, depending as it does on love, undermines the rationality of the route to that acquisition in terms of which we can understand considerations of fairness to be already a part of the child's subjective motivational set.

Williams does not, of course, claim that there must be such a deliberative route in terms of which we can understand a child's acquisition of a concern for fairness; his claim is only that such a route is required if we are to be able to say that the child has an internal reason to develop that concern. He acknowledges the existence of cases in which a person might have no

---

[13] Indeed, my account, sketched in Ch. 6, of how we can deliberate about values and priorities through dialectical processes of self-interpretation and the elucidation of concepts in light of our emotional responses, processes in which we necessarily have a degree of autonomy in determining the outcome, fits neatly into Williams's conception of the sort of reasoning that can extend one's subjective motivational set.

internal reason to do so, and claims that in such cases there are no reasons at all for him to do so: internal reasons are the only reasons there are. John McDowell disputes this, arguing in favor of the possibility of *external reasons*: reasons that are in some sense binding on an agent even though they cannot be located within his subjective motivational set.[14]

McDowell agrees with Williams that for a consideration to be a reason is for someone in accepting it to come to see things correctly, other things being equal. However, whereas Williams thinks that a reason must also be something a subject can come to accept as the result of deliberating correctly from within his subjective motivational set and therefore must be potentially motivating, McDowell thinks this is not necessary: that someone is unable to deliberate so as to arrive at a particular reason and so is unable to be motivated by it in no way undermines its status as a reason for him.[15] So although one way of coming to accept the reason is via correct deliberation, it may be that she instead comes to accept it as the result of some non-rational process of conversion; in such a case, we could say that she had external reasons all along, and the conversion was merely a non-rational process by which she came to accept these reasons. As McDowell puts it:

> The idea of conversion would function here as the idea of an intelligible shift in motivational orientation that is exactly *not* effected by inducing a person to discover, by practical reasoning controlled by existing motivations, some internal reasons that he did not previously realize he had.[16]

One form of such conversions, a form which we all undergo, consists in our being brought up more or less well: in being thus brought up, in becoming enculturated, we acquire access to reasons that we had all along, reasons to be kind, considerate, fair, just, courageous, and the like.

Now it might seem, in spite of the looseness in Williams's notion of a sound deliberative route, that the case of my daughter fits McDowell's description of someone with an external reason nicely. Insofar as she is not yet in a position to understand or even come to understand considerations of fairness through a process of reasoning, she does not have any internal reason to be fair. Still we might expect that after she is properly brought up

---

[14] John McDowell, "Might There Be External Reasons?", in *Mind, Value, and Reality* (Cambridge, MA: Harvard University Press, 1998), 95–111. I shall briefly discuss Williams's response to McDowell below.

[15] Ibid., 100.   [16] Ibid., 102.

she will acquire access to such reasons by coming to see things correctly as a result of her upbringing. This means that prior to this upbringing she has an external reason to be fair. Nonetheless, I do not think this characterization of her is quite apt, in part for reasons Williams brings out.

Part of what makes intelligible the idea that my daughter has an *external* reason to be fair is that she does not properly understand the concept either of fairness or of related concepts in terms of which we might try to explain what it is to be fair; after all, this lack of understanding underwrites the idea that she could not undergo some rational process to come to see things correctly in light of fairness. Yet, Williams argues, in order for my daughter to have a *reason* to be fair, it must be that she "*has reason to use that concept*, to structure . . . her experience in those terms."[17] Indeed, we might think, this is precisely the issue with my daughter: given that she is not yet inducted into our form of life and with no reasons forthcoming for why she ought to be so inducted, she seems to have no reason to use the concept of fairness (as opposed to shmairness), and so it is not clear what kind of claim fairness itself could have on her. Similar things could be said about the amoralist: being outside our form of life, what reason could he have to convert and so come to use the moral concepts that he lacks? Consequently, Williams argues, the status of any such external reasons as reasons is utterly mysterious given their complete disconnection from any potential explanation of the subject's actions. (I shall return to this worry below.)

It should be clear that Williams and McDowell are construing the notion of an external reason in slightly different ways. Williams thinks that what is important about externality is the way in which purported external reasons are essentially disconnected from motivation, and he thinks the notion of an external reason implies that one could believe that one has it without that belief having any potential effect on one's motivation. McDowell, on the other hand, construes the externality of external reasons in terms of the subject's inability to access that reason, so that his inability to be motivated by an external reason is a consequence of its externality, not what makes it be external in the first place. In each case, however, Williams and McDowell seem to think that someone who lacks an internal reason to be

---

[17] Bernard Williams, "Internal Reasons and the Obscurity of Blame," in *Making Sense of Humanity and Other Philosophical Papers, 1982–93* (Cambridge: Cambridge University Press, 1995), 38.

concerned with fairness, for example, can therefore bear no responsibility for acquiring or failing to acquire that concern. Moreover, in the case of bringing up a child to acquire such a concern, they seem to think that we adults can only use the sort of two-pronged strategy outlined by Schapiro, a strategy I argued above leaves us relatively impotent against a recalcitrant child. This requires further defense.

Williams suggests that when faced with a "hard case"—an adult who completely lacks within his subjective motivational set anything we can use to reason with him about the matter—all we can do is throw up our hands, give up trying to reform him or even to blame him, and take pains to protect ourselves from such a hopeless character.[18] Yet surely with a child we cannot simply give up even before he begins to have the kind of character we can reason with. Perhaps Williams thinks we can utilize his natural trust and respect of his caregivers: his "disposition to do things that people he respects expect of him."[19] This would be an addition to the two-pronged strategy Schapiro outlines, yet as was the case for that strategy such a disposition only seems to provide the child with the wrong sort of motive for acting: because that is what we expect of him rather than because that is what fairness demands. Hence it remains mysterious how we can inculcate in a child a concern for fairness itself, especially when the child is not naturally inclined to have such a concern.[20]

McDowell's understanding of how we can raise a child is somewhat more developed. He suggests:

If we think of ethical upbringing in a roughly Aristotelian way, as a process of habituation into suitable modes of behaviour, inextricably bound up with the inculcation of suitably related modes of thought, there is no mystery about how the process can be the acquisition, simultaneously, of a way of seeing things and of a collection of motivational directions or practical concerns, focused and activated in particular cases by exercises of the way of seeing things.[21]

McDowell's claim here is that our motivations to act in certain ways are inherently interconnected with our abilities to perceive the world in certain terms: in terms of fairness, for example. Thus, perceiving your circumstances as unfair ought to motivate you to respond in certain ways, by sharing or

---

[18] Williams, "Internal Reasons and Blame," 43. [19] Ibid., 42.

[20] Again, part of the difficulty here lies in the looseness of Williams's specification of what a sound deliberative route might consist in. I shall return to this point in §7.2.2.

[21] McDowell, "Might There Be External Reasons?" 100–1.

protesting or seething or sympathizing, say. The force of this "ought," Mc-
Dowell thinks, comes from your understanding of what fairness consists in,
for to fail generally to be moved to action or emotion in these ways when
the circumstances warrant it is to fail properly to understand the relevant
evaluative concepts.[22] So the acquisition of the evaluative concept and the
acquisition of suitable habits of response to the world perceived in terms of
that concept must be simultaneous, with neither conceptually or ontologically prior to the other. This means that a child must gradually acquire both
habits of perception and attention to discriminate circumstances that are fair
from those that are unfair, as well as habits of responding appropriately to
such perceptions; it is only once these habits are more or less fully in place
that it becomes appropriate to say that the child understands what fairness is
and that he responds in the ways he does because the circumstances are fair
or unfair. This understanding of the inculcation of a concern for fairness in
a child conceives of that concern as a complex holistic pattern of cognitive-
cum-motivational skills, so that its acquisition, and the acquisition of the
relevant set of interrelated concepts, must be holistic as well.

Nonetheless, without further elaboration, this holism on its own does not
seem to help us understand how to cope with recalcitrant children. Suppose
we begin to instill in a child the ability to discriminate circumstances
according to their fairness, and that we simultaneously try to instill in
him certain habits of responding appropriately to these discriminations.
We may find that he resists our attempts to get him to respond in these
ways, even though he can, with increasing accuracy, make the relevant
discriminations. What can we do? Here it seems that we are stuck with the
two-pronged strategy Schapiro describes. Thus, first, we can talk to him,
explaining and justifying particular responses in the face of the fairness or
unfairness of the circumstances, and yet these explanations and justifications
may have no rational purchase on him insofar as he has not yet acquired
the relevant concept of fairness: the only reasons accessible to him for
making these responses would be internal reasons, which he simply does
not have given that he lacks a concern for fairness as an element in his
(extended) subjective motivational set. Second, we can try to get him to
have such a concern by applying external sanctions, praising and rewarding,

---

[22] John McDowell, "Are Moral Requirements Hypothetical Imperatives?", in McDowell, *Mind,
Value, and Reality*, 87.

or condemning and punishing him so as to provide some incentive for him to respond appropriately. Yet as before, although such sanctions may succeed in motivating him to respond as we want him to when he correctly identifies circumstances as being fair or unfair, it may be that he does so for the wrong reason: to receive the reward or escape the punishment rather than because of considerations of fairness.

The root problem here lies in McDowell's understanding of the sort of conversion required in order to recognize external reasons as an arational process. For if we have no rational purchase on anyone to make this conversion, then to a significant extent responsibility has been lost for success or failure here insofar as the cause of success or failure would be largely beyond anyone's control, simply a matter of constitutive moral (cultural?) luck. Children in particular would seem to bear absolutely no responsibility for acquiring concerns they have only external reasons to acquire inasmuch as such reasons are utterly inaccessible to them, thereby undermining the possibility, which Schapiro rightly acknowledges in her setting out of the predicament at the heart of the problem of childhood, that they have some say in determining the cares and concerns central to their evaluative perspective, a say that can make this perspective authoritatively their own. If this is accepted—if children could not be responsible on their own for acquiring such concerns insofar as they have no access whatsoever to reasons for them—then to accept as well the individualist conception of autonomy is to preclude the possibility of solving the problem of childhood. So much the worse for the individualist conception of autonomy. Moreover, on McDowell's account (as for Williams's) it should make no necessary difference whether or not those who provide the reinforcement and explanations to help a child undergo this conversion themselves have any particular relationship with the child: a stranger capable of instilling trust with the right rhetorical flourishes and capable of supporting that rhetoric with appropriate sanctions should be no less effective at inspiring such a conversion than a loving parent.

All of this conflicts with the intuition (which I shall defend) that children can best be enculturated when they have loving relationships with caregivers, for it is only within such relationships that the caregivers can directly make apparent the point of certain concerns (for fairness, say) in such a way that the children themselves can recognize that they ought to take up these concerns. Such an intuition grounds our sense that we are far from helpless even in the face of recalcitrant children and provides the basis for caregivers and children to share significant responsibility for the children's upbringing. As I shall argue, by exploiting the rational interconnections among parents and children involved in a loving relationship, the parents are able not only to provide access to thick evaluative concepts like fairness but also more directly to shape and inculcate concerns informed by these concepts in their children. Because these are rational interconnections, we can see how the children themselves can be held partially accountable for successes or failures in their upbringing. Moreover, I shall argue, these rational interconnections are distinctively interpersonal in a way that both begins to undermine the individualist conception of autonomy and brings into question whether the route to acquiring such concerns can properly be understood as deliberative in nature, and so whether the reasons at issue here are to be understood as internal or external. In the end, I shall suggest, the nature of these reasons themselves is much clearer than their status as internal or external.

7.2 Reciprocal Love and Access to Reasons

In normal love among equals, as I have argued, the lover ought to trust and respect the beloved, finding her cares and values to be reasons for him to care and value similarly for her sake; in this way the lover identifies with her in the way characteristic of love. In the case of an adult's love for a child, however, things are different given the child's immaturity. Of course, the loving adult ought still to respect the child's autonomy or potential for autonomy in defining her identity and well-being, and, where the child's identity has been properly and autonomously determined, the adult ought to trust that identity as well. Yet children, especially young children, do not typically have determinately formed identities; indeed, children young enough not to be able to feel pride, shame, and other person-focused emotions will therefore be unable to love themselves in the way necessary for establishing their own identities and well-beings as persons. Even when the child expresses strong views about what is best for her, the loving adult may with good reason feel and judge that he has a better sense of the child's well-being than the child does, and so may refuse in particular cases to accept the child's sense of import as defining either her own well-being or what he should care about for her sake. Indeed, this is the case for my paternalistic love for my daughter: she understands her well-being selfishly, and I refuse to accept her selfish concerns either as defining her well-being or as binding on me.

Nonetheless, in loving my daughter paternalistically I need to have some sense of what her well-being consists in if I am to be concerned with that well-being in the way that love demands.[23] Thus, assume that I find her well-being to consist in part in a concern for fairness among other things: I find that the life worth her living consists in part in her being fair, even though I recognize that she is not yet, due to her immaturity, in a position to be able to understand what fairness demands. This is for me to be concerned for her sake with her caring about fairness, and my concern is constituted in part in my feeling the relevant emotions focused on her and subfocused on fairness. I ought, therefore, to be proud of her for sharing one of her prized possessions with a friend, disappointed in her for (unfairly) demanding that her twin brother and sister give her some of their goodies, and so on. Moreover, I ought to be motivated to act so as to instill in her the sort of concerns that would enable her to understand her own well-being similarly. Such paternalism, therefore, lacks the sort of trust that characterizes love among equals, and it is proper only when the beloved displays a diminished capacity for autonomy or a diminished understanding that prevents her from seeing the reasons she has for adopting such concerns.[24]

It should be clear that in loving her paternalistically, I am investing myself in her in a way that goes beyond the sort of intimate identification with her that I argued was a part of ordinary love. For I do not simply track, other things being equal, her sense of her well-being but rather come to take responsibility for her well-being more directly through my caring that she become a certain kind of person and so valuing certain things for her sake that she does not yet value. Indeed, as a part of my acting on

---

[23] Of course, if the child is very young, she will not already have a determinate well-being as this person, and so it may not be possible for me to love her in the full way I can someone whose identity is well formed. For now, this distinction does not matter; I shall return to the role a parent can play in developing a child's capacity to value—and so in developing her identity as this person—in §7.3.

[24] Such reasons may be what Williams and McDowell call "internal" reasons, insofar as she may be able to get herself to acknowledge them through a process of reasoning from within her subjective motivational set, or they may be "external" reasons, inasmuch as such reasoning may not be possible for her. I shall discuss these possibilities in §§7.2.1–7.2.2, respectively. For the moment, it suffices that they are reasons for *me* to understand her well-being in this way.

behalf of these values, I ought normally to value my role in guiding and shaping her life, so that I ought to feel pride or shame at my successes or failures in this aspect of my life. The investment of myself in someone I love paternalistically, then, normally involves my finding her growth and development to be a part of the kind of life worth my living.

So far, such properly paternalistic love does little to address the problem of childhood and the dispute concerning internal and external reasons. When the child reciprocates this love, however, things are different, for it is only in a loving relationship that the adult's paternalistic understanding of the child's well-being can make accessible to the child the reasons underlying that understanding. This is because, in short, for my daughter to love me is for her to identify with me in such a way that she shares my cares and values for my sake.[25] Now one thing that I care about is her, including especially that she care about fairness. This means that she ought to care, as a part of loving me, that she care about fairness, and this may seem to establish the requisite connection between my paternalistic understanding of her well-being and the reasons she has to adopt a similar conception and so take on the concerns it involves. This requires further explanation.

One obvious worry about this account is that it does not provide any genuine reasons for my daughter to care about fairness. After all, it may seem, she may simply reject my paternalistic conception of her well-being: "I don't care about being fair!" she may respond to my expression of disappointment in her. It may therefore seem that my account provides no further route to overcoming this sort of resistance than the two-pronged strategy advocated by Schapiro and McDowell—an approach that I criticized on the grounds that it can provide no reasons for her to care about fairness itself rather than merely behaving as if fairly but for the wrong reasons: to avoid punishment, for example. Indeed, in the case of my account it might seem that the strategy is doomed insofar as she cares that she cares about fairness for my sake, as a part of her love for me, rather than caring about fairness for its own sake.

---

[25] As was the case earlier (note 23), I am oversimplifying here. If the child is very young, she may be incapable of the sort of person-focused emotions constituting such love. In such a case, she may nonetheless be capable of caring about me as an agent (rather than as a person), and so caring about the things I care about as a part of caring about me, without distinguishing between my cares and values. I shall ignore this complication here, as it does not affect the main lines of my argument.

Two replies are necessary. First, this worry too quickly assimilates my account to the two-pronged strategy by ignoring what is crucial about the loving relationship. For insofar as my daughter loves me, she has a concern for my well-being that ought, other things being equal, to include a concern for the things I care about and value inasmuch as these affect my well-being. When I love her paternalistically, so that I invest myself in her and make my well-being depend on her developing in a certain way, she ought, as a part of loving me, to care about herself in this way, albeit for my sake. The 'ought' here signals a pro tanto reason, which may be overruled by other, contrary reasons she might have. Thus, it may be that my paternalism is unwarranted, so that I am inappropriately infringing on her autonomy; in such a case, she has good reason to reject my paternalistic attitude toward her (and to try to reform my love for her). However, when there are no such overriding reasons, our loving relationship imposes rational pressure on her to conform to my conception of her well-being, pressure which ought to lead her to share my desire that she come to care about fairness and hence to share both my disappointment in her when she knowingly acts unfairly[26] and my pride in her when she begins to recognize and respond appropriately on her own to considerations of fairness. In this way, our loving relationship provides a further route to overcoming her resistance than that provided by the two-pronged strategy.

Second, this understanding of our loving relationship grounds her having reasons to care about fairness for its own sake and not merely for extrinsic reasons. To see this, we must more carefully specify the contents of the concerns at issue. After all, in loving her paternalistically, I care that she care about fairness for its own sake, and my consequent desire that she come to care about fairness for its own sake would be unsatisfied were she to care about fairness merely for the sake of avoiding negative (or receiving positive) external sanctions, including my approval or disapproval. For her to share this care is for her to care, as a part of caring about me, that she come to care about fairness for its own sake. Although she cares about coming to care about fairness as a part of caring about me, it is only this

---

[26] Care needs to be taken in precisely how this is understood: how can she *knowingly* act unfairly when, as I am presupposing, she is not in a position to understand what (un)fairness is? My claim, to be developed in §7.2.2, is that she can come to know this in particular cases through her relationship with me (as when I warn her in advance that acting like that would be unfair), even while not understanding the general concept.

second-order care that is undertaken for my sake; the first-order care is for fairness for its own sake. The structure of our relationship and her second-order care therefore provides her with a reason to care about fairness for its own sake, contrary to what is claimed in the objection. Or so I shall argue.

Of course this sketch is not yet a solution to the problem of childhood. In particular, I need to show how a child can plausibly care about something like fairness even when he is now incapable of understanding what fairness amounts to. Before addressing this issue directly in §7.2.2, I shall first fill in some details about how, in cases in which the relevant conceptual resources are not beyond our children's grasp, we adults can use our loving relationships with them to provide them with reasons for having certain cares and concerns and thereby help instill these concerns in them. Consequently, my aim in §7.2.1 is, as a kind of warm-up exercise, to think about how within loving relationships parents can help their children recognize what Williams and McDowell would understand to be "internal" reasons for caring about something.

7.2.1 Warm-up: "Internal" Reasons

Consider my paternalistic desire that my son come to care about neatness: how can I instill such a concern in him? Of course I can adopt the two-pronged strategy and talk with him about the benefits of neatness ("You can always find where you put things") and reward or punish him for his successes or failures here. Yet this strategy is one anyone can adopt for any child, and I have claimed that it is not likely to be effective against children who resist that concern. What distinctive strategies are made available to me by virtue of my loving relationship with him? The answer, I shall argue, is that these strategies emerge through my engaged activity with him and my interpretations of my and his responses to that engaged activity.

Recall that in an ordinary case of love among equals, my concern for your well-being involves my sharing your cares and values, and this implies not merely that I share your emotional responses to your circumstances but also your desires. This means that I will normally be motivated to act on your behalf in support of your desires, as a part of my concern for your overall well-being. Of course in desiring something for your sake, I ought not to simply jump in and do it in your stead; rather, I ought to pay special attention to you and the way my participation in this activity affects your well-being. For you may desire not simply that something gets done, but that you be the one who does it, so that for me to take over from you would be to harm you and so would be contrary to my motives in so acting. Even in such cases, I ought nonetheless to offer you encouragement, an ear to listen to your complaints, a shoulder to cry on, and so be a partner in your joys and sorrows, hopes and frustrations—all emotions I share with you for your sake. In other cases in which your caring permits me to help you more actively, my sharing your desire may even result in our having a shared intention—to play tennis or go to the opera together, for example.[27] Yet once again my engaging in this activity with you must be shaped and guided by my love for you: in going to the opera together, we do not merely coordinate our plans and intentions; we coordinate our emotions, as I take my emotional cues from you, coming to share your appreciation of this activity. It is this overall attunement to you and your agency (including not just your actions and desires but also the underlying cares that motivate them) as a part of my loving you that constitutes my *engagement* with you in your (or our) activity.[28]

In the case of a properly paternalistic loving relationship, the adult can use that relationship and their consequent engagement with each other to try to instill in the child certain desires and cares the child does not presently have. This will require some explanation.

Assume that I care that my son care about neatness and so that he has certain desires motivated by that care: to clean his room, for example. Consequently, he ought to care, as a part of loving me, that he care about neatness, and so he ought to care that he has the relevant pattern of emotions and desires constituting that concern for neatness. So far, he may not have much motivation to clean his room, especially if, as I am supposing, he does not yet care about neatness. I can impose some rational pressure on him by expressing my disappointment (or pleasure) in him for failing to respond (or succeeding in responding) as he ought to the import neatness ought to have to him. For given our loving relationship he ought to share these emotional evaluations of himself and so to motivate himself to act as neatness demands.

---

[27] Here, I am, of course, alluding to work on shared intention such as that of Tuomela, *The Importance of Us*; Tuomela, "We-Intentions Revisited"; Tuomela, *Philosophy of Sociality*; Velleman, "How to Share an Intention"; Bratman, "Shared Intention"; Gilbert, *Sociality and Responsibility*.

[28] See §3.3.

I suspect that Schapiro would say that this is a matter of my acting as a "surrogate conscience" for him, for by communicating to him my disappointment or pleasure I am trying to "awaken" in him "a sense of [his] own freedom and responsibility rather than to remind [him] of [his] subjection to an external authority."[29] However, the notion of "surrogacy" suggests that my praise or blame here somehow stands in for the way in which he ought to praise or blame himself, taking the place of his own self-evaluation. Such a notion perhaps seems most applicable to the way we might reward or punish someone, applying a kind of disciplinary force from outside; indeed, this is precisely what Schapiro intends. Yet it does not seem applicable to the sort of shared emotional evaluations at issue here: my son does not simply allow my emotions to substitute for his but rather feels (or ought to feel) these emotions himself. Hence, my emotional evaluations do not substitute for his; rather, given our relationship, the pattern in my emotions imposes rational pressure on him to feel likewise, thereby "inspiring" his emotions through the kind of sympathetic identification characteristic of love. Such a direct connection to his evaluations of himself makes intelligible, in a way that the surrogate disciplinary force does not, how he can come to take responsibility for himself. For insofar as he cares, as a part of caring about me, that he care about neatness, he ought not simply mirror my emotional evaluations of him; the rationality of the pattern of emotions constituting his second-order care means that he ought to experience these emotions even when I do not (as when I am not around to see his success or failure here). This is a matter of his developing the sort of critical self-understanding that just is his *conscience*.

Of course, we should not expect such second-order emotional evaluations to have significant effect motivating a recalcitrant child to care about neatness or to be neat. Thus, my son may simply retort that he does not care about neatness and the motivation he has to do other things may simply override the motivation he gets through these second-order evaluations to get himself to care about it. What is needed is (seemingly paradoxically) for me to show him that he cares about neatness as a way of getting him to care. This requires getting him to feel not merely the second-order evaluations discussed so far, but also first-order evaluations focused directly on neatness itself. It is here that engaged activity becomes relevant.

[29] Schapiro, "What Is a Child?" 736; see p. 217, above.

In order to instill in my son not merely the second-order care that he cares about neatness but the first-order care for neatness itself, I need to get him to experience first-hand not only the frustrations of having a messy room but also the pleasure of having a neat room, the satisfaction of tidying up, and so on. I therefore engage him in activities designed to get him to have these experiences: "Come on," I say, "let's go clean up your room! It'll be fun." Insofar as this is something I want to do—and, indeed, do with him—and insofar as he loves me, he has reason to engage me in this activity. So we make a game of it: seeing how fast he can make his bed, putting his books back on his shelf in order from tallest to shortest, racing to see who can match the most socks, singing songs, and so on. In the process, he has a variety of emotions whose precise content may be indeterminate. Thus, is his pleasure at matching more socks than I did focused on winning, on me (inasmuch as his initial motivation to undertake this activity was to engage me as a part of his loving me), or on neatness (insofar as matching socks is instrumental to being neat)? Indeed, exactly which emotion he feels—its formal object—may be indeterminate, depending on how its focus gets interpreted: is he pleased at winning, does he enjoy doing things with me, or is he satisfied because of his action's contribution to being neat? Such interpretations likewise go hand-in-hand with interpretations of his actions: was he simply playing a game, supporting me, or tidying his room?

We should not assume that these are exclusive options: my son may simultaneously experience all of these emotions (and engage in all of these activities) or only two or one. Nonetheless, what is important for present purposes is the viability of the last option. In getting him to engage me in this activity, my aim is two-fold: to get him to care about neatness for its own sake and to neaten up his room, and my understanding of the activity which I engage in with him has been informed all along by these aims: we have been both getting him to care about neatness and tidying up his room, and I would not have acted as I did if it did not have that effect. My desire, therefore, has a *dual focus*: my son, insofar as my wanting this is a part of my paternalistic love for him, and neatness itself.[30] Given that my son shares my desires as a part of his engaging me in this activity, it is

---

[30] Alternatively, we could say that I have two desires to do the same thing, each with its own focus; this is a distinction without a difference.

proper for me to interpret his emotions at least in part in terms of the focus of my desire: the pleasure he feels is at least in part focused on neatness, just as mine is, so that his desires and emotions ought to be informed by my understanding of what we have been doing.

At this point, one might object, my interpretation here is tainted by the ulterior motive of getting him to care about neatness, and that taint would seem to undermine the validity of the interpretation. Consequently, we might ask why we should think that *his* emotions and actions are focused on neatness itself just because *I* interpret our emotions and actions in this suspect way? Shouldn't the question of how we should interpret his emotions depend on those emotions themselves rather than on my ulterior motives?

The answer lies in the kind of paternalistic loving relationship we have. By virtue of our loving relationship, he ought to share, as a part of his caring about me, my desire that we clean his room, and in sharing this desire he ought to share my interpretation of it and of the particular actions it motivates. Thus, his desire is subfocused on neatness and, because it is one he shares with me as a part of caring about me, focused on me. In addition, however, the "ulterior motive" informing my interpretation of him is one that he ought to share with me by virtue of his caring, as a part of caring about me, that he care about neatness for its own sake. This reason to care about neatness for its own sake gives him a reason to want to clean his room for the sake of neatness: such a desire, motivated by his caring that he care about neatness for its own sake, is therefore focused on neatness itself. This means that his desire to clean his room is one he has both for the sake of neatness and for my sake: like my desire, it has a dual focus. My interpretation of his emotions, desires, and actions, therefore, is not "tainted" by an "ulterior motive," as the objection suggests, because it is informed by a concern he shares with me and that has motivated our actions all along.

Of course, it would be too much to expect my young son to appreciate all these fine-grained distinctions in, and interconnections between, our motivations and so to recognize all on his own that this is how his emotions are to be interpreted. Instead, I must make these interpretations explicit: "That was fun! It sure is satisfying to have such a neat room, isn't it?" The upshot of this remark is to get him to understand his emotions in this way against the backdrop of what we have been doing all along. Once he understands his emotions in this way, he comes to be committed, by virtue of the commitment to the import of neatness now made explicit in this understanding, to feeling other emotions and desires also focused on neatness. In this way, as I claimed, I can show him through engaged activity and interpretation that he cares about neatness as a way of getting him to care.

I have, of course, painted a rosy scenario of my son being extraordinarily responsive to the reasons he has, through our loving relationship, to respond in this way to the import of neatness. In actual cases, he will likely be resistant at various points to engaging with me in such activities, to enjoying these activities and their consequences, to interpreting this enjoyment in particular ways, and so on. Consequently, I may need to work hard at each stage, and over long periods of time, to overcome this recalcitrance through explanations, rewards, threats, and punishments so as to get him to start engaging in the sort of activity that can reveal to him the import that neatness can have.[31] My point, however, is that as a result of our having the kind of paternalistic loving relationship we do, there are kinds of rational pressure I am able to bring to bear on him through engaged activity and interpretation that are simply not available outside such a relationship and so that are simply absent from the two-pronged strategy, which ignores such relationships.

7.2.2 Access to "External" Reasons

So far I have presented an account of how I can try to instill a concern for neatness in my son. Here, we might expect, Williams would point out that this account fits quite well with his understanding of "internal" reasons: it is only because my son loves me—because this is internal to his subjective motivational set—that he has reason to care that he cares about neatness. Part of what makes this plausible is that my son seems already to understand the concept of neatness, at least well enough that we would not hesitate to say that he is using *our* concept of neatness, even if he may subtly misunderstand it in certain ways (by thinking, for example, that books ordered by height are somehow neater than books

---

[31] Indeed, understanding threats and punishment in this way is crucial to understanding how it can result, as Schapiro hopes, not merely in the child's "subjection to external authority" but rather to his awakening to a critical perspective on himself and what has import. I shall return to this in §7.2.2, below.

ordered by subject matter or author's name). However, the account so far is inadequate to make sense of cases like my earlier example of my daughter and the concern for fairness, in which the adult aims at inculcating in the child concerns the child is not yet in a position to understand, even after deliberation. Such cases are cases of allegedly "external" reasons.

Consider, then, the example of my daughter and the concern for fairness. If considerations of fairness are to provide "external" reasons for her, Williams argues, it must be clear that the concept of fairness is one she ought to have. What reasons can there be for her to possess this concept? The answer once again revolves around her loving relationship with me. For given my paternalistic love for her, in which I care that she cares about fairness for its own sake, and given her love for me, she ought to care, as a part of caring about me, that she care about fairness for its own sake. Because this second-order care is one she shares with me, the relevant concept of fairness informing both it and the first-order care is mine, not hers.[32] Moreover, because she does not yet understand the concept of fairness, a necessary condition of her coming to care about fairness is that she come to have that concept, and this will be something she ought to care about as a part of having the second-order care. Consequently, our loving relationship provides her with a reason to possess this concept.

This is, of course, too fast. For given my daughter's lack of understanding of what fairness is, how can we credit her with even the second-order care that she care about fairness? The answer depends on the way in which she is rationally accountable to my caring about her, a caring that is informed by my concepts. Thus, in caring that she care about fairness, I feel pride in her for standing up for one of her friends when considerations of fairness are at stake (or disappointment in her when she fails to do so); I am ashamed of her when she exploits another's inexperience and naivety for her own gain; and so on. These emotions and related desires are rationally interconnected precisely because they are all subfocused on, and so are informed by the concept of, fairness. In sharing this second-order care as a part of loving me, she ought to experience a pattern of related emotions and desires that likewise is rationally structured in accordance with their subfocus on fairness as such; indeed, the rational structure of this pattern is such that she ought to experience these emotions even when I do not.

---

[32] Of course, she may protest; I shall address the status of such protests below.

To deny that the second-order concern she shares with me in virtue of our loving relationship is about fairness is illegitimately to ignore the patterns of rationality that structure that concern. Consequently, her concern, as a part of her love for me, that she care about fairness for its own sake is informed by my concept of fairness, which, given her present inability to understand that concept, she must take on faith, deferring to me on matters of its use. Thus, my conception of fairness has a kind of *authority* for her, such that were I to change my understanding of fairness and therefore of that about which I care that she cares, she ought to as well. In this way, she comes to be beholden to my concept in a way that is not true of the conception of fairness of others, who nonetheless might provoke her to questioning my conception of fairness in ways that might provoke me to revise my understanding of it.[33]

As before, we should not expect these second-order evaluations to motivate a recalcitrant child to care about fairness or to be fair, for the reasons they provide to come to care about fairness may be simply outweighed, at least so far as she is able to understand, by other concerns. Once again, what is needed to overcome this recalcitrance is to get her to feel not merely the emotions and desires constitutive of her second-order concern but also those constitutive of the first-order concern for fairness for its own sake: emotions and desires focused directly on fairness itself. Thus, I must engage her in activity designed to get her to feel emotions that can reasonably be interpreted as focused on fairness, thereby imposing further rational pressure on her to display the entire pattern of emotions with that focus, a pattern that is constitutive of her concern for fairness for its own sake (and as a part of her caring about me).

The complication, of course, is her lack of understanding of fairness. As I argued in Chapter 2, caring about something in general requires both vigilance for when it is affected favorably or adversely and preparedness to respond, both emotionally and in action, when it is thus affected. What my daughter lacks in her misunderstanding of fairness, therefore, is both the ability, required by vigilance, to identify situations reliably that are relevant to issues of fairness and the ability, required by preparedness, to identify reliably what sort of response is required by such situations.

---

[33] I say "provoke" here to signal that she cannot reason with me about it, insofar as I am presupposing that she cannot yet understand the concept; nonetheless, she may use examples of what Jones says about fairness or parrot putative reasons that Smith gives for understanding fairness differently.

Moreover, if she is to acquire the relevant pattern of emotions, these identifications must be ones she makes not merely explicitly in judgment but as the result of coordinated dispositions: she must have the habit of making the appropriate response immediately upon identifying the situation as of the relevant type.[34]

My claim is not that her coming to make these identifications and even to have these emotional responses is possible only if she is taught by someone who loves her paternalistically. Rather, it is that through such a loving relationship she can come to have access to reasons for caring about fairness and so for making these identifications habitually—reasons that are lacking outside of such a relationship. For given that we share the second-order concern that she care about fairness, my attempts to point out to her ways in which particular circumstances are fair or unfair have a kind of authority for her that similar attempts by others lack. Thus, if we set aside my loving relationship with her and consider simply her disputes with others over the proper use of the word, 'fair,' which she is just beginning to use, it may be best to interpret such disputes as merely verbal: she means something different by the word than they do (such as schmairness: the equal distribution of goodies when this is advantageous to me), so that she and they are simply talking past each other. For given the assumption that she is as yet unable to be reasoned into an understanding of what fairness consists in and given the clear conflicts between her understanding of it and the public, linguistic concept, the mere fact that she uses the same word is not enough to show that her use is the same as theirs.

However, given the way in which my concept of fairness essentially informs her emotions and judgments concerning what is fair or not, apparent conflicts between her and me will be genuine and, given the nature of our loving relationship, normally require her to defer to my understanding of the concept. Thus, in particular, were my understanding of fairness to be idiosyncratic, she would have reason, through sharing my second-order concern and absent any independent understanding of fairness, to follow my understanding rather than the public one. On the other hand, if my understanding of fairness itself is an understanding of the public, linguistic concept, then it is only because her use of 'fair' is parasitic

---

[34] For details on how such coordinated dispositions can result in genuine emotions, see Helm, *Emotional Reason*, Ch. 6.

on my understanding that we can make sense of her dispute with others as genuine rather than merely verbal. Thus, the authority my concept of fairness has for her is part of what provides her, within the context of our loving relationship, with a distinctive reason to come to make these identifications, both of situations relevant to considerations of fairness and of appropriate responses to those situations.

I can exploit the authority my concept of fairness for her in part by engaging her in activities—games of various sorts—in which issues of fairness are likely to arise, using these activities not merely as occasions to praise or blame her when she acts fairly or unfairly, as just anyone might be able to do, but also to impose rational pressure on her, both through my emotional responses focused on her and subfocused on fairness and through my interpretations of her emotions, to respond appropriately to the import fairness can have for her. Thus, I may engage her in her activity of playing soccer in part by being supportive and sympathetic of her play. Attending one of her games, I may get angry at her coach for telling her and her teammates to be more aggressive against the opposing team, which is bigger and more skilled than theirs, and so to throw elbows as they fight for the ball. My anger here is, at least in part, focused on her and subfocused on fairness: to play like this is contrary to the place fairness has in her well-being, as I paternalistically conceive of it, so that she therefore has a reason to feel similarly. In addition, when she gets angry after a teammate gets called for a penalty that results in a goal, I can interpret her anger to be focused on fairness: she's angry at her coach for telling them to play unfairly rather than at her teammate for getting caught. Just as I argued in the example of neatness in §7.2.1, she has reason, stemming from her second-order concern, to accept this interpretation and thereby make determinate her emotions as focused on fairness in this way.

I can further exploit the authority of my concept of fairness for her in part through the imposition of sanctions on her in such a way as to overcome the difficulty with the use of sanctions that arose for the two-pronged approach. Recall that the difficulty was to see how the imposition of sanctions can result in something other than the disposition to behave as if the child cares about fairness merely for the sake of those sanctions. In hard cases, in which the child responds only to sanctions, rebuffing proffered explanations as irrelevant, the two-pronged strategy has nothing more to say about how sanctions can act as a "surrogate conscience." Thus, when another child tattles on the recalcitrant child, claiming that he's not sharing with her, he may respond, "I was going to give it to her after I was done." Here, if we set aside as irrelevant (the way the two-pronged strategy does) any loving relationships he finds himself in, this desire seems to be best understood as motivated by fear of punishment given its origins in a past pattern of punishment: he did not come to have this desire until he realized that punishment was in the offing. Thus, his desire is focused on punishment. Were my daughter to make a similar claim, however, the origins of her expressed desire in a past pattern of punishment does not so clearly determine that it is focused on punishment precisely because of the alternative motives afforded by her loving relationship with me. For in virtue of our shared concern that she care about fairness for its own sake, an alternative interpretation can make better sense: she did not come to have the desire to share until she came to recognize that considerations of fairness were at issue. Interpreting her this way, I say, "I'm glad you want to be fair, but you need to tell him your plans." This provides her with reason both to be pleased with herself for her subsequent sharing of the toy as a part of her concern that she care about fairness and to desire to be fair, all as a part of her caring about me. Moreover, the reasons she has to care about fairness for its own sake as a part of caring about me just are reasons for her to desire this for the sake of fairness itself. As before, then, her desire is properly understood as being focused simultaneously on both me and fairness itself.

In general, therefore, the desires and emotions that sanctions give rise to can be interpreted by the loving parent as focused not on the sanction but rather on the paternalistic value itself, thereby providing the child with reasons to feel these desires and emotions with that value as their focus. In this way, the parent can provide the child with reasons and motivation to develop her own conscience in a particular way.

It is important to recognize that the rational impact of these interpretations of her emotions extends beyond these individual cases. For once such emotions are in place, they provide further rational pressure for her to feel subsequent emotions and desires with the same focus so as to acquire the complete pattern of such emotions constitutive of her caring about fairness. In this way, the reasons my daughter has for feeling these emotions and so coming to care about fairness itself allow for her emotions and subsequent caring to be informed by my concept of fairness: such reasons apply to her and so ought to be motivating to some degree even though she does not now understand what fairness consists in and is not yet in a position to be able to arrive at that understanding through a process of deliberation. Thus, the authority my concept of fairness has for her is such that my concept necessarily defines and structures the rationality of the patterns of her responses constitutive of her caring about fairness.

Given this, how should we understand the sort of reasons considerations of fairness provide for my daughter: are they internal or external reasons? Recall that Williams understands this distinction primarily in terms of motivational effectiveness: internal reasons are those that could move us to act (were we to recognize them, possibly after some deliberative process), whereas external reasons are essentially disconnected from motivation. McDowell, on the other hand, understands the distinction in terms of the potential access the subject has to the reasons: internal reasons are ones the subject can access through a deliberative route, whereas external reasons are ones the subject not only does not understand but is not yet in a position to be able to understand even as the result of correct rational deliberation. Against this background, what are we to say about the kind of reasons I have claimed considerations of fairness provide my daughter? On the one hand, they seem like internal reasons insofar as they are potentially motivating: she feels rational pressure, other things being equal, to be moved by considerations of fairness not only to feel the relevant emotions but also to have the relevant desires focused on fairness itself and so to act accordingly. On the other hand, it may seem, they are more like external reasons because the route through which she comes to respond to these reasons as reasons is hardly a matter of deliberation, at least deliberation of the relevant sort. This needs clarification.

Initial resistance to the idea that considerations of fairness are merely external reasons for my daughter might take the following form. Everything she does, including her trust in my sense of her well-being, turns out to be motivated by elements of her subjective motivational set. After all, it is only because she already loves me that she has reason to trust me as a kind of expert with respect to what constitutes her well-being. Such trust, the objection continues, is directly analogous to the trust I have in scientific experts on whose judgments I rely in coming to believe that gluons exist or that space is non-Euclidean, even though I do not understand (and perhaps am incapable of understanding) the relevant conceptual background necessary for properly assessing these claims. For in the scientific case, my reliance on the experts comes through my desire to believe what the experts tell me to believe, whereas my daughter's reliance on me comes through her desire to care about what I think she ought to care about. Consequently, such reasons just are internal reasons after all.

In reply, I do not want to deny that at each stage my daughter's responses are motivated by elements that are at least partially within her subjective motivational set (suitably extended via deliberative processes). This fact alone, however, is not enough to say that the reasons supporting that motivation are internal, for the question is in part whether we can properly explain these responses by appeal merely to such elements. This raises questions concerning precisely what that internality comes to: can we understand my daughter's responses as already a part of her subjective motivational set? Precisely what is the nature of the sort of deliberation that can extend a person's subjective motivational set? (What does that subjectivity amount to?) As I have noted, Williams is notoriously loose in his understanding of the notion of deliberation. Keeping with this looseness, we should construe deliberation as a matter of proceeding from one thought to another, where such thoughts encompass not only beliefs, judgments, and intentions but also perceptions, imaginings, emotions, and the like. Consequently, we need to consider whether the relevant thought moves my daughter undergoes should count as deliberation of a sort that extends her subjective motivational set and so makes considerations of fairness be internal reasons for her. I shall now offer two reasons for thinking that this is not the case.

First, insofar as what is at stake is the constitution of her *subjective* motivational set, it might seem that the sort of deliberation through which she comes to be induced into having certain thoughts must be the result of her own mental states and abilities. After all, for me to impose a thought on her from the outside might be considered a matter of brainwashing, whatever reasons I might have for doing this, such that this thought would not genuinely belong to her subjective motivational set. Indeed, such a conception of deliberation as essentially being from within one's subjective motivational set is an instance of the individualist conception of autonomy. Consequently, it seems, thoughts arrived at as the result of thought moves that are essentially *interpersonal* do not count as subjective in the relevant sense. This is precisely how my daughter comes to have access to and be motivated by considerations of fairness, a kind of access and motivation she would not have all on her own. For such access and motivation essentially depend on her loving relationship with me: it is an essentially interpersonal matter in which, through both my paternalistic concern for her and her concern for me, my concept of fairness itself informs her emotions, desires, and judgments, so that she thereby has reason to have the whole pattern of emotions, desires, and judgments focused on fairness in the relevant actual and counterfactual situations. In this way, I provide something like a scaffold that enables her access to and motivation by considerations of fairness, access and motivation that are not intelligible simply in virtue of her mental states and abilities. Such scaffolding seems inconsistent with the kind of individualism at issue in talk of a subjective motivational set.

Now surely Williams would accept the possibility that extending my motivational set in a particular way may be the result of my talking things out with someone else, so that such extensions would count as already internal; indeed, given certain psychological facts about me, it may be that I never would have come to see things this way and so to extend my motivational set accordingly had I not talked things out with someone else. Yet such deliberation together with another person is not ordinarily essentially interpersonal insofar as we could imagine my being capable of making the relevant thought moves all on my own, perhaps by imagining what my interlocutor would say or what perspective she brings. In the case of my daughter, however, the thought moves required to provide her with new motives are, I have claimed, *essentially* interpersonal: what makes considerations of fairness themselves (rather than her love of me or her fear of punishment) be the reasons for her to have particular emotions and desires, and so what makes these emotions and desires be focused on fairness itself, is the way my concept of fairness comes to inform her emotions and desires as the result of the particular loving relationship we have and so the way in which I actively shape her emotions and desires through interpretation. Consequently, her ability to respond to considerations of fairness is made possible by our loving relationship.

Does the fact that the deliberation required to extend one's motives is essentially interpersonal in this way disqualify the reasons that deliberation uncovers from being internal reasons because they are not "subjective" in the relevant sense? As I indicated, this might be suggested by the idea of a subjective motivational set, where such subjectivity—perhaps grounded in the individualist conception of autonomy—may seem to require that whether or not a reason is internal to this set is a matter of the individual's mental states and abilities. Even so, the answer is not clear if only because of Williams's broad and loose understanding of what deliberation involves. Nonetheless, to the extent to which we accept such essentially interpersonal deliberation as capable of defining the extension of one's subjective motivational set, we weaken both the relevant notion of subjectivity and, therefore, the claim that something is an internal reason. I shall return to this point shortly.

A second reason for thinking the kind of thought moves my daughter makes in responding to considerations of fairness are not instances of deliberation of the relevant sort concerns the role of habituation. Part of what is behind McDowell's understanding of conversion as involving the subject's coming to acknowledge what had previously been merely external reasons is that conversion, at least of the sort involved in enculturation, involves the acquisition of new skills through habituation. Just as we would not say that the process of learning to ride a bike is deliberative, so too we would not say that the process of learning to recognize colors or oak trees or even valid inferences is deliberative.[35] The same goes for recognizing when considerations of fairness are in play and for responding appropriately to these considerations: in each case, acquiring the relevant recognitive capacities is possible only through habituation—practice and training—and as such are to be acquired only gradually. McDowell rightly claims that acquiring thick evaluative concepts like fairness is possible only through acquiring these habits of perception and response, habits which, when they are in place, can properly be said to be informed by those concepts. Indeed, he understands the two-pronged approach as a method of training whereby the parent aims to get the child to acquire the relevant cognitive-cum-practical skills. It is this role of habituation and training in such conversions that explains why conversions are not processes of deliberation, so that the reasons one comes to recognize in this way were not, in one's "preconversion" state, internal reasons.

The same moral seems to apply to my understanding of a child's upbringing in the context of a loving relationship. The ways in which I

---

[35] On the latter point, see Lewis Carroll, "What the Tortoise Said to Achilles," *Mind* 4 (1895): 278–80.

can exploit the authority of my concept of fairness for my daughter so as to provide her with reasons to act accordingly depends in part on this two-pronged strategy, augmented with the role my interpretations of her in light of my concept of fairness can play in disambiguating her emotional and desiderative responses. Moreover, although I have described my daughter as having access to *reasons* for accepting the authority of my concept and my interpretations of her, the effect of this authority is a transformation of her habits of perception and response that is intelligible only as a part of a larger process of habituation and training that taken together seems not to be intelligible as a process of deliberation.

So again: are these reasons my daughter has to respond to considerations of fairness internal or external reasons? I have offered two arguments for thinking that the process she undergoes in acquiring a concern for fairness is not one that can be understood solely or even primarily as deliberative, or at least deliberative in the relevant sense. Of course, we could stipulate that insofar as there are reasons in play for my daughter to make the relevant thought moves at each stage—indeed, reasons to which she has access—these moves are deliberative, so that considerations of fairness provide her with internal reasons after all. Such a stipulation, however, would seem to weaken the notion of an internal reason to such a degree as to make the distinction between internal and external reasons, and so Williams's claim that all reasons are internal, all but meaningless. In the end, perhaps, it does not matter: we can now see that there is a nebulous middle ground between internal and external reasons, and the kind of reasons adults can provide for children within a paternalistically loving relationship lies somewhere in that middle ground. Getting clear on the nature of these reasons as essentially interpersonal is more important than trying to force on them a label of "internal" or "external."

7.3 Developing Persons

In the account of the sort of rational influence loving caregivers can have on their children presented so far, I have ignored the fact that very young children do not yet have the capacity for person-focused felt evaluations, cannot fully love themselves (or others), and so have no determinate identity as persons. This raises the question of how young children can acquire this capacity in the first place and so can become full-blooded, autonomous persons. Indeed, this is ultimately the problem of childhood.

Loving yourself, as I have argued, presupposes that you have the capacity for person-focused felt evaluations; when focused on yourself, these felt evaluations evaluate particular actions, omissions, and motives in terms of their bearing on the kind of life worth your living. Of course, having the capacity for such felt evaluations requires that you not only are capable of feeling, say, pride, but that you are capable of feeling a broad spectrum of positive and negative, epistemic and factive person-focused felt evaluations, including in addition shame, anxiety, and self-assurance (see §4.2). For a condition of the possibility of having the capacity for any of these felt evaluations is that your felt evaluations are by and large warranted, and such warrant is possible only if they come in projectible, rational patterns constituting the import of their common focus—constituting your love for that focus.

Part of what makes these felt evaluations distinctive is their focus on persons: to have the sense of a particular person's well-being that these felt evaluations involve requires that you be capable of evaluating particular motives or actions in light of their contribution to that well-being, so that these evaluations are second-order and involve your identification, either with the thing valued or with another person (see Chapters 4–5). The question, then, is how children can acquire the capacity for such evaluations and so the capacity for love and self-love. In particular, how can they acquire the concepts informing the formal objects of person-focused evaluations—concepts like those of nobility and degradation—that distinguish these felt-evaluations from their non-person-focused counterparts, like pleasure and displeasure?[36]

Of course, the two-pronged strategy can help. Offering praise or condemnation, providing honors or requiring public apologies, all backed up by suitable explanations and justifications ("How dare you exploit him like that! You ought to be ashamed of yourself") can gradually inculcate

---

[36] In approaching this question, we should not assume that a child first acquires the concepts of nobility and degradation and then comes to be capable of person-focused felt evaluations like pride and shame. For given that these are concepts of thick evaluative properties, it would seem that a child would not properly understand nobility, for example, without being already capable of feeling or anticipating pride and being motivated to act accordingly. Thus, possessing these concepts presupposes having the capacities for person-focused felt evaluations, including second-order desires, as well as vice versa: they form a conceptual package that must be acquired simultaneously or not at all.

suitable habits of response in a child and begin to provide him with an understanding of the relevant evaluative concepts and, simultaneously, the capacity for person-focused felt evaluations. However, even setting aside the worries already raised about the impotence of the two-pronged strategy in the face of recalcitrant children, there is a further problem that emerges in the context of getting a child not merely to care about something but to value it and so to find it a part of the kind of life worth his living. If we are to provide the child with an adequate conceptual grasp of the formal objects of the relevant person-focused emotions so as to make possible a more "authentic" self-love, the child must recognize the place of individual autonomy in determining the kind of life worth one's living. For at stake here, in the context of thinking about a person's identity, are not universal values that everyone ought to share (such as moral values), but *personal* values that are relative to the individual and serve to distinguish one person's identity from those of others. Consequently, we cannot simply impose characteristically personal values on a child from the outside via the two-pronged approach, for to do so would be to undermine or at least fail to develop the very capacity for autonomy that is central to his taking responsibility for his own identity as this person and so to his properly loving himself: in adopting the two-pronged strategy, he is being held accountable to others rather than for and to himself. How, then, can we instill not just cares but also personal values in children in such a way as to preserve their responsibility, without simply imposing those values on them? In answering this question, it is once again crucial to recognize the loving relationships children can have with adults.

Assume that my daughter starts to take an interest in science and mathematics and discovers that she is very good at them; as she learns more and more, she increasingly comes to take pleasure in it. This vague description leaves it open precisely what her feelings are and so what she cares about: is this mere satisfaction in something that is not really that important, or is it a pride in this facet of her intellectual abilities, reflecting the newfound value science and math have to her? Of course, she may be unable to formulate the question in these terms in part because she may not yet have a clear grasp of the distinction between caring and valuing and so of the distinction between, for example, satisfaction and pride. Indeed, her inability clearly to distinguish these possibilities may leave her open to peer pressure: she may sense that others think that girls should not take science and math—or their intellects—too seriously, thereby leading her to interpret her concern as mere caring. Such peer pressure, as for the application of punishment and reward of the two-pronged approach, potentially bypasses her autonomy and responsibility for developing her own identity.

Here I can use my loving relationship with my daughter to shape her evaluative responses and so potentially to instill in her a value for science. Against the background both of explanations to her of the value of intellectual activity in general and science and math in particular and of consistent engagement with her in the relevant sorts of activities, I can offer interpretations of her felt evaluations as person-focused. Thus, as she completes a working model of the solar system or demonstrates mastery of long division, I may say, "You're really proud of these, aren't you," thereby interpreting her evident pleasure as person-focused. Informing my interpretation here is my understanding not only of what values are (and so of the concepts of the various formal objects of person-focused felt evaluations, such as nobility and degradation) but also of what are permissible or even worthy candidates as objects of value. Once again, given both her relative lack of understanding of these issues and the paternalism that characterizes our loving relationship, my understanding has a kind of authority for her by informing her felt evaluations and so her sense of import, thereby providing her with reason to accept this interpretation of her pleasure as person-focused and so her concern as valuing rather than caring.

Of course, to provide her with the concepts of nobility and degradation, I'll need to use these concepts in contexts other than those relevant to the value of science. In part, this is a part of the normal process of moral education, identifying particular traits, such as courageousness, as modes of a worthy life for anyone precisely because such a life involves a kind of nobility worthy of pride. Yet, as I have noted, insofar as what is at stake are ultimately personal rather than moral values, I must also find other occasions in which to bring out the idea that these can be personal choices. Reading literature together can help: we can talk about *Charlotte's Web* and whether she would like to be like Charlotte or Templeton (the rat) and why, coming to the conclusions that Charlotte ought to be proud of herself for her selfless courage in her final hours and that Templeton ought to be ashamed of himself for his greed and egotism. Here we can see that

Schapiro is right, in her discussion of the transition from childhood to adulthood, to emphasize the role of trying on another's persona in play. However, such play is not the normal mode of childhood in which all of their actions in the course of their daily lives have a merely provisional character; it is rather a distinctive exercise of imagination that provides an opportunity, in part through the influence and authority of parents, for children to learn not merely the relevant evaluative concepts, like nobility and degradation, but also the possibilities for response in action, felt evaluation, and judgment, as these responses are informed by those evaluative concepts.

This appeal to the authority of a loving parent may seem contrary to my claim that through loving relationships we can instill values in children without undermining their autonomy. However, it should be clear that the kind of rational authority at issue here ought to be sensitive to the child's capacity for autonomy. For, on the one hand, this authority derives not simply from the existence of a loving relationship between the adult and child, but from the character of this relationship as properly paternalistic. Thus, we have been assuming that my daughter so far fails to have an adequate understanding all on her own of the relevant concepts informing her felt evaluations, so that the concerns she shares with me in the context of our relationship rationally require that her felt evaluations be informed by my concepts. In part this implies that in the early stages of her development into a person my daughter will not yet have acquired the ability to decide what does and does not form a part of her identity and so will not yet have acquired a capacity for autonomy;[37] consequently, in these early stages it does not yet make sense to speak of her capacity for autonomy as being undermined by my authority. Yet, on the other hand, I ought to be sensitive to her growing capacity for autonomy as a part of my love for her, for to love someone is to be concerned with her well-being as this person, where this well-being crucially depends on her having and exercising a capacity for autonomy. This requires not merely that I generally offer explanations (in part clarifying the relevant evaluative concepts) to justify my attempts to shape her values in a particular way but also, as her capacity for autonomy gradually develops, that we constantly readjust our relationship so that I ought to allow her increasing latitude in

[37] Contra Schapiro, "What Is a Child?" 729; see n. 4.

exercising her autonomy in appropriate ways, and so I ought thereby to come more and more to trust her growing sense of her own identity.

The relevant standards of appropriateness here are ill-defined in ways that can be quite hazardous to the loving relationship between an adult and child. The adult, concerned for the child's well-being, may find that she makes poor choices concerning what to value (even if these choices are otherwise morally permissible) and so may try to be more proactive in shaping her values.[38] In the face of these attempts, the child may rebel, perhaps becoming even more entrenched in her evaluative perspective as a result. There is, of course, room for culpable irrationality on both sides: the adult may overreach and abuse his authority by failing to be sensitive to the ability of the child properly to exercise her autonomy, and the child may fail to be properly sympathetic to the adult's concern for her for her sake and to the authority his concepts ought to have for her. Although rational conflict may be inevitable (as it is within an individual), the key is how such conflict gets resolved. In his attempts to instill particular values in the child, the adult ought to be properly constrained by his concern for her well-being, including her autonomy, so that in the face of resistance from the child these attempts take into consideration to an appropriate degree the child's growing sense of her own identity. Likewise, the child's cares and values ought to be properly informed by the more sophisticated conceptual understanding of the adult, an understanding that leads the adult to intervene on the child's behalf. When this is so, the adult and child can share responsibility for the values the child comes to have in a way that allows us to retain the idea that these values are authentically the child's own. As the child's identity as this person comes to be increasingly determinate, and so as her capacity for autonomy develops more fully, the balance of this responsibility shifts more and more completely to the child herself.

7.4 Conclusion

In this chapter, I have begun to examine reciprocal loving relationships, in particular those loving relationships that are characterized by a kind of

[38] This is not a matter of the adult's identifying limited domains in which the child's decisions and activity are not merely provisional, as Schapiro thinks, but is rather based on the adult's substantive conception of what is in the child's best interests.

proper paternalism as a result of an antecedent inequality in status between the participants. In such a relationship, I have argued, the child ought to share certain concerns the parent has for her for her sake, and so the child's concerns ought to be informed by the relevant thick evaluative concepts of the parent. Consequently, the parent's evaluative concepts have a kind of authority for the child insofar as it is these concepts that inform the child's shared cares. In this way, the parent's paternalistic understanding of the child's well-being provides a kind of scaffold for the child that provides her with access to reasons for caring she could not now have all on her own. Given the mediation of the loving relationship, we can say that such access to reasons is essentially *interpersonal*.

This understanding of paternalistic loving relationships enables me to solve the problem of childhood. A child can acquire an evaluative perspective in terms of which she can make autonomous choices not simply as the result of external, arational forces acting on her, as the two-pronged strategy would have it. Rather, I have argued, through a properly paternalistic loving relationship the parent can impose rational pressure on the child so as to instill certain cares and values in her; given the shared concerns and the way in which the parent's concepts inform those concerns, such an imposition is not the result merely of external forces acting on the child but is rather a means of enabling the child's conscience, her sense of responsibility for her cares, her actions, and her identity. Moreover, it is only because reasons are at stake (rather than mere external force) that we can make sense of those having access to those reasons as being potentially responsible for the outcome. To the extent that the child's access to these reasons is essentially interpersonal, so too is the responsibility for her coming (or failing to come) to care about or value appropriate objects: that responsibility is to that extent shared between the child and the parent. Without this, we parents can have no rational purchase on our children as they develop, so that we and they can only abdicate responsibility for the cares and values they ultimately come to have—for their identities as persons.

As I indicated, the interpersonal nature of the access to reasons a child can have within a paternalistically loving relationship, together with the nature of the transition the child undergoes to caring about fairness, for example, calls into question the importance of the distinction between internal and external reasons. For what makes that distinction seem important, I suggested, is a notion of subjectivity that seems to presuppose the individualist conception of autonomy, which my account thus far begins to undermine. For a child's responsiveness to reasons in virtue of which she can exercise some control not only over her actions but also over her feelings and thereby her cares and values, can depend essentially on her personal relationships with others. Consequently, the distinction between what belongs and what does not belong to an agent's subjective motivational set, and so the distinction between internal and external reasons, is not nearly as sharp as Williams and McDowell seem to think.

This conception of the role of paternalistic love in developing a child's identity as this person resonates with some things Marilyn Friedman says about how romantic love can "promote the growth of competencies for autonomy." As she puts it:

The shared activities and projects of love in particular engage us jointly with our lovers over the whole trajectory of agency: attending to situations, evaluating circumstances, making decisions, expressing our concerns in action, and living with the consequences of our choices. One's more autonomous lover might be able to show how to maintain one's commitments in the midst of difficult situations or how to imagine alternatives to them.[39]

Once again,[40] this is quite suggestive, though Friedman has done little to provide an account that can explain how this is possible. To a limited extent, that is what I have provided in the context of paternalistic loving relationships. This account, however, will have interesting implications for other sorts of loving relationships, including not only romantic relationships but also relationships of friendship. Indeed, exploring these implications and what they tell us about the essentially social nature of persons is my aim in Chapter 8.

---

[39] Friedman, "Romantic Love," 175–6.   [40] Cf. §6.4, p. 209.

8

Friends Are Other Selves

I have claimed that providing an adequate account of loving relationships like friendship requires significant revision to our ordinary conception of persons. In particular, we must come to understand persons as essentially social in ways denied by the ordinary conception, with its insistence on the individualist conception of autonomy. I shall now argue for these claims by offering a positive account of friendship in which at least certain kinds of friends are understood to be "other selves," such that they, to a certain extent, share a capacity for autonomy.

To motivate this account, I shall first, in §8.1, examine a variety of alternative accounts of friendship and, in particular, their understanding of the kind of intimacy characteristic of friendship. My tentative, suggestive conclusion will be that the intimacy of friendship crucially involves the friends being uniquely able to shape each other's thoughts, feelings, and lives, at least within particular domains defined within their friendship. They do this by "sharing," in a stronger sense than that required by reciprocal love, not only their evaluative perspectives but also their activity and so their lives (within that domain). To start to make sense of such "sharing," I turn in §8.2 to examine standard accounts of shared activity, arguing that these accounts fail to do justice to the kind of shared activity characteristic of friendship. In §8.3, I provide an alternative account of this sort of shared activity, which gets expanded, in §8.4, into a general account of friendship.

8.1 Intimacy and Standard Accounts of Friendship

As I indicated in §1.5, a loving relationship like friendship must involve something more than just reciprocal love among equals: adult siblings may love each other and yet fail to be friends. For, it seems, an essential part of friendship is the way in which friends are involved in at least portions of each other's lives, dynamically influencing and shaping each other in the process. Indeed, it might seem, such involvement constitutes a kind of intimacy not merely in the attitudes each has for the other, as for love, but rather in the relationship itself. I shall now argue that making sense of this intimacy requires rethinking the way in which the relationship of friendship involves activity on the part of the friends. In so doing, it will be useful to examine alternative accounts of friendship and the ways they try to cash out such intimacy; as we shall see, such accounts typically (and, I shall argue, mistakenly) understand such intimacy largely in terms of a kind of passive response of the friends to each other.

Laurence Thomas claims that we should understand what I am calling the intimacy of friendship in terms of mutual self-disclosure: I tell my friends things about myself that I would not dream of telling others, and I expect them to make me privy to intimate details of their lives.[1] The point of such mutual self-disclosure, Thomas argues, is to create the "bond of trust" essential to friendship, for through such self-disclosure we simultaneously make ourselves vulnerable to each other and acknowledge the goodwill the other has for us. Such a bond of trust is what institutes the kind of intimacy characteristic of friendship.[2]

Dean Cocking and Jeanette Kennett have caricatured this as the "*secrets view*," arguing:

It is not the sharing of private information nor even of very personal information, as such, that contributes to the bonds of trust and intimacy between companion friends. At best it is the sharing of what friends care about that is relevant here.[3]

Their point is that the secrets view underestimates the kind of trust at issue in friendship, conceiving of it largely as a matter of discretion (of a sort we expect from our therapists and lawyers). Given the way friendship essentially involves not just discretion but also mutual love, each ought to care about the other's well-being for the other's sake and so act on behalf of that well-being. Entering into and sustaining a relationship of friendship will normally involve considerable trust in your friend's goodwill toward

---

[1] Thomas, "Friendship"; Thomas, "Friends and Lovers"; Thomas, "Friendship and Other Loves."
[2] A similar account can be found in David B. Annis, "The Meaning, Value, and Duties of Friendship," *American Philosophical Quarterly* 24 (1987): 349–56.
[3] Cocking and Kennett, "Friendship and the Self," 518.

you generally, and not just concerning your secrets; such trust would be in addition to the kind of trust I have argued is central to love (on which, more below). Consequently, Thomas fails to acknowledge the way in which friendship normally involves trust in your friend's judgment concerning what is in your best interest, for when your friend sees you harming yourself, she ought, other things being equal, to intervene, and through the friendship you can come to rely on her to do so.

Given this, we might try to cash out the kind of intimacy characteristic of friendship in terms of the normal effects of such enhanced trust: in terms of "shared interest or enthusiasms or views . . . [or] a similar style of mind or way of thinking which makes for a high degree of empathy."[4] Elizabeth Telfer finds such shared interests central to the "sense of a bond" that friends have.[5] For trusting your friend's assessments of your own good in this way seemingly involves trusting not only that she understands who you are and *that* you find certain things valuable and important in life but also and centrally that she understands the *value* of these things that are so meaningful to you. That in turn seems to be grounded in your in some sense sharing a sense of what is important with your friend. Such a shared sense of importance therefore provides a richer sense of the intimacy essential to friendship than that offered by Thomas.

Nonetheless, it matters precisely how we understand the sharing of such concerns. If we follow Telfer in understanding such sharing as a kind of empathy, as something like the kind of shared cares and values I have argued are a part of love and the sort of trust that is normally a part of love, then we seem to have an inadequate basis for the intimacy of friendship. For, again, adult siblings can love each other without being friends, and so mere reciprocal love among equals cannot be sufficient for friendship. We can, perhaps, see this more clearly by considering the *mirror view* of friendship, which has its origins in Aristotle's claim that a friend is a kind of mirror of yourself. If we construe the sense in which we share concerns with our friends in terms of similarity of character, then an examination of our friends ought to provide us with some insight into our own qualities of character: they reflect our own

---

[4] Elizabeth Telfer, "Friendship," *Proceedings of the Aristotelian Society* 71 (1970–71): 227.
[5] This is similar to the "solidarity"—the sharing of values and a sense of what is important—that Richard White thinks is central to friendship. See White, *Love's Philosophy.*

character and so provide a mirror for our selves.[6] The idea is not simply that your friend's character is exactly like your own, so that to know your friend is to know yourself. Rather, minor differences between you and your friend, as when your friend occasionally makes a choice or responds emotionally in ways you would not, can lead you to reflect on whether this difference reveals a flaw in your own character that might need to be fixed, thereby reinforcing the similarity of you and your friend's evaluative outlooks and so, one might think, establishing the intimacy needed for friendship.[7]

On this reading of the mirroring view, your friend plays an entirely passive role: just by being himself, he enables you to come to understand your own character better. Cocking and Kennett argue that this appeal to the friend's role as a mirror in understanding the intimacy of friendship involves assigning too much passivity to the friend, for our friends play a more active role in shaping us than the mirroring view is able to acknowledge.[8] In particular, they argue, what your friend provides is not so much a passive reflection as an interpretation of you, through which he can actively shape your perception of yourself and thereby change your character. Thus, your friend may admire your tenacity (a trait you did not realize you had), or may be amused by your excessive concern for fairness, and you may come as a result to develop a new understanding of yourself, and potentially change yourself, in direct response to his interpretation of you. The mirror view therefore distorts the relationship between the friends by ignoring the active role your friend can play in shaping your self.[9]

In addition to the effects a friend can have on you through interpretation, Cocking and Kennett think your friend can actively shape you in another

---

[6] Indeed, if we follow Aristotle in thinking that we can have only imperfect direct knowledge of ourselves, such mirroring will be indispensable in understanding ourselves.

[7] For an elaboration of this argument, see, e.g., Badhwar, "Love."

[8] Cocking and Kennett, "Friendship and the Self," 513.

[9] This criticism of the mirror view applies as well to Elijah Millgram's account of the role of mirroring in shaping your friends (Elijah Millgram, "Aristotle on Making Other Selves," *Canadian Journal of Philosophy* 17 (1987): 361–76). According to Millgram, in mirroring my friend, I am causally responsible for his coming to have the virtues he does; this makes me, in a sense, my friend's "procreator." However, in offering this account, Millgram seems to confound my being *causally necessary* for my friend's virtues with my being *responsible* for them: to confound my passive role as a mirror with that of a "procreator," a seemingly active role. Millgram's understanding of mirroring does not, therefore, escape Cocking and Kennett's criticism of mirroring views as assigning too much passivity to the friend as mirror.

way: by *directing* you—imposing his interests, values, and so on on to you. Thus, your friend may suggest that you and he go to the opera together, and you may agree to go, even though you have no antecedent interest in the opera. Through his interest, enthusiasm, and suggestion ("Didn't you just love the concluding duet of Act III?"), you may be moved directly by him to acquire an interest in opera because he is your friend. Thus, according to Cocking and Kennett, to be friends with someone is for each of you to be receptive to interpretation and direction from the other, so that "the self my friend sees is, at least in part, a product of the friendship."[10] This they call the *drawing view* of friendship.[11]

Although Cocking and Kennett are right in understanding your friend to play an active role in shaping you through the friendship, and although this is an improvement over the secrets and mirror views of friendship, they do not go far enough in making sense of the place of activity in understanding the intimacy of friendship. Notice that it is unclear what your role is in being thus directed and interpreted by your friend. Is it a matter of merely passively accepting the direction and interpretation? This is suggested by Cocking and Kennett's use of the word, 'receptivity,' and by their apparent understanding of this receptivity in dispositional terms; indeed, it is what lies behind their sense that friendships can be potentially morally dangerous insofar as a friend can direct you to do something you ought not do: "I am just as likely to be directed by your interest in gambling at the casino as by your interest in ballet."[12] Here they seem to be insufficiently sensitive to the way in which the friends' concern for each other's well-being is reciprocal, so that there is the potential for a conflict between a friend directing you to do something wrong and your interpretation of him as acting or desiring badly: if you understand gambling to be wrong, then you fail in your concern for your friend if you blindly go along with him. Indeed, blindly to allow yourself to be directed by your friend would seem to be a matter of simply ceding your autonomy to your friend, and that surely is not what they intend. Indeed, Cocking and Kennett explicitly acknowledge that we are somehow selective in the ways in which we allow our friends to direct and interpret us, and we can resist other directions and

---

[10] Cocking and Kennett, "Friendship and the Self," 505.
[11] Such a view is prefigured in Rorty, "The Historicity of Psychological Attitudes."
[12] Dean Cocking and Jeanette Kennett, "Friendship and Moral Danger," *Journal of Philosophy* 97, no. 5 (2000): 286.

interpretations.[13] Yet although it surely is possible for our friends to have morally dangerous influence on us, this selectivity of interpretation and direction might lead us to wonder whether we are as impotent concerning this influence as their account suggests—and so whether the worry they raise about moral danger in friendship therefore is overblown.

A more important question is this: on what basis are we selective in allowing our friends to direct and interpret us in this way? One type of answer would be that we allow it because we recognize the independent value of the interests of our friends, or that we recognize the truth of their interpretations of us. Yet such answers would not explain the role of friendship in direction and interpretation, for we might just as easily accept such direction and interpretation from a mentor or possibly even a stranger. For friendship to play the role Cocking and Kennett rightly recognize it as having, the answer must rather be that our receptivity to direction and interpretation is to be understood not in dispositional terms but rather in normative terms: we *ought* to accept direction and interpretation from our friends as providing us with defeasible reasons precisely because they are our friends—because as friends we offer such direction and interpretation from within an evaluative perspective on what it is worth doing and who it is worth being that we come to share by virtue of our dynamic interaction as friends. The sharing of concerns, then, would seem to be a sharing of evaluative perspective, so that understanding the intimacy of friendship requires making sense of the dynamics of the friendship relationship in essentially normative terms, contrary to what Cocking and Kennett claim.

This is not, of course, a knock-down argument for the idea that the intimacy of friendship is to be understood in terms of the sharing of an evaluative perspective. Nonetheless, it is suggestive in a way that intersects with my conclusion drawn in §1.5 from a discussion of the nature of sort of shared activity characteristic of friendship: to make sense of such shared activity, we must understand the friends not merely to coordinate their activity in pursuit of a common aim but rather to be capable of deliberating together in a way that is closely analogous to how an individual does so: from within a single evaluative perspective they share in common. Indeed, the dynamic interaction just described is presupposed by the kind of shared activity characteristic of friendship. Alternative accounts of friendship often

---

[13] See Cocking and Kennett, "Friendship and the Self," 524–5.

pay lip service to the idea of shared activity, claiming that friendship involves or requires that the friends engage in shared activity with each other. This lip service, however, is never supported by an explicit account of what the shared activity characteristic of friendship consists in, and (as I argued in §1.5) existing accounts of shared intention, designed as they are to make sense of a much broader and therefore weaker phenomenon, are inadequate to the task in this context. Consequently, the implications of such shared activity for our understanding of persons generally, and the individualist conception of autonomy in particular, have gone unexamined. My aim, therefore, is to provide (in §§8.2–8.3) an explicit account of shared activity and so to use this account (in §8.4) as a way of cashing out the kind of intimacy characteristic of friendship.

8.2 Agency v. Goal-Directedness

As I already suggested in §1.5, existing accounts of shared activity or shared intention seem ill-suited to making sense of friendship. For such accounts are intended to cover many kinds of cases, including cases of shared activity that arise and dissolve within the space of a few minutes, as when two strangers go on a walk together and then never meet again;[14] as such, they have no special place for the kind of stable, loving relationship that friendship is. In order to avoid this limitation of alternative accounts, my aim will be to discuss a distinct kind of social phenomenon, which I call "plural agency," that is richer and more intimate than any so far articulated. For, I shall argue, standard accounts of shared activity and shared intention largely ignore a crucial dimension of our social lives—our emotional attachments to each other—and by doing so fail to make a crucial distinction between what I shall call "plural goal-directedness" and "plural robust action." I shall argue that the failure to make this distinction stems from the failure to recognize the social dimension emotions can have, as when we feel fear, joy, disappointment, and the rest on behalf of others.[15] This requires some explanation.

[14] See, for example, Margaret Gilbert, "Walking Together," *Midwest Studies in Philosophy* 15 (1990): 1–14.
[15] Of course, some accounts of the "emotion" of love make an appeal to this phenomenon. (See, for example, Nozick, *Examined Life*; Frankfurt, *Necessity, Volition, and Love*.) However, none of these

In §2.1, I claimed, following Daniel Dennett,[16] that a mere intentional system is a creature that is intelligible as having goals and pursuing them by virtue of displaying a projectible pattern of instrumental rationality in its behavior. Thus, a chess-playing computer is an intentional system and has the goal of winning the game by virtue of the way in which its moves are, by and large, rational as attempts to achieve that goal. I argued, however, that such an account falls short of being an account of robust agency because it fails to address the problem of import: (robust) agents do not merely exhibit goal-directedness but rather pursue these goals because they find them *worth* pursuing—because they have import. Given my account of what it is to be a subject of import, this means that we can make sense of the distinction between goal-directedness and robust agency only in terms of the emotional capacities of agents in virtue of which things have import to them, so that the exercise of their agency is in part an exercise of their emotional capacities.

This distinction between goal-directedness and agency, between mere intentional systems and robust agents, can be used in making sense of social action as well: we need to distinguish between plural intentional systems and plural robust agents in much the same way. Thus, a *plural intentional system* will exhibit a pattern of goal-directedness in the collective behavior of the individuals that make it up, behavior that is mediated rationally through "its" informational states—through the group's overall responsiveness to its environment. There are at least three distinct kinds of plural intentional systems. Ant or termite colonies, for example, are plural intentional systems insofar as the goal-directedness of the colony as a whole is constituted by the activity of the individual intentional systems (the insects) that make it up. A more interesting kind of plural intentional system would be a pack of wolves hunting together; here the group exhibits goal-directedness by virtue of the activity of the individual wolves, who are

accounts provides a detailed analysis of the sociality of emotions. This is complicated by the typical assumption that love is itself an emotion, which I think is a mistake (hence my scare quotes above); it is, as I have argued, an evaluative attitude.

Margaret Gilbert is an exception, for she tries to offer an account of how a group can be the common subject of a single emotion. (See Gilbert, *Living Together*; Gilbert, "Obligation and Joint Commitment.") However, Gilbert aims to use an antecedent understanding of the sociality of persons to provide an account of shared emotions, whereas I shall argue that an understanding of the sociality of emotions is central to (albeit not intelligible wholly independently from) an account of social action.

[16] See, for example, Dennett, *The Intentional Stance*.

themselves robust agents. Finally are those plural intentional systems whose members are persons and so, for example, are able explicitly through their use of language to deliberate about the best means to take to achieve their collective end; thus, committees are typically plural intentional systems with (hopefully!) a particular goal they aim to achieve.

It might be tempting to understand these latter two kinds of plural intentional systems to be engaged in plural action rather than mere goal-directedness. After all, the individuals that make up the plural intentional systems in these cases themselves are agents, and so their contributions to the behavior of the group will take the form of actions.[17] Nonetheless, in none of these cases does the group itself care about the goal its activity aims at (though in the latter two kinds of cases individuals may); that is, in none of these cases is that activity engaged in because of the import that goal has to the group. Because we normally think of actions and agency as essentially tied to agents, talk of "plural action" in these cases would seem to be misplaced: there is no plural agent here that cares about its actions, even if the individual agents that make it up do, albeit for potentially diverging reasons.[18] So as not to invite confusion, therefore, I shall continue to describe these as cases of plural intentional systems whose members are agents (or persons).[19]

By contrast, a *plural robust agent* will care about at least some of its ends by virtue of displaying the relevant projectible patterns of rationality in its behavior. That is, there will be some things that have import to the group as such—to *us*—and these things will motivate group activity because of that import. A plural robust agent, therefore, will be a more complex sort of thing than merely a plural intentional system because it is also a subject of import. Thus, whereas a plural intentional system will simply have ends that it pursues, without there being for that system anything other than instrumental reasons to have these ends, a plural robust agent can pursue ends because they are worth pursuing *to the group* by virtue

---

[17] Thanks to Angelica Krebs for help clarifying this point.

[18] On such diverging reasons, see my discussion of Bratman's account of shared intention in §1.5.

[19] Velleman makes what may initially seem like a similar distinction between a group's exhibiting mere goal-directedness and its acting from an intention: what is needed for the latter, he claims, is having "shared discretion" in whether and how the goal will be achieved, and not merely a goal they hold in common (Velleman, "How to Share an Intention," 35–6.). However, Velleman's distinction is within the class of plural intentional systems: that the members share discretion in this way does not imply that the group itself cares about anything—that it is a plural robust agent.

of what has import to it. This requires that the plural agent itself has a particular evaluative perspective from within which such import can be disclosed, and this is possible only when this evaluative perspective is in some sense shared in common by the individuals who constitute that plural agent.

Given this distinction, it becomes clear that standard accounts of social action[20] aim at understanding what it is for a group of people to exhibit in their collective behavior, in a way that is coordinated through planning and deliberation, the sort of instrumental rationality that is characteristic of mere goal directedness: they are accounts of plural intentional systems whose members are persons. Thus, these accounts are incomplete in that they fail to make sense of a distinctive and important part of the landscape of social phenomena—important especially for making sense of our most intimate relationships with others.[21]

To understand plural robust agents as I have characterized them—as caring about particular things by virtue of having their own evaluative perspective from which decisions about what to do derive—might seem to require that plural agents have their own minds, which are separate from the minds of the individuals that make them up. After all, it is plausible that evaluative attitudes like caring are attitudes only things with minds can have, and if a plural agent is the subject of such caring, then it must have a mind of its own. Yet this may seem crazy, an idea that we, like Searle, can dismiss without further ado:

I find this talk [of "group minds, the collective unconscious, and so on"] at best mysterious and at worst incoherent.[22]

---

[20] Raimo Tuomela, *A Theory of Social Action* (Dordrecht: Reidel, 1984); Tuomela, *The Importance of Us*; Tuomela, *Philosophy of Sociality*; Gilbert, *On Social Facts*; Gilbert, *Living Together*; Gilbert, "Obligation and Joint Commitment"; Margaret Gilbert, *A Theory of Political Obligation: Membership, Commitment, and the Bonds of Society* (Oxford: Oxford University Press, 2006), Searle, "Collective Intentions and Actions"; Velleman, "How to Share an Intention"; Bratman, "Shared Intention"; Bratman, "Shared-Valuing"; Abraham Sesshu Roth, "Shared Agency and Contralateral Commitments," *Philosophical Review* 113, no. 3 (2004): 359–410.

[21] It may seem that Bratman aims at something more like my notion of a plural robust agent insofar as he offers an account of shared values. (See Bratman, "Shared-Valuing.") However, by "values," Bratman does not intend evaluative attitudes that constitute their objects as having import to the subject; he rather means "shared policies about what to treat as a justifying reason in the context of [the group's] shared activities" (§7). Thus, the account of "valuing" Bratman provides is in terms of how people in fact behave and the ways in which they in fact try to enforce conformity; by contrast, the sort of import I am after in speaking of caring and valuing provides a normative constraint on how people ought to behave.

[22] Searle, "Collective Intentions and Actions," 404.

Since society consists entirely of individuals, there cannot be a group mind or group consciousness. All consciousness is in individual minds, in individual brains.[23]

Bratman similarly disparages this idea, again without much argument:

[A] shared intention is not an attitude in the mind of some superagent consisting literally of some fusion of the two agents. There is no single mind which is the fusion of your mind and mine.[24]

In the face of these dismissals, is it possible to understand there to be such a thing as a plural agent the way I have described it, which seems to involve there being something like a "fused" or "group" mind?

As I shall argue in §8.3, there is a sense in which plural agents have their own emotions, desires, beliefs, and cares, and perhaps this is enough to say that they have their own minds. As Velleman says in defense of Gilbert's notion of a plural subject, "whether there are collective minds depends on whether there are collective mental states,"[25] a possibility that he leaves open and which I plan to defend. Nonetheless, there are clearly important differences between plural agents and individual agents that ought not be obscured in speaking of collective minds. For the patterns of rationality a plural agent will exhibit in its behavior will tend to be confined to particular regions of the lives of its members, and these regions can be small enough that, were we to focus on these limited patterns of rationality alone, Davidsonian worries about whether the plural agent has any real content to its mental states could be raised.[26] Consequently, it seems, for the mental states of plural agents to have determinate content, this content will in general be parasitic on the (already determinate) content of the mental states of the individual agents that are its members; this means that plural agents are ontologically dependent on individual agents, contrary to what Gilbert says about plural subjects.[27]

---

[23] Ibid., 406.

[24] Bratman, *Faces of Intention*, 111.   [25] Velleman, "How to Share an Intention," 38.

[26] See, for example, Donald Davidson, *Inquiries into Truth and Interpretation* (Oxford: Oxford University Press, 1984), especially chs. 9–12.

[27] Gilbert, *On Social Facts*, 432. Of course, I do not mean to imply that the contents of the mental states of individual persons do not depend on those of other persons. In the context of the literature on joint activity, Annette Baier has argued persuasively for such dependence, as is especially clear in the case of our ability to speak language and other abilities that depend on language, such as that for explicit deliberation; for details, see Annette C. Baier, "Doing Things with Others: The Mental Commons," in *Commonality and Particularity in Ethics*, ed. Lilli Alanen, Sara Heinämaa, and Thomas Wallgren (New York, NY: St. Martin's Press, 1997), 15–44. My claim is that the mental states of plural agents depend on those of their members in a different way, though I shall not explore those differences here.

8.3 Plural Robust Agents

What is it for a group itself to care about things—to be a subject of import—and so to be a plural agent? Applying my account of agency directly to groups yields the following: to be an agent, the group must care about things by virtue of the appropriate projectible pattern of rationality in the group's felt evaluations and evaluative judgments. Thus, if we are to act as a plural agent in building a house, we the group must exhibit a pattern of hope, fear, frustration, anticipation, disappointment, joy, relief, and so on, for the most part at the appropriate times and for the right reasons: because we (the group) feel the import the house has for us. Is this really an intelligible possibility?

One aspect of joint[28] agency on which Margaret Gilbert has rightly insisted is the idea that the individuals engaged in joint agency are each accountable to the others in a way that allows the others to demand compliance from them.[29] The relevant kind of accountability to the group must be a rational accountability analogous to that within an individual agent; indeed, because we are concerned not merely with plural intentional systems but with plural agents, it must be an accountability not merely to act but also to care and to feel. We can call an individual (including ourselves) to task for failing to act in ways demanded by their individual aims: "Hey! Why aren't you exercising? I thought you wanted to get in shape. Get a move on it!" Similarly, we can call a particular member of a plural agent to task for failing not merely to act but also to care or feel in certain ways demanded by the group's aims—for failing, that is, to care

---

[28] I shall be careful here to distinguish between states and actions that are *shared*, in that they are those of individuals which they have in common non-accidentally, and those that are *joint*, in that they are those not of the individuals but of the group. Authors working on what I am calling plural intentional systems tend to be insensitive to this distinction, using the two terms as synonyms, perhaps because they reject the possibility of "group minds." Margaret Gilbert is an exception here.

[29] See Gilbert, "Obligation and Joint Commitment." Gilbert's account, however, does not enable us to make sense of the inevitable cases in which there is ambiguity in the precise content of that to which we are jointly committed nor, therefore, of how to resolve this ambiguity. Such resolution, it seems, will require joint deliberation so as more precisely to articulate both what we are jointly committed to doing and what our individual obligations to the plural subject are; such deliberation, it seems, must be undertaken in light of joint reasons, and that raises the question of what the source of the relevant normative standards for such reasons is. On these points, Gilbert is silent; consequently, her account might better be described as an account of *coordinated we-commitments* rather than plural subjects. (Similar criticisms apply to Bratman, "I Intend That We *J*"; Bratman, "Shared Intention"; Bratman, "Shared Intention and Mutual Obligation," in Bratman, *Faces of Intention*, 130–41.)

about certain things because the group does, thereby sharing the group's cares: "What's wrong with you? Why aren't you happy that we've finally done it?"[30]

Nonetheless, if we are to make sense of the notion of a plural agent, the group itself must be the subject of these felt evaluations and cares, so that we can say that the group acts because of the import things have to it. The key question is: why should we attribute these felt evaluations and cares not to the individuals but rather to the group? Answering this question requires articulating more clearly the way in which the mental states of individual agents are rationally interconnected in a plural agent so that individual agents have felt evaluations as a result of their responsiveness to what has import *to us* and not merely to those individuals—so that they have these felt evaluations *as one of us*. As I shall now argue, the relevant rational connectedness, and so plural agency itself, emerges out of the way in which the members of the plural agent care about what the group does as a part of caring about the group itself as an agent. I shall lay out the account in broad strokes in §8.3.1, filling in the details of the relevant rational connectedness that must be in place among group members in order for the group to be a plural agent in §8.3.2.

8.3.1 Groups as Subjects of Import

I just claimed that the plural agent itself—the group as a whole rather than the individuals that make it up—must be the subject of import, such that the group as a whole has the relevant felt evaluations and makes the evaluative judgments. For only if this is true can we make sense of the group itself non-metaphorically as a (plural) robust agent. Yet this might seem just crazy: how can *the group itself* feel emotions, and so experience the relevant pleasures and pains that emotions are, in a way that does not simply amount to each of the members of the group feeling them? This brings us back to Searle's and Bratman's worries over the idea of a fused mind (see p. 264–5): surely there is no additional mind there, over and above the individual minds of the members, that can feel mental states that are themselves distinct from the mental states of the members, is there?

---

[30] It should be clear that at issue here is not merely behaving as if they have the relevant emotions, but actually feeling them. I shall ultimately argue, however, that this analogy breaks down: the sort of accountability members have to the group is more analogous to the accountability you have to yourself than the accountability you have to an outsider.

As I indicated in my initial response to that worry, there is a genuine, non-metaphorical sense in which plural agents have their own felt evaluations, albeit a sense that is not exactly the same as that in which individual agents do. Thus, according to the Davidsonian account I have adopted in which rationality is the constitutive ideal of the mental, what it is for something to have particular mental states is for there to be a single, appropriately robust, projectible pattern of rationality in its responsiveness to the world that is properly interpretable in terms of those mental states. Thus, if the group itself exhibits the appropriate projectible pattern of rationality, then the group itself has the mental states. Key to this account is the rationality and projectibility of the pattern: it will not do for the individual members of the group to exhibit a responsiveness to the world that merely happens to coincide in such a way that there is an overall pattern for the group itself. Rather, if we are members of the group, then my responsiveness to the world must be rationally tied to your responsiveness to the world, such that were your responsiveness to change then, other things being equal, mine ought to change as well. Moreover, how we respond to the world (both actually and counterfactually) must vary non-coincidentally with changes in the world (both actual and counterfactual) in such a way as to preserve that overall pattern of rationality. Nonetheless, the precise nature of this interconnectedness among our responses needs to be clarified, and I shall return to this shortly and in §8.3.2.[31]

In claiming that the group is the subject of import and so of various felt evaluations, I am not denying that the individual members of the group also have the relevant felt evaluations. It may seem that the response to

---

[31] A variant of this objection to the idea that the group itself has emotions stems from an understanding of emotions as essentially experiential states: there is "something it is like" to undergo an emotional experience, and we can classify emotions broadly as pleasant or painful. Yet, it might seem, surely the group itself does not undergo any such experiences—surely there is nothing "it is like" for the group to have an emotion—and so surely we cannot in any real sense understand the group as having any emotions at all, contrary to my claim. However, this variant of the objection gains its force from an understanding of the nature of qualia that I have rejected elsewhere. The nature of the pleasure and pain central to emotional experience, I have argued, is not something we can identify as a potentially separable "component" of the emotions, such as a bodily sensation. Rather, to feel fear, for example, just is to be pained by danger: to have the negative import of one's circumstances impress itself on one in this way. Indeed, as I have argued, we ought to understand bodily pleasures and pains in terms of this model of emotional pleasures and pains: they are all species of the genus of felt evaluations. (For details, see Helm, "Felt Evaluations.") This means that the group itself does feel pleasure or pain—at success or danger, for example, for such pleasure and pain just are satisfaction and fear. If this is all that is intended by the locution "something it is like to undergo the experience" then I reject the premise that groups themselves cannot have such experiential states.

the world made by an individual member must be either his own response or the response of the group, so that either the group is the subject of the relevant emotion or the individual is, but not both. However, to understand these options as mutually exclusive is a mistake, as is clear once we consider the nature of the relevant patterns of rationality constitutive of being a subject of import. A particular response when interpreted one way, by virtue of its rational interconnections to other responses we all make or would make, may fall within a pattern of rationality constitutive of the group's caring about something, while what is in some sense the same response interpreted another way, by virtue of its rational interconnections to other responses I make or would make, may simultaneously fall within a pattern of rationality constitutive of my caring about something. Thus, my jumping up and down as the last shingle is nailed in place may be simultaneously an expression of my joy, insofar as I care about the house being built, and an expression of the group's joy, insofar as we care about its being built. In this way, the rationality of that response is, so to speak, overdetermined: I ought to make it both because of the import the house has for me and because of the import the house has to us. As such (and given my earlier account of emotions as intentional feelings of import in §2.2), my behaving this way is the result in these circumstances of both (a) my feeling the import the house has *to me* and (b) our feeling the import it has *to us*, feelings which are identical to the emotions that (a) I feel and (b) we feel.

It may be, of course, that an individual who is a part of a group that cares about something does not on her own care about it, as when Mary is a part of a group that cares about building this house, even though she herself does not, perhaps because she believes it is a mistake for the group to be involved in this project. In such a case, she may find herself, with some justification, jumping up and down with the rest of us in celebration of the house's being completed.[32] However, such behavior would not be rationally overdetermined: it would be false to say that she ought to respond

---

[32] This example differs from other cases in which one might get "infected" by the emotional responses of others, as when you walk into a crowd of angry people and feel yourself coming to be angry as well, even though you may not know exactly what they—and you—are angry at or why. As the metaphor of "infection" suggests, in such a case your coming to feel as others do is *arational*, a sort of reflexive response we find ourselves making without that response being to anything which could provide a reason for it. By contrast, the joy Mary feels is a response to a reason: the import this has for the group of which she is a member.

that way because of the import the house has for her. Indeed, she may on her own behalf feel ambivalent emotions in line with her assessment of this project as a mistake. So in this sense the joy she feels is not "Mary's own": the house does not have this import *for her*; it has this import *for us*, and so the emotion is in this sense *ours*.

Nonetheless, it may seem, in a different but still straightforward sense Mary is the subject of the emotion. After all, she is the one jumping up and down, and this behavior of hers is responsive to the import (to us) of the house and is therefore expressive of the relevant emotion; insofar as this responsiveness to import is exercised through her body, we might say that she is the one experiencing the emotion. However, it must be clear that she is experiencing this emotion *as one of us* and not merely all on her own, for two reasons. First, the import she feels is the import the house has *to us*, and not to her. Consequently, second, the emotion is intelligible as warranted only because she is one of us and so has reason to respond in ways that are demanded by what has import to us. Indeed, if Mary were to fail to respond with joy to the completion of the house, her failure would be a rational failure, subject to rational criticism in light of her status as one of us; moreover, her status as one of us would be undermined were such failures widespread in her responsiveness to what has import to us.

Another objection might be raised at this point: why should we think that the pattern of rationality we exhibit as a group must be different from the aggregate of the patterns of rationality we each exhibit individually? Of course, there must be some coordination among us in order for those patterns to mesh non-accidentally and so be projectible, but why not think that Tuomela, Gilbert, and Bratman have given adequate accounts of the appropriate sort of meshing? Granted, none of them speak about caring and the emotions, but can we not just assume that once motives for action (as are provided by, for example, desires) are in the picture, caring and the emotions go along for the ride? In short, can I justly claim to offer an account of a distinctive kind of social activity, namely that of plural robust agents, that is not captured by alternative accounts?

The answer lies in the kind of shared evaluative perspective characteristic of a plural agent and provided by the relevant pattern of felt evaluations and evaluative judgments, a perspective that is the group's own, held jointly by all its members. Thus, as I have just claimed, a particular member of the group ought to have the relevant felt evaluations (as one of us) *because* he thereby feels the import something has *to us*—because, that is, he shares the evaluative perspective that is the group's—and not because he feels the import it has *to him*. This means that we cannot simply assume, as the imagined objector does, that once the desire to act is in place, emotions and caring will naturally follow, for the central question is not simply *whether* he cares at all but *how* he cares: as one of us or not. It is only when the members each care as one of us, such that they share the group's evaluative perspective, that we have a case of a plural agent rather than merely a plural intentional system.

Just what it means for the members of a group to share the group's evaluative perspective can be clarified by considering cases either of disagreement within the group or of the resolution of indeterminacy in the precise focus of that import. Thus, return to the example of you and me going to the beach, initially discussed in §1.5 (p. 36–8), only this time assume that we form a plural agent and so jointly care about going to the beach together. Nonetheless, as before, assume that we start off with different motives: I do so intending to relax together with you in a quiet spot on the beach, whereas you do so intending that we immerse ourselves in the crowd on the boardwalk. The question then arises as to what we jointly want—what we jointly care about—in going to the beach together, for so far we have no determinate conception of what precisely it is we (the plural agent) want in going to the beach. How, then, can we resolve this conflict so as to determine more precisely what we want?

When an individual is faced with a similar problem, the typical solution is to try out different conceptions of the object of one's care to see which, all things considered, "resonates" best with one's evaluative perspective. As I briefly outlined in §6.1, at issue here are not only those evaluations and reasons one explicitly articulates in judgment but also one's sense of import as found in one's felt evaluations. Thus, even if one is unable to articulate clearly why one specification of the object of one's care is better than another, one's felt evaluations can nonetheless provide access to reasons one has for making a choice one way rather than another. In deliberating about what to do, one must balance these competing demands against each other, groping toward a clearer sense of what has import to one by trying to achieve something like an equilibrium within one's evaluative perspective.

The same is true of the plural agent: we must together aim at achieving an equilibrium within *our* evaluative perspective, a perspective which includes not only our evaluative judgments but also our felt evaluations (that is, the judgments and felt evaluations each of us makes or has as one of us). Consequently, insofar as we are a plural agent the enthusiasm you feel *as one of us* at the thought of our people-watching while munching on greasy boardwalk fare is a reason, albeit a defeasible reason, for me to feel likewise, and it ought to be given due weight in my rational responsiveness to the import things have to us, potentially sparking in me some anticipation of the cheesy pleasures this would afford us. Conversely, my utter distaste (again, as one of us) for our making a meal out of that stuff is a defeasible reason for you to be less enthusiastic here: such food has less import to us than it initially seemed to you. In short, in deliberating jointly each of us ought to seek to delineate more clearly what has import to us by being rationally responsive to the evaluative perspective comprised of the evaluations both you and I (each as one of us) feel emotionally and make in judgment. The evaluative perspective of a plural agent is thus held jointly by us, its members, insofar as we are rationally bound to that perspective and to each other in this way, and such rational interconnection is constitutive of the emotions of each being felt as one of us.

Given that the members of a plural agent must share a single, joint evaluative perspective, the nature of the kind of the deliberation they undertake as a plural agent is of a very different character than that of plural intentional systems, which do not hold such a joint evaluative perspective; indeed, this can be so even when the individual members of a plural agent have somewhat different conceptions of the group's aims. For, as I indicated in §1.5, the members of a plural intentional system must deliberate through bargaining and compromise, in which each individual has her own evaluative perspective from which she tries to maximize, in some sense, the good to be realized. By contrast, within the sort of joint deliberation among members constituting a plural agent, there is no such competition between diverse evaluative perspectives; there is only one evaluative perspective from within which they together attempt to forge a decision for shared reasons. This does not mean that there is no room for some members to attempt to foist on others their own views (views not held as one of us) as if in a competition; however, such an attempt would be an abuse of that joint evaluative perspective, an abuse that is subject to rational criticism by others. Indeed, this reveals that whether or not an individual's responses are made as one of us is determined not simply by the individual who makes the response but rather, at least in part, by whether or not others of us accept it as a defeasible reason to think or feel likewise as one of us.[33]

8.3.2 Being One of Us

So far I have provided a basic account of what must be the case if there are to be plural agents: there must be a projectible pattern of rationality in the group's responses constitutive of an evaluative perspective held jointly by members of the group, such that each of us can be held rationally accountable for his or her responses in light of that joint evaluative perspective. Nonetheless, more needs to be said about how this rational pattern binding the individuals into a group can come into place: how are we to understand in detail the kind of rational beholdenness individual members must have to the group and so to each other in order for the group to come to be a plural agent at all?

Return to the beach example discussed above (§8.3.1, p. 271–2), this time making some additional assumptions about our relationship. Thus, as before, you and I each want that we go on a day trip to the beach together, but we each have different understandings of what this involves. However, do not presuppose yet that we form a plural agent; instead, assume that we each care about the other as an agent. This means in part that, insofar as I care about you and insofar as you want and so care about our eating the greasy boardwalk fare, I ought, other things being equal, to care about this too as a part of caring about you. Of course, it might be thought that in this case other things are not equal, for I find such food distasteful, perhaps because it gives me heartburn or for other health reasons. Thus, I find it to have negative import inasmuch as I care about not eating it for the sake of my health, which seems to conflict with my finding it to have positive import insofar as I care about eating it for your sake. So what should I desire and care about?

What is important for present purposes is not whether I come to care about eating the boardwalk food with you; after all, you are in a similar

---

[33] The issue is actually much more complicated than this makes it seem, for it is ultimately a normative issue of whether or not the rest of us *should* accept it as a defeasible reason, and so whether or not it has a place within our joint evaluative perspective. This implies that the rest of us could all be mistaken in our acceptance or refusal to accept this response as a reason, and so the matter is not simply settled by what the rest of us actually do. Nonetheless, given that the import things have to us is in part a subjective matter, determined by what we think and feel, our actual acceptance or rejection of this response as having a place within our evaluative perspective will not be irrelevant.

predicament with respect to our eating food we take with us, given that you care about me and I care about this. Rather, what is important is that, as a result of our each caring about the other as an agent, we each are faced with a rational conflict and so come to feel some rational pressure to give up our own desire for that of the other. It may turn out that my concern for my health, given my family history of heart disease, is much more important to me than the pleasure you would get from eating greasy fries, and in recognition of this you change your mind and thereby eliminate the conflict. Consequently, we each come to want to eat a picnic lunch and so to respond in felt evaluation in the appropriate ways when things go well or poorly; thus, for example, we each come to feel disappointment when, as we are carrying our picnic lunch to a spot on the beach, the basket handle breaks, spilling our food on to the sand.

It should be clear that at this stage each of us is merely responding to what has import to himself, individually, and not, as is required for plural agency, to what has import to us jointly: insofar as you come to care about our having a picnic lunch, this is only because of the import I have *to you* (and, consequently, the import this has to me). Indeed, although each of us is responding to the emotional and judgmental evaluations of the other, allowing the other's views to exert some rational influence on his own, and although this means that we each have come to be rationally constrained by the evaluations of the other, even if we disagree, it may seem that this is just a happy coincidence that might too easily be dissolved. Thus, it might be that when push comes to shove our individual interests for the most part take precedence over those of the other, so that disagreements tend not to be resolved harmoniously but, if at all, only grudgingly, with conflicts remaining between your and my evaluative responses (as when you respond with concealed joy when the picnic basket handle breaks—a joy that suppresses the disappointment you would otherwise feel for my sake). In such a case, the pattern of responses you and I each make would not cohere together well enough to be identifiable as a single pattern we share in common. Because there are so far merely individual evaluative perspectives involved, there is no joint evaluative perspective from which things come to have import *to us*, and so there is consequently no plural agent.

It would be false to conclude, however, that there is no interesting sense in which we come to share an evaluative perspective and so that no progress has been made in understanding plural agency. For it may instead turn out that when push comes to shove we each care about the other enough that the rational pressure we each feel from the other's evaluations (both felt and judged) succeeds in imposing a kind of harmony among our evaluative responses that constitutes a single pattern. Of course, once again the pattern of responses here derives from our individual evaluative perspectives and commitments to the imports things have to each of us, and so we do not yet form a plural agent. Nonetheless, we share an evaluative perspective in a sense analogous to that in which I share your cares as a part of caring about you and not merely in the relatively weak sense that there is an answer, at some level of description, concerning what our aims are that we each agree to (as for plural intentional systems). For although the precise focus of our evaluations will differ in that, sometimes, mine will be focused on some object and yours will be focused on me and subfocused on that object, and *vice versa* at other times, we each make what is in a clear sense the same evaluations, and our doing so is projectible because rationally demanded from within each of our evaluative perspectives: we each ought, other things being equal, to modify our individual evaluations (both felt and judged) in the face of newfound disagreement in order to accord with the evaluations of the other. Thus, given this shared—but not yet joint—evaluative perspective, you ought to be disappointed when our picnic lunch spills on to the sand because this has become important to you insofar as you care about me and I care about it.

This is not yet enough to say that *we* care about it, however. In addition to our sharing an evaluative perspective in the sense just defined, in order for us to become a plural agent we must extend this shared evaluative perspective in such a way that our individual evaluative attitudes are transformed into attitudes we each have as one of us. This means that as we come to be a plural agent, each of us must simultaneously come to be responsive not merely to that which has import to himself but rather to that which has import to us, the plural agent.[34] Yet in order for me to be responsive to what has import to us, I must care about these things for *our* sake, as a part of caring about us, so that my emotions and desires must be focused not on the things themselves but rather on us, the plural agent.

---

[34] Of course, this does not preclude the possibility that I might also find these things to have import to me. In such a case, as I claimed in §8.3.1, my responsiveness will be rationally overdetermined.

Becoming a plural agent therefore requires that the members each care about the group as an agent, and this begins to change the sense in which we share this evaluative perspective. For once this happens there will no longer be the disparity just noted between the focus of your evaluations and that of mine; rather, the evaluations of each will be focused on us, the plural agent, and subfocused on what has import to us. Nonetheless, the way we each must care about us as an agent must take a distinctive form. To be a plural agent we must not merely each care about us as an outsider, such that these evaluations are simply responsive to an already formed and largely independent agent. Rather, each of us must do so with an understanding that he is *one of us*—that he is a member of a plural agent whose evaluative perspective he both shares and helps constitute; that is, we each must care about us *as a plural agent.*[35] This in turn requires a transformation in the way in which we are each rationally beholden to the other. This needs further explanation.

Setting aside for the moment the possibility of the transformation of us into a plural agent, it was assumed that I care about you as an agent. This means that I exhibit a projectible pattern of rationality in my responses to import that rationally demands that I respond in certain ways in particular situations: I ought to be pleased by your success, frustrated at setbacks to your plans, motivated to help you when appropriate, and so on. Given this, it is possible for you or anyone else to criticize me for failures to have these responses in light of these rational demands. However, my failures in these cases will be largely failures of consistency with the projectible pattern of rationality constitutive of my caring,[36] and so the criticism (from a third party) might take the following form: "Why aren't you happy for her? I thought you cared about her." In this sense, I am answerable not to the agent about whom I care, nor to the critic calling me on it, but ultimately to myself: to my own evaluative perspective.

---

[35] My claim is not that a member of a plural agent must have a conscious understanding of her status as one of us; that thought need never have crossed her mind, and she certainly need not have made any explicit verbal commitment to that effect. Rather, as I argued in §3.2, such an understanding can be implicit in the overall pattern of rationality constituting the evaluative perspective that the members hold jointly and constituting their each caring about us as a plural agent.

[36] Of course, in appealing to failures of consistency, I do not mean to imply that there can be no standards for what we ought to care about beyond simply those imposed by the other things we do care about. This complication does not affect my point.

Once we each come to understand ourselves as one of us and so to care about us as a plural agent, however, things are different because we together constitute, and each as one of us is answerable to, the evaluative perspective of us, the plural agent. Thus, just as I can fail myself in failing to seize an opportunity to accomplish something I care about, so that I ought to be disappointed in or frustrated with myself as a part of my answerability to my evaluative perspective, so too I can fail us so that we ought to be disappointed in or frustrated with me as a part of my answerability to *our* joint evaluative perspective. This implies that each of us ought to feel that disappointment or frustration, and so each of us has the standing to criticize me not merely as an outsider pointing out a failure wholly internal to my evaluative perspective but rather from within the evaluative perspective we share.[37]

Indeed, it is such an extension of our shared evaluative perspective that makes intelligible the idea that this evaluative perspective is not merely shared in the sense described above but that it is ours *jointly*, the evaluative perspective of us, the plural agent. What is at stake here is not merely the sharing of an evaluative perspective with someone you care about, so that you come to feel frustrated with or disappointed with him when he fails himself. For in contrast to such a case, here we each care about us as a plural agent, so that the focus (and subfocus) of our cares and the felt evaluations that constitute them will be the same: they are focused on us, the plural agent, and subfocused on what we care about. Consequently, it is by us members of the group forging agreement among ourselves concerning the subfocus of our emotions that we together constitute that about which

---

[37] This issue of the standing we have to criticize each other is discussed in Gilbert, "Shared Values, Social Unity, and Liberty." Gilbert's answer is superficially similar to mine: we each have the standing to criticize the other insofar as we have made a joint commitment to a shared value, where it is this joint commitment that binds us together into a plural subject. There are, however, some important underlying differences between her account and mine. Most obviously is the difference in our understandings of what values consist in, and the consequent understanding of what it is to be committed to a value. I have argued against the sort of account of value Gilbert assumes (as being a matter of belief), and the alternative conception of value I offer (in terms of projectible patterns of rationality in one's felt evaluations and evaluative judgments) has important implications for how we are to understand the resulting commitments: our answerability to each other, I claim, must be fundamentally emotional if we are to be able to distinguish between plural intentional systems and plural agents. For it is only with such a rationally structured pattern of emotions that we can make sense of the idea that *we* jointly care about something rather than that each of us cares about it individually and is committed to the coordination of our individual actions. (These implications run contrary to Gilbert's claim that it does not matter what account of values is in the offing; see ibid., end of §2.1.)

278 FRIENDS ARE OTHER SELVES

we jointly care. In such a case we have each thereby become rationally beholden to the same evaluative perspective and so answerable to ourselves jointly. This evaluative perspective is most properly speaking not mine nor yours individually but ours jointly, and it is that which constitutes things as having import to us and so, finally, us as being a subject of import. The simultaneous transformation both of our individual evaluative attitudes to attitudes we each have as one of us and of us into a plural robust agent is now complete.

One implication of this account is that the members of a plural agent must, as a part of their joint evaluative perspective, hold a joint sense of which individuals constitute this plural agent. For an understanding of oneself as one of us involves also an understanding of others as likewise one of us and therefore not only as jointly holding this evaluative perspective but also as having standing to criticize and be criticized from within that perspective. Moreover, this understanding of who the members of the plural agent are must, by and large, be held jointly by its members in order to retain the singleness of evaluative perspective necessary for robust agency. Of course, with presumed plural agents consisting of two members, as in the beach example, any disagreement on this score will undermine the requisite evaluative perspective; with larger groups it is possible that some such disagreement can be tolerated so long as it remains merely "noise" in what is otherwise a robust pattern of rationality constituting that perspective and does not itself destroy that pattern.[38] Thus, the members of a Philosophy Department[39] meeting the criteria for plural agency just given might disagree whether a recently hired junior colleague ought to be given a full say as one of us in certain policy or hiring decisions, such as how precisely to define the needs of the Department in an upcoming job search. Nonetheless, so long as there is otherwise widespread agreement concerning who the members of this plural agent are, his status as one of us or not can be left indeterminate without undermining our plural agency.

[38] This metaphor of "noise" in the pattern is one Dennett uses to good effect (Daniel C. Dennett, "Real Patterns," *Journal of Philosophy* 88 (1991): 27–51). Thus think of the way in which some static on the radio can be tolerated as noise in an otherwise robust pattern of sounds constituting a performance of a piece of music; too much noise, however, can destroy that pattern.

[39] In choosing this as my example, I do not mean to imply that philosophy departments typically are plural agents; indeed, it would be the rare—and probably only relatively small—department or other such group that could achieve the kind of intimacy among its members required for them to constitute a plural agent. Nonetheless, it is, I believe, possible.

This point about disagreement can be generalized: the joint evaluative perspective of a plural agent need not be fully determinate and harmonious any more than it needs to be so for an individual agent. After all, an individual agent may be unable to reach a decision about some matter of import and so be "of two minds" concerning the issue insofar as she has not yet settled on a single evaluative perspective with respect to it that is determinately her own; in such a case it is to some extent indeterminate precisely what she cares about. Moreover, even when she has made up her mind, she may find herself, irrationally, making contrary evaluations from time to time—evaluations which appear as "noise" in light of the robustness of the relevant pattern of her evaluations overall. Similarly, we members of the Department may be unable to reach a decision about how to cash out what "best qualified" means in the context of a job search, even against the background of what is overall a joint evaluative perspective. In such a case, the Department does not yet have a precise understanding of what being the "best qualified" candidate consists in, and, as in the individual case, there is rational pressure from within our joint evaluative perspective to resolve the matter.[40] Moreover, the Department as a whole can decide that it cares more about research quality than precise fit with Departmental needs and so make an offer to one candidate over another, even if isolated members of the Department disagree, perhaps because they are uneasy about the direction the Department will now take.[41] Thus, even if I disagree in this case, I am now bound by the evaluative perspective I share as one of us to feel anxious as the candidate drags her feet in responding to the offer, relieved when she accepts, etc., and so to care about this as one of us even when I don't care about it individually (see §8.3.1). For me to fail to feel these emotions as one of us

---

[40] So long as this failure of agreement does not become widespread—so long as it does not, by and large, affect our joint understanding of what the Department stands for—it does not affect the status of the Department as a plural agent. If, however, this failure is widespread throughout the various aims of the Department, then there is no joint evaluative perspective that we share each as one of us, and the Department fails to be a plural agent.

[41] Applying my account of deliberation about import (from §6.1 and Helm, *Emotional Reason*, Ch. 7) to plural agents provides some content to the idea Gilbert raises of a "re-assessment of these values at the collective level" being provoked by "a disparity between one's personal values and those one collectively shares with one's fellows" (Gilbert, "Shared Values, Social Unity, and Liberty," end of §7.1). (I shall have more to say about how this application works in §8.5, in the context of a discussion of the justification of friendship.) Again, my complaint against Gilbert (see n. 29) is that she needs to articulate more clearly the kind of rationality governing group agency and the way in which that rationality connects to the rationality of its members—something I aim to have done here.

and so to fail to care in this way would be a rational failure given that I am one of us.[42]

I have been focused thus far on the way in which the evaluative perspective of a plural agent must be held jointly by its members, each as one of us. It should be clear, however, that the jointness of this evaluative perspective has broad implications. First, it is this joint evaluative perspective that defines the well-being of the plural agent as such, so that the members of the plural agent must therefore have a joint understanding of that well-being that is at least implicit in the evaluative perspective each shares as one of us. For without such a joint understanding, there would be no single focus of their various evaluations and so no single evaluative perspective they hold jointly. As will become clear in §§8.4–8.5, such a joint understanding of the well-being of the plural agent is central to understanding the nature and justification of friendship.

Second, in holding such a joint evaluative perspective the members of a plural agent are each thereby committed not merely to making evaluations (whether judged or felt) as one of us but also to acting in ways that promote the well-being of the plural agent; this is a consequence of the understanding of import I have offered as involving not merely worthiness of attention but also worthiness of action. Indeed, inasmuch as we each are one of us, we together are responsible for such actions, where this is a responsibility we each have to us, the plural agent. Other things being equal we can each be held accountable by the others for successes or failures to act appropriately as one of us. Thus, other members of the group may feel irritated with or resentful of me for not upholding my responsibilities as one of us or may feel obliged to me for my notably satisfying them; in each case, these emotions target me but are focused on us, the plural agent, for it is the import we have to ourselves that makes intelligible the evaluation of me that is implicit in these emotions' formal objects. In this way, our subjecting ourselves to such responsibility and accountability is itself a part of what it is to care about us as a plural agent, for it is a matter of your coming to have a place in both defining and executing the group's agency and so of attaining the status as able to criticize and

---

[42] This way of putting the point, I believe, can be understood as a way of cashing out in the context of my notion of a plural agent what Gilbert means in talking about our "joining forces" in a "pool of wills" (Gilbert, *On Social Facts*, 411) insofar as it provides a clearer understanding of the kind of "joint commitment" we have as members of a plural agent.

be criticized by others, each as one of us, for successes or failures in this regard.

Of course there can be tensions between an individual's commitment to the well-being of the plural agent and her commitment to herself.[43] In particular circumstances, other things I care about may conflict with what we the plural agent care about in a way that may justifiably lead me to fail to act on behalf of us. Others ought to be sensitive to such a possibility; indeed, the criticisms each makes or feels of others must be tempered in part by the understanding each must have of the others' individual agency insofar as each cares about the others as an agent. Nonetheless, conflicts can remain: even when I think I am justified in failing to act as one of us (given my circumstances and priorities), others may nonetheless be resentful of me, a resentfulness that I can contest from within our joint evaluative perspective. When conflicts of this sort are widespread, they can begin to undermine the overall evaluative perspective that makes us intelligible as a plural agent. Consequently, to be a plural agent we must have a joint conception, however rough, not merely of the plural agent's well-being as such, but also of the place that plural agent is to have within each of our lives.

One might object that this account of plural agency is viciously circular, potentially in two ways. Thus, first, we might wonder whether the answerability of each member of a plural agent to the plural agent itself is a consequence of our having a joint evaluative perspective or whether it instead constitutes our having that perspective. Which of these comes first in the analysis? Indeed, we might generalize this somewhat in a second case. If my being a member of a plural agent involves in part my caring about the group as a plural agent, then the group must already be a plural agent, and yet the group's being a plural agent is constituted by precisely such attitudes on behalf of its members toward the group; consequently, it may seem, in order to be constituted as a plural agent, the group must already be a plural agent, and this circularity may seem vicious. In reply, the supposed difficulties here arise from a presupposition of conceptual or

---

[43] Here I disagree with Carol Rovane's account of group agency (Carol Rovane, "Personal Identity, Ethical not Metaphysical," in *McDowell and His Critics*, ed. Cynthia Macdonald and Graham Macdonald (Malden, MA: Blackwell Publishing, 2006), especially §II), for Rovane assumes that the individuals constituting a group thereby lose their individual identities as persons. I see no reason to make that assumption so long as we can distinguish as I have between those evaluations we make on our own and those we make as one of us.

ontological priority. Thus, in the first case it is presupposed that either my answerability to the group or our having a joint evaluative perspective must be prior to the other; in the second case it is presupposed that either my caring about the group or the group's existence as a plural agent must be prior to the other. The solution, already implicit in my account, is to reject such priority insofar as each comes into existence simultaneously. As the members' individual concerns come to be coordinated appropriately, it becomes simultaneously intelligible both that they jointly hold an evaluative perspective that defines the plural robust agent as such and that they each care about that plural robust agent itself and so are answerable to it. Such is the nature of holistic patterns quite generally, and nothing is unusual about this one.

8.4 Plural Agency and Friendship

I have argued that the distinction I made in Chapter 2 between intentional systems and agents can be applied as well to social groups: some social groups can be understood as plural intentional systems (whose members, potentially, are themselves agents or persons), whereas other social groups can be understood as plural agents. I have now provided an account of how plural agency is possible by focusing on the ways in which the patterns of felt evaluations of individual members of a group can become rationally intertwined in such a way as to constitute things as having import to the group itself. By ignoring the difference between mere intentional systems and robust agents, and so by leaving out these emotional entanglements, alternative accounts of social action fail to capture a whole range of social phenomena involving plural agents.

As I hope is now apparent, this account of plural agents is important for understanding friendship. Indeed, my central example of two people as a plural agent seems to be a case of what we might call *ordinary friendship*. For not only do the members of a plural agent each care about the other as an agent and so each identify with the other by sharing each other's cares and concerns for the other's sake, but insofar as they form a plural agent they will also share certain cares and concerns in a more robust sense: jointly, by means of a joint evaluative perspective. Moreover, in addition to their affection for and commitment to each other that is a part of their caring about each other as agents, they each also care about, and so have affection for and commitment to, them, the plural agent and in this way each identify themselves with that plural agent. That is, we might say, they each care about and have affection for and commitment to their "relationship."[44] Finally, of course, insofar as they are members of a plural agent, they engage in joint activity. All of these features of a relationship are marks of friendship commonly raised in the literature. The members of a plural agent, therefore, are friends in this rather ordinary sense.

I have described this as *ordinary* friendship in part to mark it off from other kinds of friendship that I shall discuss shortly. What makes such friendship be ordinary is the way in which the friendship is limited in both scope and depth. Thus, ordinary friendship as I have characterized it is of limited depth inasmuch as it is grounded in the friends each caring about the other as an agent (rather than each loving the other), and it is of limited scope insofar as the friends' joint conception of the plural agent they form involves only a limited range of joint cares and activities. This limited scope is defined by the set of cares and concerns of the plural agent itself—by, that is, the friends' joint conception of their relationship. This requires further explanation.

In order to be a plural agent, I have argued, the friends must together hold a joint (albeit possibly implicit) understanding of the well-being of that plural agent as such and so of the joint cares and concerns that constitute it as a plural agent. For example, the friends might understand the plural agent they form in a very limited way as caring merely about playing tennis, say, and about otherwise maintaining their relationship so as to make such joint caring possible. That is, the friends understand their relationship in terms of this joint activity of playing tennis: they are, and understand themselves to be, tennis buddies, and each identifies herself not merely with the other as an agent but also as one of "us." Of course, plural agents can have a broader range of cares and concerns than this. It may be that the cares of a plural agent are organized around a common theme: perhaps the friends pursue joint activities involving many different sports (or kinds of music or . . .),

---

[44] This echoes the central theme of Niko Kolodny's account of love; see Kolodny, "Love as Valuing a Relationship." I have already criticized Kolodny's account in §1.4.2, largely on the grounds that it is unable to make sense of how loving relationships like friendship can be justified; I shall have more to say about how my account does better in §8.5.

both as participants and observers. In such a case, this theme will provide a kind of unity to the various cares of the plural agent and so to the plural agent itself. Such a thematic unity thus enables us to understand what friendships of pleasure or of utility are:[45] they involve plural agents whose cares are thematically organized around pleasure or utility. This does not mean, however, that the cares of a particular plural agent must have some such thematic unity. Thus, it might be tempting to infer that two people who jointly care about both tennis and gardening must therefore form two distinct plural agents rather than just one that cares about both. Such an inference would be a mistake because it ignores a more fundamental rational unity that structures the friends' actions and interactions. After all, sometimes playing tennis will conflict with gardening, and the friends must be capable of exercising their rational capacities from within their joint evaluative perspective to resolve such conflicts. In this way, these two cares can be integrated into a single, joint evaluative perspective that constitutes them as a plural agent.[46]

This account of friendship provides some substance to Marilyn Friedman's federation model.[47] Thus, recall, Friedman claims that the interaction of the friends produces a new, unified entity,

one which involves the lovers acting in concert across a range of conditions and for a range of purposes. This concerted action, however, does not erase the existence of the two lovers as separable and separate agents with continuing possibilities for the exercise of their own respective agencies.[48]

With this understanding of friendship in terms of the account of plural agency, we can now see how this can be true. For the plural agent itself is the third, unified entity that nonetheless does not involve the sort of unification that would destroy their separateness as individual agents or persons.

This account so far begins to make sense of the varying degrees of closeness that are possible within a friendship. For the more they the plural agent care about, the more substance there is to their joint evaluative

[45] See Aristotle's *Nicomachean Ethics*, Bk VIII, in, for example, Richard McKeon, ed., *The Basic Works of Aristotle* (New York, NY: Random House, 1941).

[46] This implies that Aristotle's notions of friendships of pleasure and of utility should not be understood to be mutually exclusive or to exhaust the kinds of friendships there are outside of friendships of virtue.

[47] Friedman offers this model as an account of love, in particular romantic love. However, insofar as her target is not love as an evaluative attitude but rather as grounding a relationship, it is a model that fits with my account of friendship generally, and I shall interpret it that way here.

[48] Friedman, "Romantic Love," 165.

perspective and so to the kind of relationship they have as friends. Thus the scope of the interests of the plural agent partly determines the closeness of their friendship. However, we must not forget that friendship is a relationship grounded in the friends' mutual caring for each other. Such mutual caring of course makes possible their plural agency, but it also makes intelligible their mutual affection for and commitment to each other, affection and commitment that extend beyond the potentially narrow scope of their joint concerns as a plural agent: in caring about each other, the friends each ought generally to care about the other's cares and values for his sake, thereby sharing these concerns in the sense outlined in Chapter 3. Consequently, another factor determining how close a friendship is is the place within their individual systems of priorities of the concern the friends each have both for their friend and for the plural agent itself. For insofar as your friend himself and your friendship with him have a relatively high priority within your life, you ought to pay more attention to, and be more prepared to act on behalf of, both the well-being of your friend and of your friendship itself, potentially sacrificing other things you care about for the sake of your friend and your friendship.

Yet the closeness of a friendship can vary also with what I have called its "depth," which can have a far more profound effect on the character of the friendship. Not only can friends care about each other as agents; they can also love each other, thereby sharing not only each other's concerns but also their identities as the person they each are. Such sharing of each other's identities leads to increased intimacy between the friends, as discussed in Chapter 5, and it thereby affects the quality of their relationship. Nonetheless, it does not on its own affect the character of their joint concerns or actions and so, we might think, is not central to the friendship itself. More interesting for present purposes are cases in which the friends not only love each other but also form a plural agent that itself not merely cares but also has values: a plural person.

Plural agents, I have argued, are formed when two or more people who care about each other transform their shared cares into joint cares by each coming to care about the group as a plural agent. Similarly, a *plural person* is formed when two or more people who love each other transform their shared cares and values into joint cares and values by each coming not merely to care about but, more deeply, to love the group as a plural person. Of course to love the plural person means that they must each have person-focused felt evaluations like pride and shame focused on the plural person and subfocused on the things the plural person values. However, such felt evaluations differ from those constituting our love for (singular) persons in that in the case of a plural person it is their joint evaluative perspective that constitutes these joint cares and values: they must value these things as a part of their love for the plural person *as such*, so that each friend's felt evaluations had as one of us will be answerable to those of the other. Consequently, the commitment each undertakes in having these person-focused felt evaluations is not merely to the well-being of the plural agent, for that well-being is not determined except by the joint evaluative perspective constituted by such felt evaluations; rather, their commitment is to living together the kind of life these joint values define as worth living. That is, the friends must have a joint conception of the kind of life worth their living together and so to have in this sense a joint identity as a (plural) person. Friendships of this sort will have the increased intimacy of love in a way that is central to the friendship, for such intimacy makes possible not only the jointness of values and identity characteristic of a plural person but also thereby the increased "depth" of the relationship.

Friendships grounded in plural personhood have an additional dimension of "depth." For we should not expect that such friendships will always be harmonious, and so in forming and sustaining such friendships, the friends will inevitably need to overcome conflicts that arise in defining what is a joint conception of how they together shall live. As I shall clarify in §8.5, this is, in effect, a matter of their jointly exercising control over their joint identity as a plural agent: a matter of exercising *joint autonomy*. This idea can provide content to Aristotle's striking yet puzzling claim that a friend is another self,[49] for such friends are each "another self" not merely in that each identifies with and so acts and feels on behalf of the other, as is the case with the sort of identification I have argued is central to love of others. Rather, their joint exercise of autonomy in defining the kind of life worth their living together and the joint actions in which they engage in pursuit of that kind of life is what makes intelligible there being a single (joint) self here in the first place, of which they each are parts. Hence, as Aristotle

[49] Aristotle, *The Nicomachean Ethics*, ed. David Ross (Oxford: Oxford University Press, 1983), Bk IX, chs. 4, 9.

roughly says,[50] my relation to you as participant in this joint exercise of autonomy and joint pursuit of our life together is the same as my relation to myself in my individual exercise of autonomy and pursuit of my own life: you are another self. It is precisely in this sense that friendships grounded in plural persons have increased "depth" relative to those grounded in plural agency.

It should be clear that although I have characterized the members of a plural person as jointly exercising autonomy over their joint identity, this need not come at the expense of their individual identities or autonomy. What I am proposing is not a variant of the union account, in which the friends' individual identities are each subsumed by the merged identity that they together form. Rather, the joint identity we, the plural person, come to have retains its distinctness from my individual identity, as is clear given the possibility of conflicts between the two. Although we may agree that we should jointly value something and agree on the joint priority it ought to have within our joint evaluative perspective, that evaluative perspective and the shared life to which it leads does not exhaust my evaluative perspective or my life. Consequently, although from our joint evaluative perspective it may be clear that I ought to act in some way, I may have sound reasons from within my individual evaluative perspective for not so acting. Our friendship is a part of my life and my identity insofar as it is a part of what I value in loving us, the plural person, but it is only a part and must have a place relative to other values that together constitute my individual identity.

Nonetheless, there is room within a friendship for my friend to contest my devotion to that friendship, arguing, for example, that I am "something of a freerider on her loving endeavors"[51] by virtue of a significant imbalance in our individual commitments to our joint identity and activity. The merit of such a complaint has its source within the friendship itself: within the conception of our friendship that we jointly hold as members of this plural agent, a conception that, as I argued in §8.3.2, includes a joint understanding of the place that plural agent—our friendship—is to have within each of

---

[50] I say "roughly" here to signal that I am not making any serious attempt to interpret what Aristotle actually meant in the brief remarks he makes about the idea that a friend is another self. Nonetheless, something like this understanding of Aristotle can be found in Sherman, "Aristotle on Friendship and the Shared Life."

[51] Friedman, "Romantic Love," 175.

our lives. Thus, my freeloading on our friendship may lead to your feeling resentment inasmuch as my doing so is detrimental to us, the plural agent; such resentment, then, is a part of our joint evaluative perspective. Indeed, insofar as in the type of friendship currently under consideration the friends constitute not just a plural agent but a plural person, at stake here is the proper self-trust and self-respect that we, the plural person, have. For my failure as a freeloader is a failure properly to rely on the soundness of our joint evaluations as these determine how I as one of us ought not only to think and feel but also to act, and it is therefore a failure to pay proper attention to the proper exercise of our joint autonomy.

I already indicated that the character of a friendship is determined in part by the friends' joint conception of their relationship; thus, two friends may have a conception of their relationship according to which they are tennis buddies, so that, while they each continue to share the concerns of the other and so participate in engaged activity on behalf of the other, their joint activity is confined largely to the domain of playing, watching, and discussing tennis. With this development of the potential depth of friendships in terms of (a) the friends not merely caring about each other but loving each other and (b) the friends forming not merely a plural agent but a plural person, it becomes possible to clarify two particularly important forms of friendship that deserve special mention: romantic love and friendships of virtue.

Consider first *romantic love*: a form of friendship in which the friends form a plural person in which the joint conception of their relationship more or less centrally involves romance. That is, the friends each love the other and form a plural person in which their joint evaluative perspective includes joint values which they arrive at through the joint exercise of their autonomy. Moreover, insofar as they jointly conceive their relationship in romantic terms, they jointly find import in certain sorts of joint activities—having candlelit dinners, seeing films or plays, having sex, and so on—that they understand to be activities each participates in exclusively with the other as a part of this plural person. Indeed, for me to engage in such activities with someone else would be to betray our joint values, our sense of our joint identity, in a way that makes intelligible your jealousy and resentment: jealousy and resentment that are internal to our joint evaluative perspective.

Of course, actual romantic relationships may well fall short of the sort of depth I have attributed to romantic love here; indeed, it is perfectly possible for a relationship to involve merely a plural agent in which the members' joint conception of the plural agent gets cashed out in these romantic terms. Nonetheless, there does seem to be a distinction in kind between the romantic friendships we might find among teenagers and those that can evolve in the best marriages. My claim is that we can understand what both kinds of relationships have in common in terms of their similar joint conceptions of their relationships while nonetheless maintaining this distinction in a way that accounts for their relative depths in terms of the distinction between plural agents and plural persons.

The other important form of friendship that I shall consider briefly is what Aristotle calls *friendship of virtue* and which he distinguishes from friendships of pleasure and of utility. As I indicated in §1.1, these types of friendship seem to be distinguished in light of the reasons we have for forming and continuing the friendships, whether because of the pleasure or utility we gain from the relationship or because of our friend's virtuous character. This seems to indicate that we have ulterior motives for having friendships of pleasure or utility that potentially compromise their integrity as genuine cases of friendship. For insofar as friendship, like love, is grounded in a commitment to the well-being of your friend for his sake, these friendships, by seeming to be at least partially contingent on your friend's remaining pleasant or useful to you, thereby compromise that commitment and so the kind of concern that is central to friendship. Only friendships of virtue, by being grounded in the qualities of your friend's character, escape this conclusion; it is therefore tempting to think that friendships of virtue are the highest or purest form of friendship, of which other forms of friendship are merely deficient approximations.

This is, I believe, a mistake. I have already offered an understanding of friendships of pleasure or utility not in terms of their grounds but rather in terms of the *content* of the joint concerns that define them. A similar understanding of friendships of virtue is also apt: such friendships are ones in which the friends' joint conception of their relationship centrally involves the pursuit of virtue—whether or not (contra Aristotle) the friends themselves closely approximate virtue. It would be a mistake, however, to think that the difference between friendships of virtue and friendships of pleasure or utility simply lie in the content of their joint concerns. For friendships of virtue are concerned with virtue not merely as one care among others but rather as a joint value defining the kind of life worth their living together; that they have such a joint value requires that friendships of virtue involve not merely plural agency but plural personhood.[52] Consequently, friendships of virtue are distinguished as well by the depth of relationship they involve—though, it should be noted, they are not the only form of friendship having that sort of depth. All of this implies first that we should not understand friendships of pleasure or utility to be deficient forms of friendship (see p. 7) and second that we should not understand friendships of virtue to be an ideal that we ought to strive to attain in all of our friendships. Friendships come in different forms and with different scopes and depths; the question of what form, scope, or depth a particular friendship ought to take is a matter for the friends themselves to determine. That—and how such determination is possible—is the subject for §8.5.

8.5 Value and Justification of Friendship

Friendship, as I have described it here, is a rather demanding relationship: demanding of our time, attention, efforts, and resources. It is therefore important to understand the value of friendship: what makes friendships worthwhile, and so how ought we to evaluate whether or not particular friendships are worthy of continuation?

Philosophical discussions of the value of friendship often appeal to the consequences of friendship in understanding its value. Thus Elizabeth Telfer claims that friendship is "*life enhancing*" in that it makes us "feel more alive": it enhances our activities by intensifying our absorption in them and hence the pleasure we get out of them.[53] David Annis adds that it helps promote self-esteem, which is good both instrumentally and for its own sake.[54] John Cooper, in offering an interpretation of Aristotle, claims that friendship promotes a flourishing life for the individual in two ways.[55] First, our friends act as a kind of "mirror," providing epistemic access to the goodness of our lives, which knowledge is required if we are to flourish; indeed,

---

[52] This implies that the depth and scope of friendships are not entirely orthogonal: whether or not the friendship is grounded in plural agency or plural personhood affects the kind of scope that is possible for them.

[53] Telfer, "Friendship," 239–40.   [54] Annis, "The Meaning, Value, and Duties of Friendship."

[55] John M. Cooper, "Friendship and the Good in Aristotle," *Philosophical Review* 86 (1977): 290–315.

given the perpetual possibility of self-deception, we can come to know this—and so to flourish—only through friendship. Second, friendship, and the shared values and activities it essentially involves, is needed to reinforce our intellectual and practical understanding of the sort of moral and intellectual activities characteristic of living well "continuously" and "with pleasure and interest,"[56] for without friendship and these shared values our interest in such activities would be difficult to sustain. Consequently, Cooper's Aristotle concludes, friendships are valuable because of the way they contribute to human flourishing.

I have my doubts about the legitimacy of these claims in every case, for friendships can be worthwhile even though they are painful, do not do much for our self-esteem, and fail to have the sort of depth or scope necessary for contributing to our own virtue. Nonetheless, more interesting for present purposes is that so far these accounts of the value of friendship understand it to be extrinsic to the friendship itself; that, however, seems inadequate since, as David Brink notes, we ordinarily understand relationships like friendship to have intrinsic value: friendships are valuable for their own sakes and not merely for the way they contribute, instrumentally or constitutively, to something else that is valuable.[57] Indeed, part of the worry here is whether our friends are fungible, for if the value of friendship is merely extrinsic then it seems we would be able to justify trading up from one friend to another who is better able to promote these extrinsic values. Consequently, as was the case for love, in order properly to capture the intimate, personal nature of friendship we need to understand its value to be intrinsic to the particular relationship. Moreover, as was the case for love, insofar as your identity is potentially at stake in who your friends are, and insofar as your identity is something for which you can be responsible through the exercise of your capacity for autonomy, we must understand questions of the value of a particular friendship to be at least partly up to you.

Ferdinand Schoeman, partly in response to the individualism of alternative accounts of friendship, argues that friendship involves "a way of being and acting in virtue of being united with another"[58] in which the

[56] Ibid., 310.
[57] Brink, "Eudaimonism, Love and Friendship, and Political Community."
[58] Ferdinand Schoeman, "Aristotle on the Good of Friendship," *Australasian Journal of Philosophy* 63 (1985): 281.

friends "become a unique community with a being and value of its own."[59] Although this claim has intuitive appeal, Schoeman does not clearly explain what that "unique community" is or why it should have the value it does. My account of friendship in terms of plural agency can help insofar as it provides a clear understanding of what such a unique community is and, I shall argue, of how we should understand not merely its import but also how that import can be at least partially up to us. Indeed, much of what is needed for an understanding of the value and justification of friendship is already in place.

As with the value and justification of love, we must distinguish between questions concerning the value of initially coming to be friends with someone from questions concerning whether we ought to sustain an existing friendship. The differences between justifying the initiation of love and that of friendship are not theoretically interesting. In each case, we do so by appealing to particular properties, including relational properties, of another. Through a dialectical process of deliberation, in which we exercise autonomy both in interpreting our responses (potentially through the elucidation of relevant evaluative concepts) and in actively attempting to shape those responses, we can arrive at an essentially personal understanding of what makes another worthy of our love or our friendship. Of course substantively the two cases are different, for the considerations relevant to love are different from those relevant to friendship largely because friendship is a relationship between people rather than simply an evaluative attitude one person might adopt. In particular, in considering whether to attempt a friendship we might worry about whether a potential friend has certain qualities of character that promote our having a certain sort of relationship with her: qualities like considerateness or loyalty. Indeed, given a particular understanding of the scope of friendship, such qualities might include her being a good sport or handy with tools. Yet such qualities cannot exhaust the reasons for friendship, for friendship must be grounded in a concern for your friend for her sake, and so part of justifying the initiation of a friendship must include the justification of such a concern. Moreover, insofar as friendship is essentially a relationship, its character is not something that one party can simply determine irrespective of his prospective friend. Precisely what that character ought to be is something

---

[59] Schoeman, "Aristotle on the Good of Friendship," 280.

that can only emerge from the interaction of the two parties as they forge and sustain their friendship. Consequently, we cannot neatly separate questions of the discernment of friendship from those of its constancy.

When we turn to the questions concerning constancy, we find once again that there is some overlap between the cases of love and friendship. Just as friendship essentially includes a concern for your friend for her sake, justifying continuing being a friend will consist in part in justifying continuing that concern. So when your friend begins to change radically so as to come to have concerns you find, upon deliberation, you can no longer share with her for her sake, you thereby have reason to end not only your concern but also your friendship. Nonetheless, the case of friendship is importantly different from the case of love precisely because of the place of plural agency in friendship. For whether the friendship itself is something you are justified in being a part of depends essentially on what exactly that friendship consists in: on how we jointly are to conceive of both our well-being as a plural agent and the place this ought to have within our individual lives. Consequently, the question of whether you are justified in continuing this friendship is not one that is separable from the question of what conception of friendship we together can endorse from within our joint evaluative perspective.

In general, joint deliberation about import proceeds in much the same way as individual deliberation, though it takes place from within a joint evaluative perspective constituted by the friends' evaluations made as one of us. Consequently, as I argued in §8.3, each friend, in making evaluative judgments and having felt evaluations, ought to be sensitive to those of the other as they try together to forge and sustain a single evaluative perspective that they can hold jointly, each as one of us. In the account of deliberation about import I sketched in §6.1, however, an important role is played by the agent's capacity for autonomy, and this requires special discussion in the context of joint deliberation: how can a plural agent itself exercise a capacity for autonomy?[60]

---

[60] Actually, what's required for deliberation about what we ought to care about is a capacity to exercise control over your felt evaluations and so over what you in fact care about. Such a capacity falls short of a full-blown capacity for autonomy in something like the way caring falls short of valuing: autonomy, insofar as it is a matter of self-determination in which a person's identity is at stake, has a kind of depth that the mere capacity to control what you care about does not. Thus strictly speaking it is only plural persons that have a capacity for autonomy inasmuch as what is at stake for them is

As I argued in §8.3, a plural agent is itself a subject of import and so has and can exercise the capacity for various felt evaluations. Of course a plural agent is not an independent entity capable of exercising any capacities wholly apart from the individual agents that constitute it; rather, it does so only insofar as we, its members, exercise these capacities on its behalf: each as one of us in a way that constitutes a single evaluative perspective we hold jointly. The same goes for a plural agent's exercise of a capacity for autonomy: we, its members, exercise that capacity on its behalf insofar as our individual attempts take place from within our joint evaluative perspective. Thus, for example, your attempts (as one of us) to reinterpret particular events in the world or even feelings I have as one of us ought, other things being equal, to exert a kind of rational pressure on my feelings, potentially altering them and so imposing a new shape on them that changes what has import to us. Although my felt evaluations may be spontaneously responsive to your interpretations, in general for such an attempted exercise of autonomy to succeed, we must have a relatively unified will: I must be willing to take up your interpretation, potentially in light of a refined articulation of the relevant evaluative concepts, and attempt to impose it on the felt evaluations I have as one of us. Indeed, such a willingness is a normal part of the joint evaluative perspective we have as a plural agent.

Within a plural agent, the jointness of our evaluative perspective makes intelligible one way in which we can each rationally motivate changes in the other's evaluations, whether felt or judged: any conflict internal to that perspective rationally motivates changes to reduce or eliminate it. Consequently, my unwillingness or even simple failure to have particular felt evaluations in accordance with your articulation of what we jointly care about ought to motivate a re-examination and potential refinement of our joint sense of import, just as within an individual agent. Of course, this does not imply that I have arbitrary veto power over our evaluations, for a rational resolution of this conflict may require that I conform my felt evaluations to your judgments. Just as within an individual, we can (within limits) exercise rational control over the evaluations we each make as one of us by focusing our attention on what has import and, if necessary, acting as if we have the requisite felt evaluations so as to establish the habit

___

not merely what they jointly care about but rather their joint identity itself. Indeed, it is partly for this reason that it makes sense in the case of a plural person to say that your friend is another self.

of response to import that just is our having these felt evaluations.[61] In a plural agent this may require your reminding me at the appropriate times what has import to us, thereby getting me to focus my attention on what matters to us, and encouraging me to respond as one of us to that import. Moreover, as one of us, you have standing to criticize me, positively or negatively, either explicitly in judgment or implicitly in felt evaluation, for successes or failures in this regard, thereby potentially further motivating me to change. Thus, you may feel (as one of us) disappointed in me when I fail to be motivated by the conception of our friendship that you have argued for and I have endorsed; such disappointment ought to call my attention to my failure here and so motivate me not only to feel similar disappointment (also as one of us) but also thereby to act accordingly. In all these ways, a plural agent's exercise of such rational control over what it cares about is analogous to that within an individual.

Things are somewhat trickier when we friends have not yet arrived at a conclusion concerning whether a particular revision to our conception of our friendship is one that we hold jointly, so that my failure to be motivated by that revised conception is not so clearly irrational. For example, when you propose that we extend our friendship into a new domain, so that we are not just tennis buddies but also take a joint interest in the opera, I may resist, a resistance that is not itself clearly irrational but instead raises the question of whether your attempted extension of our friendship is appropriate. Faced with this situation, you may encourage me to give the opera a try; so, as much as I care about you and you care about this, I have some reason to do so for your sake.[62]

Assume, then, that I allow myself to be drawn into going to see an opera in response not to the import we jointly find it to have (since it is not yet determinate whether this is something that has import to us) but rather in

---

[61] I have discussed how such rational control over our felt evaluations is possible in Helm, "Freedom of the Heart."

[62] Of course, I might have better reason to resist this suggestion, as when you want us to come to rob banks together, and my better reasons ought to lead me not merely to refuse to go along with you but also to change your mind out of my concern for your well-being. It is precisely because the rational influence friends can have on each other goes in both directions that Cocking and Kennett's worries about our being drawn into morally dangerous situations by our friends are overblown. (See Cocking and Kennett, "Friendship and Moral Danger.") In less dramatic cases, my reason to resist this suggestion may simply be a matter of priorities: although I do care about you, I find other things to be more important than engaging with you in this activity given the place you have within my evaluative perspective and the place going to the opera has within yours.

response to the import this has to you as a part of my caring about you. As I argued in §3.3, §6.2, and §7.2, to engage in this activity with you is not merely to exercise my will so as to get myself to do this; rather, it is to be motivated to do so in part through sharing the import it has for you for your sake, and so it requires being attuned to your emotional responsiveness, so that I ought, other things being equal, to share your appreciation of it and so to try to get myself to do so when I find myself initially unable. Assume, on the one hand, that my sincere attempts to get myself to share your appreciation of opera might be unsuccessful. In the context of my concern for you, such recalcitrance is, other things being equal, a kind of irrationality. In the context of our friendship, however, we cannot pin the rational conflict between my evaluations and yours (each as one of us) on either side; rather, that very irrationality is indicative of there being no clear pattern of felt evaluations constitutive of our caring jointly about opera: this is not something we care about.

Of course, on the other hand I might be successful in getting myself to share your appreciation of the opera. In this case my felt evaluations are subfocused on the opera, and yet they may have an indeterminate focus: are they focused on you so that I feel them as a part of my caring about opera for your sake, or are they focused on us, the plural agent, so that I feel them as one of us—as a part of our joint caring about opera?[63] At this point it is possible for you to interpret these felt evaluations as ones I feel as one of us, and such an interpretation can make determinate my present felt evaluations in such a way as to alter their future shape, thereby instilling in me—in us—the joint concern for the opera.

All of this is much like what happens in cases of paternalistic love in which the parent interprets the felt evaluations of the child so as to try to impose a particular shape on them. Nonetheless, it should be clear that the paternalism is replaced in this case by plural agency, so that the rational interconnectedness of our evaluations that would motivate my adopting this interpretation for my own is not that of paternalistic love but rather that of our joint evaluative perspective. Consequently, in the case of friendship what motivates your interpretation is not a paternalistic concern for me but rather your tentative extended conception of our friendship. Such an

---

[63] These are not mutually exclusive options; as I indicated in §7.2, felt evaluations can have a dual focus.

interpretation, therefore, cannot simply be imposed on me irrespective of my own understanding of these felt evaluations and of our relationship, an understanding that also contributes to our joint evaluative perspective and that you therefore ought to trust and respect. So I may resist your interpretation by saying something like this: "Yes, I did find the opera interesting and even exciting and uplifting, but the interest I took in it was really for you. Although I understand you'd like a fellow enthusiast who can sustain and deepen your interest, it is not something I can see myself engaging in on a regular basis. There's just too much for me to learn in order to really understand and appreciate the opera, and I already have too many other projects on my plate."[64]

The upshot is that we friends can exercise joint control over what we care about through the kind of give and take just described within a joint evaluative perspective in which we aim together to articulate and refine our understanding of what is important to us jointly and, thereby, of the character of our friendship. This just is to arrive at a joint conception of the import the plural agent we form has to us: a joint conception of the intrinsic value of our friendship. In arriving at this joint conception through the rational process just described, we have thereby come to justify our friendship. The justification of friendship, therefore, is something we friends can undertake only together, from within our joint evaluative perspective.

One might object that although I may have provided an account of the value and justification that friendship has to the friends jointly, I have left out the friends' individual evaluative perspectives. Why not think that the justification of friendship can also be an individual matter that each of the friends takes up on her own? For surely we can separate questions of the import the plural agent has to itself and so the correctness of a description of what we jointly stand for from questions of the import the plural agent has to each of its members. This objection is clearly correct insofar as there must be conceptual room for the concerns we each have as one of us to diverge from our own individual concerns; indeed, I have argued that we can care jointly about something even if I personally disagree with our doing so.

---

[64] Of course, this trust and respect goes both ways: seeing your crestfallen face, I may realize that I have underestimated the importance to you of this conception of our friendship and so add, "but we'll see. Let's try again, give it a little time, and see if it works out."

Nonetheless, the objection presupposes that the plural agent's well-being is something that can be fixed within our joint evaluative perspective independently of the individual friends' determinations of whether to continue that friendship, as if we first check to see what the friendship amounts to and then decide individually whether to continue it. This is clearly false, for it ignores the way in which we are each one of us and so constitute the joint evaluative perspective that defines the plural agent and what has import to it. When we actively seek to alter that evaluative perspective, we do so in a way that not only must be sensitive to the overall shape of our current joint evaluative perspective but also cannot be dissociated from each of our willingness to continue the friendship thus defined. Consequently, for us jointly to justify a particular conception of our friendship requires that we each have thereby justified continuing that friendship. Of course, the friends' individual evaluative perspectives can over time drift apart from their joint evaluative perspective, so that the joint concerns they formerly could get on board with they now cannot sustain, thereby leading to rational conflict. Yet it should be clear that such conflict is at least partially within their joint evaluative perspective, for it will lead to failures to feel as one of us the felt evaluations that would formerly have been called for by their joint evaluative perspective. It may happen that the plural agent's evaluative perspective then drifts with those of the individuals, or it may happen that such conflict results in disagreement that the friends must jointly address. In either case, we again find the presupposition of the objection is false.

A related objection runs as follows. In friendships grounded in plural personhood, I have argued, the friends have a joint capacity for autonomy, a capacity they can use to determine the kind of life it is worth their living together. However, such a joint capacity for autonomy involves an undesirable limitation on the friends' individual autonomy, so that in forming such a close friendship I must give up the ability to determine who I shall be as an individual. This, it may seem, is too high a price to pay for friendship, and that is surely a *reductio* of my account.

The objection is right that a friendship grounded in plural personhood does in a way limit individual autonomy. Once in such a friendships, we are not simply free to do what we please without giving due consideration to our friends or our relationships. However, our freedom is constrained in this way whenever we come to care about something: we are rationally bound by our cares and values to respond in certain ways on behalf of that which we care about or value. Indeed, it is such rational constraints that, by constituting import, provide a point to our activities in the first place, and it is moreover only in terms of such constraints that we can intelligibly exercise a capacity for autonomy in the first place. Thus, far from undermining our autonomy, such cares and values make it possible, a possibility which we can use to change those very cares and values.

This might seem an inadequate response to the objection, for the objection gets its apparent force from the thought that once I have entered into such a deep friendship, it is no longer simply up to me to determine what I care about or value. Instead, it may seem, my friend comes to have a potentially quite significant role in determining what I can or cannot value, and to that extent this is for me simply to surrender my autonomy to my friend and abdicate responsibility for my own identity. It now becomes clear that what is behind this objection is the individualist conception of autonomy: my autonomy is a capacity that only I can exercise, and I can do so only when I am not being unduly influenced by others, as the objection presupposes is the case with plural personhood.

In reply, it should be clear, first, that whether or not I become friends with or continue a friendship with someone is something over which I have a say, so it is not as if I am somehow being forced into surrendering my autonomy. To a proponent of the objection, however, this merely sounds as though I am freely surrendering my autonomy, which is bad enough. An adequate reply therefore requires showing how being a member of a plural person involves not simply an abdication of individual responsibility for who we each are as individuals but rather the rejection of the individualist conception of autonomy, so that we can see plural personhood as involving an *extension* of our autonomy to include the autonomy we exercise jointly with others.

To see this, consider first the way in which being a member of a plural agent involves an extension of the possibilities for action of each of its members. For by forming a plural agent and so taking on the rational constraints of our joint evaluative perspective, we acquire a new possibility for acting jointly with others. Of course, the capacity for joint action is not one that we can undertake simply as individuals, but that does not change the new possibilities the individual has acquired by being a part of the plural agent: she can now act *as one of us*, which was not possible previously. Furthermore, in acquiring this new possibility for joint action, she does not give up her ability to act as an individual. Although her individual actions are in part rationally constrained by the joint evaluative perspective of the plural agent, this constraint is a part of her concern for us as a plural agent, and such a constraint is in principle no different than the way in which her individual actions are constrained by coming to acquire any new concern. Consequently, becoming a member of a plural agent and so coming to be rationally constrained by that plural agent is far from a limit on our freedom of action; it is rather that which makes possible the new freedom of joint action, thereby extending our freedom into the social realm so that I am no longer simply an individual who interacts with others simply as an individual.[65]

The same is true for the way in which becoming a member of a plural person provides an extension of the possibilities for autonomy that we each have. For it is precisely by coming to be rationally constrained by the joint evaluative perspective of a plural person that we acquire the new capacity for joint autonomy in addition to each of our capacities for individual autonomy. As before, joint autonomy is not a capacity that we can exercise simply as individuals; nonetheless, we each acquire new capacities to deliberate about and change what we jointly feel, capacities we each exercise as one of us. In acquiring these new capacities, each member of the plural person does not give up his individual autonomy, for although the subsequent exercise of individual autonomy will be constrained by our joint evaluative perspective, such constraint is merely the result of our each coming to love us as a plural person. Indeed, it is this very constraint that makes possible the extension of our individual autonomy into the social realm so that we each are no longer simply individual persons with individual identities but rather each find the life worth our each living includes a life lived jointly with another.

In short, the individualist conception of autonomy involves an undue restriction of those capacities which make us be persons at all. Although we persons each do have a capacity at least partially to determine our own identities as the particular persons we each are, we ought not understand

---

[65] For a detailed discussion of how such rational constraints can make possible new freedoms, see Robert Brandom, "Freedom and Constraint by Norms," *American Philosophical Quarterly* 16, no. 3 (1979): 187–96.

this to exhaust the kind of autonomy that is possible for us nor to limit the kinds of identity in which we can participate. Rather, we persons are essentially social in a way proponents of the individualist conception of autonomy cannot acknowledge.

In this way, this account of friendship, especially that grounded in plural personhood, can make sense of how particular friendships can be centrally important in our lives. To see this, consider how the loss of a friend can strike deeply at our sense of who we are in a way that goes well beyond the sort of mourning and sorrow or yearning discussed in §6.3. For in losing a friend you lose not merely a loved one, but someone with whom you have forged a particular relationship that includes a joint identity—a joint conception of how you ought to live together—through which we can understand your friend to be another self. Such a joint identity is not merely one that you share with a loved one for her sake, as a part of loving her; rather, insofar as this identity is joint, it is one you hold together with your friend, each as one of us: as a part of loving us as a plural agent that you together thereby constitute. Of course such a joint identity is at least in general something you yourself have come to endorse as a part of your participation in this joint evaluative perspective, so that to lose such a partner in a joint life is to lose a central part of what you find makes your life worth living: a central part of your identity. However, we should not think that such a value made intelligible from within my individual evaluative perspective exhausts the kind of value a friendship can have. For in addition we must consider its value from the perspective of us, the plural agent, and so of each friend *as one of us*. In losing the friendship, each friend has thereby lost that on the basis of which he can act and judge and feel as one of us and so has lost the capacity for joint freedom or even joint autonomy. The result will be not simply the dissolution of the plural agent but a dissolution the friends may each feel as something like an identity crisis—an inability to know what evaluative sense to make of things quite generally—insofar as you each have lost that joint identity of which you were a part.

Postscript

I claimed in Chapter 1 that there are two common tendencies in recent philosophical thought about persons that block an adequate account of love and friendship: the cognitive–conative divide, and the individualist conception of persons. As I have argued at length against the former elsewhere, my focus in this book has been the latter.

The individualist conception of persons, recall, has two central components: the egocentric conception of intimate concerns, and the individualist conception of autonomy. The egocentric conception of intimate concerns is an attempt to understand the intimacy of our concern for other people in terms of a kind of identification in which we incorporate their interests and concerns into our own. Such a conception of intimacy, I argued, forces a choice between two unacceptable alternatives: understanding love in terms of intimacy, which results in the union account of love, or rejecting the idea that intimate identification has a place in love, resulting in the robust-concern account. I have argued that we can reject this false choice by rejecting the implicit egocentrism behind it: the intimate identification at issue in love ought to be understood in terms of your having a concern for your beloved's identity that is the same in kind as your concern for your own identity. Thus, as I argued in Part II, your concern for your own identity is constituted by a projectible, rational pattern of person-focused emotions focused on yourself and subfocused on the things you thereby value. Likewise, your concern for your beloved's identity is constituted by a projectible, rational pattern of person-focused emotions focused on him and subfocused on the things he values; this just is for you to value these things for his sake. This account of intimate identification and of love is non-egocentric in a way that retains the distinctness of the identities of the lover and the beloved and yet enables us to make sense of our loving concern for others as deeply personal in a way that lays the groundwork for a rejection of the individualist conception of autonomy.

The individualist conception of autonomy understands our autonomy, our ability to exercise control over our identities as the persons we each are, as a capacity we each have and exercise as individuals, such that our autonomy is undermined to the extent that our identities are shaped by others without our consent, thereby setting up rather strict boundaries between persons. My account of love begins to undermine this conception of autonomy and so to break down these boundaries. This first became clear in Chapter 7, in which I argued that for paternalistic loving relationships the parent and child can share responsibility for the development of the child's identity as well as his capacity for autonomy itself. Centrally important in this account was the understanding of how the parent can provide the child with access to reasons for caring about or valuing something, reasons to which the child does not have independent access. Consequently, it becomes difficult to understand which evaluations are "internal" and which are "external" to the child's subjective motivational set—difficult to understand, that is, what such subjectivity amounts to in this context—precisely because these boundaries between persons are not as clear cut as may initially have seemed.

Somewhat more radically, I argued in Chapter 8 for a conception of plural agency and plural personhood as the basis for friendship. According to this conception, a plural agent is defined by an evaluative perspective that both is held jointly by its members and yet is distinct from their own individual evaluative perspectives. In holding this evaluative perspective jointly, the friends not only jointly care about particular things but also jointly determine what to care about—not through a process of bargaining and compromise but rather in a way that is analogous to how individuals deliberate about import from within a single evaluative perspective. The result is that it becomes possible for the friends to exercise a new kind of freedom of action that is essentially interpersonal. In the case of friendships grounded in plural personhood, the friends jointly hold not merely certain cares but also certain values that define a joint identity—a joint conception of the kind of life worth their living together—so that in determining what their joint identity shall be, the friends together exercise joint autonomy. In this way, the boundaries between the individual friends have been blurred so that, at least within the scope of their friendship, it is most proper to say that they together, rather than either of them individually, are the subject of what they think, feel, do, and value.

On its own, this is a coherent alternative to the individualist conception of autonomy; why should we believe it? Ultimately my claim is that the justification for the account is the sense it is able to make overall of a variety of related phenomena. Thus, in providing this account of love and friendship I have provided explicit accounts of what it is to care about and value something for the sake of another person or agent, of the phenomenology of love and the place of the emotions within it, of the intimacy of love, of the rational role of loving parents in the enculturation of their children, of the nature of plural agents as distinct from plural intentional systems, and of a solution to the fungibility problem for both love and friendship in the context of an overall account of their value and justification.

In addition, the account of love and friendship I have provided is intended to be the basis for an understanding of a variety of loving relationships, and the strength of this account comes from its success in providing such an understanding. As I indicated in Chapter 1, my intent has been not to provide an account of *philia* rather than *eros* or even to claim that *philia* is somehow more fundamental than *eros*. Rather, the account of plural agency I have provided is intended to be the genus of which both *philia* and *eros* are species. Thus, the precise form the relationship takes, I have argued, depends on the scope and depth of the plural agent: on, that is, the well-being of the plural agent as this is determined by its members' joint conception of their relationship. In this way, the account can handle different forms of interpersonal relationships, from being tennis buddies to various forms of romantic relationships to relationships in which one's friend is "another self"—relationships that vary not only in their scope but also in their depth. In so doing, the account enables us to understand the similarities and differences among these types of relationships in virtue of which we can understand them to be more or less distinct species of a common genus.

Bibliography

Annis, David B. "The Meaning, Value, and Duties of Friendship," *American Philosophical Quarterly* 24 (1987): 349–56.

Aristotle. *The Nicomachean Ethics*, ed. David Ross (Oxford: Oxford University Press, 1983).

Badhwar, Neera Kapur. "Friends as Ends in Themselves," *Philosophy and Phenomenological Research* 48 (1987): 1–23.

—— ed. *Friendship: A Philosophical Reader* (Ithaca, NY: Cornell University Press, 1993).

—— "Love." In *Practical Ethics*, ed. Hugh LaFollette (Oxford: Oxford University Press, 2003) 42–69.

Baier, Annette C. "Doing Things with Others: The Mental Commons." In *Commonality and Particularity in Ethics*, ed. Lilli Alanen, Sara Heinämaa, and Thomas Wallgren (New York, NY: St. Martin's Press, 1997) 15–44.

—— "Unsafe Loves." In Solomon and Higgins, *The Philosophy of (Erotic) Love*, 433–50.

Blum, Lawrence A. *Friendship, Altruism, and Morality* (London: Routledge & Kegan Paul, 1980).

—— "Friendship as a Moral Phenomenon." In Badhwar, *Friendship: A Philosophical Reader*, 192–210.

Brandom, Robert. "Freedom and Constraint by Norms," *American Philosophical Quarterly* 16, no. 3 (1979): 187–96.

Bratman, Michael E. *Faces of Intention: Selected Essays on Intention and Agency* (Cambridge: Cambridge University Press, 1999).

—— "I Intend That We J." In Bratman, *Faces of Intention*, 142–61.

—— "Shared Intention." In Bratman, *Faces of Intention*, 109–29.

—— "Shared Intention and Mutual Obligation." In Bratman, *Faces of Intention*, 130–41.

Bratman, Michael E. "Shared Valuing and Frameworks for Practical Reasoning." In *Reason and Value: Themes from the Moral Philosophy of Joseph Raz*, eds. R. Jay Wallace et al. (Oxford: Oxford University Press, 2004) 1–27.

Brentlinger, John. "The Nature of Love." In Soble, *Eros, Agape, and Philia*, 136–48.

Brink, David O. "Eudaimonism, Love and Friendship, and Political Community," *Social Philosophy and Policy* 16 (1999): 252–89.

—— "Rational Egoism, Self, and Others." In *Identity, Character, and Morality: Essays in Moral Pshychology*, eds. Owen Flanagan and Amélie O. Rorty (Cambridge, MA: MIT Press, 1990) 339–78.

Carroll, Lewis. "What the Tortoise Said to Achilles," *Mind* 4 (1895): 278–80.

Cocking, Dean and Jeanette Kennett. "Friendship and Moral Danger," *Journal of Philosophy* 97, no. 5 (2000): 278–96.

—— "Friendship and the Self," *Ethics* 108, no. 3 (1998): 502–27.

Cooper, John M. "Aristotle on Friendship." In *Essays on Aristotle's Ethics*, ed. Amélie O. Rorty (Berkeley, CA: University of California Press, 1980) 301–40.

—— "Aristotle on the Forms of Friendship," *Review of Metaphysics* 30 (1977): 619–48.

—— "Friendship and the Good in Aristotle," *Philosophical Review* 86 (1977): 290–315.

Darwall, Stephen. *Impartial Reason* (Ithaca, NY: Cornell University Press, 1983).

Davidson, Donald. *Essays on Actions and Events* (New York, NY: Clarendon Press, 1980).

—— "Hume's Cognitive Theory of Pride." In Davidson, *Essays on Actions and Events*, 277–90.

—— *Inquiries into Truth and Interpretation* (Oxford: Oxford University Press, 1984).

—— "Mental Events." In Davidson, *Essays on Actions and Events*, 207–25.

Delaney, Neil. "Romantic Love and Loving Commitment: Articulating a Modern Ideal," *American Philosophical Quarterly* 33, no. 4 (1996): 339–56.

Dennett, Daniel C. "Intentional Systems," *Journal of Philosophy* 68 (1971): 87–106.

—— "Real Patterns," *Journal of Philosophy* 88 (1991): 27–51.

—— *The Intentional Stance* (Cambridge, MA: MIT Press, 1987).

Dilman, Ilham. "Shame, Guilt, and Remorse," *Philosophical Investigations* 22, no. 4 (1999): 312–29.

Dray, William. "The Rationale of Actions." Ch. V in *Laws and Explanation in History* (London: Oxford University Press, 1957) 118–55.

El-Wafi, Aïcha, Matthias Favron, and Sophie Quaranta. *Mon Fils Perdu* (Paris: Plon, 2006).

Fisher, Mark. *Personal Love* (London: Duckworth, 1990).

Frankfurt, Harry G. "Autonomy, Necessity, and Love." In Frankfurt, *Necessity, Volition, and Love*, 129–41.

—— "Freedom of the Will and the Concept of a Person," *Journal of Philosophy* 68, no. 1 (1971): 5–20.

—— "Freedom of the Will and the Concept of a Person." In Frankfurt, *The Importance of What We Care About*, 11–25.

—— "Identification and Externality." In Frankfurt, *The Importance of What We Care About*, 58–68.

—— *The Importance of What We Care About: Philosophical Essays* (Cambridge: Cambridge University Press, 1988).

—— *Necessity, Volition, and Love* (Cambridge: Cambridge University Press, 1999).

—— "On Caring." In Frankfurt, *Necessity, Volition, and Love*, 155–80.

—— "On Love, and Its Reasons." In Frankfurt, *The Reasons of Love*, 35–68.

—— "The Question: 'How Should We Live?' " In Frankfurt, *The Reasons of Love*, 1–32.

—— *The Reasons of Love* (Princeton, NJ: Princeton University Press, 2004).

Friedman, Marilyn A. "Friendship and Moral Growth," *Journal of Value Inquiry* 23 (1989): 3–13.

—— "Romantic Love and Personal Autonomy," *Midwest Studies in Philosophy* 22 (1998): 162–81.

—— *What Are Friends For? Feminist Perspectives on Personal Relationships and Moral Theory* (Ithaca, NY: Cornell University Press, 1993).

Fromm, Erich. *The Art of Loving* (New York, NY: Harper Perennial Library, 1974).

Gilbert, Margaret. *Living Together: Rationality, Sociality, and Obligation* (Lanham, MD: Rowman & Littlefield, 1996).

Gilbert, Margaret. "Obligation and Joint Commitment." In Gilbert, *Sociality and Responsibility*.

—— "Shared Values, Social Unity, and Liberty," *Public Affairs Quarterly* 19, no. 1 (2005): 25–49.

—— *On Social Facts* (Princeton, NJ: Princeton University Press, 1989).

—— *Sociality and Responsibility: New Essays in Plural Subject Theory* (Lanham, MD: Rowman & Littlefield, 2000).

—— *A Theory of Political Obligation: Membership, Commitment, and the Bonds of Society* (Oxford: Oxford University Press, 2006).

—— "Walking Together," *Midwest Studies in Philosophy* 15 (1990): 1–14.

Gordon, Robert M. *The Structure of Emotions: Investigations in Cognitive Philosophy* (Cambridge: Cambridge University Press, 1987).

Greenspan, Patricia S. *Emotions and Reasons: An Inquiry into Emotional Justification* (Boston, MA: Routledge & Kegan Paul, 1988).

Hall, Richard J. "Are Pains Necessarily Unpleasant?" *Philosophy and Phenomenological Research* 49, no. 4 (1989): 643–59.

Hamlyn, D. W. "The Phenomena of Love and Hate." In Soble, *Eros, Agape, and Philia*, 218–34.

Harman, Gilbert. "Desired Desires." In *Explaining Value and Other Essays in Moral Philosophy* (Oxford: Oxford University Press, 2000) 117–36.

Helm, Bennett W. *Emotional Reason: Deliberation, Motivation, and the Nature of Value* (Cambridge: Cambridge University Press, 2001).

—— "Emotions and Practical Reason: Rethinking Evaluation and Motivation," *Noûs* 35, no. 2 (2001): 190–213.

—— "Felt Evaluations: A Theory of Pleasure and Pain," *American Philosophical Quarterly* 39, no. 1 (2002): 13–30.

—— "Freedom of the Heart," *Pacific Philosophical Quarterly* 77, no. 2 (1996): 71–87.

—— "Integration and Framentation of the Self," *Southern Journal of Philosophy* 34, no. 1 (1996): 43–63.

—— "Love, Identification, and the Emotions," *American Philosophical Quarterly* 46, no. 1 (2009): 39–59.

—— "Plural Agents," *Noûs* 42, no. 1 (2008): 17–49.

—— "The Significance of Emotions," *American Philosophical Quarterly* 31, no. 4 (1994): 319–31.

Helm, Bennett W., Yaroslava Babych, and Aleksandra Markovic. "Moods as a Sense of Priorities," talk given to MidSouth Philosophy Conference, 1999.

Hume, David. *Treatise of Human Nature.* 2nd edn., ed. P. H. Nidditch (Oxford: Oxford University Press, 1978).

Humphrey, Nicholas and Daniel C. Dennett. "Speaking for Ourselves: An Assessment of Multiple Personality Disorder," *Raritan: A Quarterly Review* 9 (1989): 68–98.

Isenberg, Arnold. "Natural Pride and Natural Shame." In *Explaining Emotions*, ed. Amélie O. Rorty (Berkeley, CA: University of California Press, 1980) 355–83.

Ishtiyaque, Haji and Stefaan E. Cuypers. "Moral Responsibility, Love, and Authenticity," *Journal of Social Philosophy* 36, no. 1 (2005): 106–26.

Kolodny, Niko. "Love as Valuing a Relationship," *Philosophical Review* 112 (2003): 135–89.

Korsgaard, Christine M. *The Sources of Normativity* (Cambridge: Cambridge University Press, 1996).

LaFollette, Hugh. *Personal Relationships: Love, Identity, and Morality* (Cambridge, MA: Blackwell Press, 1996).

Liddell, Henry George et al. *A Greek-English Lexicon.* 9th edn. (Oxford: Clarendon Press, 1940).

McDowell, John. "Are Moral Requirements Hypothetical Imperatives?" In McDowell, *Mind, Value, and Reality*, 77–94.

—— "Might There Be External Reasons?" In McDowell, *Mind, Value, and Reality*, 95–111.

—— *Mind, Value, and Reality* (Cambridge, MA: Harvard University Press, 1998).

McKeon, Richard, ed. *The Basic Works of Aristotle* (New York, NY: Random House, 1941).

Millgram, Elijah. "Aristotle on Making Other Selves," *Canadian Journal of Philosophy* 17 (1987): 361–76.

Montaigne, Michel. *Essays of Montaigne*, ed. William Carew Hazlitt, trans. Charles Cotton (London: Reeves & Turner, 1603/1877).

Newton, Natika. "On Viewing Pain as a Secondary Quality," *Noûs* 23 (1989): 569–98.

Newton-Smith, W. "A Conceptual Investigation of Love." In Soble, *Eros, Agape, and Philia*, 199–217.

Nozick, Robert. *The Examined Life: Philosophical Meditations* (New York, NY: Simon & Schuster, 1989).

—— "Love's Bond." In Nozick, *The Examined Life*, 68–86.

Nygren, Anders. "*Agape* and *Eros*." In Soble, *Eros, Agape, and Philia*, 85–95.

Pitcher, George. "Pain Perception," *Philosophical Review* 79 (1970): 368–93.

Rorty, Amélie O. "The Historicity of Psychological Attitudes: Love is Not Love Which Alters Not When It Alteration Finds." In Badhwar, *Friendship: A Philosophical Reader*, 73–88.

Roth, Abraham Sesshu. "Shared Agency and Contralateral Commitments," *Philosophical Review* 113, no. 3 (2004): 359–410.

Rovane, Carol. "Personal Identity, Ethical not Metaphysical." In *McDowell and His Critics*, eds. Cynthia Macdonald and Graham Macdonald (Malden, MA: Blackwell Publishing, 2006) 95–114.

Schapiro, Tamar. "What Is a Child?" *Ethics* 109, no. 4 (1999): 715–38.

Schoeman, Ferdinand. "Aristotle on the Good of Friendship," *Australasian Journal of Philosophy* 63 (1985): 269–82.

Scruton, Roger. *Sexual Desire: A Moral Philosophy of the Erotic* (New York, NY: Free Press, 1986).

Searle, John R. "Collective Intentions and Actions." In *Intentions in Communication*, eds. Phillip R. Cohen, Martha E. Pollack, and Jerry L. Morgan (Cambridge, MA: MIT Press, 1990) 401–15.

—— *Intentionality: An Essay in the Philosophy of Mind* (Cambridge: Cambridge University Press, 1983).

Sherman, Nancy. "Aristotle on Friendship and the Shared Life," *Philosophy and Phenomenological Research* 47, no. 4 (1987): 589–613.

Singer, Irving. "From *The Nature of Love*." In Solomon and Higgins, *The Philosophy of (Erotic) Love*, 259–78.

—— *Philosophy of Love: Partial Summing-up* (Cambridge, MA: MIT Press, 2009).

—— *The Pursuit of Love* (Baltimore, MD: Johns Hopkins University Press, 1994).

Smith, Michael. *The Moral Problem* (Oxford: Oxford University Press, 1994).

Soble, Alan, ed. *Eros, Agape, and Philia: Readings in the Philosophy of Love* (New York, NY: Paragon House, 1989).

—— *The Structure of Love* (New Haven, CT: Yale University Press, 1990).

—— "Union, Autonomy, and Concern." In *Love Analyzed*, ed. Roger E. Lamb (Boulder, CO: Westview Press, 1997) 65–92.

Solomon, Robert C. *About Love: Reinventing Romance for Our Times* (New York, NY: Simon & Schuster, 1988).

—— *Love: Emotion, Myth, and Metaphor* (New York, NY: Anchor Press, 1981).

—— *The Passions* (New York, NY: Anchor Press, 1976).

Solomon Robert C. and Kathleen M. Higgins, eds. *The Philosophy of (Erotic) Love* (Lawrence, KS: Kansas University Press, 1991).

Stephens, G. Lynn and George Graham. "Minding Your P's and Q's: Pain and Sensible Qualities," *Noûs* 21 (1987): 395–405.

Taylor, Charles. *Human Agency and Language: Philosophical Papers 1* (Cambridge: Cambridge University Press, 1985).

—— *Sources of the Self: The Making of the Modern Identity* (Cambridge, MA: Harvard University Press, 1992).

—— "What Is Human Agency?" In Taylor, *Human Agency and Language*, 15–44.

Taylor, Gabriele. "Love," *Proceedings of the Aristotelian Society* 76 (1976): 147–64.

—— *Pride, Shame, and Guilt: Emotions of Self-Assessment* (Oxford: Oxford University Press, 1985).

—— "Shame, Integrity, and Self-Respect." In *Dignity, Character, and Self-Respect*, ed. Robin S. Dillon (Boston, MA: Routledge & Kegan Paul, 1995) 157–78.

Telfer, Elizabeth. "Friendship," *Proceedings of the Aristotelian Society* 71 (1970–71): 223–41.

Thomas, Laurence. "Friends and Lovers." In *Person to Person*, eds. George Graham and Hugh Lafollette (Philadelphia, PA: Temple University Press, 1989) 182–98.

—— "Friendship," *Synthese* 72 (1987): 217–36.

—— "Friendship and Other Loves." In Badhwar, *Friendship: A Philosophical Reader*, 48–64.

—— "Reasons for Loving." In Solomon and Higgins, *The Philosophy of (Erotic) Love*, 467–76.

Tuomela, Raimo. *A Theory of Social Action* (Dordrecht: Reidel, 1984).

—— *The Importance of Us: A Philosophical Study of Basic Social Notions* (Stanford, CA: Stanford University Press, 1995).

—— *The Philosophy of Sociality: The Shared Point of View* (Oxford: Oxford University Press, 2007).

—— "We-Intentions Revisited," *Philosophical Studies* 125 (2005): 327–69.

Tuomela, Raimo and Kaarlo Miller. "We-Intentions," *Philosophical Studies* 53 (1988): 367–89.

Tye, Michael. "A Representational Theory of Pains and Their Phenomenal Character," *Philosophical Perspectives: AI, Connectionism, and Philosophical Psychology* 9 (1995): 223–39.

Velleman, J. David. "How to Share an Intention," *Philosophy and Phenomenological Research* 57, no. 1 (1997): 29–50.

—— "Love as a Moral Emotion," *Ethics* 109 (1999): 338–74.

Vlastos, Gregory. "The Individual as Object of Love in Plato." In *Platonic Studies*, 2nd edn. (Princeton, NJ: Princeton University Press, 1981) 3–42.

White, Richard J. *Love's Philosophy* (Lanham, MD: Rowman & Littlefield, 2001).

Whiting, Jennifer E. "Friends and Future Selves," *Philosophical Review* 95, no. 4 (1986): 547–80.

—— "Impersonal Friends," *Monist* 74 (1991): 3–29.

Wilkes, Kathleen. *Real People: Personal Identity without Thought Experiments* (Oxford: Oxford University Press, 1988).

Williams, Bernard. "Internal and External Reasons." In *Moral Luck: Philosophical Papers 1973–1980* (Cambridge: Cambridge University Press, 1981) 101–13.

—— "Internal Reasons and the Obscurity of Blame." In *Making Sense of Humanity and Other Philosophical Papers, 1982–93* (Cambridge: Cambridge University Press, 1995) 35–45.

—— *Shame and Necessity* (Berkeley, CA: University of California Press, 1993).

Wollheim, Richard. *The Thread of Life* (Cambridge, MA: Harvard University Press, 1984).

Index

Lightning Source UK Ltd.
Milton Keynes UK
UKHW010641130223
416869UK00003B/239